Mass Communication

Issues and Perspectives

Second Edition

Edited by

Robert Abelman
Robin Ross

Cleveland State University
Department of Communication

GINN PRESS
160 Gould Street
Needham Heights, MA 02194

Printed in the United States of America

10 9 8 7 6 5 4 3 2 1

ISBN 0–536–58182–7

BA 0118

 GINN PRESS

160 Gould Street/Needham Heights, MA 02194
Simon & Schuster Higher Education Publishing Group

Copyright Acknowledgments

Table of Contents

Preface

Since the introduction of movable type to the western world in the 1400s, mass communicated messages have generated their share of controversy and criticism due to the very fact that they are, indeed, mass communicated. The large-scale distribution and simultaneous reception of media information has fostered much concern by those who ponder the impact of modern media technology on daily human interaction, those who wonder about the ability of a society to digest and use massive amounts of free-flowing information, and those who fret over the implications of readily accepting information created by largely unknown, unseen, inaccessible, unaccountable sources.

Needless to say, significant concern has also been raised about the nature and quality of the information, entertainment, and advertising presented through mass media. Over the years, numerous citizen groups have staged protests and initiated legal actions in response to what they believe to be either excessive or inadequate, conservative or liberal, explicit or subliminal, pluralistic or biased, insensitive or overly sensitive portrayals of violence, sex, politics, religious faith, old age, and ethnicity, among others. Various extremist groups have gone so far as to wage boycotts and employ terrorist strategies to get the attention of the general public and express their discontent to the "powers that be," shaking their fists in blind fury all the while. Still others simply shake their heads in frustration as they sit in silent vigilance in the privacy of their homes. They see no change in sight and can not envision any action that might alter the face of contemporary culture as expressed through TV and radio programs, popular movies and magazines, and the daily paper.

Of course, there also exists a large, contented portion of the mass media audience who neither question where the fare comes from, worry about what impact it may or may not be having on their lives, or understand what the big deal is for all those angry activists. "After all," they sigh between programs, "it's just media." "If you *are* concerned or worried," they note while standing in line at the Multiplex, "shut the TV off, cancel your subscriptions, don't buy a ticket. What you don't see can't hurt you."

This book is for all of the above groups of people, most of which are represented within the pool of students taking Introduction to Mass Media courses. These groups rarely engage in dialogue to share each others' views about media, and large introductory classes further prohibit interaction and exchange. Consequently, this book offers a collection of readings about mass media from popular and trade publications that support highly divergent perspectives. Just as you cannot know what is being shown on Channel 3 when you are watching Channel 5, members of one group often cannot put themselves in their neighbor's shoes and see things from another perspective. In a sense, this book offers you your neighbor's shoes. Try them on. Take them around the block. You don't have to buy these perspectives, but you can certainly get the feel for them and see how they fit with your own views and vantage point. Hopefully, intellectual growth will result.

This book is meant to compliment a primary, required text; it does not stand on its own. Most introductory books do a wonderful job of offering the history and development of mass media. Many examine the paramount issues that have resulted from this evolution, and discuss the primary findings from social science research. No one text, however, can cover all of the important issues related to a phenomenon so complex, varied, and far-reaching. Similarly, no one text can address these issues from the wide variety of perspectives of societal reaction to these issues. Indeed, most texts pride themselves in not taking a voice, so that the readers can simply be informed rather than persuaded. Of course, what can also result from this approach is that readers fail to experience the dynamics of the mass communication process, fail to consider the important implications of a media-dependent society, fail to reflect on their own views. The readings provided here are meant to stimulate thought, generate dialogue, and provide avenues for reflection. Readers will realize that they are active participants in the mass communication process, whether they engage in mass media consumption or not.

The seventeen chapters in this book address the most controversial and contemporary areas of concern and criticism, although not all of these areas are examined in every Introduction to Mass Media course. This book was purposefully designed to provide enough variety and breadth so that most of the chapters are applicable to every course offering. Regardless of which chapters are assigned, each contains several applicable to every course offering. Regardless of which chapters are assigned, each contains several short essays. Essays typically come from different publications and offer divergent perspectives. Each chapter contains a brief introduction and a worksheet containing four questions about the readings. This worksheet can be used as a class assignment or for extra credit, as a vehicle to facilitate class discussion, or as away for the readers to register reaction to the essays for their own edification and reference.

Those who produce mass mediated messages and have written the enclosed critical essays on the mass communication process have done so with the investment of much time and mental energy. We hope that the reader will respond in kind.

Thanks must be extended to our colleagues in the Department of Communication at Cleveland State University, past and present, who have taught the basic mass media course. They have created one of the most popular and valuable courses in the college, which has inspired the production of this book. We are confident that these pages will meet their expectations and serve their needs. Special thanks to Ellen Huber, Research Assistant Extraordinaire, for her time, energy and resourcefulness in the coordination of this Second Edition.

Robert Abelman
Robin Ross

I

Media Industry–Print

Slightly more than 550 years ago, a German craftsman invented a machine that introduced to the then-civilized world what is now known as mass media. Johannes Guttenberg and his colleagues little realized that moveable type and the primitive, hand-operated printing press would initiate what ultimately became the "communication revolution," which has affected virtually everyone throughout the world.

Today, modern versions of Gutenberg's technology produce some 63 million copies of approximately 1,700 daily newspapers that are being circulated in the United States alone. This week, more than 50 million copies of some 7,500 weekly newspapers will be distributed. This month, nearly 10,000 magazine titles will reach the marketplace. This year, some 45,000 new book titles (including what you hold in your hands) will compete for readers.

In addition to technological changes and the subsequent increase in audience, there has been an economic upheaval and reconfiguration of media ownership. We are currently in a time of mergers and acquisitions, a concentration and reorganization of much of the print industry. Indeed, companies are buying both print and broadcast properties, blurring the distinction between the print and broadcast media and eliminating the number of voices heard in the marketplace. "Mom and Pop" publications have been purchased by corporations, forming a "chain" of ownership in the industry. These corporations, in turn, are being bought out by even larger, more powerful, and often international conglomerates. Cities that once possessed a vibrant and competitive market of several newspapers are now left with one.

Interestingly, while the number and diversity of newspapers are dwindling, the world of magazines reflects the opposite extreme. More than any other medium, the magazine anticipated the age of information and emphasized discrete "target" audience segments through specialization. However, magazines are currently facing stiff competition from other media (e.g., cable television) attempting to reach the same audience. Consequently, magazines are also increasingly becoming party to corporate mergers and buy-outs, risking autonomy and independence for financial security.

The three essays provided in this section reflect the changing times in the print industry. The first, "Time: The Counterattack," examines one of the largest and most high-profile examples of the contemporary economic upheaval. It paints a portrait of the existing reconfiguration of media ownership, in all its complexity. The second essay, "The Revival of the Alternative Press," reflects upon a day in the not so distant past when the American press was highly diverse, somewhat radical, and more concerned with the bottom line than the bottom dollar. It offers us peek of what the print industry was, so we can gain better perspective on what it has become. The third essay, "The Newsweeklies: Is the Species Doomed" explores the changes in the magazine industry described above. In particular, it discusses the struggle of the three largest, general interest news magazines in a time of specialization and medium segmentation.

Time: The Counterattack
John Schwartz, NEWSWEEK

Up at the command center on the 34th floor of the Time & Life Building, the generals looked drawn. In the aftermath of battle, a stream of reporters was trooping through. For the final interview of the day, Time Inc. chairman J. Richard Munro, president N.J. Nicholas Jr. and Warner Communications chairman Steve Ross offered fruit or cookies, and then trotted out the latest figures for the marriage of Time and Warner. Despite their exhaustion, they seemed exuberant, almost giddy, like fraternity boys who had pulled off their first all-nighter. "We're the walking wounded," said Munro, smiling bravely.

Two weeks ago it seemed that the empire founded by Henry Luce in 1922 had all but soldiered itself into the ground. The planned friendly merger with Warner, intended to protect Time Inc. from takeovers, had in effect put it into "play" on Wall Street. Martin Davis, CEO of Paramount (formerly Gulf + Western), entered a stunning $10.7 billion bid for Time, killing the delicate deal with Warner. Stock in all three companies fluctuated wildly as each fell victim to rumored takeover plots by such players as Rupert Murdoch and General Electric. When The Nation offered its own satirical "white knight" takeover of Time, it was about the only potential entry that didn't cause the ticker to jump.

Behind closed doors, Time and Warner boards pored over options. Warner went by the code name "Batman," the studio's planned summer blockbuster. "Batgirl" was the Time subsidiary being formed to buy Warner stock. Time Inc. was "Joker." Then last Friday Time and Warner announced their counterattack: Time would buy Warner outright for $14 billion instead of merging with it. Time hoped to make itself too big for Paramount to buy, and continued to defend the Warner deal as America's answer to global competition in the media industry. Others saw it a different way. Andrei Shleifer, professor of finance at the University of Chicago, says executives of Time and Warner are doing little more than "trying to keep their jobs . . . it's not clear what this merger is going to accomplish for shareholders."

Has Time snatched victory from the jaws of corporate restructuring? Far from it. "You're in a play with many endings," says money manager Mario Gabelli. "This is only the third act." Several scenarios could be written, any of them ultimately changing the face of Time Inc. Another bidder could surface who would offer a higher price for Time alone, scotching the merger with Warner. Or Paramount could line up a buyer—perhaps Warner shareholder Herbert J. Siegel—to outbid Time for Warner. And though it would likely take a whopping $24 billion to buy the combined Time Warner, such sums have been spent before: the megadeal that took RJR Nabisco private totaled nearly $25 billion. The only certain outcome is that the deal will be entangled in drawn-out court battles—with Paramount and perhaps disgruntled Time shareholders leading the charge.

Short term: The titanic struggle for control of one of America's most prestigious companies marked another chapter in the corporate warfare of the 1980s. The wave of mergers and acquisitions has forced companies to take on crushing burdens of debt. The Time fight underscores again the questions over "revolving-door capitalism": are companies only run to get the highest price for shareholders—and is that the best prescription for making America competitive in the global marketplace? Should managers work for the long term or simply churn out the highest overnight returns for stockholders? The takeover advocates argue that much of the "long term" talk is simply cover for managers who haven't performed well enough. Most managers counter that their colleagues who decide to look long term find their companies squarely in the gunsights of investment bankers and takeover lawyers. And many shareholders are also playing for the short term, whether they are arbitrageurs looking for a quick killing or fund managers obligated to grab the highest profit for their investors.

Those issues had already ensnarled Time, ensuring that the company that emerges from the fray will look very different from today's. On Sixth Avenue, Time Inc. employees, wary of the first Warner merger, noted caustically that their company would be spending $14 billion—only to complete virtually the same deal that *Time* magazine had linked to "restoring U.S. competitiveness in the 1990s." On the executive floor, a sign referring to a "34th-floor crossover" had been vandalized to read, "the 34th-floor doublecross . . ." The staffers feared that the debt Time is about to incur will cause new rounds of cost cutting, threatening the quality of Time's products and curbing the development of new magazines—harsh realities in a corporate culture that once had a reputation for such lavish spending that it carried the nickname "Paradise Publishing". Clearly irritated by questions about discontent, Munro responded, "You know journalists—they're cynical guys." Nicholas, by his side, quickly added, "A certain amount of skepticism is essential for a journalist."

Time Inc. has taken the budget knife to its editorial products before. It closed down the weekly version of *Life* magazine in 1972 and shuttered the more than 100-year-old Washington Star in 1981. Like many other companies, Time has undergone a range of belt-tightening measures in the '80s. Time executives claimed that a Paramount takeover would endanger its editorial integrity, but by that logic it seemed that the debt-driven Warner acquisition posed a similar threat. "Wherever there are good, successful journalism values," laments media watchdog Ben H. Bagdikian of the University of California, Berkeley, "sooner or later they're going to become more impersonal and money people begin to take over." With either partner, Time would become more and more an entertainment company. Says Ellen Berland Gibbs, an investor and consultant with CRI Media Partners: "Whatever happens, the print part of the business will never be dominant again."

How did Time Inc. get itself into this mess? Analysts say the company must share the blame for its problems. Although Time has long been considered a prime takeover target, they say, Time's management did not take the steps that might have pumped up the company's stock price. Until the Paramount bid, the company was selling at prices below $130 per share. That was far less than its estimated "breakup value" of as much as $240, the price its parts would bring if sold separately. The company was especially attractive because of recent interest in media properties generally to put it in raw consumer terms, Time's respected publications and cable operations carry strong "brand names," such as *Time, Fortune* and HBO. Because Time was successful, it was vulnerable.

Time looked to the Warner merger as its salvation, but the plan, announced last March, merely turned up the heat. Supporters of the merger praised its debt-free nature—it would entail a share-for-share sway of the two companies' stocks. However, critics soon began to attach the merger as a raw deal for Time shareholders and as too sweet for Warner, which would end up owning some 60 percent of the merged company. Worse, say some Time staffers, the merger announcement cast doubt on the company's longstanding argument that it was in the national interest for the media giant to remain independent. One editorial employee grumbles that "to enter a sweaty embrace with Steve Ross" took Time off the high road. "What did it say, that we can merge with anybody? You didn't have to be a rocket scientist to figure out that it was inviting another bid."

The Warner deal, which gave little to Time's existing stockholders, served only to provide the opening to other potential bidders. A growing backlash in Washington over the RJR Nabisco deal had cooled takeover fever for several months, but now Time had practically put itself into play. "Everybody is looking at it," one investment banker said at the time. Their only reluctance in mounting a hostile bid against Time was the "front-page syndrome"—the stigma of being portrayed in the press as a raider. "No one wanted to play the bad guy," said one adviser to potential bidders for Time. Even Davis was initially reluctant. "Time is something that Marty Davis has always talked about," says one acquaintance. Rebuffed once by Time management, Davis still wanted a deal, but not the bad reputation. Davis also worried the $10.7 billion purchase would undercut Paramount's earnings. Still, he prepared his bid for Tuesday, June 6—just two weeks before the Time Warner merger was to be ratified by shareholders. "He was agonizing over it throughout that final weekend," said an investment banker close to Davis.

Grim directors: Davis's bid threw Time Inc. into internal turmoil and sent its stock price shooting up 44 points in a single day. As rumors of other bidders advanced, some Time employees grew fatalistic. Toward the end of the week, one editor joked to his secretary as he left for lunch, "If my boss calls, ask him to leave his name." Time's board of directors, which boasts heavyweight members such as former IBM head John Opel and Xerox CEO David Kearns, struggled to find ways to avoid Paramount's hostile move. The directors were grim. Said one: "Time is a national institution with an awful lot of identity . . . Paramount proposed just to swallow us up . . . fire everyone . . ." Time also says it communicated with other parties who were interested in snapping up parts of Time, or considered making a play for Paramount. The directors even weighed a reverse-takeover attack on Paramount—the "Pac Man defense." It didn't take long for them to realize that their best hope was to buy Warner—if Ross would go along.

A Warner sale was essentially the deal that Ross had first proposed to Nicholas and Munro when they began their negotiations two-and-a-half years before. Still, the specifics took days to negotiate. Time's two dozen merger advisers moved into the 34th floor, with three catered meals a day and very little sleep. On Thursday Warner and Time management spent seven hours hammering out the final agreement, with bankers and lawyers shuttling between Time's offices on Sixth Avenue and Warner's on Rockefeller Plaza. Shortly before 7 p.m., the parties came to an agreement: Time would pay $70 per share, a sharp premium over its Thursday close of $55.50 per share. The management scheme central to the original merger plan—shared responsibility between Munro and Ross, with an eventual passage of power to Nicholas—was preserved. Time and Warner also invoked another anticipated takeover defense: a stock swap that gave each company about 10 percent of the other. Yet one element investors expected was missing. No dividend to Time shareholders was announced. (Munro, Nicholas and Ross flatly state that none is in the works—though a source close to the deal does not rule it out.) The lawyers worked through the night writing up the contracts. "There was no moment of jubilation," recalls a director. "How could there be? The whole thing occurred because of a threat."

By now it was too late for Time to take the steps that might have prevented the battle in the first place. It could have bought up more of its own stock ("recapitalization"), which would concentrate control back on Sixth Avenue instead of Wall Street. It could also have plunged deeper into cable operations. That move would have forced Wall Street to evaluate Time like other cable giants: with a greater focus on the value of assets than on earnings. (Cable companies can be cash cows, but they periodically dilute earnings while constructing their cable networks.) Looking at Time like a cable company would have boosted its stock price, says media analyst John Bauer of Kidder, Peabody, but publishing snobbery kept the company from recognizing its strengths. "They've always had a distrust of their best business," Bauer says. "They are a tomato but kept calling themselves a rutabaga." And while either recapitalization or a bigger cable investment would have plunged the company into greater debt, analysts say a little red ink would have helped Time on Wall Street, where companies with too healthy a balance sheet become prime takeover candidates. Wall Street's love of debt "doesn't make sense, but it's there," says analyst John Reidy of Drexel Burnham Lambert.

Indeed, Wall Streeters seemed confused by the bid. Despite the drawbacks of going deeply into debt to pay for Warner, Time's stock slipped back only 6 1/2 points on the day the deal was announced. Some investors were clearly betting that the bidding war would continue. Other, like Gordon Crawford of The Capital Group (the largest shareholder of Time and Paramount and second largest of Warner) found the Warner buy preferable to Paramount's takeover. The stock of a combined Time Warner, he said, was likely to rise solidly into the future. Other Wall Streeter lambasted Time. Fund manager Ron Baron calls the Warner deal an "outrage" that will sink Time's stock price back to $130 per share. "It's very clear to see that the management of this company isn't working in the interest of shareholders," he says. (Baron sold most of his sizable chunk of Time at $120 per share.)

Despite numerous statements about the synergistic benefits of combining Warner's global distribution system with Time's varied media offerings, some skeptics contend that size alone is not a strategy. "I don't care how big you are," says Alfred Rappaport, a consultant and a professor at the Kellogg Graduate School of Management at Northwestern University, "if you don't behave in ways that earn you points in the consumer market, somebody else is going to come in and do better." As media analyst Boer put it, "This is a lot of empire building cloaked in terms of global international media competition."

Big winner: What's next? It appears that Time has bought itself a little time, if nothing else. It has taken its immediate fate out of the hands of its shareholders, and it has also complicated the life of Paramount's Davis, who would have to add Time's new $14 billion in debt to this bid in order to mount a new attack. Paramount still has arrows in its quiver: if it can line up a buyer for Warner at a higher price, Warner shareholders could reject Time. The companies are now fighting their hottest battles in court. In Paramount's suit against Time, the courts will have to balance Paramount's still standing offer against the long-term earnings potential of the newly debt-laden Time Warner. Time also filed suit Friday against Paramount for interfering in its merger plans, accusing Paramount of lying in its tender offer. Paramount called the suit "a continuation of the publicity campaign Time has been waging."

Even if last week's counterattack succeeds, the victory would not be without its ironies. One of the biggest winners could prove to be Steve Ross. Not only would he gain substantial control over the newly merged company, he would also reap a fortune on the increased value of his 830,000 Warner shares. As for Time Inc., the company that had campaigned bitterly against Paramount's debt-driven takeover attempt would get the upper hand only by going massively into debt itself. In mounting its defense, Time has been forced to turn its back on what in Mr. Luce's day passed for sound accounting. The founder would not have liked it, but those seemed to be the terms of trade in the closing years of the American Century.

The Revival of the Alternative Press
Shirley Biagi, MEDIA/IMPACT

In the 1800s, the abolitionist and emancipation movements used alternative newspapers to voice their social arguments. Like their predecessors, people who supported the alternative press in the 1960s felt that the mainstream press was avoiding important issues, such as the anti-Vietnam War movement and the civil rights movement.

In 1955, journalist I. F. Stone anticipated the trend that created 1960s alternative newspapers. As an articulate critic of the government, Stone began *I. F. Stone's Weekly,* which he researched, wrote, and published virtually by himself. Filled with valuable insider information about the federal government that only Stone seemed to know, *I. F. Stone's Weekly* outlasted many of the weeklies created by the social protest movements of the 1960s. (Citing poor health, Stone stopped his Weekly which had by then become biweekly—in 1972.)

In 1964, as a way to pass along news about the antiwar movement, the *Los Angeles Free Press* became the first underground paper to publish regularly. The *Barb* in Berkeley, *Kaleidoscope* in Chicago, and *Quicksilver Times* in Washington, D.C., soon followed.

In his book *Uncovering the Sixties: The Life and Times of the Underground Press,* Abe Peck describes the alternative voice: "Mainstream newspapers ran crime news and arts reviews and Dick Tracy. Underground papers ran demonstration news and rock reviews and the *Fabulous Furry Freak Brothers,* a comic about three amiable 'heads' Tracy would have busted for their rampant potsmoking."

Cornell University professor Theodore J. Lowi, who calls the '60s activists "extreme reformists," says that one reason the alternative press declined is that the causes these newspapers espoused became part of the mainstream. In 1971, for example, the *Los Angeles Times* editorialized against the Vietnam War, and the *Boston Globe* followed a year later.

These reformists "used radical action to gain attention," says Lowi, "but their demands and hopes were for the present society to live by its own ideals. . . . And the Sixties movement succeeded to a large extent. Universities reorganized themselves: there is more public access to agencies; there have been civil rights advances; there is more pacifism. Success is one reason for the decline of the movement."[1]

What the 1960s underground press did prove had been proved two centuries before—that in America, causes need a voice, and if those voices are not represented in the mainstream press, publications emerge to support alternative views.

---

[1]Abe Peck, *Uncovering the Sixties: The Life and Times of the Underground Press* New York: Pantheon Books, 1985), p. xiv.

The Newsweeklies:
Is the Species Doomed?

Bruce Porter, COLUMBIA JOURNALISM REVIEW

For all the popularity of the three newsweeklies, as measured by a combined readership of some 50 million people, their editors in recent years have been haunted by the vague feeling that, like the doomed dinosaurs, the magazines' existence on earth was not guaranteed to last forever, maybe not even far into the 1990s. Economically, the picture has been distinctly gray, with sales of ad pages slipping by around 20 percent in the last decade, mostly from the loss of ads formerly taken out by cigarette and liquor companies. Circulation has risen only marginally since 1970, compared to the 1960s, during which it nearly doubled, and what increases there were had to be bought at great expense, by fire-saling subscriptions or giving away fancy gifts such as telephones and underwater radios. Most disturbingly, the crucial figure for newsstand sales—the number that media buyers along Madison Avenue have always seen as an index of how "hot" a book they were being sold—plummeted more than 25 percent in the last twenty years, from a combined total of about 615,000 copies sold each week in 1968 to 455,000 last year.

The main problem, ironically, seemed to be that *Time* and *Newsweek* and, to a lesser extent *U.S. News & World Report,* had become the prime victims of their own success. Where once the newsmagazines stood alone in offering readers a colorful, well-written digest of the week's events, larded with sufficient interpretation to put the news into clear perspective, in recent years this endeavor has drawn a heavy amount of competition from week-in-review sections of newspapers, as well as from television talk shows, magazine shows, and weekend insider programs about economics and Washington politics. Where once the newsmagazines were the general public's only source of news about special areas, such as the law, medicine, the press, and the environment, today all the large dailies, including *USA Today,* also employ back-of-the-book specialists dealing in these subjects. And where once the newsmagazines provided residents of small towns with virtually their only source of sophisticated analysis of national and international developments, nowadays practically everyone in the country can get home delivery of *The New York Times,* as well as *The Wall Street Journal,* not to mention being able to tune in to the substantive news programs coming over National Public Radio and the Public Broadcasting Service or to flick on the wall-to-wall coverage provided by Cable News Network.

"The question it has suddenly become quite urgent for newsmagazines to ask is, 'What are we giving readers that they can't get anywhere else?'" says Roger Rosenblatt, a former Harvard English professor and essay writer for *Time* who was hired late fall as the most recent in a fairly rapid succession of editors trying to turn *U.S. News & World Report* around. "You have to ask yourself why a reader needs us if he gets told a fact on Monday and you tell him the same fact a week from Monday."

Why indeed? Which might explain why the three newsweeklies these days are engaged in one of the biggest and most frantic renovations in their histories, trying to discover a new formula for success that, in the words of a hopeful-sounding promotional announcement to readers of *Time,* will yield "a magazine for the 1990s, a vital print companion to the electronic age." Not only have they souped up their graphics, added new departments, and tinkered with the designs of their covers, but they have also altered the content of their magazines, both in the manner in which they write about the news and in the kind of news they write about. "One thing became remarkably clear in the 1980s, and that was that what the newsmagazines were doing was all-consumingly boring," says Walter Shapiro, senior writer at *Time,* formerly of *Newsweek* and *The Washington Monthly.* "And telling readers what they already knew, but telling it with a sprightly lead, that was *still* boring."

Time: chummier, airier . . . sharper?

The most recent set of changes was promulgated with great fanfare last October by the editors of *Time* and amounted in part to yet another effort by a publication to engage in "user friendliness." "Our analysis," says *Time* managing editor Henry Muller in a by-now familiar complaint, "is that people have less time to themselves and are more harassed and under pressure to give more time to their jobs, their families, and their communities, and they simply have less time to read us." To try to forge a closer relationship with its reader, *Time* began running reader surveys, asking people, for instance, if they would be willing to separate garbage into cans, bottles, and papers if such action would help conserve the environment. It now features readers' opinions in headlined quotes in the letters column ("I will continue to eat oat bran for the rest of my life." Harry G. Vredenbregt of Watertown, Wisconsin, brayed in twenty-four-point type in response to a *Time* cover story on cholesterol). It introduced a human interest department called American Ideas that regularly dishes up warmhearted portraits of "people who are not household names but who do make a difference." Early samples: a Texas nun battling the state to get drinking water to poor families along the Mexican border; a retired New York advertising executive doling out wool gloves to derelicts on the Bowery.

To get information more rapidly "off its pages into the minds of its readers"—Henry Luce put it in his prospectus the year before *Time* made its debut in 1923—the magazine expanded its index from one page to two, added a Critics Choice page with quick recaps of book, music, and movie reviews, and instituted a host of design changes. Their purpose is both to air out the pages and to allow editors to feature the salient parts of stories in devices like blurbed quotes, thumbnail picture captions, and boxes—nicknamed "factoids," by staff writers irritated at having to write stories in several different bits—all with the aim of insuring that readers get a fast idea of what a story says without having to undergo the inconvenience of actually reading it.

Although the editorial side was given a little extra space to play with, what *Time* gained in bigger art, lighter pages, and jazzier graphics it necessarily had to take away from text. Cover stories were cut from an average of nearly 1,000 lines to 600. Actual written copy in the issue of last December 5 filled about 100 fewer column inches than was the case in the issue of December 6, 1968, almost all taken away from the Nation and World sections. The shrinkage occurred despite the fact that the news hole in the 1988 issue contained twenty-one columns more than did the one in 1968. And with a greater number of departments and features these days among which to divvy up the increasingly scarce words, stories in *Time* can get pretty thin. Before the magazine was redesigned, for instance, a two-page spread, with a modest amount of art, would provide readers an average of about 300 lines of copy. But last December 5, a two-page Travel section, equipped with a triple-banked headline, whopping pictures, and four separate factoids, had room for only 102 lines of regular text. "There's just less in *Time* these days than there used to be," complains one editor. "I get through reading the magazine and I feel hungry."

Indeed, the new expanded two- to three-page People section—with its lopsided title and wacky assortment of type, the section struck one staff member as looking "like a ransom note"—is so devoid of actual information that it makes one nostalgic for the old fever-pitch *Time*-ese, which for all its use of reversed sentences, piled-on adjectives, and parenthetical asides, packed an awful lot of facts into a tiny space. Here's a People item that ran in 1958 about the pianist Van Cliburn:

> Surrounded by Russian souvenirs, including a 6-foot lilac bush, mop-topped Pianist Van Cliburn, 23, fresh from victory in Moscow's International Tchaikovsky Competition, flew into New York to clasp his happy parents with bearhugs, gab about his Russian hosts ("They're very much like Texans"), shake hands with fans (among them, one 7-year-old who rapturously referred to him as "Moving Van") and settle down for a concert tour.

Total elapsed space: about 1-1/2 inches.

Compare that with a People piece that ran last October. Printed in gargantuan type and accompanied by a huge picture of Johnny Carson and David Letterman, it took up a full half page of the magazine for the sole apparent purpose of repeating a limp Dan Quayle joke borrowed from a Letterman interview with *Rolling Stone* magazine. There was nothing at all in the item about Johnny Carson.

More significant, however, than providing its audience a quicker read and a different feel in its news columns is the degree to which the new *Time* has turned up the decibel level of its editorial product. In recent years, says Muller, a former chief of correspondents who was appointed managing editor in the spring of 1987, the magazine had grown somewhat bland, straying too far from the feistiness Luce imbued it with back in the beginning.

In the years since, the magazine traversed its notorious phase in the two decades after World War II, during which it served more or less as a mouthpiece for the Eastern Republican Establishment: then it tried to right itself during the period of Henry Grunwald's editorship, from the late 1960s to late 1970s, when he discarded much of its ideology in an effort to recapture intellectual respectability. The price it paid, Muller believes, was to become dull, "I think we overcompensated slightly during that period," Muller says, "by rounding off the edges of a lot of stories—adopting the 'Yes, but' formula in which you would quote two professors with opposite points of view and end up the story by saying, 'Whatever the case . . . .' What we want to restore to *Time is* the edge without the ideology."

One way of doing this is to pitch coverage of major news events at a sharper angle to make it, in a word that seems to be on everyone's lips at all three newsmagazines, "provocative." Now, assuming that readers already know most of the news, *Time is* putting new emphasis on telling them what they should think about it. "I accept the fact that people get their news from TV and other sources," Muller says. "But they're confused. Our singular strength is that we can bring thought and analysis to the news, not just a packaging of what happened the previous week. . . . We've got to help readers think."

To this end, *Time's* cover story the week after the stock market crash of October 1987 showed columns of people marching behind an American flag being carried by no one. "Who's in Charge?" the headline asked, the implied judgment being that the president was sitting on his hands. Its cover on Dan Rather's famous interview with then candidate George Bush called the shouting match "The Ambush that Failed" and Rather himself a "gunslinger." And last April, after Jesse Jackson won the Michigan primary, there he was on the cover of *Time,* depicted in a painting as grinning with a "Gotcha" expression, behind a headline that said simply: J E S S E!? "In the old days," Muller says, "the headline would have been more noncommittal." Adding the exclamation point, he says, "means we're saying, 'Holy shit—Jesse!' Which we couldn't really say, of course."

In an even sharper break with its past, the magazine has begun bringing in special voices from the outside—people who have built reputations as analysts and critics—and to encourage those on staff to speak their minds more freely under top-of-the-story bylines. Thus, historian Garry Wills provided *Time* with an analysis of George Bush's election victory; financier Felix Rohatyn told readers what to expect in the post-crash economy. The magazine hired Michael Kramer from *New York* magazine and Margaret Carlson from *Esquire* and recruited Michael Kinsley and Charles Krauthammer of *The New Republic* as essayists. Correspondents in the bureau have been encouraged to write their own stuff as well as report it—"writing to space," it's called—as opposed to producing the voluminous files the bureaus have traditionally supplied to the writers in New York. "Henry Muller wants us to speak with a voice and to make judgments," says Walter Isaacson, a former *Nation* editor and now a senior writer. "We're using the news as a springboard, a jumping-off place to get to the things readers can't get elsewhere."

Describe it how you will, the typical new *Time* takeout starts with something that sounds mighty like a plain old editorial. "Democracy is an optimistic faith." *Time* writer Walter Shapiro stated in his introduction to the magazine's post-election coverage, "and the choice of a new president cannot help inspiring a flicker of faith. . . . The promise of a Bush administration lies in the hope that the new president will soon inspire America to forget the manner in which he was elected." And some of the new-style writing sounds chauvinistic enough to have come right from the pen of old man Luce. "In the age of Gorbachev," Isaacson opined after the Soviet president's visit to New York last December, "'new thinking' has become a Soviet monopoly. If Bush hopes to define an age of his own he must start by reminding the world that new thinking also happens to be an American specialty."

Not every newsmagazine aficionado is convinced that the new, or old, voices of *Time*, provocative though they may be, are what readers really want to hear. "The question is, do readers buy *Time* or *Newsweek* because they want to hear what the editors have to say about last week's events, or do they buy them to hear exciting voices making exciting points?" says one former *Time* editor. "If I want to hear exciting voices I can find them in a lot of places. If I want to read *The New Republic*, I'll go out and buy it. But what I can't get in a lot of places are the resources *Time* and its editors can bring to reporting the news."

U.S. News: thriving the briar patch

One competitor who thinks *Time's* new direction puts him at an advantage is Roger Rosenblatt editor of *U.S. News*. With an editorial budget just 40 percent larger than what *Time* spends on photography alone, *U.S. News* cannot hope to provide as comprehensive a treatment of the week's events as either *Time* or *Newsweek* can. Instead, it has chosen to stake out a sophisticated form of service journalism ("News You Can Use") emphasizing stories having to do with personal finance health, nutrition, and education. It encourages its correspondents to do thoughtful pieces about their beats ("I know it sounds impossible," wrote David Lawday from Paris, "but I'm just beginning to start to like the French"). It also is less likely to get suckered into non-stories by paying slavish attention to the glitzy end of the news. Just before the Gorbachev visit, for instance, there was a moment when he was going to pay a visit to real estate developer Donald Trump's complex of lavish stores on Fifth Avenue, a prospect to which both *Time* and *Newsweek* gave a lot of free publicity and to which *U.S. News* gave none at all. The visit, of course, never came off.

U.S. News also comes up with offbeat ideas for covers that don't seem to fit into the format of its two competitors. One such effort last December examined the children of four "Amazing Families," and tried to show what circumstances had led to their success. "What *I can't* do," says Rosenblatt, "is what *Time* does so well, and that is to say to the reader. 'We have apprehended this tremendous mass of information that occurred in the last seven days and are giving it back to you in a form that you can readily understand and that gives you what you need to live in your world.' There will always be room for at least one magazine that does that, and *Time* can take the room, in fact, it is the room. But if they want to stress individual voices and provocative writing instead, I say, 'Great, throw me into that briar patch,' because that puts them on a par with me. I'm doing it now and I think I can do it better than they can."

If success depends on rivaling *Time's* battery of clever writers, however, one voice US. *News* might usefully consider doing without is that of its publisher, Mortimer B. Zuckerman, the real estate developer and owner of *The Atlantic,* whose back-page bromides would send the worst-case insomniac off to dreamland. Example: "America can view the world these days and feel satisfied and even inspired by the clear triumph of the American philosophy. . . . No country provides easier access to the marketplace of opportunity. . . . It is this culture—regularly refreshed by immigration—that brings out the best in a diverse people . . ." etc., etc. On the other hand, if providing Zuckerman space for his editorials is what it takes to insure his continued support, the deal is probably a fair trade. The magazine was barely breaking even when he purchased it in 1984; since then he's almost doubled the editorial budget. But because he made the publication into a privately held corporation, no outsider knows for sure what shape it's in today. Advertising people at *Time* and *Newsweek* estimate that *U.S. News* must be losing somewhere between $7 million and $10 million a year. Zuckerman says it is "moderately profitable." In 1988 *U.S. News* did post a

10 percent increase in ad pages. Sources at *Time,* whose pages rose 6 percent, and at *Newsweek,* where they dropped by 3 percent, claim that Zuckerman sells his pages cheap; Zuckerman says that he offers "volume discounts," as do all magazines.

Newsweek: Staying hip while running scared

Whatever the case, *US News,* assuming Zuckerman's continued support, is probably in better shape than *Newsweek,* whose imminent sale by its parent, the Washington Post Company, is a subject of constant rumor. "People around here are so nervous," one senior editor says, "that last week when the cleaners came in and vacuumed the carpet twice everyone freaked out. They thought the guys with the blue suits were about to come in to look over the merchandise." *Newsweek's* contribution to the earnings of its parent company dropped from 30 percent twenty years ago to 6 percent in 1987. And although the magazine boasted of a circulation increase in 1988 of 200,000, much of it was bought dearly. Insuring that cheap subscribers come back as renewals at regular rates always gives circulation directors headaches. To keep circulation from dropping requires the constant giving away of copies at bargain prices, which is an expensive proposition, especially considering that these days magazines are trying to shift some of their cost burden from advertisers to readers. Rather than paying the cost of trying to keep its own circulation up, for instance, *Time* decided last fall to lop 300,000 people off its lists.

The troubles at *Newsweek* may explain why it preceded *Time* by several years in effecting its own face-lift, part of which included hiring a batch of outside writers, six of them from *The Washington Monthly* alone, to try to ream out its newsmagazine prose. About half of the stories these days are written by the person who did the reporting. While the buzzword at *Time* is "provocative," *Newsweek* editors talk about being "smart," meaning that stories are pitched at a slightly hipper, more urban set of readers, people in their thirties and forties. "I edit for people the same age as myself, the people who grew up on rock'n'roll," says Sarah Crichton, thirty-four, the magazine's cultural editor, who had formerly headed *Seventeen* magazine, and, before that, had been an editor at *The Harvard Crimson.* "*Time* follows the old rules and just reports on what's new," she adds. "At *Newsweek* we're tracking a generation." In the last two years, for instance, *Newsweek* has had four cover stories on the problems of bearing or raising children. In culture coverage, *Newsweek* was alone in doing a takeout on Keith Richards, lead guitarist for The Rolling Stones, on the occasion of the release of his first solo album, and a cover on John Lennon at the time a controversial biography of him was published last fall. Crichton was also well ahead of *Time,* and *The New York Times* for that matter, with a story about Dennis Potter, who wrote the innovative British television film *The Singing Detective.*

Newsweek's election coverage was particularly noteworthy for its pursuit of a hip voice, a tone that would be familiar to readers of, say, *Esquire* or New York's *Spy* magazine. In delineating the campaign, *Newsweek* did not report so much on what the candidates did or said as on the ways in which their staffs tried to manipulate the public and the press. Both *Time* and *Newsweek,* for instance, produced the obligatory cover story on the Iowa caucuses but the one in *Newsweek,* "Adventures in Campaignland, Where the American Dream Becomes a Hallucination," was remarkable for giving readers a surrealistic, heavily cynical view of the process that exposed the manipulators to public view, as if a curtain had suddenly been pulled back from a puppet show. The piece was accompanied by an insider's glossary of campaign terms ("Bluehead gig: n., meeting between candidate and elderly voters") and illustrated by a running satirical cartoon by Mark Alan Stamaty of New York's *Village Voice.* Sample balloon talk from staffer to candidate Dan Dazzle: "Okay, Dan, here's your list of buzzwords for tonight's debate. They're all carefully targeted. The first three should resonate well with pig farmers . . . and these next two phrases are aimed at under 30 convenience store clerks. . . . We hope to harden up some of our soft support and soften Senator Fuzz's hard support."

In a weekly column called Conventional Wisdom the magazine also tracked not how candidates were actually doing but how political pundits *felt* they were doing; arrows showed whether someone's stock had risen or declined. "In 1984, we did the best we could to try to report the conventional wisdom as news; this time we lampooned it," says Jonathan Alter, an alumnus of *The Washington Monthly who*, with Dickey Kaus (since returned to his former employer, *The New Republic*), helped sharpen the magazine's political cutting edge. "We tried to show readers that a lot of the punditry coming from politicians and writers in Washington was fallible." Including some of what was said by *Newsweek*. In one piece Alter and Kaus reminded readers that after Jackson's primary victory in Michigan the magazine had called Jackson the "new front runner" and said that an effort by Dukakis's staff to pump life into the governor's lagging primary campaign "was going to be hard to do." *Newsweek* has also experimented with personal journalism in a way uncharacteristic of newsmagazines. In one cover story, senior writer Jerry Adler told about his and his wife's anguish over raising a handicapped child; in another, correspondent Frank Maier shared his heart problems with readers. "On a gray afternoon two weeks before Christmas, my doctor told me I was dying," he wrote. "To me, unpredictable is not a dirty word at all," says editor-in-chief Rick Smith, who is responsible for most of the changes at the magazine. "The reason our readers love the magazine is that we don't write from formulas and we don't think on the basis of conventional wisdom."

Another way *Newsweek* has always tried to distinguish itself from *Time* has been to get off the mark a lot faster in reporting the news, typically to go after news exclusives and to "crash a cover" late in the week when events seemed to dictate it. *Time,* on the other hand, when confronted with a scoop, "is like a whore with a baby," as its late managing editor, Roy Alexander, put it a few decades ago. "She just doesn't know what to do with it." When it comes to choosing among news events, for instance, *Newsweek* is more likely to go with the still-breaking story than to push a piece whose effect on people may be more profound in the distant future. Both magazines geared up for cover stories on Gorbachev's trip to New York, but when the earthquake hit Armenia and the Soviet president broke off his visit, *Newsweek* instantly switched its cover to the earthquake while *Time* stuck with its story about Gorbachev and the cold war. "We try to figure out this Wednesday what people will be talking about next Wednesday," says executive editor Stephen Smith. "Impact journalism" is what the promotion department calls it—evidence that the magazine is living up to its current slogan, which has it that "No one reports it like *Newsweek* reports it."

Some of *Newsweek's* last-minute cover switches have committed it to stories of at least questionable taste, one example of which was a quickie cover on "Trash TV" last November that took only a day to report and write. Filled with a good amount of tongue-clucking disapproval of the loud-mouthed talk shows, sensational programming, and the occasional on-camera brawl, the story was illustrated with the battered, discolored face of syndicated television personality Geraldo Rivera, in effect using the same tawdry appeal as the programs it condemned in order to sell magazines—successfully, as it turned out. The cover ended up being the biggest newsstand hit of the fall. Then, barely four weeks later, *Newsweek* crashed another cover on the Joel Steinberg trial, this one illustrated with a shot of a battered Hedda Nussbaum—setting a record of sorts by having put two people with prominently broken noses on the front of the magazine in a month's time.

"One criticism of *Newsweek is* that they often fail to distinguish between what's on *Nightline,*" says Walter Shapiro, who spent three years at *Newsweek* before becoming a senior writer at *Time* in 1987. In their rush to be trendy—and much to the irritation of their staff—the "Wallendas," as the top three *Newsweek* editors have long been called in honor of the editorial balancing act they perform each week, leap nimbly from idea to idea, often leaving the matter to be settled, not by editorial judgment, but simply by having time run out on them at the end of the week. "On Tuesday," says Shapiro, "you knew that if they assigned you to write a 300-line violin ['violin' being newsmagazine parlance for the introduction to the lead national or international story], the same story would be reduced to a forty-line box by Friday, depending on who was on Ted Koppel or in *The New York Times* on Thursday."

For these and other reasons, morale in general at the magazine has sunk pretty low these days. In the last two years, for instance, a dozen staff members, including Washington bureau chief Mel Elfin, have defected to *U.S. News*. Not only is there the natural pall that settles on a place plagued by rumors of a sale, but senior editors in particular grouse that their ideas are often ignored. "The basic senior editors' complaint is that the top editors don't listen to them," one senior editor says. "They hire you for your supposed expertise in a certain area, then they don't do what you suggest."

Then there are the cutbacks. At *Time*, where editorial perquisites always existed on a slightly more sumptuous level than at *Newsweek*—executive editor Smith recalls that when he ran the Nation section at *Time* the senior editors there were only gently admonished one year for having spent $39,800 on Friday night peanuts and cheese—the staff was pared down to more or less fighting weight two years ago. One of the last vestiges of the old days, plenty of free stock for the liquor cabinets kept by senior editors for use in lightening the end-of-the-week editors chores, was not done away with until the end of 1987. "The practice," read a staff memo, "is increasingly inappropriate in an operation that is putting a premium on quality, efficiency [and] speed."

At *Newsweek*, the editors trimmed twenty-three people from the editorial staff who last fall accepted tempting early retirement packages. Other cuts have gone deeply into the researcher and fact-checking level and are being achieved somewhat less magnanimously. "What they're doing," one editor says, "is just not giving researchers any promotions or raises and if they get pissed off and leave, that's fine with them." Partially as a result of losing fact-checkers, as well as a few copy editors, some fairly horrendous gaffes have begun appearing in *Newsweek's* copy, errors being considered a greater sin at a newsmagazine than at a newspaper, given the time and resources the weekly publication has to get things right. In a picture caption last fall *Newsweek* told readers that Nancy Reagan and Raisa Gorbachev were shown smiling during their meeting in Reykjavik, Iceland, which must have been news to Nancy since her husband had gone to that summit conference without her. In a column about Club Med, the magazine managed to spell the word "alcoholic" in three different ways. And just before he was nominated as Republican vice-presidential candidate *Newsweek* told its readers that Dan Quayle represented the state of Iowa. "If you'd like me to," says editor-in-chief Smith, sounding somewhat testy, "I could find just as many typographical errors in *Time.*" But on the cover? In a story on the political demise of Gary Hart written by historian journalist Garry Wills, a last-minute change in design resulted in the author's name appearing on the cover of *Newsweek* spelled with only one *r*.

In the end, however, whatever throes *Newsweek* and its two competitors are going through to try to assure their survival into the 1990s—whether it's being super smart, extra provocative, or oriented toward service—the question arises whether they aren't also guilty of subscribing to a conventional sort of wisdom that has about as good a take on the American reading public as it does on political candidates. For one thing, not everyone thinks the long-term newsmagazine economics are so gloomy. "Some say there's just not room for three newsmagazines; I think quite the opposite," says Mort Zuckerman of *U.S. News*, "In fact, I can imagine even more than three. When advertisers look at TV, with all the channel zapping and switching that goes on in that medium, I see continued and strong support for the high demographics at all three newsmagazines."

As for readers who don't read, the assumption that educated Americans won't bother with any information that is not done up in boxes and packaged in circus rings seems even more questionable. "If people don't read anymore, why do you have *to* fight your way to the cash register in bookstores?" asks Ray Cave, a former managing editor of *Time*. "I don't believe for a minute people don't read. The problem is there are so many good magazines out there that they've become more demanding. To get readers these days you had better be good. People have a half dozen alternatives and if you don't deserve attention you're not going to get it. People still read, but they don't tolerate a lot of damn foolishness."

Bruce Porter, an associate professor at Columbia's Graduate School of Journalism, worked at Newsweek from 1967 to 1972.

Media Industry–Print
Worksheet

1. In the essay "Time: The Counterattack," we see that the print industry is big business, and that much of its business has little to do with print (e.g., Time Inc.'s holdings in film and cable TV). In your opinion, how do you think this might impact on the quality of contemporary journalism? Give one example of a positive impact and one example of a negative impact.

2. The essay notes that "the history of the American press is full of dark pages where capricious press lords corrupted the news." Multimillionaires Joseph Pulitzer and William Hearst, for example, used their newspaper holdings as playthings during the late 1800s. Today's press lords are multi-billion dollar conglomerates. Which is worse for the editorial quality of the press? Why?

3.   As we enter into the 1990s, the alternative press—as described in the essay "The Revival of the Alternative Press"—is all but deceased. What contemporary cause or issue could most benefit from a resurgence of underground/alternative newspapers? In what way could this form of mass communication aid in public knowledge or generate public reaction?

4.   Is there still a need for news magazines in the 1990s? If you subscribe to this medium, what does it provide that other media do not? If you do not subscribe, what media seem to serve the same function as news magazines? In what ways are they better or worse?

II

Media Industry–Broadcasting

In the early 1800s, if you wanted to send a message from one point to another, you had the choice of two prosperous industries. You could hire the pony express which took (for example) ten and a half days to travel the 1500 miles from St. Joseph, Missouri to San Francisco, California. Or, you could go through the stagecoach line, which needed approximately thirteen and a half days to travel the same distance.

In the mid- to late-1800s, you could go to the local telegraph or telephone offices and deliver your message through wires from your location to your destination. Delivery was faster, more reliable, and considerably more expensive. In the early 1900s, you could go to a local radio station and pay a fee to broadcast a message over the air. While mostly beneficial to advertisers and office-seeking politicians, who wanted their messages received by a large group of people, the airwaves were nonetheless in the public domain and accessible. Much like the pony express, stagecoach, telegraph and telephone before it, the broadcast industry was developed to serve the public.

Today, the airwaves are still public—that is, radio and television stations are mandated to operate "in the public's interest, convenience, and necessity"—but the airwaves are far from accessible. In the last half century, public access has been limited to *receiving* messages from radio and television; those having regular access to message production and delivery have been limited to four distinctive groups—station owners, professional production houses, commercial advertisers, and network executives. Consequently, much money and power can be had by the one group with the most control over the messages that get delivered to the general public.

The four essays in this section examine the battle between these four groups since the formation of the television industry in the 1940s. The first essay, "Commercial Television: How it Works," defines the function of each group and how these functions have evolved over the past fifty years. While noting that the battle for power and control has often been ruthless, this essay suggests that these four groups are nonetheless mutually dependent, functionally interwoven, and *collectively* comprise the broadcast industry. The second essay, "Save CBS," examines one of the current casualties of war within the television network structure. Once the most proud, powerful, and profitable of networks, CBS has fallen upon troubled times. "Autumn of the Networks' Reign," our third essay, suggests that CBS is not alone. Rather, all three networks are facing increased competition that threatens to challenge their collective lock on television entertainment. The author of this essay suggests that a "fifth wheel"—the "ad hoc network"—is shaking up the industry and bringing new life to broadcasting. The final essay, "The Fourth Network," gives a name to this "fifth wheel." The name is ... FOX.

Commercial Television: How It Works
Robert Abelman, MASS MEDIA AND SOCIETY

Despite the increasing prevalence of cable and home videocassette recorders, valiant efforts by the Public Broadcasting Service, and the threat of a fourth commercial network by corporate moguls Rupert Murdoch, Ted Turner, and others, American television is ABC, CBS, and NBC. Together these three networks reach over 80 million households on any given night. According to a recent CBS report, by 1990 the three networks will have an estimated combined revenue of over $15 billion as a result of their capacity to capture a mass audience. Les Brown (1982, p. 26), editor of *Channels* magazine, refers to commercial television as a "beautiful business: three networks in one vast sellers' market. . . . The networks' main challenge has been in dividing up the audience. One year, NBC ran a poor third and still made record profits. Quite a business—sweet and failure-proof." That is why Capital Cities paid $3.5 billion for the acquisition of the ABC network in 1985, and General Electric purchased RCA, NBC's parent company for which it generates 40 percent of the corporate profits, for $6.3 billion in 1986.

Upon close examination, however, the heartbeat of commercial television does not resound from the networks alone. Rather, the networks are one of four interrelated, mutually dependent components of the American television industry. Commercial broadcasting would not be successful without nationwide distribution, but it would not be feasible without production houses to make programming, advertisers to buy airtime within programming, and the over 700 TV stations through which to deliver this fare to the masses. Over the years, the networks—the carriers and distributors of programming—rose to power, prestige, and accumulated wealth.

How did this happen, and how do the production houses, advertisers, and TV stations benefit from their role in this multibillion dollar industry? As we shall see, the current structure and stature of the television industry is the result of a multiphase evolution in the relationship among these four components, an evolution still in the state of flux.

The Beginning, 1948–1955

During the early days of television, the advertisers were in control of the industry. As a carry-over from radio, companies and corporations, through advertising agencies, owned and sole sponsored programming. They selected a program that best suited the company's image or, more likely, promised to be the most lucrative, and produced it themselves or had it made by independent production houses. These programs bore the company's name when they were broadcast on the air, and, because they were the sole sponsor, the companies were in a position to control program content. Consequently the networks, TV stations, and production houses were dependent on advertisers for programming and revenue.

For making these programs, production houses typically received the cost of making the program plus a 10 percent profit from the advertising agency. Producers did not retain ownership of the programs or program idea they generated for advertisers. However, in the hope of making a greater profit and retaining ownership, producers often sold their wares directly to individual TV stations or to regional or local sponsors. As television became more popular and the number of stations across the country increased, producers were able to negotiate price with a growing supply of interested buyers. All in all, it was a seller's market for producers.

Owners of television stations obtained their revenue by selling their sole commodity, airtime, to advertisers. The stations received 30 percent of the fee they would charge local advertisers when they aired network distributed programming. The 70 percent loss of potential revenue was easily justified by local broadcasters, for they received a better-quality show than would have been produced locally, they were the recipients of the prestige that came with being part of a nationwide network, and they received all this without having to solicit business. They simply signed a contract, received the network feed through telephone wires (now received through microwave and satellite), aired the program to their local viewers, and reaped the benefits. Their biggest decision was with which network to affiliate.

Affiliation was a tougher decision than it is today for, in the beginning of television, numerous television networks surfaced in an effort to capitalize on the promising future of the new medium. Clearly ABC, CBS, and NBC were in the forefront, having gained prominence and experience in the radio industry and early experimentation with television technology. The Dumont Television Network and the Westinghouse corporation, however, attempted to jump on the bandwagon and serve as go-between for the stations and the advertisers.

Indeed that was the early function of networks: to serve as national sales agents. They cleared time with the stations, collected fees from the advertiser, and arranged for the program to be distributed to participating stations. In return, the network collected a fee for its services. For several years, this symbiotic relationship among advertiser, producer, broadcaster, and network was mutually satisfactory. Each component stood to make money, and the function of one component was dependent on the others.

Eventually, however, the networks came to realize that they were the most depended upon component as the all-important link between these other parties but did not generate the most money or have the greatest control over programming.

Transition 1: Creative Control, 1955–1958

The networks first attempted to generate creative control over the programs they distributed and in so doing created problems for advertisers. According to David Sontag, former vice-president of 20th Century Fox and self-proclaimed "survivor of the Golden Age of television" (Newcomb and Alley 1983, p. 12), it was relatively easy for the networks to take control: "Program and time costs were relatively inexpensive . . . allowing the networks the option of accepting or turning down programs which advertisers had bought directly and were attempting to place on the network."

The shift in control created some problems for producers. Because the networks started pulling their weight in terms of approving or disapproving material they disseminated, the advertiser would buy the program from a producer subject to network approval. This problem was confounded when the networks began expanding the news and sports programming they produced to include more popular fare, such as daytime soap operas, thus competing with the producers who were seeking approval for their programs. Often the networks found the programs they produced more acceptable for distribution through their stations than programming offered by an outside producer. Many production companies quit, others learned the new rules, which included paying the networks a fee in return for creative counseling and advice to make their programs more acceptable for distribution.

Transition 2: The Quiz Show Scandal, 1959

The networks' next step toward control was to remove advertisers from programming decisions completely and require the producer to deal directly with them. At about the time network executives were trying to figure out how to go about such a dramatic move, a major scandal broke involving one of television's most beloved genre, quiz shows. Several winners of CBS's *The $64,000 Question*, one of the most popular programs on television from 1955 to 1958, confessed that the shows were staged and scripted rather than truly intellectual and legitimate contests.

One of the results was the removal of all intellectually based prime-time quiz shows from the airwaves. (Only recently, over twenty-five years later, have these programs resurfaced with some level of success.) The first major consequence of the scandal affected producers. CBS took advantage of the public uproar by reminding their audience and government officials that the quiz shows had been made by independent producers, not the networks, and were brought in by advertisers. The other networks claimed that they too had no control and did not know what was going on in programming. They followed CBS's lead by taking control of the programs they distributed to their affiliated stations.

From that time forward, producers with a program to sell had to go directly to one of the three networks rather than to any of the hundreds of potential advertisers. Furthermore, the networks limited their use of independent producers in an effort to cut down on the cost of program production. Instead they established relations with major film studios, which could produce programs faster and for less money because of their expansive facilities. The networks would then become the owner of the program or go into partnership with the film studio and control the program's future. Before long, the networks owned, at least in part, nearly every show they telecast.

By this time, many programs were recorded on film (videotape came later) rather than performed and aired live, and their future consisted of national and international syndication (reruns). Ownership entitled the networks to sell their programs to individual stations across the globe. It also meant that they could withhold U.S. syndication of a popular program in order to prevent the program from cutting into the ratings of their first-run shows.

The second major consequence of the scandals concerned advertisers. Many advertisers, having lost faith in television and perceiving the scandals as the first sign of television's demise, placed their advertising dollars elsewhere. Advertisers still interested in investing in television had to do so under the control of the networks. Rather than offering a program to the networks, the advertisers now found themselves in the position of being offered a series of shows over which they had no control or ownership. Thus, they paid money to the networks not only for the airtime of the TV stations but also for the programs themselves. With fewer advertisers interested in television, the networks found it more expedient and profitable to do away with sold sponsorship and offer numerous advertisers one-minute pieces of the same programs. Thus, in the course of just a few years, advertisers found themselves going from sole ownership and sponsorship of programs to competing for airtime with other advertisers on network-owned programming.

The third major consequence concerned the TV stations. With advertisers now buying pieces of programs, the companies wanted some guarantee that they were reaching as large an audience as possible during their commercial minutes. Consequently national ratings became more important than ever before, and the networks charged advertisers on a dollars-per-thousand viewers basis. The networks then paid their affiliated stations on the basis of the average number of people the stations were capable of reaching. For a successful show, the advertiser paid an increased amount for gaining access to so many viewers. The broadcasters received no additional monies from the networks for airing a popular program than they did for running a poorly attended program.

Independents, or nonnetwork affiliated TV stations, were also influenced by the scandal. Independent stations survive on the selling of local and national advertising for movies, locally produced programming, and, primarily, off-network programs purchased through syndication. When the networks gained control of syndication rights, they also controlled the existence of these independent stations. When the networks limited syndication distribution, they cut off the life's blood of many of these stations.

Transition 3: FCC Intervention and Deficit Financing, 1971

Eventually the Federal Communications Commission (FCC) and committees of both houses of Congress expressed an interest in the demise of syndication and the subsequent reduction of competition in the marketplace. Of paramount concern was the fact that the networks controlled both the production and distribution of television programming. In 1970–1971, the FCC initiated and enforced a series of unprecedented rulings designed to disrupt the growing network monopoly.

First, the FCC forced the networks out of major involvement in entertainment program ownership through the financial interest and syndication rule. This rule prohibited the networks from producing and owning its own prime-time programming and acquiring any interest or ownership in a program produced by an outside party beyond the right of exhibition. Second, the FCC mandated that the networks would no longer acquire syndication rights, called back-end profits, or engage in the selling of programs to anyone, anywhere in the world. Instead the network retained the right to show a program twice (typically during the regular season and again during the summer), and the production houses received syndication rights. Third, the FCC adopted the prime-time access rule, imposing a limit of two and a half hours that affiliates in the top fifty markets would be allowed to clear for network entertainment each weeknight in an effort to allow network-affiliated stations to choose alternative programming. The intention was to inspire locally produced programming and form a new market for producers without network interference.

Much of the good intention behind these rulings resulted in problems for producers and benefits for the networks. By the 1970s, the cost of producing a network-quality prime-time program had skyrocketed. The networks were finding it expensive to maintain big studios and the staff necessary for producing nearly two dozen programs for weekly distribution. They were already farming out productions to private companies to cut costs when the FCC ruling to get out of production came into play, which then served as a final release of what had become the financial burden of production.

The prime-time access ruling was also beneficial for the networks, for it reduced the amount of available prime-time commercial time below advertiser demand and drove up the rates the networks could charge their advertisers. This ruling was especially advantageous for ABC, which had been running hopelessly behind the other networks in the ratings. Forced to cut its schedule to two and a half hours, ABC happily discarded seven series from its large roster of losers, thereby narrowing the gap between it and its rival networks, and allowing it to become a full-fledged competitor for the first time.

Although it appeared as if the producers would greatly profit from getting back the business of program production and obtaining back-end profits, it was actually one of the worst things to happen to producers since the inception of television. Because the producers now owned syndication rights, the days of cost plus 10 percent were over, and the networks were just paying producers the average cost of producing a program—typically $400,000 for a situation comedy and $900,000 for an action-adventure show in today's market. And the networks were once again in control of accepting or rejecting a producer's program.

Consequently, in order to make a program more attractive to the networks and increase the likelihood of its acceptance, producers often created one episode of a program (*pilot*) that cost twice what they received as payment from the networks. Producers made up the difference of this deficit financing from their own pockets, an acceptable expense for the possibility of having a hit show and making a fortune from syndication. And fortunes were to be had. When *M*A*S*H* went into syndication in 1977, stations paid $250,000 per episode; today episodes are being sold for $900,000, and there are eleven years of episodes. *Magnum P.I.* went into syndication in 1986, its producers receiving $1.7 million per episode. NBC's popular program *The Cosby Show*, which will be going into syndication in 1989, is expected to accumulate $3 million per half-hour episode in national revenues (Brown 1986b, p. 72).

Here is where the problems come in. Approximately 5 percent of all pilot programs are accepted by the networks. Consequently the producers run the risk of losing $400,000 to $900,000 for every pilot episode that fails. And if the program is accepted by the networks and is successful, the networks continue to pay the standard rate for a program but expect the same quality program they received in the pilot episode. As a result, the producers find themselves having to pay twice what they receive from the networks for every episode they produce. It is not uncommon for a producer to lose $5 million to $15 million a year producing a successful program while the network makes a profit in advertising sales. For example, the producer of the successful TV drama *The Waltons* was paid approximately $275,000 per one-hour episode; the network received $600,000 in advertising revenue for that same one-hour program (Reel 1979). It is not until syndication that the producers make their money.

Herein lies the biggest problem of all: very few shows get to the point where they can be syndicated. In order to be syndicated, there need to be about one hundred episodes so individual stations can *strip* the show (that is, place an episode of the program at the same time every weekday). It usually takes from four to five years before a producer has generated that many episodes. Of ten shows that get on the air as a series, seven will be immediate failures, two will run for just a year, and only one will be a lingering success. That means that producers have no back-end profit on nine out of ten shows made. They literally lose fortune after fortune in the hope that a program lasts four or more years. And the duration of a program's run is dependent on the network's perception of the program's ability to attract a large audience of 20 million people or more.

Only extremely large production houses, typically film studios, can afford to lose millions of dollars in the hope of eventually striking it rich with one success. All totaled, television program syndication in 1985 amounted to a $1.7 billion industry (Guttenplan 1986), led by the following production houses and their 1985 syndication revenues: Coca-Cola, which owns Columbia Pictures and Embassy Communications ($400 million); Paramount Studios ($375 million); Universal Studios ($275 million); 20th Century Fox ($225 million); and Lorimar/Telepictures ($216 million) (Brown 1986a). Clearly syndication is a lucrative business, but it has led to the near elimination of small production houses.

It was originally thought that the prime-time access ruling would enable small production houses to sell programs directly to individual stations and survive. According to the FCC, the aim of the ruling was "to make available for competition among existing and potential program producers, both at the local and national levels, an arena of more adequate competition for the custom and favor of broadcasters and advertisers" (FCC 1970, p. 326). In order to make this type of arrangement feasible and the cost to producers affordable, however, the program must be sold to stations in the largest markets in the country that would pay the largest fee. Unfortunately for producers, the largest stations in these markets (New York, Los Angeles, and Chicago) are owned and operated by the organizations that kept them off the air to begin with—ABC, CBS, and NBC.

Although the prime-time access ruling seemed to have helped TV stations by lessening the networks' hold over prime-time entertainment programming, it too hurt the stations in the long run. Rather than produce local programming, broadcasters took financial advantage of this access period by buying off-network syndicated programming. This type of programming did not reflect the intent behind the ruling but was more attractive to local advertisers and thus generated a greater profit for stations than the production of their own programming or the purchase of original programming from producers. However, in response to this ruling and the reduced number of hours stations carried actual, on-network programming, the networks decided to modify their pay scale to local stations. Rather than simply paying the stations on the basis of the size of audience they were capable of delivering, the networks created the network-station rate (NSR) for each individual station.

The NSR is a figure negotiated by the network and the station based on how much money the network will pay for each equivalent hour that the station carries a network program. Prime time (8–11 P.M.) has the greatest audience and is worth one equivalent hour. Early evening (5–7 P.M.) typically has half the prime-time audience and is worth 50 percent of an equivalent hour. Daytime (9 A.M.–5 P.M.) has the smallest audience and is worth only 35 percent of an equivalent hour. The actual NSR is determined by the size of the market in which the station exists. The NBC station in Cleveland, Ohio, for example, gets approximately $5,000 per equivalent hour; the NBC affiliate in New York City gets approximately four times that amount.

The network then figures out the total equivalent hours based on the total number of hours of programming the station carries across the various time periods. Twenty-four equivalent hours are automatically subtracted every month to compensate the network for overhead costs of providing their programming service. The total number of equivalent hours are then reduced to 30 percent. (Recall that since the beginning of network-station affiliation, broadcasters received 30 percent of the fee they would charge local advertisers when they aired network distributed programming.) The remaining equivalent hours are then multiplied by the NSR, and that is the amount of money the station would receive for carrying network programming, minus 3.59 percent for artist royalty costs. This was quite a dramatic change from the early days but still worth the trouble for local broadcasters. Aside from being an independent station, network affiliation was the only game in town—until the next transition occurred.

Transition 4: Ad Hoc Networks, Early 1980s

Traditionally programs canceled by the networks are given up for dead by producers. Unless enough episodes were generated for syndication, the producer absorbed the substantial financial loss, and the program went out of production. Similarly advertisers for canceled programs simply sought new vehicles for their commercials. TV stations whose local audiences loved a program that the networks subsequently cancelled had no recourse. Recently, *Ad hoc* networks have been forming that give promising but cancelled programs a second chance to make money, offer advertisers and TV stations new episodes of cancelled favorites, and are giving ABC, CBS, and NBC a run for their money.

Ad hoc networks are comprised of organizations that own and operate stations in at least three of the largest U.S. cities and four stations in other major markets (at this time, seven television stations—five, VHF, two UHF—is the maximum number a company can own). Most stations are independents, allowing them to be relatively free to take on programming from non-network sources. Independent stations reach only 65 percent of U.S. homes, however, so it is also necessary for an Ad hoc network to get a substantial number of network affiliates to join the club in order to establish a truly nationwide network. With these stations lined up, the Ad hoc network encourages producers to continue production of their well-known but cancelled programs and then proceeds to distribute that programming to the various stations and sell time to national advertising.

Metromedia Television, an example of an organization setting this trend, resurrected *Fame,* which was canceled by NBC after two years of generally lukewarm ratings, and *Too Close for Comfort,* which had three respectable seasons on ABC when it was released (Zuckerman and Brown, 1983). Note that Ad hoc networking is not being referred to as a new trend, for this phenomenon has all the components of the TV industry through its various stages of transition. As with the beginning of television, the Ad hoc network is merely serving as a clearinghouse and distribution agent. Producers own their product, advertisers buy pieces of the program, and stations purchase the program as they would with any other form of syndication.

In addition to the resurrection of off-network programming, Ad hoc networks are generating original programming. Operation Primetime is one example, distributing such distinguished programs as *A Woman Called Golda,* with Ingrid Bergman, and *Smiley's People,* with Alec Guinness. Films rejected by the networks and cable movie channels are also being distributed by Ad hoc networks.

There is evidence that Ad hoc networks are having an impact on the TV industry, though minuscule in scope. At the NBC affiliate convention in 1982, the network announced that its prime time program availability had fallen to 97 percent of all television homes; in the daytime, NBC was off by as much as 5 percent. According to network president Pierson Mapes (Zuckerman and Brown , 1983, p. 46), that translates into millions of dollars in lost revenue each year. This effect afforded greater revenue and creative freedom for producers, however, who had felt restricted by the limited in the amount of nonnetwork programming they could accept without raising the wrath of their mother network. Furthermore, the prevalence of Ad hoc networks no doubt made the networks less cavalier about cancelling programs that still showed signs of popularity, thus offering greater security to producers. Similarly, Ad hoc networks offered stations greater variety of programming, although network-affiliated stations were somewhat limited in the amount of nonnetwork programming they could accept without raising the wrath of their mother network.

Transition 5: FCC Deregulation, Mid-1980s

The current FCC chairperson, Mark Fowler, is committed to deregulating broadcasting as much as possible, a stance quite the opposite of that held by the FCC during its era of intervention in the 1970s. The FCC has recently relinquished some of its early forms of restrictive regulation of the networks and created new avenues of entrepreneurialism for those with enough money to play the game.

One such form of deregulation has been to expand the limit of corporate television station ownership from seven to twelve stations. Furthermore UHF stations, because they do not typically attract as many viewers as VHF stations, count as only one-half of a station in the scheme of ownership. Consequently it is possible for a corporation to own as many as twenty-four (UHF) television stations across the country.

While this ruling affords Ad hoc networks a greater opportunity to expand their services and opens uncharted territories for independent producers, it also allows the already powerful networks to further their strong hold on the television industry. Each network can now reach 25 percent of the total television audience through its twelve owned and operated stations alone. As a result, the networks not only collect the national advertiser's fee (as it would for all network program distribution) but receive the income from local advertiser fees sold by the station and do not need to pay the station for carrying network programming.

It is no surprise, then, that television stations are currently being bought and sold for enormous prices and at breakneck speed. Boston's WCVB-TV was recently bought for $450 million, more than doubling in value in only three years. Los Angeles' KTLA-TV sold for $510 million in 1985, more than doubling in value in only two years. In Houston, the eleventh largest media market, KHOU-TV sold for $342 million in 1984. Even in smaller markets, such as Minneapolis, KITN-TV sold for $25 million, over twice its going price just sixteen months earlier. Consequently owning a television station stands to be more lucrative than ever. Because of the escalating prices, however, only large corporations can afford to partake in these endeavors. As was the case with program production for the networks, where the smaller production houses were slowly eliminated from participation, small-time broadcasters are being pushed out of the industry by large conglomerates.

Another form of deregulation focuses on program production. The FCC loosened the financial interest and syndication ruling, permitting the networks once again to engage in prime-time program production and ownership, albeit on a much more limited basis than was previously permitted. Once again the networks are given permission to compete with producers for the valuable commodity of prime time. And once again, the networks have some voice in the well-being of syndication-dependent independent stations.

The Outlook

Although cable and various forms of new technology have not yet dramatically transformed the television industry, it is safe to say that yet another transition is in the making. Proponents of direct broadcast satellite claim that they will render the networks obsolete by providing households with programming direct from production houses via satellite transmissions. Similarly efforts are being made to bypass network programming and off-network program syndication through the creation of regional television, in which either individual television stations or a corporation that owns several stations contribute to the overall cost of program production. In return they receive limited partnership of the program and a network-quality program for a cost similar to local production.

Clearly the power of cable is not to be undermined when it reaches its estimated 65 percent national saturation in 1990.

There is every indication that the evolution of the relationship among the four key components of the industry is continuing and prone to dramatic change and the introduction of other key components. The industry is still in a state of flux, but it is certain that television will remain one of the most active and volatile communication industries in the future.

Robert Abelman is an associate professor in the Department of Communication at Cleveland State University.

References

Brown, L. 1982. "Are the Networks Dinosaurs?" *Channels of Communication* 2(2): 26–29, 57.

_____. 1986a. "Running the Numbers." *Channels of Communication* 6(1): 72.

_____. 1986b. "Running the Numbers." *Channels of Communication* 6(2):72.

Brown, M. 1986. "The Real Action in TV—Station Trading." *Channels of Communication* 5(5):25.

Federal Communicator: Commission. 1970. "Amendment of Part 73 of the Commission's Rules and Regulations with Respect to Competition and Responsibility in Network Television Broadcasting." Washington, D.C.: Government Printing Office.

Guttenplan, D.D. 1986. "Syndication's New Superteam." *Channels of Communication* 5(5): 58–61.

Newcomb, H., and R. S. Alley. 1983. *The Producer's Medium.* New York: Oxford University Press.

Reel, A. F. 1979. *The Networks: How They Stole the Show.* New York: Charles Scribner's Sons.

Wellesley, A. 1980. "Behind TV's 'Angelgate' Mess: How Shady Deals Work—and Why Hollywood Loves Them." *Panorama* 1(9):34–39, 93.

Zuckerman, L., and L. Brown. 1983. "Autumn of the Networks' Reign." *Channels of Communication* 3(3):45–48.

Save CBS

Mark Harris, ENTERTAINMENT WEEKLY

First things first: CBS is not dead. Ailing, flailing, perhaps even failing, but still (subject to sudden changes of fortune, takeover bids, and the weekly Nielsen ratings) alive. However, if words of praise for the broadcasting giant have taken on a eulogistic ring in recent months, the reason is obvious. The house that Paley built may be standing, but viewers by the millions have decided they'd rather spend the night somewhere else. And things may get worse before they get better. There's no question that CBS deserves to be rescued from its present fate. What's astonishing is that it *needs* to be rescued.

Even now, CBS' schedule has a few bright spots. *Murphy Brown*, the treasure of its Monday lineup, has become television's smartest and most engagingly acted comedy series. With many years of life left, it could become the linchpin of a revitalized roster of sitcoms, always one of the network's strongest suits. The critically esteemed, innovative crime drama *Wiseguy* has a core of devoted fans; *Designing Women*, in its fourth season, has never been more popular; and newcomers, *Major Dad* and *City* show promise. The news division, despite problems, continues to provide the ever-renewable *60 Minutes* and the up-and-coming *48 Hours*. But if CBS is to survive, most of what's left has to go. *Hasta la vista, Paradise*. You're shot, J.R. War's over, *Tour of Duty*. Right now, at least a third of CBS' schedule is past its prime, and another third never had a prime.

So far, here's what the CBS of the '90s has offered: *Grand Slam, Max Monroe: Loose Cannon, His & Hers, Island Son, The People Next Door, A Peaceable Kingdom*. Desperate measures that reeked of cynicism and defeat the moment they were conceived. Of course, CBS doesn't have a monopoly on rotten shows—just on rotten shows that nobody wants to watch.

At the top of the prime-time ratings just five years ago, CBS is likely to end this season in third place, achieving the lowest Nielsen rating for any network in 36 years. During an average hour of prime time this season, only 12 percent of households with TVs have been tuned to CBS programs—fewer than NBC, fewer than ABC, and sometimes fewer than Fox.

The network's precipitous decline is all the more startling because CBS has had so much further to fall than its competitors. For television's entire first generation, when NBC was an also-ran and ABC was laughed off as the Almost Broadcasting Company, CBS *defined* television, with shows that lodged themselves in the national consciousness and then went to rerun heaven for an eternal reign. In the 1950s, that meant Lucy and Ricky, Burns and Allen, Jackie Gleason, Ed Sullivan, Alfred Hitchcock, Perry Mason, and Lassie. Sublime or ridiculous, these were the series around which Americans arranged their leisure time. A decade later, some new faces—Andy Griffith, Dick Van Dyke, Carol Burnett—joined the schedule and helped to consolidate CBS' hold on the viewing public.

Even in 1970, when the network briefly slipped to second after 15 years at the top, it anticipated the needs of a new audience and began replacing its sagging rural sitcoms. Out went *Green Acres* and *Hee Haw*; in came *M*A*S*H, Mary Tyler Moore, All in the Family, Kojak, The Waltons*—a fabled lineup that brought CBS back to first place, pulled entertainment television into the modern age, and dominated the medium for much of the following decade. And in the '80s, *Dallas* legitimized prime-time serial storytelling with an impact still felt in series from *L.A. Law* to *The Wonder Years*.

But *Dallas*, once America's most popular series, has become a dwindling relic, and CBS has lost its finger-on-the-pulse acuity, falling to second place in 1986 and then, in 1988, to third. This season, the network's attempts to revitalize its lineup were unnervingly wide of the mark. CBS tried to draw younger viewers into a schedule that included 10 new series. When the shows made their debuts, the network's lineup looked like a suicide mission, not a strategy. CBS' "youth appeal" schedule included Lindsay Wagner, Richard Chamberlain, and William Shatner. Six months later, seven of the new shows are gone; of the remaining three, the most successful, *Major Dad*, ranks 40th out of 96 series. CBS' pessimism runs so deep that it seems to have conceded an entire night as lost, renewing its Saturday lineup of leftovers—*Paradise, Tour of Duty*, and *Saturday Night with Connie Chung*—for the entire season.

The network can find little cause for cheer on the rest of its schedule. A number of CBS' few successful shows—*Murder, She Wrote; Knots Landing; Newhart; Dallas*—are among its oldest; by 1991, they'll almost certainly cease production and leave the network with more gaping holes. CBS long has been unwilling to let its series end gracefully, squeezing one, two, or three more years out of exhausted concepts (remember the back-from-the-dead season of *Magnum, P.I.*, or *Dallas*' season-long dream sequence?) Meanwhile, the development of new shows has been ignored. If the arthritic dud *Falcon Crest* had been put out of its misery a couple of years ago, CBS might be building a new Friday hit. As it is, *Crest* and series like it limp on until the last viewer departs. That kind of lazy programming exacts a steep price, and the network is about to pay it.

Outside of prime-time, the outlook is equally gloomy: Except for the network's success in daytime programming, where it continues to be No. 1, there isn't a single area where CBS isn't in deep trouble.

Take CBS News. Once the only network news organization that mattered, it now carries an air of fallen nobility, having ceded preeminence, both in the ratings and by reputation, to ABC. From the abuse of cutbacks under sword-wielding CEO Laurence Tisch in 1987 to the use of reenactments on Connie Chung's so-called news hour, its agonies have been noisy and public, a litany of gaffes and inept decisions that generated a library shelf full of postmortems whose titles—*Who Killed CBS?; Bad News at Black Rock; Prime Times, Bad Times*—tell it all.

Here, CBS faces still competition from its own ghosts and gray eminences. By the time Walter Cronkite vacated the *CBS Evening News* anchor seat in 1981, he was venerated as the avuncular repository of all that was trustworthy and sensible in the journalistic world. How can it be that at 58, after nearly a decade as Cronkite's successor, Dan Rather still seems new on the job? In Rather's hands, the broadcast is a guessing game: Will he sit or will he stand? Will he wear a sweater or wear a jacket? And when the news comes out of his month, will it be quickly or slowly, with a frozen smile, a furrowed frown, or perhaps a self-consciously down-home Texasism to top it off?

When something Rather says or does off-camera makes news, it usually triggers editorial cartoons and comic monologues. If audiences do pick their newscast for its anchorman, it's hardly a surprise that in 1989, CBS fell to second place after 20 years at the top. This year, the broadcast often finishes third, a nightly symbol of the network's misfortunes.

In the morning, the consistently poor performance of CBS' news programs has been a series of setups and punch lines lasting the better part of a decade. Some of them—notably the Phyllis George and Mariette Hartley fiascos—were obvious blunders. But other shakeups seem to follow George Steinbrenner's fat-contracts-and-hot-air philosophy: It's always the team's fault, never the owner's. Last month, just as CBS was gaining substantially on the second-place *Today* show, host Kathleen Sullivan was fired. No wonder CBS remains third in the morning; it has never demonstrated a bit of confidence in its morning shows, and the audience has followed suit.

And then there's late-night, where CBS already has demonstrated too much confidence in *The Pat Sajak Show*, despite its firm and permanent rejection by viewers. Now suffering through a period of frenzied tinkering, *Sajak* only looks more desperate to please. CBS won't wait forever for Sajak's ratings to pick up, but until the ax falls, it is locked out of the race.

But it is CBS' prime-time series that define its success or failure, and yes, things really are as bleak as they appear. The last long-term resident in the ratings basement was NBC, which occupied third place for nine years in the 1970s and early '80s. Heading into the 1990s, CBS is in even worse shape—the competition is tougher, more varied, and ready to step in and take the network's place whenever it falters. Although its parent company, the CBS Broadcast Group, is comfortably in the black—its operating profits were close to $300 million in 1989—the network's woes are the kind that whet the appetite of people like Ted Turner and fuel speculation that CBS will be the target of a merger or takeover. Most recently, the Walt Disney Co. reportedly has taken a long look at the network; last month, Disney chairman Michael Eisner issued a less-than-categorical denial of his company's interest. Changes in the business of television in the last decade have made third place a vulnerable location. Consider:

- In 1979, the networks were competing for a much larger piece of the pie—more than 90 percent of all prime-time viewers were watching CBS, NBC, or ABC. Even third-place NBC mustered better than a one-in-four share of viewers. Today, with competition from cable, independents, Fox, and videocassettes, one in three TV viewers skips the networks' primetime lineups entirely. That leaves CBS' nighttime shows with an average of just one in five viewers in what some experts say has become a system that can't support three traditionally structured networks.

- Audience demographics, ever more important to the ratings, cast CBS in an especially unappealing light. CBS' audience always has been significantly older than that of its competitors, and now NBC and ABC have seized the interest of 18- to 49-year-olds. Many shows with middling ratings—ABC's *thirtysomething* is one—are cherished by advertisers because of the kinds of viewers who tune in—baby boomers with disposable income. Even CBS' most successful entertainment program, *Murder, She Wrote,* has an older-than-average audience and is losing viewers and advertiser appeal to Fox and ABC.

- When NBC was deep in third place during the early '80s, its adventurous lineup grew to include *Cheers, Hill Street Blues, Family Ties, Remington Steel, St. Elsewhere,* and *Fame.* Suddenly, NBC had low ratings in spite of its shows, not because of them, and viewership began to build. By contrast, CBS' program development has been its weakest area, and the breakout potential for most of its newer series is slim.

To fill the void with more than just creaky retreads, CBS has to go in a new direction. Institutionally averse to admitting mistakes, CBS has enough shows "on hiatus" (*The Famous Teddy Z, Island Son, Max Monroe: Loose Cannon*) to stock the USA Network for years to come. But why pretend that failures aren't failures? A cruddy buddy show like *Grand Slam* shouldn't be given a first chance, let alone a second. To change its ways, the network also will have to quit going to the well of revivals; Movies such as *Return to Green Acres* only demonstrate CBS' programming weakness.

But there are positive signs. Installed two months ago as president of CBS' entertainment division, the well-regarded Jeff Sagansky hasn't had a chance to put his imprint on the prime-time lineup. But he's made it clear he wants to hold on to some of CBS' best producers and writers while attracting new talent. "I hope what we're about in the 1990s is that we take a lot of chances," he recently told *Advertising Age* magazine. Sagansky, who worked under NBC's Brandon Tartikoff as senior vice president of series programming until 1985, has drawn praise even from his former boss, who says Sagansky "understands how to program for a young adult audience."

And any doubts about CBS' commitment in one area—sports—have been erased by a series of bold, big-money purchases, including the renewal of rights to NCAA basketball and the acquisition of the 1992 Winter Olympics and the next four years of major league baseball. That gives CBS a valuable opportunity to showcase its new programs during next fall's playoffs and World Series, when the network's viewership is almost guaranteed to be high. Those series may be the best hope for a badly battered network to get back some of its lost glory.

We wish it better luck this time. CBS is too great a part of television's past to be left out of its future.

The Demise of CBS

February 1983
The end of an era: CBS broadcasts the final episode of *M*A*S*H* to the largest single audience in TV history. It is the last series from CBS' acclaimed lineup of '70s comedies to leave the air.

January 1984
The beginning of an error: *Airwolf,* starring Jan-Michael Vincent, Ernest Borgnine, and a helicopter, makes its deput.

October 1984
CBS attempts to capitalize on the growing music-video craze with *Dreams,* featuring John Stamos as a rock musician. It lasts one month.

May 1985
CBS Morning News anchorwoman Phyllis George interviews Gary Dotson, freed after six years' imprisonment on a rape charge, and Cathleen Webb, who recanted her accusation against him. First she makes them shake hands. They do. Then she has an even brighter idea. "How about a hug?" she suggests: A nation stares in disbelief. Dotson and Webb decline.

July 1985
Ominous turning sounds are heard emanating from the grave of Edward R. Murrow.

August 1985
After eight months on the job, Phyllis George leaves under pressure.

April 1986
After six straight years as the top-rated network, CBS finishes the 1985–86 season in second place.

May 1986
Under chairman Thomas Wyman, CBS decides to eliminate 700 jobs.

August 1986
In a nationally syndicated column about the cutbacks, *60 Minutes* commentator Andy Rooney writes, "CBS, which used to stand for the Columbia Broadcasting System, no longer stands for anything. They're just corporate initials now."

September 1986
As a new season of Dallas begins, Pam Ewing wakes up, and her husband, Bobby, informs viewers that the entire previous season was a bad dream. A nation groans.

September 1986
Beleaguered anchorman Dan Rather unexpectedly ends an evening newscast with the sign-off "Courage." A nation giggles.

September 1986
A few days laer, Rather amends the sign-off "*Coraje*" ("courage" in Spanish). A nation guffaws.

September 1986
Elliott Gould and Dee Wallace Stone play a married couple in the new CBS comedy *Together We Stand.* Its ratings are poor. In true comic tradition, the network decides that the series would be funnier if one of the characters was dead. A revamped version, called *Nothing Is Easy,* bombs just as quickly.

January 1987
Polaroid pitch woman and ex-bride-of-the-Incredible Hulk, Mariette Hartley, begins a run as host of CBS' new morning show. Her most memorable question, to Rep. Joseph Kennedy 2nd: "I was wondering about your feelings about guns." Other guests include Hartley's dog, Daisy.

April 1987
At the end of the seventh season of *Magnum, P.I.,* Magnum (Tom Selleck) dies. Ratings are high. Suddenly, CBS decides he wasn't so dead after all. Magnum returns, healthy as ever, the next fall.

September 1987
CBS announces its plan to drop Mariette Hartley and cancels *The Morning Program.*
September 1987
Stars of tomorrow in the fall lineup include Paul Sorvino, Jerry Orbach, William Conrad, and Anne Jackson.
September 1987
Infuriated when a tennis broadcast runs into his time slot, Dan Rather walks off the set of the *CBS Evening News* and, for the seven longest minutes in its history, CBS goes black.
January 1988
Rather gets into an on-air shouting match with then-Vice President Bush. "How would you like it if I judged your career by those seven minutes when you walked off the set?" Bush says. "Would you like that?"
January 1988
During an interview in connection with Martin Luther King Day, *NFL Today* commentator Jimmy the Greek decides to moonlight as a racial theoretician. "The black is a better athlete . . . because he's been bred to be that way," he tells a reporter. "This goes back all the way to the Civil War, when . . . the slave owner would breed his big black to his big black woman so that he could have a big black kid."
January 1988
The network fires Jimmy the Greek.
April 1988
CBS finishes the season in third place for the first time in its history.
September 1988
After changing its time period approximately 225 times in one year, CBS cancels its acclaimed series *Frank's Place.*
October 1988
Venerable CBS stars Mary Tyler Moore and Dick Van Dyke return to the network in new situation comedies. Nobody watches.
January 1989
Aware that it's in deep ratings trouble, CBS combs the entertainment world in search of the one man who can turn its fortunes around. The result of the network's efforts, *The Pat Sajak Show,* makes its debut shortly thereafter. A nation gets up and changes the channel to *The Arsenio Hall Show.*
September 1989
CBS This Morning anchor Kathleen Sullivan makes a joke about her employer—calling it "the Cheap Broadcasting System"—into a microphone that, to her surprise, is open. The comment is heard on CBS' closed-circuit system in New York. Nobody laughs.
September 1989
Saturday Night with Connie Chung begins its run and becomes the first CBS News series to use reenactments. Somewhere, Edward R. Murrow stirs again.
October 1989
The Pat Sajak Show shrinks from 90 minutes to one hour per night.
November 1989
Doomstruck on *Donahue.* Kathleen Sullivan tells Phil's audience, "The ax is right there ... I know that, and I'm a grown-up. I can take it."
December 1989
The on-again, off-again cult series *Beauty and the Beast* returns, with a special valentine to its fans: Beauty gets murdered. Four weeks later, the show is canceled for good.
December 1989
For the first time, the *CBS Evening News* fails to finish the year in first place, falling to ABC's *World News Tonight* with Peter Jennings.

December 1989
In a prime-time year-in-review news special, Andy Rooney comments that "homosexual unions … lead quite often to premature death."

December 1989
After CBS' highly promoted slate of new series fails, Kim LeMasters is replaced by Jeff Sagansky, who inherits a slate of replacement shows that includes vehicles for Shadoe Stevens and Moon and Dweezil Zappa.

January 1990
Finally, a piece of luck for CBS: the Super Bowl. Unfortunately for the network, the game turns out to be the lowest-rated ever in prime time.

February 1990
If you thought the insult was bad, wait until you hear the apology: In an explanation of his views on homosexuality in *The Advocate*, a gay magazine, Rooney is quoted as saying that blacks have "watered down their genes."

February 1990
The Pat Sajak Show changes its set and format, concluding each evening with round-table discussions among the guests. After a one-year grace period, Arsenio Hall starts making fun of him.

Autumn of the Networks' Reign
Laurence Zuckerman and Les Brown, CHANNELS

When the networks had television all to themselves, the conceit of every new season was that it would revitalize our popular culture. Every September a score of newly minted series promised, in the promotional slogans, to raise enjoyment to greater heights if we but reorganized our nightly viewing regimen.

The pitch is the same this year, but times have changed. The future of our popular culture doesn't so much ride with the fate of the networks' heavily hyped new offerings as with the destiny of two shows the networks canceled last spring and gave up for dead. For those two shows, *Fame* and *Too Close for Comfort*, in defying the old laws of survival by continuing on special satellite hookups of their own, could upset the whole television system, diminish the power of the three networks, and change forever what a new television season is all about.

In the past, with very few exceptions, when a network series was canceled it went out of production. If it was lucky enough to have a run of at least five seasons, it would have amassed a library of reruns sufficient to give it an afterlife in syndication on local stations. In this kind of syndication—which is where the production companies make their big profits—there have to be enough episodes for a station to "strip" the program into the same time period five days a week. Any canceled series that falls short of affording a full season of stripping can forget about an afterlife and all the residuals that go with it.

Fame, an hour-long comedy-drama series with music, was cut loose by NBC after two seasons of generally lukewarm ratings. But for MGM/UA, the producing company, it seemed a pity to let the program fade away when it was so popular in Europe and Australia. So with a foreign sale assured for a third season, but no network interest here, the studio decided to try a new route to keep the series going and expand the precious library of episodes. *Fame* will continue in production for distribution on a so-called "ad hoc network," one that has lined up its own stations and advertisers.

Too Close for Comfort had three respectable seasons on ABC when it was axed; producer D.L. Taffner wasn't going to let it go at that and miss out on the lucrative syndication market. He too elected to resume production of the sitcom for an ad hoc network, betting that *Too Close*, as a known quantity, would appeal to enough stations to cover most of the country, and that viewers would continue to think of it as a network show.

Ad hoc networks are not a recent invention. They date back to the '50s, when certain advertisers created their own temporary networks built around programs that wished to place in select markets. They are, in fact, a form of syndication. The 1975 David Frost interviews with Richard Nixon went out over an ad hoc network, put together especially for those broadcasts. Mobil Showcase Network, which has presented such serials as *Edward and Mrs. Simpson*, *Ten Who Dared*, and *Nicholas Nickleby*, is an ad hoc network. So are SFM's Holiday Network and Paramount's daily soft-news magazine, *Entertainment Tonight*.

Perhaps the biggest and best-established ad hoc network is Operation Prime Time, which has presented such distinguished programs as *A Woman Called Golda*, with Ingrid Bergman, and *Smiley's People*, with Alec Guinness. This fall, OPT will offer *Sadat*, a four-hour docudrama on the late Egyptian leader, and *Helen Keller: The Miracle Continues*, a two-hour made-for-television movie.

But if ad hoc networks are nothing new, their significance this season is that there are more of them than ever and that, for the first time, they are carrying genuine network programming on a weekly basis, posing direct competition to the networks—in many cities, their programs air on network-affiliated stations. If *Fame* and *Too Close for Comfort* succeed in the fall, with their scattershot scheduling, the three big networks will have something to worry about besides competition from HBO, direct-broadcast satellites, and video recordings.

You cannot start an ad hoc network without a base of stations in the country's largest markets, and there is no better base today than Metromedia Television. Metromedia has something only the three networks have: owned-and-operated stations in the three largest cities—New York, Los Angeles, and Chicago. As this has been the key to the networks' strength, it is also the key to Metromedia's strength. Metromedia owns seven television stations in all, which together cover around 25 percent of the nation's television homes.

Most of the Metromedia stations are independents—that is, they have no network affiliation. This means they're relatively free to take on, or initiate, interesting projects. At a time when most other media companies are diversifying into cable, videotex, direct-broadcast satellites, and other new forms of television, Metromedia has been concentrating on expanding in old-fashioned broadcast television. When it acquired Boston's WCVB-TV for a record price of $220 million in 1981, it also acquired the president of Metromedia Television. More recently, it purchased the Chicago independent, WFLD-TV, clinching its entree to the top markets.

Metromedia is positioned now to emerge as the fourth great force in commercial television, after CBS, ABC, and NBC. It has been laying plans to distribute movies, news, and first-run entertainment programming in prime time and daytime, and will make an important competitive foray this fall into late-night entertainment, as part of a consortium producing the 90-minute nightly variety show, *Thicke of the Night*. As part of another consortium, it is also behind a new weekly talent-scout series, *Star Search*.

The vehicle carrying Metromedia into television's major league is the ad hoc network. "If *Fame* and *Too Close for Comfort* can work," says Bob Bennett, "then the producer of every show that gets canceled is going to say, 'Wait, see if we can sell it through Metromedia.' "

The trick in setting up an ad hoc network is getting a substantial number of network affiliates to buy programs; otherwise, it would be impossible to achieve the national coverage most television advertisers require. The independent stations around the country are sufficient to reach only 65 percent of the homes, so it is necessary, in markets with no independent outlets, to enlist affiliates willing to preempt their networks in prime time. This is relatively easy to do on a sporadic basis, with shows like *Nicholas Nickleby* and *Blood and Honor,* but it is extremely difficult for series that are intended to have a protracted weekly run, such as *Fame* and *Too Close for Comfort*.

Bonded by years of tradition and handsome profits, the major networks and their affiliates have a symbiotic relationship. Affiliates give the networks access to the local airwaves; in return the networks pay these stations for the use of their air-time, and give them a core of popular programming around which to sell advertising. Nevertheless it is a business relationship, and stations, like the networks, are under corporate pressures to increase their profits.

Presented with an opportunity to join an ad hoc network, an affiliate is usually faced with the paradox of improving his own revenues by weakening the network that sustains him day by day. It is a bit like risking a good marriage for a night on the town. But when a network falters in the ratings, as NBC has the last few years, affiliates find it easier to slip away.

At the NBC affiliates convention in Los Angeles last spring, the network's top officials repeatedly implored their "local partners" to air as many NBC programs as possible. The network's clearance of programs in prime time had fallen to 97 percent of all television homes, one percent behind ABC and CBS. In daytime, NBC is off by as much as 5 percent. As the network's president, Pierson Mapes, pointed out, that translates into millions of dollars in lost revenues each year.

Don Taffner, whose company produces *Too Close for Comfort*, which will be reactivated early next year, expects most of the affiliates joining the ad hoc network to carry the program in a fringe time period, perhaps 7 P.M. Saturdays. "No one can preempt the networks in prime time," Taffner says. "They're just too strong."

Metromedia's Bob Bennett disagrees: "If a guy is sitting with a network show that is doing poorly at 10 o'clock and wrecking his lead-in to the local news, he just might want to put *Fame* in there."

Some observers of the scene believe *Fame,* as a one-hour show, will find its niche on affiliated stations at 7 P.M. Sundays, where it would compete head-on with *60 Minutes.* This time period carries a restriction imposed by the Federal Communications Commission more than a decade ago. Under the Prime Time Access Rule, that early-evening hour on Sundays can only be used by the networks for children's programming, or news and public affairs. *60 Minutes* qualified as news, and one reason for its great success on Sundays is that it has been protected by the FCC's rule from having to compete with typical network entertainment programming. On ABC and NBC the time period is off-limits to the likes of *A Team* and *Magnum.*

Fame would get around the rule, because technically it is no longer a network show. Emanating from the syndication market, albeit on an ad hoc network, it is considered a local station's program. Thus the NBC and ABC programs slotted against *60 Minutes* appear highly vulnerable to preemption, especially since neither network's Sunday-evening program choices have had much success against the CBS newsmagazine in the past.

Monitor is the obvious soft spot in the NBC schedule. It had fared poorly in the ratings last season and now has been shifted into competition with *60 Minutes.* A number of affiliates have indicated a desire to live without the network's newsmagazine.

While the fortunes of *Fame* and *Too Close for Comfort* in network-dominated prime time remain to be seen, there is no doubt about the potency of *Thicke of the Night* as an ad hoc offering. A coproduction of Metromedia, MGM/UA, and Fred Silverman's company, Intermedia, the 90-minute late-night show starring Canadian comedian Alan Thicke has already cleared 85 percent of the country's television homes on more than 100 stations. Along with the independents, the stations include 24 ABC affiliates, 11 from NBC, and 6 from CBS. At least two of these, WMAR-TV in Baltimore and KTWO-TV in Casper, Wyoming, have elected to bump Johnny Carson's *Tonight Show* for *Thicke of the Night.*

If the new entry should prove popular with the viewers, the lineup of stations for *Thicke of the Night* could double in a matter of months and place the profitable late-night franchises of all three networks in serious jeopardy.

And if *Thicke of the Night* looks like a network show, is distributed like a network show, and is sold to advertisers as a network show, who's to say it is less than a network show?

To set up an ad hoc network for *Nicholas Nickleby,* Mobil sent a sample tape and proposal to every station in the largest television markets. Mobil's method is to buy the air-time on the stations it chooses. There were more than a hundred responses, and Mobil selected 61 stations. More than one-third were affiliates of ABC, CBS, or NBS that agreed to preempt their networks for nine hours of prime time on four consecutive nights. The networks, which hate to lose any links, were not pleased. When WEYI-TV, a CBS affiliate in Flint, Michigan, accepted an offer to carry *Nickleby* and suddenly reneged, Mobil vice president Herb Schmertz sent a letter to CBS Broadcast Group president Gene Jankowski protesting alleged network pressure against the affiliate. "I can sympathize with your inability to sell your program," Jankowski replied, "and I suggest you try other stations in the marketplace."

The *Nickleby* network proved to be something of a watershed. Within weeks of its telecast, four different proposals for new ad hoc networks were floated. Two were from movie studios and two from station-group consortiums.

The idea of an ad hoc network is especially attractive to film companies because this method of television distribution allows the studio to share in the advertising revenues. In the long run, this could be more lucrative than simply leasing movies to the big networks for a flat fee. Certain film companies have proposed offering their films on ad hoc networks soon after their exposure on pay cable.

"If the networks can each have their *Night at the Movies*, why can't we?" says Gary Lieberthal, president of Embassy Telecommunications, which plans to air one of its theatrical features each quarter via an ad hoc network. "If we can line up the stations and sell directly to advertisers, we don't have to pay the middleman."

The irony of the matter is that the proliferation of ad hoc networks has been spurred not by technology but by the actions of the Big Three networks themselves. For many years, ABC, CBS, and NBC have enjoyed a sellers' market. With the demand for advertising time consistently exceeding the supply of 30-second spots, the networks have routinely hiked their rates every year. Last season, the ad rates went up a record 13 to 16 percent, with the average 30-second prime-time spot on ABC selling for $91,000. This season's rates are reported to have risen another 15 percent. Advertisers have been driven to finding less expensive ways of reaching national audiences through television.

Meanwhile, ABC, CBS, and NBC have been lobbying hard in Washington for repeal of the financial-interest and syndication rules, under which they are barred from owning even part of the programs they buy, and from engaging in the domestic syndication of programs. Independent stations have flourished under this rule, since it allowed them to buy the reruns of shows like *M*A*S*H* and *Laverne & Shirley* while those programs were still running on the networks and still at the peak of their popularity. Fearing now that repeal of the rule would let the networks again control the flow of programs to the syndication market and impair their ability to compete, Metromedia and other independent groups have begun to seek new sources or programming, and are even producing shows themselves.

The needs of the advertisers and the independent television operators have thus converged, elevating the ad hoc network to a new position of power in commercial television. According to Henry Siegel, chairman of Lexington Broadcast Services, a leading company engaged in what he calls "advertiser-supported syndication," the revenues in this field have grown from $30 million in 1972 to $300 million in 1982. Siegel believes the market will be worth $1 billion by the end of this decade.

A new entry this fall, *Star Search*, illustrates the reasons behind the growing advertiser enthusiasm for ad hoc networks. The weekly hour-long talent scout show, laden with guest stars, has lined up more than 170 stations—less than 30 short of the number the big networks generally provide. The stations pay nothing for the program, but in exchange for carrying five minutes' worth of national advertising in the show, they receive an equal number of commercial spots to sell locally. And here's why it all works: A national advertiser can buy a 30-second spot on the full ad hoc network for around $42,000, or less than half the price of a spot on ABC, CBS, or NBC. This clarifies why the bulk of the advertising time for *Fame* and *Thicke of the Night*, as well as *Star Search*, was sold months before the shows' ad hoc premieres.

Independent stations may not have the resources to go head-to-head with the networks in producing first-run programming, but they do have the advertisers' blessings and a strong show of interest today from the more venturesome production companies.

With *Fame* and *Too Close for Comfort*, the networks are being challenged by their own castoffs. And if nothing else comes of the refusal by those two shows to die in the time-honored way, it should at least make the networks less cavalier about canceling programs that still show signs of life.

Laurence Zuckerman is associate editor of the Columbia Journalism Review.

The Fourth Network

Ronald Grover and Susan Duffy, BUSINESS WEEK

Hollywood producer Michael J. Weithorn figured Fox was his only bet. He was looking for a home for *True Colors,* a sitcom about an interracial marriage that merges two families, pitting an angst-filled white mother-in-law against a jive-talking black stepson. He decided not even to show it to ABC, NBC, or CBS, where a few years ago, he had circulated a pilot about a black man and a white woman in their 20s who shared an apartment. "I got the coldest shoulder I have ever felt," recalls Weithorn, a former producer of the NBC hit *Family Ties.* "No one," he explains, "could sell an interracial couple to their affiliates."

No one, that is, but Barry Diller. The Fox Broadcasting Co. chief jumped at *True Colors.* In early September, he slipped it into Fox's 7 p.m. Sunday slot—when his rivals air family-oriented fare. For Fox, the specter of an interracial family squabbling over the kitchen table is family entertainment. It's standard Fox: go with the unexpected, even the unthinkable. While the jury is still out on *True Colors,* Fox has already produced some surprising hits. Its raunchy *Married . . . With Children* finished regularly among the top-20-rated shows toward the end of last season, and its animated series *The Simpsons* is a frequent member of the top 10.

The upshot? While industry veterans said Diller could never make it happen, Fox has emerged as the nation's fourth network. It may be a ragtag band of seven Fox-owned stations and 126 independent affiliates—mostly dinky, low-power UHF stations. Yet it can now reach 91% of the country (compared with 99% for the three majors) and has finally wooed enough viewers and ads to turn a neat profit. That's good news for Australian owner Rupert Murdoch, whose far-flung media empire is showing big losses elsewhere.

Now, Diller is pulling out all stops in his assault on the Big Three. This fall, he's expanding from three nights of programming to five. He has spent millions more on 10 new shows. And he is moving his biggest hit, *The Simpsons,* from its secure position on Sunday night into the Thursday night fray immediately opposite NBC's aging but No. 2-rated *The Cosby Show.*

All this could be as big a gamble as starting the network in the first place. Producing a few big hits in neglected time slots is one thing. But going head to head on two more nights, especially when the competition is finally taking you seriously, is quite another. Fact is, Fox could hit a rough patch this season. By spreading more shows across more nights, Fox will be hard-pressed to show the huge ratings gains of past seasons. "Up to now, Fox has been engaging in guerrilla warfare," says television consultant David Smith of Frank N. Magid Associates, a media consulting firm. "Fighting a broad, land-based battle is far different."

Besides, the Big Three have adopted some Fox tactics. Early on, Diller targeted Saturday and Sunday nights first because they were littered with TV's most uninspired shows. No longer. The other networks have filled up those slots with their own fresh new shows.

In 1988, Diller blindsided the Big Three when he aired his new lineup weeks before the traditional mid-September start of the TV season. Viewers, particularly kids, teens, and young adults, dumped reruns for Fox. Once exposed to Fox's hip, offbeat programming, they kept watching.

Now, though, the other networks are hip to Diller's game plan. Fox first got attention by flouting convention: Its *Married . . .With Children* provoked controversy with toilet jokes and gibes at the loose morals of Al Bundy's bimbette daughter. Its hit *In Living Color* is a black, more outrageous version of *Saturday Night Live.* Suddenly, everybody is trying to be provocative. Even CBS, which for years contented itself with staid stuff for older folks, is pushing the envelope: Its *Uncle Buck* specializes in flatulence jokes. And CBS Inc. programming chief Jeff Sagansky recently tried to deflect criticism over the first episode—in which a 6-year-old tells another kid: "You suck."

None of this scares Diller, although he is characteristically intense and fidgety as he reflects on his show-biz showdown. These days he spends most of his time at his command post in the Fox studios in Hollywood, which is dominated by a huge board that details all of the four networks' schedules. And he clearly relishes the intensifying battle: "We could have taken the conservative approach—and maybe gone to four nights and steered clear of *Cosby*," he says. "But that's not the way we intend to play this game." Diller's ultimate goal is to establish a seven-nights-a-week prime-time lineup, a one-hour network news show, some game shows, and maybe even soap operas.

The 48-year old Diller has been girding for this moment for most of his adult life. The son of a wealthy Beverly Hills real estate developer, he worked his way up in true Hollywood fashion, starting as a mail clerk at the William Morris Agency. He got the job with the help of a neighbor, comedian Danny Thomas, after dropping out of both Stanford University and the University of California of Los Angeles. He joined ABC in 1967, first as a programming assistant. Rising quickly, he took over the programming chores and pioneered the development of made-for-TV movies and miniseries. One of his first big hits: *Roots*.

"He was the single most determined guy I ever saw," recalls ABC founder Leonard Goldenson. "He'd just as soon run through a door than open it." Gruff and impatient, Diller demanded long hours and unswerving devotion from his staff. As he would repeat at Fox, he hired bright young people, pitted them against one another in stormy closed-door sessions, and walked out with top-notch creative ideas. Among those who survived the ordeal was Walt Disney Co. Chairman Michael D. Eisner.

Operating out of a programming office above a tailor shop in New York, ABC quickly became a ratings force, rising to the top in the mid-1970s with such shows as *Happy Days* and *Laverne & Shirley*. In fact, Goldenson thinks Diller is repeating history. ABC also took off by playing to young, urban audiences. And as Diller has done with *The Simpsons*, Goldenson put his quirkiest show, the tongue-in-cheek western *Maverick*, up against the top-rated *Ed Sullivan Show*. Sullivan lost a few viewers, but ratings soared for *Maverick*.

By 1974, Diller had jumped to Paramount Pictures Corp. He was joined again by Eisner, and the two tripled Paramount's profits within six years, making hit films such as *Raiders of the Lost Ark* along with top TV shows such as *Taxi* and *Mork & Mindy*.

Diller got the itch to start a fourth network in 1977, figuring he could launch it with new episodes of the cult hit series *Star Trek*. He began lining up affiliates. But advertisers didn't come running, and Paramount's parent, Gulf & Western Inc., pulled the plug. Diller quit in 1984 after an unrelated blowup with Paramount Chairman Martin S. Davis, and he joined Fox with a lucrative contract that gave him $3 million a year plus 25% of any appreciation in the then-struggling studio's assets.

'No censorship.' As the new Fox chairman, Diller found a kindred spirit in Rupert Murdoch. Murdoch controlled Fox after buying out his partner, oilman Marvin Davis, in 1985. Diller and Murdoch thought they saw trouble ahead for the Big Three, as prime-time audiences began defecting to independent TV stations and cable. So they began looking for stations that would form the backbone of a new network. Media baron John W. Kluge sold them his six Metromedia Inc. stations in 1986 for nearly $2 billion. Located in major cities, they would reach enough viewers to persuade advertisers to sign up.

By late 1986, Murdoch and Diller had lined up another 96 independent TV stations around the country. For an "indie," the idea of a new network was appealing: Rather than paying stiff fees for old movies and sitcom reruns, the station owners would get their programming free. In return, they had to give up eight of the eleven 30-second spots that are aired each hour.

Fox soon became a haven for TV producers who wanted to experiment. "Diller told me that I could do anything I wanted, that there'd be no censorship," says James Brooks, the creator of the acclaimed ABC show *Taxi*. Over lunch, Diller agreed to bankroll and air whatever show Brooks wanted to make. The result was *The Tracy Ullman Show*, a modest hit.

Brooks was joined by such well-regarded TV producers as *The A-Team* creators Steven Cannell and Ed Weinberger, who created the sitcom *Amen*. The producers, however, turned out to be hotter than the shows they did for Fox. Within a year of Fox's 1987 launch, its shows were hovering at a mere 2% share of the 91 million television households. Test patterns in many cities got higher ratings. And by the end of its first full year, Fox had lost some $95 million. Worse yet, rumblings of discontent were coming from Fox's affiliates, the customers Diller and Murdoch could least afford to lose.

The problem was that Fox ended up copying rather than competing with the other networks' shows. Eager to give their new affiliates network-quality programs, Fox had served up clones such as *Mr. President, Karen's Song,* and *The Dirty Dozen.* All of them bombed. By the end of its first season, most were canceled.

But the angry letters Diller received from restless affiliates still hang in some executives' offices. "They told us that we were stupid, didn't know how to run a network, and wouldn't know a good show if we saw it," recalls Diller." And you know what? They were right."

Fox's big break came in mid-1988, when Hollywood writers went out on strike. With the Big Three forced to run third and fourth reruns of their shows, America found *Married . . . With Children, 21 Jump Street,* and other previously ignored Fox shows. They also found "reality-based" shows that use actual news footage and few actors. For many viewers, the gritty *America's Most Wanted* and *Cops* were a welcome relief from the ubiquitous slick cop shows. Cheap to produce, they helped Diller cut the average cost of his half-hour shows from $350,000 to less than $200,000.

Ratings for *Married . . . With Children* and *21 Jump Street* moved into double digits, a rarity for Fox. And by late 1987, Fox showed its first profit, a modest $400,000 for its second quarter. More important, Fox had found a formula. By introducing its new shows during the summer, it was able to build hits without much competition. Since 1988, in fact, Fox's competitors have lost 7.7% of their audience during the summer months, according to Larry Gerbrandt, a senior analyst with Paul Kagan Associates Inc. in Carmel, Calif. Barry Diller's crew, says Gerbrandt, has picked up almost all of the defections.

Bonanza. The rest is ratings—and advertising—history. The *Cosby* matchup was not only an attention-getter but also one designed to help bring in ad revenue. Thursday is an important TV night for retailers—and the big movie companies. And *The Simpsons* commands a breathtaking $300,000 per 30-second spot from national advertisers, roughly 40% more than ABC's *Monday Night Football* and only slightly behind *Cosby.* That was no small factor in the bonanza Fox enjoyed during this summer's commercial time-buying period for next season. Advertisers threw about $550 million Fox's way—almost twice last year's take. That may not be much compared with top-rated NBC's $1.5 billion haul or the $1.4 billion raked in by ABC. But both NBC and CBS lost billings from the year before—to ABC, Fox, and cable. And the $900 million sold for CBS's faltering prime-time schedule puts it perilously close to being overtaken by Fox not too far down the road.

Advertisers had been looking for a real alternative to the Big Three. Their standard beef: The three networks keep losing viewers—and they keep raising prices. Advertisers were particularly incensed during the summer's time-buying spree, when ABC and NBC announced they would ignore traditional ratings guarantees—while asking for double-digit rate increases. "That scared dollars to Fox," says American Telephone & Telegraph Co. advertising director Robert Watson. But the upstart's biggest draw, he says, is its young, free-spending audience. Fox has grabbed nearly 50% of TV viewers aged 12 to 34. Says Fox advertising sales chief Jon Nesvig: "We're selling the next generation of customers."

Fox Broadcasting is finally out of the red. After past seasons produced $128 million in losses, Fox made $35 million in operating income on $320 million in revenues in the year ended June 30. Murdoch projects earnings at $70 million to $80 million on more than $620 million in revenues in the current year.

Along the way, movie studios Paramount and Universal tried to outfox Fox. They hankered to control outlets for their movies and TV shows and tried to launch a fifth network. Diller sent executives scurrying to deliver some tough talk to the affiliates—warning them not to defect, even on those days when Fox wasn't programming. The threat? That Fox would cut them loose. "We reminded them that we were going to get to seven nights soon enough," says Jamie Kellner, Fox Broadcasting's president. The rivals didn't get anywhere and pulled out. More recently, Fox pressed affiliates into passing on Walt Disney Co.'s weekday afternoon cartoon show, *Peter Pan*. Disney slapped Fox with a lawsuit.

Indies' Delight. Disney may be irked, but Fox's affiliates couldn't be happier. The network's higher ratings have boosted profits. Like most indies, they were saddled with pricey shows and low ratings. Now, according to Pat Mullen, station manager of WXMI in Grand Rapids, his Fox affiliate will see earnings increase by 30% this year despite generally flat ad spending. That's because he gets Fox programs for free and can charge more for local spots for its hits. "I can get $2,000 for 30 seconds on *Simpsons*," says Mullen. "That used to be an entire Sunday night for me."

And improved ratings have generally made it far more attractive to own a Fox affiliate. Well-heeled investors such as TV producer Norman Lear and record executive Quincy Jones have focused on buying up Fox affiliates in the past two years, confident that margins will begin to edge toward the 50% other network affiliates can command. "Just being Fox increases the value of an independent," says Barry Barker, who bought Fox affiliate KDNL in St. Louis and is looking for more.

Fox's success has also been a windfall for its own seven TV stations and its movie studio. The stations earned more than $134 million last year, a 23% hike over the previous year. The chief reason for the improvement: putting on more Fox network shows, for which advertisers pay the freight. Then there is Fox's studio, which this year will produce one-third of the 15 shows and all of the movies that the network will air. But if it means more money for Fox, the studio sometimes bypasses its own TV network. It produces *L.A. Law* for NBC and syndicates its popular *A Current Affair*.

Television producers that stuck with Fox are now cashing in on the syndication market, where highly rated sitcoms still command hefty payments. Columbia Pictures Entertainment Inc.'s TV unit, which made *Married . . . With Children*, will probably clear more than $100 million this fall from selling reruns of the show. "Don't let anyone tell you this is a startup network any longer," says Gary Lieberthal, who heads the Columbia TV unit. "Not with the kind of money we're going to make on this show."

How much larger Fox will grow is still unclear. The Big Three are restricted under 1970 rules by the Federal Communications Commission that forbid them to own and syndicate any shows that they air. The rules, however, allow newcomers such as Fox to own and air up to 15 hours of programming.

On May 4, the FCC gave Fox a one-year exemption, allowing it to program up to 18 hours a week. That's enough for five nights a week and weekday and Saturday morning cartoons. Fox argued that its very survival was at stake. By early 1991, the regulators should decide whether to approve Fox's request to increase that to 30 hours.

The Big Three have vehemently fought any change that would allow Fox the added hours. "It's unfair and uncompetitive," says NBC Inc.'s Ellen Agress, vice-president for legal policy and planning. "We think it's ridiculous that Fox is trying to portray itself as a poor little emerging business," she scoffs. "It owns as many TV stations as we do, has a major production studio, is a major syndicator, and has the might and muscle of News Corp. behind it." Meanwhile, the networks are also asking to be freed from the 1970 rules.

If the FCC rules against Fox, says Diller, he would shrink back to 15 hours rather than lose the rights to syndicated shows such as *M*A*S*H* and *L.A. Law*. That would still be enough to air prime-time programs on all seven nights, giving up any thought of Saturday cartoons, game shows, and news.

How long can Fox continue its hot streak? Even Diller, known for hyperbole, is cautious. "What we are doing is a risk," he says, "and there is going to be a long, difficult road ahead of us." Does he think *The Simpsons* can overtake *The Cosby Show* on Thursday nights? No. But he does think that when the aging *Cosby* eventually goes off the air, Fox could inherit the night.

A solid second on Thursday night still means a lot of money for Fox. But that doesn't mean everyone agreed with the decision. The idea to move *The Simpsons* was first raised by Murdoch this summer and quickly seconded by Diller. "Everyone else thought we were on an ego trip," recalls Murdoch. "But Barry and I voted our shares, and that was it."

For *The Simpsons'* Thursday night debut on Aug. 23, *Cosby* came out swinging with a special show, complete with highlights from best previous shows and a special intro by the star. Bart and his scruffy family finished a respectable second, luring 16% of TV viewers, compared with 28% for the Huxtable clan. But that's still a far cry from the 24% *The Simpsons* had averaged the previous three Sundays.

Fox has predicted to advertisers that *The Simpsons*, the cartoon show developed by counterculture artist Matt Groening, will be seen in 27% of the homes using TV's on Thursday nights. That's about the same as on Sundays. Advertisers generally disagree. Paul Schulman, one of the industry's savviest media buyers, says it will lure 19% of the audience, although it will steal some younger viewers from *Cosby*. "I for one am worried," says James Brooks, who produces *The Simpsons* and who argued against the Thursday move. "I have never had a show that has done better after it has been moved."

Indeed, Fox probably killed off one of its early hits, *21 Jump Street*, by moving it from Sunday to Monday nights. And it deep-sixed *The Tracey Ullman Show* by moving it from Sunday to Saturday. But neither show was *The Simpsons*, which has become such a favorite that singer Michael Jackson recently asked Diller for a cutout of Bart Simpson. Fox complied, painting a glove on one of the character's fists.

Watch the Flops. Thursday is only one of several risky nights on the Fox schedule. It still can't generate sizable ratings on Monday, where it has canceled *21 Jump Street* and *Alien Nation* in favor of movies. And it is trying to lure male audiences to Friday night by moving *America's Most Wanted* from Saturday.

Fox's biggest problem now is delivering the average 7% market share that it has promised advertisers. Fox currently averages well above that on Sundays but is only just above it on Saturdays and Mondays. Adding two new nights could drag all the show's numbers down. Considering that three out of four new shows flop, and that Fox is debuting 10, that's a real possibility. As insurance, the network is holding in reserve nearly one-fourth of its ad time and would give it back to advertisers if it missed its targets.

In the end, Fox's biggest hurdle may be success itself. In its early days, after all, it could afford to alienate advertisers with racy, off-the-wall stuff. It had so few to lose. As it becomes more successful and attracts more advertisers, it's going to be harder to take such chances. "Now that Fox is a network with a capital 'N'," predicts former production chief Garth Ancier, now at Disney, "they are going to play it safer." Maybe. But with Diller calling the shots, don't count on it.

III

Media Industry–Film

The modern motion picture evolved from humble beginnings. Developed essentially from the technology of still photography, "movies" began as a series of still images attached to a cylinder which, in turn, was mounted on a vertical spindle. When this zoetrope, or "wheel of life," was in motion, it produced the illusion of natural movement. The viewer, typically at a traveling side show, circus or penny arcade in the late-1800s, peered through the slits of the spindle as it spun. The popularity of this visual curiosity gave way to short features in the early-1900s and then longer movies with simple plots, much slapstick humor, bigger-than-life acting and, of course, no sound. Sound was not added until the late 1920s. Color was added in the 1930s. Since then, the motion picture industry has experimented with 3-D, "smell-o-vision," Dolby stereophonic sound, and other innovations to facilitate what many believe to be the primary function of film—escapism.

Today's consumer is used to all the technological innovations that have become an integral part of modern motion pictures. Indeed, we tend take them and the technology of motion picture itself for granted as we escape into the big screen. The first essay in this chapter, "A Revolution in the Movies," is presented to give the reader some sense of the wonder of these innovations upon their inception. Written in 1935, on the cusp of the demise of black and white films, this piece discusses the wonder of color. The second article, "The Color of Money," argues for the artistic integrity behind the old black and white films and addresses a current and heated controversy—the move toward the colorization of old movies.

Above and beyond technological developments and escapism, the cinema has always spoken to broader issues and offered some form of social commentary. Films like "Casablanca," for example, told us that any individual's problems are tiny compared to the threat of fascism. "To Kill A Mockingbird" showed us that it can be worth risking our lives for justice. The third essay in this chapter, "Pretty Worthless," suggests that today's movies no longer urge us to consider such universal values. Rather, unadulterated, mindless escapism seems to reign supreme. The show may go on, says the author, but is it worthy watching or just pretty worthless? The fourth essay, an editorial from the feminist magazine "On the Issues," offers a very different opinion of contemporary film in general and one movie in particular—"Thelma and Louise." Rather than offering mindless fare, the author argues that the cinema is still providing morality plays worth serious consideration.

Whether or not Hollywood films are or ever were hotbeds of complex moral thinking, one change in American cinema is blatantly obvious—the demise of the independent movie theaters that show these films. The final essay "Reel Politick," examines the reasons behind this occurrence and its impact on the media landscape.

A Revolution in the Movies
Robert Edmond Jones, VANITY FAIR

Something new and strange and exciting is happening in Hollywood.

Color is coming to the screen. And it is coming to stay.

Already the blurbs on the newest "trailers" are carrying the legend, *See your favorite star in her true colors, see the honey of her hair, the peach-bloom glow of her skin, the azure of her eyes, her ruby lips . . . all in glorious new Technicolor.*

For once the blurbs are not exaggerated. The Technicolor makes it possible to see your favorite star in her true colors, far larger than life and many times as natural. The new Technicolor camera can reproduce with startling fidelity, every tone and shade of color that is put before it. It can give you the wine-dark sea, the rosy-fingered dawn, the Royal Family, your Aunt Minnie, your baby boy. There is literally no end to the possibilities of this new medium. For color, like music, has no limitations. The color film is a creation in the true sense of the word. Something alive is in the world that was not there before.

The advent of color in pictures, it seems to me, is only the next step in an inevitable law of growth. First, there were black-and-white images of ourselves preserved in our family albums. Then, miraculously, these images began to move on a screen before us. Then they began to speak. Now they are taking on all the colors of life. Soon they are going to come to you in your own homes. Presently they will step off the screen and appear before you in the round—all but living. These things will happen. They have to happen. They are all a part of our raging modern thirst for discovery. For the first time in history we seem to have become actively impatient of our physical limitations.

Every day we surpass yesterday's speed records, every day the telephone and telegraph and the radio and the motion picture draw us all closer together—the ultimate aim being, one supposes, to make every human being on this earth immediately present to every other human being. I cannot say why this should be so. But it is the way in which things seem to be moving.

At any rate, this next step—color in motion pictures—will soon be a matter of cinema history. By the time this issue of *Vanity Fair* reaches its readers the first feature film to be produced in color, *Becky Sharp*, will be showing in various parts of the habitable globe, and you will see Miss Miriam Hopkins, one of the screen's very gifted actresses, appearing to better advantage than she has ever appeared on the screen before, and nearer to you, more real. (I may say that the frontispiece to this issue—the portrait of Miss Hopkins, was made by straight color photography—that is not by Technicolor.)

The first thing that strikes one about these new color films is that, once we have seen them, they seem to be the most natural thing in the world. The ordinary black-and-white films seem, by comparison, not only pallid and anaemic, but artificial. The reason for this is simple. Our eyes naturally see color just as our ears naturally hear sound. We do not live in a silent world, neither do we live in a black-and-white world. You would not bring up your children in a black-and-white nursery, nor give them only black-and-white toys to play with. We hardly see anything, *except on the screen*, that is not alive with color. True, we have great etchings, great cartoons, great black-and-white drawings. But imagine the cathedral of Chartres with all the color abstracted from the windows! Or imagine Wagner's Fire Music played in front of a black-and-white fire!

But it is not enough merely to have lovely color in motion pictures. If that were all, they would still remain caviar to the general. There is a real reason for the appeal of these colored films. It is this: Color is not only pleasing to the eye: it affects us emotionally; it *means* something to us; it has what we call significance. Light bright colors make us feel sad. We see red; we get the blues; we fall into a brown study; we become purple with rage; green with envy. Orange and black, used together, bring to our minds hobgoblins, witches on broomsticks, and Ichabod Crane; red and green make us think of Christmas presents, the Star of Bethlehem, the Prince of Peace.

There are cheerful colors, low, sad colors, reds like battle-cries, calm, faraway blues, rosy tints of romance, dark purples of death. Beautiful color is pleasing to our eyes, just as beautiful sound is pleasing to our ears. But, more than this, beautiful color, properly arranged and composed on the screen and flowing from sequence to sequence just as music flows from movement to movement, stirs our minds and our emotions in the same way that music does. Color on the screen—mobile color, flowing color—is really a kind of visual music. Or rather, it is an art for which there is as yet no name.

Here is the fundamental difference between the old black-and-white pictures and the new Technicolor films. It is not only that color has been added to black-and-white. Color has been added for a reason—to enhance the action of the drama. As a matter of fact, the difference between a black-and-white film and a Technicolor film is very like the difference between a play and an opera.

You will get a clear idea of what I mean if you will think first of Maeterlinck's *Pelleas and Melisande* as a play, and then of the same play with the addition of Debussy's music. Color on the screen, shifting, flowing from sequence to sequence—*largo, allegro, fortissimo, scherzo, grave*—is an orchestral, symphonic accompaniment to the melody of the drama. Color enlarges the drama, supports it, enhances it, actually impels it; becomes an organic part of it, just as Wagner's music becomes an organic part of the great emotional surge of the love motif of *Tristan*.

Within us all is a deep, unconscious response to the rhythms and harmonies of color, just as there is an unconscious response to rhythms and harmonies of sound. To give an obvious illustration: Someone is singing a song, to the accompaniment of a piano. Now, if the accompanist suddenly and arbitrarily shifts the key in which he is playing, we are instantly aware that something is wrong. We don't have to be musically educated to be aware of this. We just *feel* it. Even a child feels it.

There is no reasoning involved in this. It is a matter of instinct. We respond to harmonies or discords of color in exactly the same manner. We may not know anything about the laws of color, but we feel the harmonies, we feel the discords. Again it is a matter of instinct, planted in us all, ages ago.

Here a gate opens and shows us vistas of power and enchantment. Not for ages has there been such an opportunity for art and for artists. Never has there been such a challenge. We are faced with a revolution in the manner of making motion pictures, in the very way we *think* about motion pictures. The screens of the world are about to blossom into a new life. They are about to bring all the actors of the cinema out of their black-and-white prison into the sunlight.

The problem to be faced now is not a technical one at all, but an artistic one. Color must be handled by colorists, just as music must be handled by musicians. A marvellous new instrument is given us, by means of which we may combine the beauty of painting and the emotional flow of music. This instrument must be *played upon*. As I have said, the Technicolor camera records, with startling fidelity, everything that is put before it. But—what are we to put before it?

Black and white thinking is of little use to us, for color is really a separate art, as different from the ordinary film technique as painting is from drawing. A color-sense is born, not made. Indeed, black-and-white thinking is a real handicap when it comes to color, for the experience of working for years in a world from which color has been abstracted atrophies one's color-sense.

One of the most interesting experiences I have had in Hollywood in connection, particularly, with the *Becky Sharp* film, has been that of reconditioning the eyes of several of the men on our staff, of bringing them back to the normal color-consciousness possessed by the man in the street. Their work among gray shadows had actually numbed their sense of color. Imagine seeing the blue of the sky and the green of the grass only as two shades of gray!

Where are we to find artists who will explore the infinite potentialities of this new medium? My own guess is that they will come from among the technicians of Hollywood rather than from the capitals of Europe. The initial difficulties of sound projection were overcome, not by learned professors of the universities of Europe, but by the men who were actually working on the lots at that time.

A color-sense is a gift and anyone may possess it, just as anyone may possess a natural singing voice, or absolute pitch. An instinct for color, combined with an instinct for drama, can work miracles. A rare opportunity is waiting for these undiscovered artists—whoever they are, wherever they may be. They will profoundly influence not only the art of our time, but the *life* of our time. For they will partake of the magic power of the motion picture to lift us out of ourselves into another world of beauty and fantasy.

We go through life, all of us, not paying much attention to color, unaware of it, or to a great degree oblivious to its effect upon us. Through experiencing beautiful and dramatic color on the screen we may learn to transfer our new color "awareness" to the varied scenes around us and to look upon the world with eyes newly awakened to its loveliness.

Robert Edmond Jones is the well-known stage scenic designer. Recently he acted as artistic director for Becky Sharp, *the first feature-length film in technicolor.*

The Color of Money
Susan Linfield, AMERICAN FILM

Remember the celebrated scene in which Jimmy Cagney shoves a grapefruit in Mae Clarke's face in the black-and-white classic *Public Enemy?* Haven't you always wondered whether it was a white grapefruit or a pink one? Probably not, but there's a lot of money in Hollywood that says you have, and that you prefer seeing the blood of thirties gangsters in red rather than black, and that you think Humphrey Bogart's color-coordinated wardrobe can hold its own with Don Johnson's in the pages of GQ. And this month, when the Turner Broadcasting System begins syndicating twenty-four "colorized" black-and-white film classics to stations across the country, you'll have a chance to see for yourself.

Not everyone is happy with this new consumer option. Art and commerce have always cohabited uneasily in Hollywood, but now they are about to square off in an epic combat that dwarfs such recent flaps as Jack Valenti's crusade against video copiers. On one side are some of Hollywood's most distinguished directors—Woody Allen, Martin Scorsese, Warren Beatty, John Huston, Steven Spielberg, and Elia Kazan—along with The American Film Institute, the Directors Guild of America, the Writers Guild of America West, and the American Society of Cinematographers. On the other are such companies as the Turner Broadcasting System, CBS/Fox Video, Hal Roach Studios, Colorization Inc., and Color System Technology, which have invested huge sums (coloring a feature costs about $250,000, or $2,000 to $3,000 per minute) in the new technology.

Almost all coloring work is performed by Colorization, Inc., a Toronto-based company partly owned by Hal Roach Studios, and Color Systems Technology Inc. (CST), a California company that process the Turner collection, which includes three-thousand-plus films from the old MGM, Warner Bros., and RKO libraries. Turner has contracted with CST to color one hundred of his library films—including *Casablanca, Father of the Bride, They Drive By Night, The Maltese Falcon,* and *The Bad and the Beautiful*—which, it is estimated, will cost approximately $18 million. (CST has already processed such films as *Yankee Doodle Dandy* and *Miracle on 34th Street.*) Roach Studios has reached an agreement with Otto Preminger Films to color *The Moon Is Blue, The Man With the Golden Arm, Saint Joan,* and *Advise and Consent,* and has already colorized such public-domain films as *Topper, It's a Wonderful Life,* and Laurel and Hardy's *Way Out West.* There are more than seventeen thousand black-and-white films in the public domain, and if Roach Studios can win the right to copyright its color version of these films, it will be well on its way to creating a valuable library of its own.

Although they utilize essentially the same technology, the two labs take different approaches toward their work. CST attempts to establish "authentic" color values. "First we try to locate someone who actually worked on the project," explains Charles Powell, executive vice-president of CST. "If we can't find someone, or someone who will cooperate, then we try to match color. We know what Humphrey Bogart's skin and hair looked like from color movies he was in. In the color movies, he wore certain types of clothes. We choose to match colors, rather than create colors, whenever we can." Powell adds, "We have an enormous research department. We tell them: 'Find out what a 1938 yellow taxi-cab looked like'. We sent someone to Macy's archives for *Miracle on 34th Street* to find out what was the red of the Santa Claus costume.'

On the other hand, Earl Glick, chairman of Hal Roach Studios, says, "We don't bother with anything like that at all. We give the pictures the modern look we think the audience would like to see to fit today's times. You know, some of the stuff people wore back then was pretty drab. It wouldn't show up good now."

Whatever their approach, colorers stress audience appeal and marketability when touting the new technology. David Copp, vice-president of marketing for Turner Broadcasting Sales, argues,

"If you look at children born after 1955 or 1960, they've grown up in a world of color television. Consequently, you've got an audience scared away by black and white. So we've opened up a whole new audience opportunity for the under-thirty-age population, and offered something new and different for those who have seen these films in black and white." CST's Charles Powell explains, "I have always viewed this as a marketing project. Colored films are not necessarily better, they're not necessarily worse, they're not necessarily anything, but *worth more*. As a marketing man you ask yourself, 'How can I take a library that has basically been grinding out the same bucks each year and make it hot, make it sexy?' You put a marketing coat of paint on it. That's how we view coloring movies."

However, there is surprisingly little in the way of market research to support the colorers' great expectations. In an advertising circular, Hal Roach Studios cites a survey by ASI, a Los Angeles polling company, which concluded that eighty-five percent of the audience prefers viewing black-and-white films in color, but Earl Glick says ASI's report is "internal" and declines to release it. Turner Entertainment says that sixty-one percent of the viewers who called WTBS after it premiered the colored Yankee Doodle Dandy said they favored the new version—but the figure is, obviously, derived from the self-selected group of people who chose to phone the station, not a statistical sample.

In fact, the public's presumed distaste for black and white remains to be determined. Ron Castel, vice-president of advertising for Erol's, the country's largest independent video chain, says he has found "no resistance" to black-and-white films among his customers. "This is a business with short memories," he says. "Black and white [films] sell less just because they're older—not because they're black and white. My ten year old doesn't want to see Laurel and Hardy, even if it's funnier than *Police Academy*."

The verdict isn't in from TV and cable programmers, either. Rob Friedman, director of programming for the Fox Television station WNYW-Channel 5 in New York, which often shows old films on its "Channel 5 Movie Club," says viewing patterns on the coloring question are "totally up in the air." But, he admits, "a measurable segment of the audience prefers to see a color movie. They bought a color TV, they want to get their money's worth." He adds, "On television, a film is not a work of art. A film ceases to be a film. It becomes a TV program."

But although it remains to be seen precisely how large, there is obviously a market for colored films. According to *Variety*, the colored *Miracle on 34th Street* was the highest rated syndicated film in 1985. Colored versions of *Topper*, *It's a Wonderful Life*, and *Night of the Living Dead* have been bought by television stations in forty-nine of the country's top fifty markets. Turner's David Copp says that advertising time for WTBS premieres of colored versions of *The Maltese Falcon* and *Forty-Second Street* is "completely sold out" months in advance. He reports that, as of last October, eighty-five stations had decided to "participate" in the Color Classics Network, including those in such major markets as New York, Los Angeles, San Francisco, and Chicago. Earl Glick claims that, as of November, between fifty-five and seventy-five thousand copies of the colored *It's a Wonderful Life* had been sold to video stores, versus a total of ten thousand copies of the black-and-white versions in 1985 and 1986. And Tower Video's Joe Medwick, who calls coloring "a crime," admits, "More people will probably buy *Wonderful Life* and see it on TV in the colored version. The almighty dollar will win out on this one." The crux of the controversy is ownership versus creative rights. "We never though [coloring] wouldn't be controversial." says Powell. "But the [copyright] owner of that film has the right to get it colored."

Here's where commerce collides with art. No one denies that, say, Ted Turner owns the MGM library. But the creative community, with unaccustomed unanimity, argues that he can no more color *Casablanca* than the head of the Louvre museum can rouge the cheeks of the Mona Lisa. Woody Allen, who shot four of this last seven films in black and white, charges, "These people will tell you anything. They will use any kind of statistic, public-opinion poll, or rationalization, but what they're really saying is they couldn't care less about what this does to film, or the artists involved, or the public. All creative artists should recognize that this is not just an assault, or an affront, to directors, but to film as an art form in general in the United States." Francis Coppola says, "If one doesn't feel that culture and art are more important than commerce, then anyone can buy a Picasso painting and cut it in half because they figure they can sell it as two." Martin Scorsese calls coloring films "a desecration," adding, "Art is not something you have to go to a museum to see and be bored! *Casablanca* is art. You don't mess around with it." "I hate it," says Robert Redford. "I don't like the reasons for it, and I don't like the results. I think in some cases it's like robbing a grave." And Frank Capra, who directed *It's a Wonderful Life*, wrote to the Library of Congress—which is currently considering whether to register copyright claims for colored films—that coloring is akin to painting the Lincoln Memorial.

Those involved in the actual coloring process insist that they are artists, not technicians. Brian Holmes, a former cinematographer who is now director of creative services for Colorization, Inc., says, "It's not done by computers, it's done with computers. I'm not a hack, I'm not painting by numbers."

Holmes adds that he could do a good job on *Citizen Kane*: "*Citizen Kane* could definitely be colored. It would be easier on the eye." Earl Glick has gone so far as to claim that Colorization, Inc. "improved on Joe Walker's original photography in *It's a Wonderful Life*." And the colorers' work has, indeed, won some fans. Cary Grant called the colored *Topper* "extremely interesting," and Nancy Reagan has said that she and the president "were most impressed with the colorization of that fun movie."

But the colorers' technical work has also come under some heavy fire. *Wonderful Life* star Jimmy Stewart has said that he was unable to sit through the entire colored version of that film: "The faces are orange-yellow, and the shadows are not there, except for great, big shadows which are blacker than black." According to Gilbert Cates, president of the DGA, the coloring process "removes shadow and substance. The first thing you'll see is that it looks lousy. It doesn't look like color, it looks like a tinted movie. It really is neutering the picture." A former employee of a coloring company who requested anonymity admits, "They needed the output rather than the quality."

Part of the coloring dispute turns on the question of the artist's intent. According to Roger Mayer, a former president of MGM Laboratories and now president of Turner Entertainment Co., none of the old films in the Turner collection were "made" in black and white. "None of those directors would know if they would've chosen black and white back then," Mayer argues. "The world is in color," Replies director George Stevens, Jr., co-chairman of The American Film Institute, "I know that John Huston will tell you that he wanted to make *The Red Badge of Courage* in black and white. Fred Zinnemann will tell you that he wanted to make *High Noon* and *From Here to Eternity* in black and white, and in fact, persuaded Harry Cohn that it was preferable to making it in color. And I, from personal experience, can tell you that color was very much available when George Stevens chose to make *A Place in the Sun* in black and white." Director Richard Brooks agrees: "When I made *In Cold Blood*, I had to tell the producers: When anyone's afraid, it's in black and white, not color. It should not be pretty. It should be stark. The footsteps that come from a candy-colored spectrum are not the same as footsteps that come in the dark." In fact, cinematographer Vilmos Zsigmond has gone so far as to say, "I would like to see some of my color films in black and white. Many of them should have been shot that way, but I wasn't allowed to."

For these directors and cinematographers, black and white is not the absence of color but, rather, represents a series of deliberate creative choices. "My two black-and-white films, *The Elephant Man* and *Eraserhead*, were shot specifically in those tones to communicate a feeling," says David Lynch. "You see things differently in black and white, you tend to look at it more closely; it's dreamlike, not reality, and both these films would be ruined in color." Robert Wise (*Somebody Up There Likes Me*), speaking as a director and not in his current capacity as president of the Academy of Motion Picture Arts and Sciences, emphasizes that "the sets, costumes, decor, cinematography [of those films] were designed for black and white, and to change that is to bastardize it. You cannot think that by laying on color you are doing anything but changing the integrity of someone else's work."

There is also sharp disagreement over how coloring will affect the availability of black-and-white films and tapes. For instance, CBS/Fox Home Video, which is distributing the Turner films, has stated that colored cassettes will not replace the black-and-white versions. But, George Stevens, Jr., notes, "The marketing people always push their new product off. If they have an investment in the color versions, black-and-white versions will be next to impossible to find." And while colorers point out that viewers who object to coloring can simply turn down the color button on their televisions, critics retort that many new sets have no such knob.

Perhaps most important, colorers emphasize that since they are not altering original negatives or prints, computer coloring poses no threat to the existence of black-and-white films. But director Nicholas Meyer (*The Day After*) argues that the real question is how films are used. "No one in this country goes to see old films in theaters. The mass perception, in our culture, is on the tube. Film is a popular art form and is now perceived almost exclusively—and certainly this is true of old films—on TV." Meyer adds, "Film, on a case by case basis, may be a business, but collectively it metamorphoses into our cultural heritage."

The cultural role of film has been stressed by The American Film Institute, which has taken a strong stand against coloring. At a press conference last October (at which everyone on the dais—including Jimmy Stewart—was clad only in black and white), AFI chairman Bonita Granville Wrather argued, "What is at stake is the film's 'life'—how a specific film is experienced by audiences, not only today in 1986, but by future generations in 2086. If fact, if 'colored' films are available in 2086, it is very likely that no one living will know the original power of *The Treasure of the Sierra Madre, Manhattan, Citizen Kane*, [and] *The Grapes of Wrath*." She warned that coloring will "destroy our national film history and the rich heritage which it represents." Jimmy Stewart spoke of "the distress and disappointment and surprise, and, I suppose, anger" that the great black-and-white cinematographers would feel "if they found that their work would all be wiped out by color."

Finally, coloring executives argue that the issue should be decided in the marketplace. "There is a small group of people who are afraid to let the public make the decision as to what should be colored," says Earl Glick. "They're afraid the public will love it, like they like gin and whiskey and God knows how many other things." "Only the public will make the choice—not the government or AFI," says CST's Charles Powell. Turner Entertainment's Mayer, in a written statement protesting the AFI's stand, argued. "Surely the audiences themselves should be allowed to decide whether the coloring process is enhancing their enjoyment." Replies Nicholas Meyer, "A work of art has its own reality. You don't vote on how you'd most like to see it."

The lines have been drawn. The Directors Guild of America is organizing—along with the Writers Guild and the American Society of Cinematographers—against coloring on what President Gilbert Cates calls "the legislative, public relations, and legal fronts, and in the court of public opinion"; Nicholas Meyer says the DGA will try "to make coloring as expensive and declasse as possible." Cinematographer Bill Fraker says he will fight for "an absolute creative rights clause" prohibiting coloring in all Hollywood guild contracts. Woody Allen already has such a clause—which also prohibits other alterations such as panning and scanning for TV—in his contract, and says, "I would certainly be willing to strike, to not work until this is resolved honorably. And I think everyone else in the industry should, as well."

But not every director has the clout of Woody Allen. Much is riding on the copyright decision that should be handed down by the Copyright Office of the Library of Congress sometime during the next few months.

The Copyright Office will not, however, base its judgment on the question of "artistic integrity" raised by concerned directors. Explains Dorothy Schrader, general counsel of the Copyright Office, "For the public, the most important aspect of the colorization question is whether you should be allowed to change [a film] without [the director's] permission." But,

Schrader says, such questions of "moral right" are not recognized by U.S. copyright laws. "The only question that we're looking at is: Is this an original work of authorship; that is, do those acts and creative judgments [necessary to color a film] involve a sufficient level of skill, or are they sufficiently creative, to constitute a new work of art?" (Interestingly, while proponents of coloring have, in their public statements, insisted that they are merely "enhancing," not changing, black-and-white films, in their briefs to the Library of Congress they argue that coloring does in fact involve such fundamental alteration and creative control that it constitutes a new work of authorship worthy of copyright protection.)

Schrader says that any existing copyright on a black-and-white film would automatically cover its colored version, and thus the Copyright Office's ruling "will have virtually no effect on films now under copyright [such as those in the MGM library]. The main impact would be on titles in the public domain. You don't ordinarily invest a lot of money into something [like coloring] that you'll have no protection for. Why spend a lot of money if anyone can do it?"

Schrader adds that questions of "artistic integrity" will probably be "fought out" in the courts and in Congress regardless of what the Copyright Office decides. Indeed, colorization is already in the courts, although the cases involve ownership, not artistic, rights: RKO Pictures has filed suit against Color Systems Technology, charging that CST's coloring of ten pre-1950 RKO films is a copyright infringement, and Turner Entertainment is suing RKO General for breach of contract.

Although no one wants to speak for the record, a compromise may eventually be in the cards, perhaps along the lines of the one that seems to be emerging in Britain. Explains Fred Zinnemann, the honorary president of the Directors Guild of Great Britain, "We found it was totally hopeless to talk about blanket rejection [of colored films]. They talked about copyrights; they saw it from a legal and business point of view. It became a question of [pushing] total rejection—which would have led nowhere—or of at least salvaging the really great movies, and then maybe going on from there." Consequently, the British guild has backed off from the demand for a total ban on coloring, and instead is seeking to protect a limited number (more than one hundred, as of this writing) of designated classics, such as *Brief Encounter, Rebecca, The Third Man*, and Olivier's *Hamlet*, to be selected by the guild in conjunction with other concerned parties. The guild has persuaded the BBC not to air colored versions of any film on this list, and has convinced Channel 4 not to air any colored films whatsoever. No agreements regarding cassettes for home use have been reached.

Despite the compromise advocated by the British Directors Guild, Zinnemann adds, "I totally support the American [guild's] position of total rejection." And for the moment, at least, the creative community on this side of the Atlantic is not giving an inch. What with all the variables involved—including public acceptance of coloring, the copyright decision, and attendant court battles further down the road—the outcome is by no means easy to predict. The arguments on both sides—which pit property rights against authors' rights (with collective cultural "rights," different from either, lurking in the background)—have larger implications that have barely been discussed. Some directors, for example, may see the battle over coloring as a way of getting a foot in the door for authors' (read directors') rights. These have been recognized in Europe more than here (the Taviani brothers, for example, fought against commercial breaks when their films were aired on French television, and won), but they raise a host of difficulties, not the least of which is determining who is a film's auteur in the American system of production. What is clear, however, is that the stakes are high—no less than the integrity of a good chunk of America's film heritage.

Susan Linfield is a senior editor of American Film. *Research assistance provided by Julie Stark.*

Pretty Worthless

Beth Austin, THE WASHINGTON MONTHLY

In the 1954 film *On the Waterfront*, Marlon Brando plays a dockworker named Terry Malloy whose brother is in cahoots with the vicious leader of the local dockworkers's union. Although he resists falling in with the crooks, Terry also has no interest in trying to stop them. When an investigator from the crime commission tries to question him, Terry more or less sums up his philosophy of life: "I don't know nothin', I ain't seen nothin', an' I ain't sayin' nothin'."

Enter Edie (Eva Marie Saint). She's educated and has a shot at escaping the tough neighborhood around the docks; if she falls for Terry, she probably never will. But much more threatening to the relationship than Terry's lack of money or brains are Edie's weird ideas. She's putting herself on the line to clean up the waterfront, and she expects no less from Terry. "Shouldn't everybody care about everybody else?" she asks him. He looks amazed. "Boy," he observes, "are you a fruitcake."

As *On the Waterfront* amply demonstrates, Hollywood has never been a hotbed of complex moral thinking. But the past few years have seen a dramatic narrowing of the issues and themes addressed in American movies. This is the cinematic legacy of the Reagan era, and it divides roughly into two categories. On one hand are what could be characterized as outward-looking films, in which the main players try to save or avenge their friends/town/city/planet. These heroes are not descendants of *It's A Wonderful Life's* George Bailey, who through example and hard work kept Bedford Falls from the clutches of Mr. Potter, or of Gary Cooper, who made it almost to the end of *High Noon* without firing a shot. Instead, they take after *Dirty Harry*, whose protagonist's readiness to blow holes through villains was legendary. No one will be shocked to hear that this bloody-buddy genre has its moral deficiencies.

The Reagan years' other moral legacy to Hollywood is more inward-looking: the exaltation of "family values," in which the family itself has become our only value, the single bright ray in an increasingly murky world. Compared to the blood-baths of the cop films, these movies are refreshing not only because they're generally fun to watch, but because of their emphasis on love and sincerity. Still, you don't have to be a graduate of NYU film school to see that the warm, fuzzy movies celebrating friendship, family, and the occasional dog are also lacking morally. In fact, as a moviegoer—and as a wife, mother, and journalist—I find them not just empty, but insidious, because they leave us feeling so good about our insulated selves. The redoubtable Edie of *On the Waterfront* would never have settled for such moral interior decorating, as Terry learns to his peril. She flings his offer of a mere relationship right back in his face: "No wonder everybody calls you a bum."

He pursues her, bewildered. "I'm only trying to help you out. I'm trying to keep you from getting hurt," Terry mumbles. "What more do you want me to do?"

"Much more," Edie fires back, almost snarling, "much, much, much more."

Much more, indeed. In trying to produce "family" movies, today's popular filmmakers have confused niceness with morality and ended up creating a moral universe that stops at the front door. Trend spotting, of course, is a risky business, and there are some recent exceptions—*Dances With Wolves, Glory, The Hunt for Red October,* and *Guilty by Suspicion*—that confuse the rule. But a look at the heartwarming blockbusters of recent years indicates that, in general, we hold these truths to be self-evident: that parents' highest responsibilities are to provide complete emotional and financial security for their children; that women exist to help men get beyond their fear of intimacy and commitment; and that personal relationships are by far the single most important facet of life.

And sometimes the only facet. In the latest afterlife extravaganza, *Defending Your Life*, Albert Brooks doesn't have to minister to lepers, save the rain forest, or even donate blood to reach a higher level of being. He just has to admit to loving Meryl Streep.

Of course, Brooks and Streep are utterly insulated from the real world—but then again, so are almost all of today's movie couples. In *When Harry Met Sally*, the seal is so tight that any real human being would surely suffocate. We barely learn what the characters do to pay for their loft apartments, grilled radicchio, and Mexican ceramic tile floors. The outside world intrudes only once, when Harry and Sally double-date with their best friends. Harry's friend Jess, an intense journalist, launches into passionate praise of Jimmy Breslin, calling his writing "a wake-up call to the city of New York": "He's saying we've actually got people in the city, people on welfare. . . ." And that's it. Sally rolls her eyes, and the conversation fades out, overlaid by Harry and Marie's discussion of window decorating.

Think back: Away from your VCR, when was the last time you heard a somber Rick reminding the audience that larger obligations give life meaning—that, when you get right down to it, "the problems of two little people don't amount to a hill of beans in this crazy world"? When was the last time you saw a Mr. Smith waving the Constitution on the Senate floor, expostulating, "I wouldn't give a red cent for *all* your fine rules, without there was some plain, everyday, common kindness under 'em—and a little looking out for the next fella"?

A little looking out for the next fella is precisely what filmmakers are leaving out of their family-oriented pictures—a dangerous signal to be transmitting to our kids (at whom most of these movies are aimed), since, as Mr. Smith puts it in his homey, gender-specific terms, "Now, we're not gonna have a country that makes these kinds of rules *work*, if you haven't got men who've learned to tell human rights from a punch in the nose. And funny thing about men—they start life being boys."

The people who start life being boys—and girls—have always looked to the screen to learn about life and love. Boys watch for what it takes for the hero to get the girl; girls learn what kind of girl is worth getting. At least the characters played by the likes of Jean Arthur, Katherine Hepburn, and Rosalind Russell had useful lives and independent minds. Today's female characters exist exclusively to bring white male stars in touch with The Things That Really Matter; once they grasp these Things, the stars win the prize.

Long before Edie pushed Terry to blow the whistle on the crooked union bosses, Hollywood has been using women to make heroes out of men. But The Things That Really Matter have changed; today, they include nothing beyond personal relationships. In *Mr. Smith Goes to Washington*, Jean Arthur urges Jimmy Stewart, "Don't quit. Don't grab a measly chance like this to save a few pieces—other men could—but not you. As long as you lived, you'd remember you ran out and threw this country of yours to the jackals!" Compare that movie to the blockbuster *Batman*. When Bruce Wayne (Michael Keaton) has to rush off to save Gotham City from poison-gas extermination, Vicky Vale (Kim Basinger) cavils, "It doesn't have to be a perfect world."

Getting the girl—in other words, doing the right thing—almost costs Terry his life in 1954, but by the time 1990's number two movie, *Pretty Woman*, rolled around, the price of a heroine had dropped to $300. Richard Gere—whose ambition is not to work on the docks but to own a shipyard—at first wins the girl, Julia Roberts, by, literally, paying for her. But keeping her, in both senses of the word, is another matter. Like Edie, Roberts wants much more from her man than he is prepared to deliver—but what, exactly? Good legislation? The defenestration of corrupt union boss? No. She wants "the fairy tale." She wants him to realize he doesn't want to live without her and then *commit*.

Gere may eventually turn to more productive work than corporate raiding, but he won't sacrifice one thread of his thousand-dollar suits to do it—which is fortunate, since, to deliver the fairy tale to Julia Roberts, he has to prove over and over again that he's her knight in platinum armor. He changes for her and he fights for her, but in the movie's most thrilling moments, he buys for her.

It's a nice '90s fairy tale, but don't try this at home. Today's movies show boys what it takes to win a girl in much the same way Steve Martin famously advised Americans on "How To Be a Millionaire and Never Pay Taxes": "First," he said, "get a million dollars."

"You know what's wrong with our waterfront?" cries Karl Malden, playing a Catholic priest also shamed by Edie into doing the right thing by the dockworkers. "It's the love of a lousy buck. It's making the love of a buck and a comfy job more important than love of your fellow man."

Women aren't the only victims of cinematic morality in the '90s. Blacks are also put on earth—or at least on screen—to help white males find out more about themselves. In films made by whites, blacks are almost universally portrayed as warm, centered, and soulful—so much so that it is positively refreshing to find that 1990's number five hit, *Total Recall*, features a lying, treacherous black man. This vision of blacks as conduits to The Things That Really Matter reaches an apogee in 1990's number one box office hit, *Ghost*, in which medium Whoopi Goldberg gives up her body to the spectral Patrick Swayze so he can get in touch with Demi Moore just once more.

Few movies take on the hard and dramatic issues that confront contemporary American blacks even as gingerly as *A Raisin in the Sun* did in 1961. Again, there are exceptions. This year's *New Jack City* takes a stab at exploring the connections between the drug culture and the underclass, but only Spike Lee seems consistently willing to confront a range of issues related to race.

But, as *Do the Right Thing* proved, tackling such issues unsettles audiences, a risk most filmmakers never run. Instead they go with what sells: a subtle validation of an "I'm OK, you're OK" view of society. Filmgoers learn that in relationships, people need never make any painful demands on each other. In *Pretty Woman*, Gere doesn't sacrifice to give Roberts what she needs; he merely realizes what *he* wants.

Consider the 1960s' *To Kill a Mockingbird*. The movie's central moral issue remains a tough one: Should Gregory Peck follow his conscience and defend a black man charged with rape, or should he turn his back on the case to protect himself and his young children from possible retaliation by an angry Southern town? As lawyer Atticus Finch, Peck never wavers, even though his obedience to his conscience nearly costs his children their lives. The legal heroes of today's films take a different tack. In *Reversal of Fortune*, Ron Silver portrays Alan Dershowitz as a loving father and a model lawyer—brilliant, dedicated, and deliberately inattentive to the moral implications of freeing Claus von Bulow, a society figure charged with killing his heiress wife.

To Kill a Mockingbird sends a message that today's movies, with their emphasis on quality time, sincere relationships, and parent-child bonding, never approach: A vital part of loving your children—of loving anyone—is living a life they will admire, which can mean risking yourself and even your loved ones to do the right thing. It's disheartening to realize that, in a '90s movie, Atticus Finch would be considered a bad parent because he risks his family's safety for his work. Today, his daughter, Scout, would quickly set him straight, convincing him to ditch the case because nothing could be more important than spending more time at home.

Children who put their parents back on track show up throughout these family-oriented movies: the triumph of the Shirley Temple genre. *Look Who's Talking*, *Honey I Shrunk the Kids*, *Dead Poets Society* and *Home Alone* all feature children struggling to bring their insensitive, inadequate, or just plain bad parents in touch with The Things That Matter. The calm, dependable, unbelievably wise and loving parents who once populated Hollywood have been replaced by a passel of unstable neurotics who need a good 12-step program—or a good 12-year-old—to bring them back onto solid family ground.

Home Alone develops this theme so cannily that it promises to replace *E.T.* (another kids-good, grownups-bad epic) as the top film moneymaker of all time. *Home Alone's* winsome little hero, Kevin, is a terrific and resourceful kid whose qualities are hidden beneath the blanket of his family's disapproval. He comes into his own only when his family accidentally leaves for Paris without him. In his parents' absence, the plucky child manages to save his home from burglars, reconcile an elderly neighbor with his son and grandchildren, and, finally, bring his own family back home—where they belong—in time for Christmas.

Ron Howard's film *Parenthood* is in many ways an exception to the kid as hero theme. Despite their flaws, most of the parents in this movie seem well intentioned. Still, when the parents make moral choices, family happiness is always the paramount issue. When Steve Martin has to pick between time at the office and time with his kids, it's a simple cost-benefit analysis: Money, although very good, is less valuable than family time.

And exactly what was Martin doing at the office, anyway? You probably don't remember, because beyond paying the bills, his job had nothing to do with his family life—or, for that matter, with anybody's life, since he was an advertising executive. Meaningful work? Don't look for it in these films. In fact, in *Honey, I Shrunk the Kids*, the parents are censured for pursuing their dreams—portrayed as an act of betrayal that can only hurt, not instruct, their children. The mother's commitment to her job leaves her children feebly attempting to create order in their chaotic home. And Dad, the nutty professor, won't get a good job at a good wage. Instead, he wastes his time fiddling with a wacky invention just because it might cure cancer.

No one is asking Hollywood to churn out a string of uplifting epics, say, *Mother Teresa: The Black Hole of Calcutta*. But it's jarring, and somewhat frightening, to see the cheerful moral flatness of one screen family after another. George Bailey would never have gone to work for Mr. Potter so he'd have more money and time to shower on little Zuzu, just as Bogie would never have let Ingrid Bergman's love for him stop her from getting on that plane.

It's equally hard to picture Gary Cooper ordering chardonnay—or Atticus Finch driving a BMW. Is everyone's moral sense blunted by materialism? Are moral people in America today truly as scarce as moral movies? As *Home Alone*'s Kevin would say: I don't *think* so.

Hollywood needs to realize, as its audience does, that good relationships require moral judgment of the highest order. It's easy for a third-grader, or a filmmaker with a third-grader's moral sophistication, to set out the relationship commandments: Be wise, loving, responsible, emotionally available, and financially secure, or your kids or girlfriend will send you to bed without your supper. But families are not all alike, and each person must find a balance between the understandable desire to seal off relationships from the world and responsibility toward the greater community. These decisions are never simple, but they are filled with excitement and satisfaction to which Hollywood these days seems oblivious.

Editorial on Feminism and Film
Merle Hoffman, ON THE ISSUES

I never really wear the things: Political buttons, T-shirts with messages, designer-labeled bags. I don't like to advertise my politics or buying habits by turning myself into a walking message for someone else's consumption—except when I conduct my own special social/psychological experiments and decide to become a political catalyst. There was the time in 1980 when I got a button that read "Impeach Ronald Reagan." Reagan had just been elected by a landslide, Carter left the White House in near disgrace, the hostages came home from Iran, the country was awash in an orgy of expectations, and I was wearing this "Impeach Reagan" button the day of his inauguration.

As a psychological test, the "Impeach Reagan" button delivered the expected results: From friends and sympathizers of the left there was agreement and approval; non-politicals thought it cute or just strange; supporters of the President had no sense of humor about it. But this year, with this button, things were not quite so predictable or consistent. The button was small with white letters on a dark blue background that proclaimed: "Thelma and Louise Live."

A stewardess handing me my jacket before landing bends down and whispers "Fantastic button—right on," a middle-aged clerk in a food store spots it and says: "They gave those bastards what they deserved;" my mother, who is renowned for sleeping through movies, loved "Thelma and Louise" and asks me if I can get her a button. Strong positive responses abound—knowing nods, winks, non-verbal "right ons" that cut across race, class, age and political affiliation. I am beginning to feel that something is definitely going on here.

The plot in brief; Thelma and Louise are women seemingly trapped in the morass of bourgeoise female suburban existence, who are suddenly catapulted into an extraordinary road adventure by the radical act of thwarting an attempted rape by killing the rapist. The film follows the unlikely heroines in their wild attempt to escape the law and shows us how, in that process, they find themselves and each other.

In a very real sense, *Thelma and Louise* is a morality play, one in which the characters are informed and driven by a sense of personalized justice rather than lawfully bound definitions of "right and wrong." It has a kind of karmic cause and effect immediacy of response. You rape me or my friend—I kill you. You mess with my freedom—I leave you. You block my escape routes—I stop you. And, ultimately, you try to kill me, I kill myself because death is superior to your laws around me. This then is not really about women taking the "law" into their own hands; it is about redefining and actualizing "justice."

Unfortunately, or necessarily, the film's ending has the two women achieving their ultimate self-revelations by speeding off the cliffs of the Grand Canyon together in a green convertible, holding hands. They achieve their freedom, transcendence and fusion through a violent death that we do not witness. Our last view of Thelma and Louise has them suspended in flight, hair blowing against the wind, stopped in time and space.

Interestingly, the two film characters, their adventures and their ending have become both metaphors and lightning rods for different populations for different reasons.

The reactions of the mainstream press to the film have ranged from discussions of whether or not it portrays the existence of a feminism turned "toxic," to sounding alarms over the film's catalytic possibilities for general female revolt. Questions and a myriad of associations abound. Are Thelma and Louise really lovers? Is their coupling, unlike Bonnie and Clyde's, a kind of mythological prototype of best friends, a female version of Damon and Pythias who would rather die together and for each other than make a date with the men—in this case the criminal justice system? Or, are the two women just another Hollywood creation whose ultimate value lies in their box office profitability?

The button, however, seems to proclaim a survival fantasy, as if by our collective wills we could rewind and reverse the tape, re-do the ending and freeze the frame where we want it so that, indeed, Thelma and Louise do not perish in the fiery crash and live to revenge themselves another day. The message is layered with symbols and symbolic meaning. It is the two outlaw women giving the ultimate "fuck you" to the patriarchy—the triumph of life over death, the oppressed over the oppressor, gender justice and Amazonian immortality. The button proclaims an essentially happy ending, and it is one that seems to strike resonant chords in the most unlikely of places.

"Thelma and Louise Live." But for what? For whom? Do we really want them endlessly chasing across the western landscape shooting and drinking their way out of negative interactions with masturbating, murderous, misogynist men? Shall the film and the fantasy then function as a counter-revolutionary co-opting force that allows all of us so-called good girls to sit back and let Thelma and Louise take care of all our dirty business? To let them become our own avenging angels?

Are avenging angels needed? Considering the war zone that millions of American women live their lives in, a massive strategic military initiative may be more to the point. Actually, when viewed in this realistic context, Thelma and Louise killing one man for attempted rape, leaving another rather than marrying him, putting a cop in a car trunk and blowing up an oil truck is relatively mild stuff.

If we search out the "law" that persued and ultimately destroyed Thema and Louise for their "crimes" against patriarchy, it is often either nowhere to be found or in hiding when it comes to crimes against women. A reflection of the society that spawned it, the criminal justice system functions more often than not as a support and reinforcer of perpetrators rather than as a protector of victims. Indeed, the system in all of its complicated intricacies, assumptions, precedents and formalized rituals has been unable to either stem or quell the ever-increasing tides of violence against women.

A study by the Justice Department found that while violent crime against men dropped about 20 percent from 1973 to 1987, violence against women has stayed constant with about 2.5 million women a year becoming victims of robbery, assault or rape. According to the study, which was recently made public, 25 percent of the violent crimes against women are committed by family members or men they have dated. (*WIN News* Vol. 17 #3 Summer)

A study of the National Crime Survey conducted between 1978 and 1982 found that an estimated 2.1 million women were victims of domestic violence at least once during an average 12 month period.

The National Woman Abuse Prevention Project reports that FBI statistics indicate 50 percent of female homicide victims are killed by their husbands or boyfriends. This translates into the fact that *every day in this country four women are killed by batterers*. In fact, murder is the second leading cause of death for young women.

For the women who are not murdered by their husbands or boyfriends, statistics report that up to three or four million experience severe beatings and batterings by their intimates.

This near-and-present danger for women is compounded by the fact that one in four college women is a victim of rape or attempted rape on campus, most often by someone known to the victim. Date rape actually accounts for 60 percent of all reported rapes with the majority of victims between 16 and 24 years of age. "Regular" or "violent" rapes (by strangers) occur every six minutes in this country, while according to FBI estimates only one of 10 rapes is ever reported. In 33 states, under certain circumstances, it is legal for a husband to rape his wife. (National Center of Women and Family Law, Aug. 1989)

If the names of all the women who are victims of all the crimes against their sex, from rape to battery, to murder, to abuse, to incest, to inadequate health care, to economic deprivation were put on a wall, the list would be far longer than the Vietnam War Memorial.

Although it was attempted rape that provoked the male killing in *Thelma and Louise*, in "real life" it is extremely rare, given the statistics on occurrence of rape and battery, that women ever fight back at all. Some studies have found that at least 40 percent of women who kill do so in self defense. (*WIN News*)

A California state prison study found that 93 percent of the women who had killed their mates had been battered by them; 67 percent of these women indicated the homicide resulted from an attempt to protect themselves or their children. (National Woman Abuse Prevention Project, 1989)

While most of these women rot in prison with long sentences, it's not uncommon for wife-killers to be acquitted on flimsy "provocation" defenses such as accusations in court that the dead woman nagged or committed adultery. Legally, these resemble post-mortem witch trials in which the victim, not the murderer is blamed.

One only has to look at the cases of Jean Harris, who killed her physician lover in a fit of drugged paranoia and rage, and Robert Chambers, the young "preppie" killer of Jennifer Levin. For Harris there was no mercy, not in the courts, not in the press, not in reality. She rots in jail—victim of two heart attacks—while Chambers received refuge and support from the Catholic church and press headlines that implied he killed Levin in self-defense; that he was a victim of "rough sex."

But pieces of rage are coming to the surface. A radical feminist, Nikki Craft formed "Always Causing Legal Unrest" (ACLU), and joined hands with a small company, "Pushing Buttons" to produce a new line of what they term "feminist male-bashing buttons." In their own type of social/psychological experiment, they say that "talking about killing men *Thelma-and-Louise* style, is protected under the First Amendment, isn't it? It should be, shouldn't it?" They describe their political action in terms of trying to see if they can "saturate the mainstream media with real man-hate," as a response to the plethora of woman-hating images. In order to frame the debate where they think it belongs and focus on the consistent institutionalized and conditioned misogyny in the society, they produce buttons with messages like "How Dare You Assume I'm Not Violent?," "I Think, Therefore I am Dangerous," "When Justice is Gone—There's Always Force," "Patriarchy: 5,000 Years of S/M—Are We Bored Yet?" "The Woman at Your Feet Today Will Be at Your Throat Tomorrow," "Stop Sucking and Start Biting."

After all, if Bret Ellis, author of *An American Psycho*, can speak about cutting and slicing vaginas and fucking women's decapitated heads, be on the best seller list and be protected by the parameter of free speech, so can messages like "Men and Women Were Created Equal and Smith and Wesson Makes Damn Sure It Stays That Way."

While experiments by their very nature and definition are not reality but attempts to elucidate aspects of reality through artificial situations, they can inform us. If there are seeds of female unrest and resistence, there is also the beginning of minimal institutional understanding. *The New York Times* reported that "following the lead set by the Governor of Ohio, William Schaefer of Maryland is commuting the prison sentences of eight women convicted of killing or assaulting men who battered them. Women's rights groups, criminal justice groups and legislators in several states have begun seeking clemency for women now in prison for such killings." "Some of these stories are hard to believe—difficult, horrible stories," said Governor Schaefer, adding that some of the women would probably have been killed themselves if they had not struck back.

However well-intentioned, these few cases are small flickers of light in a very dark tunnel. If a film merely depicting a fantasized version of a woman striking back against her attacker can be so threatening, the reality strikes a blow at the heart of not only the established power structure but of most women themselves. Alone, isolated from each other, facing economic inequality, lack of support services for their lives and their children, continual assaults on multiple political fronts, women are in a consistently defensive posture—a posture requiring that most energies be used for personal survival as opposed to pro-active political strategies that can benefit their sex. Additionally, there are many voices in the media that continue to blame feminists for the problems that women face. Camille Paglia, Associate Professor of Humanities at Philadelphia College of Performing Arts, who has enraged feminists for her theories of classical biological determinism, becomes a media heroine for writing things like "Rape is a mode of natural aggression that can be controlled only by the social contract," and "Modern feminism's most naive formulation is its assertion that rape is a crime of violence but not of sex. Sex is power and all power is inherently aggressive. Society is woman's protection against rape." Meanwhile a young "feminist," Susan Jane Gilman, in *The New York Times'* "Voices of the New Generation" writes that "We need to improve the way we communicate. Today, universities are the hotbed for feminist discourse. Yet, much of this discourse is irrelevant to everyday life. If women are uncomfortable with the connotations of feminism, it is up to us to stop perpetuating the stereotypes."

But feminism has no corner on stereotypes. Indeed if there are any at all, their power to coerce, control or dictate behavior is minimum compared to the stereotypes perpetrated and institutionalized by the system. Particularly the one in which the view and role of women is determined by their biological reality. When we lift our heads from the "hotbeds of the universities" to the pillows of our bedrooms we find that women no longer have a constitutional right of reproductive freedom and that poor women can't even hear the "A" word in federally funded clinics. We now stand at the precipice of looking at a country that will be a patch-work quilt of slave and free states, where a woman's personal liberty will depend on her geographic location, her degrees of freedom measured by the distance she lives from a free state. And even this legal access is no guarantee of service. Last year alone there were, according to National Abortion Federation statistics, 36 incidents of abortion clinic bombings, 56 reports of arson, 44 attempted arsons, 275 invasions, 79 death threats to health care workers, two kidnappings and 22 burglaries. At the time of this writing, Wichita, Kansas is being besieged by Operation Rescue supporters who sport T-shirts with the message "Support Our Unborn Troops," No subtlety there—keep those fetuses alive and growing so that they can become the cannon fodder they are supposed to be. Meanwhile, four state challenges wend their way up to the Supreme Court in a Kafkaesque race to see which one will become the final nail in *Roe's* coffin.

The crushing reality is that the Supreme Court—the highest "law" in the land—through its political direction and radical judicial activism will make outlaws of us all, creating a world where women will run from one state to another, where underground railroads and "safe houses" will permeate the American landscape. Unlike Thelma and Louise who run for their lives with the "law" on their backs, women in slave states will have the law on all sides—and will wish they could be Thelma and Louise, forever suspended in time and space—above and beyond the laws of men.

Reel Politick
Michael Bronski, Z MAGAZINE

On any April night in 1973 you had your choice of 17 independent and foreign films playing at eleven Boston-area theaters. Now your choices are down to eight films at three art theaters.

So what happened? It's the phenomenon of the incredibly shrinking independent movie theater. Reliable sources have estimated that between 1984 and 1989 the number of independent art and repertory theaters shrunk nationwide from 290 to a meager 60 and remains at that low figure today. Going to see the new Kevin Costner movie is as easy as driving to your local shopping mall—in fact, if the film is a megahit, it may well be playing on 2 of the 12 screens in a multiplex theater. But if you have a hankering for a double bill of Ingmar Bergman, you may have to wait until the local museum or university decides to do a Swedish film retrospective.

The demise of the independent art and repertory house is the product of a constellation of cultural, social, and economic forces. While the pre-production work may have been put in motion by changing audience attitudes toward movies in general, and by gradual shifts in the nature of Hollywood and European filmmaking, the final direction and packaging of the situation is purely a matter of economics: Corporate mergers of big film production companies, theater chains, and distribution companies are simply forcing smaller theaters out of existence.

The heydey of foreign films started in the mid-1950s when such movies as Bergman's *Wild Strawberries* (1957) and Federico Fellini's *Nights of Cabiria* (1957) found a willing and eager American audience tired of the superficiality and inanity of Hollywood movies. As film imports proliferated and the audience for them grew, certain theaters, particularly in urban areas, garnered the reputation for being "art houses." As time went on and there was enough of a backlog of available "art" films, the repertory house, which sometimes played several different movies a week, came into being. As more and more venues became available, the feasibility of importing more foreign films became a reality. Eventually even independently produced, non-Hollywood films from the United States found their way into the art houses.

By the late 1960s to the mid-1970s, art films and rep houses were flourishing. The legendary Orson Welles Cinema in Cambridge was discovering little-known films and lesser known directors—among them Werner Fassbinder and Joan Micklin Silver—and bringing them to larger audiences. And other rep houses across the country—ranging from the Elgi, the Thalia, and the New Yorker in Manhattan to the Varsity in Des Moines—were not just keeping the films of Rossellini, DeSica, Bergman, and Cocteau in the public light; they were also showing classic American films, and in some cases rediscovering and helping to re-evaluate portions of the American cinema that had been overlooked.

Although business was good, the financial position of many of the houses was precarious. Distributors looking for the widest possible audience and the largest possible returns were always looking for the biggest, most popular houses in which to show their films.

During this period, another change was occurring: A generation being raised on television—those just past the baby boom—began approaching movies from quite a different perspective. Interested less in ideas than in sensation, younger movie bulls viewed films to experience physical thrills rather than mental stimulation. Beginning with the disaster movies of the late 1970s and continuing to the visceral adventures of starship heroes, younger movie fanatics have been fascinated by the technical wizardry of filmmaking rather than by its ability to convey ideas. There is still, of course, an art house crowd (comprised of people of all ages), but the cultural events of the past 20 years have tended to minimize rather than maximize its number.

Even with these broad cultural changes, the independent art and repertory houses might have thrived. But in the early 1980s independent theaters—the repertory houses, because they were in a more fragile financial position, going first—began to close, the victims of an increasingly ruthless series of industry moves and the skyrocketing of real estate prices in most urban areas.

The problems independent theaters face with real estate prices, uncooperative distributors, and always-rising costs seem small when compared to the larger problems: the monopolization of the American movie theater. Larger theater chains such as Loews and Cineplex-Odeon have created a virtual hammerhold on film exhibition. Although once forbidden by antitrust laws, the acquisition of smaller companies and theaters by a single holder was allowed in the massive deregulations of the Reagan administration.

"The bottom line," explains Marianne Lampke, owner of Cambridge's venerable independent Brattle Theater, with some exasperation, "is that this is a political issue. Whenever we have been interviewed about running an independent repertory house we say this to reporters but no one wants to hear it. Whenever anything is written up it is always that we didn't get some movie that we wanted, or they bring out the tired idea that VCRs are ruining independent theaters. We actually find that we do *better* business when we show a film that is already available on video."

As more and more independent theaters close—and given the trend it is hard to think that the already dwindling number is going to stop at 60—there will be fewer and fewer outlets for small, non-commercial movie projects, as well as overtly or implicitly political films, or anything deemed not marketable by the distributors and the larger exhibitors. The argument—always put out by the larger chains that feature art houses in their complexes—is that more money and more screens will mean more varied films for the public. This is almost never the case.

Without independent houses willing to take a chance, most unknown, small, or slightly different films will never have a showcase or a chance to reach the general public. The loss of a healthy, vibrant, and economically sound network of independent theaters will leave moviegoers with fewer options than ever before and will ultimately affect the efforts of filmmakers, producers, and distributors whose work falls outside of the mainstream. The silver screen is beginning to look a little more tarnished than usual.

IV

Media Regulation

In 1791, the First Amendment was added to the Bill of Rights and stated:

> Congress shall make no law respecting an establishment of religion, or prohibiting the free exercise thereof; or ABRIDGING THE FREEDOM OF SPEECH, OR OF THE PRESS; or the right of the people peaceably to assemble, and to petition the Government for a redress of grievances.

It was not long after this amendment that even the framers of the Constitution were dissatisfied with how the press was using its newfound freedom. In 1803, for example, Thomas Jefferson mused that "the abuses of the freedom of the press here have been carried to a length never before known or borne by any civilized nation. But it is so difficult to draw a clear line of separation between the abuses and the wholesome use of the press." Musing soon turned to rage for, in 1814, Jefferson stated that: "I deplore . . . the putrid state into which our newspapers have passed, and the malignity, the vulgarity, and the mendacious spirit of those who write them. . . . These ordures are rapidly depraving the public taste."

Ever since, the federal government has been engaged in an on-going battle over control of information with the press. From time to time—particularly in time of war—the government has won the battle in the form of restrictions and regulations on the way the press may operate. The Sedition Act of 1798, The Sedition Act of 1917, and the Smith Act of 1940, for example, required the press to submit stories for government censors and/or approval. During the Cold War congressional investigations of Communists in the late 1940s and early 1950s, the House Un-American Committee thought the media industry to be a hot-bed of communist activity. Numerous media professionals were "black listed" from the industry, several were sent to prison. Each of these acts were short-lived, however, due to the circumstances of their formation (e.g., war) and the realization that they may have been unconstitutional.

Government intervention is also likely to occur when new and innovative media technology is generated. The Communication Act of 1934 formulated a unified and comprehensive regulatory system—including the granting, denying, modifying, and revoking of licenses for the operation of stations—"in order to protect the national interest involved in the new and far-reaching science of broadcasting." While the Act was created for radio, it has applied to the television industry as well. Broadcasting continues to be the only form of expression consistently under direct governmental supervision and regulation.

Interestingly, in more recent times, there has been a move toward government *deregulation*. The Reagan Administration, in particular, was devoted to dismantling onerous regulatory controls and restoring to broadcasters the freedom of action they had lost to previous government bureaucrats. Unleashed media entrepreneurialism, promised advocates of the deregulation movement, would generate productivity, increase diversity, and raise the level of quality of media content.

The first essay in this section, "The End of an Era/Dalton Trumbo of the Hollywood Ten," reflects back to the days of extreme government intervention of American media activities. It offers a point of comparison for the second essay, "The Strange Politics of 'Fairness'," which addresses the cornerstone of contemporary deregulation—the Fairness Doctrine. The Fairness Doctrine required broadcasters to devote air time to controversial issues and to air contrasting views of those issues. This essay examines the pluses and minuses of deregulation, from the broadcaster's perspective. The Fairness Doctrine was officially eliminated on August 4, 1987, shortly after this essay was written.

The third essay, "Aladdin's Lamp Goes Dark," examines the possible impact of deregulation on children's programming. Typically perceived as a low priority among broadcasters and a haven of exploitation for the toy, cereal and candy industries, children's programming has typically been an area of concern for consumer advocates, who have sought greater regulation to protect children. This essay traces the history of governmental intervention (or the lack thereof) with regard to children and television.

The final essay, "How to Separate the Men From the Boycotts," offers a case study of extremist citizen reaction to government deregulation of the media. It examines the activities of the National Federation of Decency—a conservative religious-political organization—and its effort to create media in its own image. Taken together, these essays offer the cost and benefit of government intervention in American media.

The End of an Era
Shirley Biagi, MEDIA/IMPACT

Before television arrived throughout the country in 1948, two other events of the late 1940s helped to reverse the prosperous movie bonanza that began in mid-1930: the hearings of the House Un-American Activities Committee and the 1948 U.S. Supreme Court Decision in *United States v. Paramount Pictures, Inc., et al.*

The House Hearings. In October 1947, America was entering the Cold War. The House of Representatives' Committee on Un-American Activities, chaired by J. Parnell Thomas, summoned ten "unfriendly" witnesses from Hollywood to testify about their communist connections. These eight screenwriters and two directors came to be known as the Hollywood Ten.

Why these ten were singled out is still debated today. Their 1930s labor activities are cited as one reason. Many of them had been involved in the formation of the Screen Writers Guild. Some of the Ten had also been members of liberal and left-wing political organizations. Another reason was that the screenwriters were visible—an easy target that could quickly send a public message that no one was exempt from the committee's scrutiny.

The Ten's strategy was to appear before the committee as a group and to avoid answering the direct question "Are you now or have you ever been a member of the Communist party?" Instead, the Ten tried too make statements that questioned the committee's authority to challenge their political beliefs. A support committee of Hollywood luminaries, including Lauren Bacall and Humphrey Bogart, flew to Washington to show their sympathies.

In a rancorous series of hearings, the committee rejected the Ten's testimony; they found themselves facing trial for contempt. All of them were sentenced to jail, and some were fined. By the end of November 1947, all of the Hollywood Ten had lost their jobs. Many more movie people would follow: In an article for the *Hollywood Review*, Hollywood Ten member Adrian Scott reported that 214 movie employees eventually were blacklisted, including 106 writers, 36 actors, and 11 directors.[1] This effectively gutted Hollywood of some of its best talent.

Dalton Trumbo of the Hollywood Ten

As a screenwriter at MGM, Dalton Trumbo was earning $75,000 per script when he was called before the House Un-American Activities Committee in October 1947. In 1948 he was cited for contempt of Congress, tried, convicted, and sentenced to a $1,000 fine and a year in jail.

When he was released, Trumbo found that the only way he could sell his scripts was to use a pseudonym. He also no longer commanded his previous salary. He wrote a friend: "It simply requires that I work three times as fast for about one-fifth of my former price."[2]

The King Brothers bought Trumbo's scripts. Writing under the name Robert Rich, Trumbo sold the King Brothers a screenplay called *The Boy and the Bull* which eventually was produced as the movie *The Brave One.* In 1957, Robert Rich won an Academy Award for the screenplay, but at the ceremony no one accepted the prize.

In 1959, 12 years after Trumbo appeared before the committee, and 2 years after Robert Rich won an Academy Award, Kirk Douglas' production company hired Trumbo to write *Spartacus,* crediting Trumbo with the screenplay. Then Otto Preminger hired Trumbo in 1960 to write

---

[1]Dalton Trumbo, *Additional Dialogue: Letters of Dalton Trumbo: 1942-1962* (New York: M. Evans, 1970), p. 301.

[2] Ibid., p. 102.

Exodus. The blacklist was broken, but many of Trumbo's blacklisted friends never worked in the movie industry again after they appeared before the committee. The only other member of the Hollywood Ten to achieve success in movies again was Ring Lardner, Jr. who won an Academy Award in 1970 for the screenplay *M*A*S*H.*

The Strange Politics of 'Fairness'
David Bollier, CHANNELS

Deep in the legal jungles of Washington, D.C., a guerrilla war of liberation is smouldering. The rebels, who invoke the spirit of the American Revolution and liken their oppressor to King George, are broadcasters and their lawyers. Previous skirmishes in Congress and the courts have left them frustrated and angry, but now they're readying themselves for what many believe will be their triumphant assault.

The citadel under siege is the Fairness Doctrine, the rules administered by the Federal Communications Commission that impose two basic obligations on broadcasters: (1) to devote a reasonable amount of their broadcast time to controversial issues of public importance and (2) to air contrasting views on those issues.

For years, most television and radio stations observed an uneasy truce with the Fairness Doctrine, providing air-time—often grudgingly—to the handful of critics, mostly citizens groups, who had legitimate complaints about broadcast fairness. But in recent months, emboldened by the deregulatory climate at the FCC, broadcasters have intensified their criticism of the doctrine. They now nourish hopes of defeating it in either of two legal challenges that may go to trail this fall.

Most of the rebels' complaints are familiar. Broadcasters claim that the Fairness Doctrine "chills" their First Amendment right of free speech by forcing them to air others' views. They say that the rules are a costly, time-consuming hassle. And now a powerful new argument has emerged: that the Fairness Doctrine is obsolete because cable television and other new media are providing a diversity of voices.

Ford Rowan, former NBC newsman and author of a 1984 book on the Fairness Doctrine, rhetorically wonders "what Madison, Jefferson, Franklin, or other co-conspirators against King George would have done. Would they have been willing to run the risk that a free electronic press might abuse its power?" (Rowan himself would take the risk.)

What makes the broadcasters' crusade so significant is that it would undercut the "public trustee" foundation of commercial broadcasting. In passing the Communications Act of 1934, Congress directed broadcasters to serve "the public interest, convenience, and necessity." The most meaningful embodiment of that standard, apart from the license renewal process, is the Fairness Doctrine.

While critics of the doctrine would like to throw out the public interest standard entirely, such an open challenge would face a strategic disadvantage: Congress simply is not prepared to jettison this fundamental premise of our broadcasting system. So broadcasters are instead seeking a radical redefinition of the standard's *meaning* by eliminating the Fairness Doctrine.

This prospect has profound implications for a constellation of other important FCC "content regulations," which govern issue advertising and response time for personal attacks. If the Fairness Doctrine is declared unconstitutional these regulations are also "doomed," according to Robert Gurss, attorney of the Media Access Project, a public interest law firm defending the doctrine. While these apocalyptic consequences are hardly imminent, many broadcasters are eager to take whatever steps possible toward transforming the publicly granted privilege of broadcasting into a corporate asset. Will the rebels succeed?

At first glance the struggle over the Fairness Doctrine seems to take place in a twilight zone in which traditional political alignments go topsy-turvy. Naderites join hands with Phyllis Schlafly because they both favor greater citizen access to the broadcast media. Staunch civil libertarians such as Floyd Abrams and Nat Hentoff make common cause with the broadcasting industry because they believe any FCC scrutiny of broadcast journalists' decision-making violates the First

Amendment (while the American Civil Liberties Union dissents from this view). And a handful of corporations such as Mobil Oil and General Motors agree with the public interest groups that the Fairness Doctrine should stay.

Now that the FCC itself has blasted the rule that it's supposed to enforce, Fairness politics have become even more bewildering. Such bizarre political alignments inspired federal appeals court judge J. Skelly Wright's famous observation that when it comes to matters of broadcast fairness, it's difficult "to tell the good guys from the bad guys." Who are we to believe when both sides claim the high ground by giving such similar names to their advocacy groups: the Center for Free Speech and the Freedom of Expression foundation? (The former defends the Fairness Doctrine, the latter attacks it.)

Despite such confusion and the unusual alliances, however, where you stand on the issue generally depends on where you sit—in the control room, or in the broadcast audience at home. Media professionals generally oppose the Fairness Doctrine; they say it infringes on their free speech. (Group W is the only major broadcast firm that actively supports the doctrine.) Citizens who have a specific message or political cause—consumers, labor unions, religious organizations—generally support it; they say it enhances their free speech. When this conflict arises locally, it's usually resolved through informal negotiations that result in free air-time for the aggrieved party. Now the conflict is flaring into a full-scale constitutional challenge to the Fairness Doctrine.

In 1982, a Syracuse, New York, television station, WTVH, sold 182 minutes of its air-time to utilities promoting nuclear power. In the eyes of the Syracuse Peace Council, a citizens group, the station failed to provide a "reasonable" counterbalance, as required by the Fairness Doctrine. The group filed a complaint with the FCC. "Even the total amount of news programming [on nuclear-related issues, not necessarily nuclear power] didn't equal the amount of advertising time bought by the utilities group," says Liam Mahoney, a peace council activist.

The FCC agreed with the antinuclear group in 1984, ordering WTVH to correct its unbalanced coverage. [See *Channels*, January/February 1985.] But the station refuses to comply with the FCC order and is now mounting a direct constitutional challenge to the Fairness Doctrine—the first such test case since 1969. "When the government ends up controlling the press," warns John DeRoache, general manager of WTVH, "we could end up in the same situation as *Pravda* in Russia. The Fairness Doctrine is an absolute threat to every broadcaster."

Using more temperate language, network journalists such as Eric Sevareid, Bill Monroe, and Dan Rather agree. Rather told the FCC: "Once a newsperson has to stop and consider what the government agency will think of something he or she wants to put on the air, an invaluable element of freedom has been lost."

Activists say that loss is greatly exaggerated; they say the free-speech rights of broadcasters and monied issue advertisers are already adequately protected by their easy access to the airwaves. Those who suffer are the majority of people, who have neither transmitters of their own nor money to buy air-time. "The Fairness Doctrine is the only reason that citizens can have First Amendment rights in the broadcast medium" says media activist Joseph Waz.

Defenders of the Fairness Doctrine also point out that its "chilling effect" has been minimal. Since only one broadcast station has *ever* had its FCC license revoked for violation of the rule—the Rev. Carl McIntyre's WXUR radio station in Media, Pennsylvania, in 1972—the industry's protestations of creeping Big Brotherism sound overwrought. Of some 6,787 Fairness Doctrine complaints and inquiries to the FCC in 1984 (about 10 percent in letters, the rest in phone calls), only six resulted in official FCC inquiries to stations. Only one case in 1984 resulted in an FCC finding that a station—WTVH Syracuse—had acted "unreasonably." It was the first such slap on a broadcaster's wrist in five years. Is that so burdensome?

Yes, says chairman Mark Fowler's FCC, quoting Judge David Bazelon of the U.S. Court of Appeals: ". . . even a governmental 'raised eyebrow' can send otherwise intrepid entrepreneurs running for the cover of conformity." In thousands of instances, says the FCC, the mere threat that citizens' groups might lodge an official complaint "creates a climate of timidity and fear" and runs up legal fees.

Some broadcasters say they'd rather avoid controversy altogether, by refusing to run advocacy advertisements, than risk contravening the Fairness Doctrine. In comments to the FCC, the National Association of Broadcasters cites 45 instances in which the doctrine has thus inhibited editorial freedom. The NAB claims the Fairness Doctrine has squelched a radio series on the B'nai B'rith in Pennsylvania, advertising for ballot propositions in Charlotte, North Carolina, and a radio show on religious cults in Southern California. Critics charge that many of the instances cited are years old and scantily documented. The real "chilling effect," they reply, is broadcasters' resistance to surrendering valuable air-time for controversies that don't pay their way.

As an imperfect means of balancing the First Amendment rights of broadcasters against those of the public, the Fairness Doctrine seems to apply a double standard. Why should broadcasters be denied the same freedom of expression print enjoys? The Supreme Court gave its first definitive answer to that question in 1969, in effect, by posing another question: Whose First Amendment is it, anyway? The landmark *Red Lion Broadcasting* v. *FCC* decision concluded that "it is the rights of viewers and listeners, not the right of the broadcasters, which is paramount." The court upheld the doctrine.

The FCC has the power to safeguard these rights, in the court's view, because broadcast frequencies are inherently scarce and selectively granted to trustees acting in the public's interest. "There is no sanctuary in the First Amendment to unlimited private censorship operating in a medium not open to all," the court said. Thus, broadcasters are free to have their say, but as public trustees they must avoid "private censorship" of others.

This unequivocal language quelled critics of the Fairness Doctrine for most of the 1970s. But with Ronald Reagan's election and his appointment of Fowler as FCC chairman in 1981, the political climate quickly changed. Fowler and many broadcasters began asserting that the proliferation of new media undermines the Fairness Doctrine's "scarcity rationale."

The first stop in the crusade to repeal the doctrine was the Senate, where Senator Bob Packwood (R-Oregon) held hearings in early 1984 on a "Freedom of Expression" bill. The legislation would have eliminated all content regulation of broadcast media, including the Fairness Doctrine and Equal Time Rule (which applies to political candidates). But the bill was defeated 11 to 6 in the Senate Commerce Committee even though it had been greatly weakened by amendment and even though Packwood then held sway as committee chairman. In the House, the repeal campaign ran up against Representative Tim Wirth (D-Colorado), chairman of the House telecommunications subcommittee, who adamantly opposes any repeal or modification of the Fairness Doctrine.

Broadcasters then tried to convince the FCC to rescind the doctrine. But this tactic ran aground on an unresolved legal question: Is the Fairness Doctrine a statutory creation that only Congress can repeal, or an administrative rule the FCC can erase?

It was first enunciated as an FCC rule in 1949, but 10 years later Congress mentioned the doctrine, in passing, as part of its 1959 amendments to the Communications Act. Now broadcasters are claiming that Congress did not *mandate* the Fairness Doctrine in 1959 but only *recognized* it as a rule. If so, the FCC would have the authority to rescind the doctrine, as it would doubtless like to do. Yet the commission last year refrained from claiming that authority. Henry Geller, director of the Washington Center for Public Policy Research, explains with a chuckle: "The FCC was scared stiff that if it made a statutory determination, 20 minutes later Congress would pass legislation telling the FCC to drop dead." Instead, the commission merely issued a report last August urging Congress to repeal the doctrine.

Stymied in Congress and half-disappointed by the FCC, broadcasters are seeking relief in the federal courts. They glimpsed an encouraging sign in two footnotes buried in a July 1984 Supreme Court decision that struck down a law against editorializing by public broadcasting stations. In *FCC* v. *League of Women Voters of California*, the court said it might reconsider its *Red Lion* decision if there were "some signal from Congress or the FCC" that new communications technologies have invalidated the "scarcity rationale" for the Fairness Doctrine, or if the commission determined that the doctrine chills free speech. The FCC virtually sent up signal flares to make both points in its August report.

It may be impossible to read the Supreme Court's mind in two if its footnotes, as Henry Geller contends, but many broadcasters regard the footnotes as the court's invitation to bring a test case on the Fairness Doctrine, and are charging ahead with two separate constitutional challenges, filed in the U.S. Court of Appeals.

The first case, brought last October by WTVH's owner, the Iowa-based Meredith Corporation, could be argued as soon as next fall. The suit represents "the most serious challenge to the Fairness Doctrine since *Red Lion*," according to opposing attorney Gurss of the Media Access Project. But the case also has its weaknesses. For example, Gurss says, "WTVH may have a hard time showing that is suffered an injury" since, in response to a later request by the antinuclear group, it voluntarily gave the group air-time.

The second case against the Fairness Doctrine was filed in the same month by the 2,200-member Radio-Television News Directors Association (RTNDA). Rallying behind the suit are the National Association of Broadcasters, Gannett, Post-Newsweek Stations, and other major broadcasters. CBS is providing most of the legal resources.

"Broadcasters agreed that this is the way to go," says Ernie Schultz, executive vice president of RTNDA. "After examining the merits of the WTVH case, we decided that it was not as good a vehicle for challenging the Fairness Doctrine." Blaming the FCC for a failure of nerve, the RTNDA seeks to force the commission to decide whether it has authority to rescind the doctrine. At the same time, the suit asks the court to find the Fairness Doctrine unconstitutional.

Defenders of the doctrine claim the RTNDA case doesn't belong in court and are seeking to have it dismissed. One reason it should be, in Geller's view, is that the court should not review the constitutionality of the Fairness Doctrine before the FCC explores alternative rules, less "chilling" to broadcasters' rights, that would achieve the Fairness Doctrine's goals.

But if the court gets past such questions and considers the merits of the RTNDA or WTVH cases, the pivotal issue may turn out to be whether the growth of new communications technologies renders the Fairness Doctrine obsolete by ending the scarcity of frequencies. Opponents say there's no need for a doctrine to assure a diversity of voices in broadcasting because there are now so many media outlets.

Defending the doctrine, Gurss looks at "scarcity" another way, arguing that there will be a scarcity of media outlets as long as there are more applicants for broadcast licenses than there are frequencies to be licensed. Those who get the licenses shouldn't be the only ones able to speak on the air.

The two definitions of scarcity are as far apart as the basic assumptions of the defenders and opponents of the Fairness Doctrine. Running a public franchise is different from running a private company. Serving the democratic process is not always as profitable as serving advertisers. The Fairness Doctrine forces the basic question: Which notion of broadcasting shall prevail.

It is not an all-or-nothing proposition, of course, because the Fairness Doctrine in practice exacts only marginal concessions from most broadcasters. They retain their First Amendment rights to have their own say on the air, while allowing others to stand on the same soapbox. They are not censored, and have great leeway in choosing how and when they will balance their coverage. Public obligations and private enterprises can coexist. Surely the Fairness Doctrine represents a small sacrifice in light of licensees' lucrative returns.

The two conceptions of broadcasting that may meet in court this fall bring to mind an old political metaphor: two teams locked in competition, one team thinking it's playing football, the other rugby. Which one is playing by the right rules? As long as a public resource, the airwaves, is devoted above all else to private profit-making, the clashes over broadcast fairness will persist. In the meantime, the Fairness Doctrine provides useful time-outs for getting the two teams together and reminding the visiting team who it is, after all, who owns the field.

"Our First Amendment right to speak on radio or television should not be limited only to those who have the money to buy the station."
Phyllis Schlafly
President of the right-wing Eagle Forum

"We simply have not found the Fairness Doctrine to be burdensome. When a company tells its managers that it should cover controversial issues of importance to their communities, all it's doing is telling them to run a good company."
Wallace B. Dunlap
Senior vice president, Group W

"There is no regulation that limits a broadcaster's right to say whatever he or she wants over the air—including personal attacks on others. The Fairness Doctrine doesn't censor them, it prevents them from censoring the rest of use."
Nicholas Johnson
Former member, FCC

"The public interest is not best served by the government telling broadcasters to whom they must give response time, or what they must cover."
Senator Bob Packwood
Chairman, Senator Commerce Committee

"The Fairness Doctrine idea—that government can improve the American media—is in brutal confrontation with the First Amendment. It is unworkable in practice, and philosophically subversive of the amendment."
Bill Monroe
NBC News correspondent

"To say that the medium of communications with the most impact in communicating news to the public should be the most regulated by Congress and least protected in its free-expression rights is to invert First Amendment values."
Floyd Abrams
Prominent attorney

Companion Rules on Broadcast Fairness

Several regulatory companions to the Fairness Doctrine developed out of FCC and court decisions over the years. Each has complex exceptions, qualifications, and ambiguities. Two of the most important:

Personal Attack Rule. When a TV or radio station airs an attack on the honesty, integrity, character, or any similar trait of a person or group, the station must notify the subject within seven days, provide a tape or transcript of the attack, and offer a reasonable opportunity for rebuttal, even if there is no paid sponsor for it. This rule does not apply to attacks made on news shows or by political candidates.

The Cullman Doctrine. If a broadcaster airs a paid advertisement that deals with a controversial issue of public importance, it must also air opposing views, even if there is no paid sponsor for those views. This rule is frequently invoked during campaign seasons, when business lobbies buy air-time to promote certain ballot initiatives or referendums.

Several other FCC rules deal with broadcast fairness during election campaigns:

Equal Time Rule (more formally known as the Equal Opportunities Rule). If a broadcaster sells or gives air-time to one candidate for public office, it must offer equal access to all candidates for the office. ("Equal" applies to both the amount of air-time and the audience size.) Again, the broadcaster cannot edit or censor the candidate's presentation. News shows are exempt.

Reasonable Access Provision. The result of a 1972 election law, this rule guarantees that candidates for federal office have reasonable access to buy unedited air-time during campaigns. The rule prevents a station from freezing out candidates it may dislike.

The Zapple Doctrine. An offshoot of the Equal Opportunities Rule, the Zapple Doctrine says that stations giving or selling air-time to the *supporters* of one candidate must provide an equal opportunity to supporters of opposing candidates.

Political Editorializing Rule. If a station endorses a candidate for public office in an editorial, the station must notify other legally qualified candidates for that office within 24 hours and offer them an opportunity to reply. If the station airs its editorial within 72 hours before an election, it must give candidates advance notice so that they can response.

Legal Landmarks in the History of the Fairness Doctrine

1929: Broadcasters are first required to air contrasting views on public issues in *Great Lakes Broadcasting Inc.*, a ruling by the Federal Radio Commission.

1934: Congress passes the Communications Act, which creates the FCC and mandates that broadcasters serve the public interest.

1941: The FCC rules in *Mayflower Broadcasting Inc.* that the public interest requires an outright ban on editorializing by broadcasters. "The broadcaster cannot be an advocate," the commission says.

1949: The FCC loosens its Mayflower decision, articulating the Fairness Doctrine as it is known today. While stations may editorialize freely, they are obligated to present "different attitudes and viewpoints concerning those vital and often controversial [community] issues."

1969: For the first time, in *Red Lion Broadcasting* v. *FCC*, the Supreme Court explicitly rules that the Fairness Doctrine is constitutional. Broadcasting's characteristics justify rules not applied to other media.

1973: In *CBS* v. *Democratic National Committee*, the court allows broadcasters to reject all opinion advertisements that individuals or groups may wish to air. There is not private right to purchase air-time. (In *CBS* v. *FCC*, eight years later, however, the court gives candidates for public office privileged access to the air during campaign season.)

1975: For the first and only time, the court forces a station (WHAR, Clarksburg, West Virginia) to cover a "controversial issue of public importance" (strip mining).

David Bollier, a political writer based in New Haven, Connecticut, is co-author of the book Freedom From Harm.

Aladdin's Lamp Goes Dark
Jane Hall, GANNETT CENTER JOURNAL

Remember *Fury,* the Saturday drama about "a horse and the boy who loved him"? *Mr. Wizard* and his science experiments? Miss Frances and *Ding-Dong School?* If you were raised in the 1950s, as I was, those network shows are likely rattling around in your memory, next to the Tiny Tears doll and the plaster-of-paris hand-mold you made for your mother. For a child in dusty West Texas, the rabbit ears of the TV antenna beckoned, first to Howdy-Doody's "Peanut Gallery" and then to a wider world beyond: Mary Martin in *Peter Pan,* Leonard Bernstein theatrically conducting the *Young People's Concert,* Walter Cronkite doing voice-over on World War II in *The Twentieth Century.*

Even allowing for nostalgic haze, it is difficult to imagine the current generation of youngsters romanticizing in the future about great kids' shows from their childhood. In the fervor of deregulation, children's television has been a prime casualty. Today, award-winning programs are the exception that prove the rule. There is no daily program on commercial TV that compares to *Captain Kangaroo.* Dramatic specials have no regular weekly time slot. TV news for children is practically obsolete. And virtually every cartoon show on independent stations stars He-Man, GoBots, or some other toy in shows that—to an adult eye—look like 30-minute toy commercials. This fall saw the introduction of the ultimate TV toy tie-in: the controversial interactive toys that allow children to play video games with the television set. Provided, of course, that the child interacts with his parent's pocketbook to buy the new toy.

What's going on here? At the same time that changes in broadcasting have made *pro bono* programming less attractive, the Federal Communications Commission has lifted its requirements for public service and its restrictions on commercialism for all audiences, including children. The theory has been "let the marketplace decide," although the Commission's studies have reported that young children, unlike adults, cannot distinguish between a TV sales pitch and a TV show. The marketplace emphasis promises to further a heated debate about the future of children's television that is already almost three decades old.

The Push for Responsible Children's Programming

Recognition of children's programming as a special category by the FCC goes back as far as 1960, when a policy statement listed children's shows as one of 14 "major elements usually necessary to meet" a licensee's public-service obligations as a trustee of the airwaves under the Communications Act of 1934. Children's television became a political cause in the late 1960s, when Peggy Charren, a Boston homemaker, formed Action for Children's Television (ACT), a parents' advocacy group. At the time, children's television was no longer a means to sell TV sets, as it had been in the 1950s, but had become a Saturday morning cartoon profit-center, with kid-appeal advertisements for candy-coated cereals and vitamins. Charren recalls, "I thought, 'Why can't children's television have as much diversity as a library?' Like proper middle-class housewives, my friends and I asked for a meeting at the FCC." In the consumerist climate of the time, Charren hit a responsive chord. After Congressional hearings, the Federal Trade Commission set guidelines to prevent deceptive ads aimed at children. The National Association of Broadcasting beefed up its self-regulating code, and the FCC began a wide-ranging inquiry into children's television, with more than 100,000 citizens writing in to express their opinions.

In its 1974 Children's Television Report and Policy Statement, the Commission concluded that broadcasters "clearly have . . . a responsibility to serve children," not only as part of their community but also because, with "their immaturity and special needs," they "require programming specifically designed for them." As part of a long-standing policy against overcommercialization, the report said, "particular care should be taken to ensure" that children are not exposed to excessive, deceptive advertisements, for "they are far more trusting and vulnerable to commercial 'pitches' than adults, and there is evidence that very young children cannot distinguish conceptually between programming and advertising." The signal to broadcasters was clear: "We expect television broadcasters, as trustees of a valuable public resource, to develop and present programs which will serve the unique needs of the child audience. . . . The use of television to further the educational and cultural development of America's children bears a direct relationship to the licensee's obligations under the Communications Act to operate in the public interest."

Noting that the Communications Act gives the FCC broad powers to regulate broadcasting but prohibits censors under the First Amendment, the FCC declined ACT's petition to mandate age-specific programming and number of hours required. But, as restated in a later FCC document, the 1974 policy statement specifically asked commercial licensees to: (1) make a 'meaningful effort' to increase the amount of programming for children; (2) air a 'reasonable amount' of programming for children designed to educate and inform and not simply to entertain; (3) air informational programming separately targeted for both preschool and school-age children; and (4) air programming for children scheduled during weekdays as well as weekends. In terms of commercials, broadcasters were expected to: (1) limit the amount of advertising in children's programming; (2) ensure an adequate separation between program content and commercial messages; and 3) eliminate host-selling and tie-in practices.

Although responsible broadcasters already were putting on shows for children, there was a veritable Renaissance of children's programming after the FCC report. "When the heat was turned on in Washington, you could feel it in what broadcasters put on," says Squire Rushnell, ABC's children's programming executive. "And, when the heat was later turned off, you could feel that, too." After the FCC report in 1974 CBS News continued to air its ambitious slate of children's shows, including *In the News*, one-minute spots that ran like commercials within weekend cartoons, special election coverage for kids and weekly magazines like *Razmatazz* and *30 Minutes*, a *60 Minutes* for small-fry. ABC started its *Afterschool Specials*, ambitious dramatic specials that treated youthful dilemmas, and jazzy one-minute "commercials" for academic subjects like *Multiplication Rock*. NBC began its afterschool specials, called *Special Treat*, and started a topical teen shown called *Hot Hero Sandwich*. At the local level, individual stations, station groups, and syndicators produced many ambitious shows. WPIX in New York had two locally produced children's shows, and WCVB, which had won its Boston license with elaborate promises for community service, had a daily half-hour show for kids and a weekly series featuring young reporters. Westinghouse produced *Call It Macaroni*, which took kids out of their own environments and sent them on adventures; Capital Cities had family specials; and Post-Newsweek stations used old mystery movies to teach reading on TV and in local schools. In an unusual public-relations move, ITT sponsored *Big Blue Marble*, an internationally syndicated series about children around the world. But, still, the FCC was not satisfied. In 1979, a task force on children's programming found that broadcasters, in general, had complied with the advertising guidelines, but not the programming guidelines.

Which Came First: The Toy or the Show?

In 1981, Mark Fowler was appointed chairman of the FCC under Ronald Reagan, and the byword was deregulation. Fowler believed that the free market—not the government—was the best determinant of what was in the public interest. In the process of the FCC's relaxing license-renewal requirements, guidelines on advertising, and other restrictions, children's television lost its special consideration. At times the rulings were about-face from the FCC under previous administrations. In 1969, for example, in a case involving an ABC show based on Mattel's "Hot Wheels" toy, the FCC found that the TV show was "designed primarily to promote the sale of a sponsor's product, rather than serve the public by either entertaining or informing it." Such a product-based show, the ruling said, subordinates "programming in the interest of the public to programming in the interest of its saleability." In 1985, however, the FCC rules that such commercial tie-ins "did not run afoul" of restrictions against program-length commercials.

As a result of deregulation, you'd be hard pressed to find many quality educational children's series in commercial broadcasting today. CBS News, for example, now programs only five minutes per week of informational spots for children, and they're ahead of ABC News at that. (NBC does the eight-times-a-year *Main Street*.) ABC has continued with *Afterschool Specials* but *Kids are People, Too*, a Sunday magazine, was cancelled. Squire Rushnell lists the cause of death as deregulation. "When we started *Kids are People* in 1978, we had 75 percent clearance on local stations. By the third season, we had 12 stations carrying it live. There was no outside pressure on stations to carry it." Without FCC encouragement, the true marketplace decides. As Rushnell point out, in order to carry the *Afterschool Specials*, stations usually are preempting the *Oprah Winfrey Show*, which costs them a lot of money in syndication and brings in big ad dollars and ratings. The network compensation for carrying the children's special, as Rushnell wryly notes, is "two pieces of bubblegum and an old sneaker." Indeed, says one network executive, the whole picture of broadcasting has changed. "In the past, broadcasters put on children's shows because it made them feel good about what they were doing." says the executive. But, in today's newly competitive environment, "Children's television is a low-profit area, and the networks are fighting it out, even on Saturday morning."

Three years after the FCC eliminated its long-standing guidelines, which, per the old NAB code, had limited commercials to nine and one-half minutes an hour on Saturdays and Sundays and 12 minutes an hour on other days, the onslaught of toy-based shows began. When the commission made its ruling that "commercial levels will be effectively regulated by marketplace forces." children's ads were not specifically mentioned, but, in response to an inquiry from the NAB, the FCC indicated that guidelines in this area have been eliminated too. Kids have always clamored for Davy Crockett caps, Flintstone lunch pails, and other merchandise featuring their favorite TV characters. Once upon a time, the TV shows created a toy. Now it's the other way around. Today, you invent the toy—then invent the TV show to sell it. According to a count by ACT, no fewer than 72 Saturday morning and afternoon cartoon shows have been toy-based. ABC, NBC, and CBS all have had plenty of shows based on popular toys, from Pound Puppies to Smurfs. But it is on independent stations that the tie-in has been refined as an art, with toy-manufacturers themselves creating the shows and syndicating them. With the right distribution windows, the profits can be enormous. Mattel's He-Man—star of stage, screen, tube, and toy shelf—is estimated to have generated $350 million in sales.

"From 20 years of research, we know that children are vulnerable to confusion between what they are seeing for education or entertainment and what they are seeing because they are being sold something." Gerald Lesser, Harvard professor of education and psychology (and co-founder of *Sesame Street*) testified this fall before the House Telecommunications Subcommittee, "To deliberately blur what is program and what is commercial and then leave it to the children to sort it all out for themselves . . . is simply not fair."

Opposing the new interactive toys, Dr. William Dietz, chairman of the children's task force of the American Academy of Pediatrics, says they disturb an important element of child's play. "Games children create for themselves teach mastery of their world, but these toys sap their imaginations," he says. "The term *interactive* should be in quotes. The television sells the toy to the child, and then the *toy* plays with the TV set. This is only the most advanced phase—after 30-second commercials and 30-minute, program-length commercials—of using TV to 'teach' kids to buy toys." Yet, despite the protests, the FCC looked into the interactives only on whether they would interfere with the television signal—and found that they did not.

The Outlook for New Commercial Guidelines

After several years in which ACT was on the losing side of regulation, the FCC's statement about commercialism gave them something to stand on. Last spring, the U.S. Court of Appeals in Washington, D.C., in an opinion written by Judge Kenneth W. Starr, a Reagan appointee, found that the FCC has overturned long-standing policy without explanation. "For almost 15 years, the FCC's regulation of children's television was founded on the notion that the television marketplace *does not function* adequately when children make up the audience," wrote Judge Starr. "As the agency has seen it, kids are different." The court has asked the FCC to explain the change.

In Congress, children's television—long a dormant political issue—is in the spotlight again. This fall, Congressman Ed Market, chairman of the House Telecommunications Subcommittee, held a day of hearings on overcommercialism in children's TV. Calling children's television "a dumping ground," Markey has introduced a bill that would require the FCC to reinstate the limits on the number of ads in children's shows. Decrying what he calls the "crassly commercial" content of children's TV, Senator Frank Lautenberg has introduced a bill that would require broadcasters to produce at least seven hours of educational children's television. The FCC and the industry "are daring us to take action," fumed Congressman Al Swift during the hearings.

In response to the recent court decision, the FCC has announced an inquiry, but no major change in policy is likely. "The federal government is not set up to protect parents from kids nagging their parents for toys," says Bill Johnson, acting chief of the FCC's mass-media bureau. "How can we determine that the *Sesame Street* toy tie-ins are better than the other ones? If kids don't object to the commercials, it's hard to show what interest it is that we're trying to protect."

That's just the point, of course, to those who want to get the FCC back into the business of regulating children's television. "Broadcasters are a public fiduciary, dealing with a unique audience, our children," says Henry Geller, the former FCC general counsel, who argued ACT's case on commercial guidelines. "Yet, this FCC has said, 'Aw, the hell with them.' If that's how broadcasters are being asked to fulfill their obligations as a public trustee, we should've auctioned off licenses—and used the millions to do shows for kids."

The prospect of Congress mandating seven hours a week of educational programming, however that could be defined, raises the specter of some governmental Big Daddy feeding kids good-for-you, brussels sprouts television and would surely be opposed by broadcasters. But, when it comes to children, it's hard to argue that deregulation has led to greater diversity and more choice. There is choice on public television, with their children's shows, and diversity on cable television, with the Nickelodeon and Disney channels, if your parents pay for it. But not on "free" TV.

Although some of her network critics think she's a content-toting nanny who expects television to do what our public schools and fissioned families cannot, Peggy Charren says she's just trying to get the FCC to get broadcasters to do what they do best. "A TV industry that sends its shows around the world knows how to do shows for kids," she says. "Television for children can be an Aladdin's lamp." Or a darkness to curse the light.

Jane Hall reports on TV and media issues for People *magazine.*

Editor's Note: Not long after this essay was published, the Children's Television Act of 1990 (H.R. 1677) was passed. The Act places restrictions on the amount of advertising in kid's shows, requires stations to serve the educational needs of children, and creates a national endowment for program creation and production. With her life's work completed, Peggy Charren retired from ACT.

How to Separate the Men
from the Boycotts
Barry Lynn, PLAYBOY

The description, in Reverend Donald Wildmon's own words, sounds harmless enough. "The N.F.D. is a Christian organization promoting the Biblical ethic of decency in American society, with primary emphasis on TV and other media." But make no mistake: The National Federation for Decency is a fanatical organization capable of much pernicious influence.

The N.F.D. is most noted for championing the Meese commission on pornography. It also figured in the recent decision by the Federal Communications Commission to broaden the definition of indecency (*The Playboy Forum*, August). It crusades against indecency; indecency in magazines, on television shows, in movies or inside bubble-gum wrappers. Its leader—Donald Wildmon. Its weapon—boycotts.

Wildmon began his odyssey one evening in December 1976, when, sitting with his wife and four children before their television set, he scanned the dial and found "skin scenes," "unbelievable profanity" and violence. He later wrote: "made up my mind to try to make TV suitable for family entertainment . . . these things were intruding in my private world."

In a sermon to his congregation a short time later, Wildmon urged that the flock turn off its televisions for one week to protest the fare. Enough complied to create some media interest—and to launch Wildmon's media career. Within seven months, he had resigned his parish pastorate and created the National Federation for Decency.

In 1978, Wildmon began serious condemnation of television networks and those advertisers who promoted their products on the most "offensive" shows (at the time, such hits as *Charlie's Angels* and *Three's Company*). He particularly condemned the advertisers: American Home Products, Ford Motor Company and Sears, Roebuck and Company. In each case, the companies withdrew commercials from programs Wildmon disliked—though they denied that Wildmon had anything to do with their decisions.

For the spring 1981 television season, he recruited the Reverend Jerry Falwell and his Moral Majority, Phyllis Schlafly and her Eagle Forum and the American Life Lobby to create a Coalition for Better Television. Planning to boycott the eight most offensive shows, Wildmon had 4000 people from these groups monitor the fall line-up.

ABC, however, cut Wildmon off at the pass by announcing the results of its own survey, which found that only 44 percent of the people who considered themselves members of the Moral Majority supported "attempts to influence programs to conform to their standards and values." Another survey—by Roper—found that even people who rated themselves to be "very high" fundamentalists were more likely than not to have favorable opinions of such steamy series as *Dallas*. Although a few timid corporate executives declared that they would no longer advertise on certain shows, the network honchos lambasted Wildmon for being out of step with America.

Wildmon went before the cameras and canceled the boycott even before it began, declaring that "we are accomplishing our goal despite the continuing rhetoric of the networks." He denied that "fear of failure" had led to the demise of the boycott.

In 1982, he tried another boycott, this time against all RCA-based companies, including NBC. RCA/NBC was condemned for failing to meet with representatives of his group, for having *Playboy* Playmates on a George Burns Christmas special, for airing anti-Christian segments on *Saturday Night Live* and for having "more leading characters depicted as homosexual than Christian." "What is at stake," said Wildmon in his statement to the press, "is much more than sex and violence on television. At stake is whether our country will turn its back on more than 200 years of Judaeo-Christian values as the foundation for law and justice . . . . The 'make-it-up-as-you-go' value system advanced by RCA/NBC as a replacement for Judaeo-Christian values is a road to chaos and confusion and a detrimental doctrine destructive to the human race."

Wildmon called for a boycott of RCA electronics, Hertz rental cars, C.I.T. Group financial corporation, Coronet carpets and Gibson Greetings cards (he withdrew that threat and apologized two days later, since Gibson was not owned by RCA). Conditions for ending the boycott required NBC to eliminate jokes about illegal drugs, to present programs dealing with "sex from the Judaeo-Christian perspective," to withdraw feminine-hygiene-product ads, and to not use the word God except in reference to the Deity. NBC also had to terminate the stereotyping of business people "as crooks and con men" and replace the offending programs with fare that promoted "the capitalistic, free-enterprise system as . . . a way to fulfill some of the needs God has placed within our hearts." Wildmon noted that the effectiveness of the boycott would be measured by "sales and financial results."

NBC did not capitulate, but months later, Wildmon claimed credit for a decline in RCA's financial picture, even though its profits rose that year by 400 percent.

Although Wildmon objects to an enormous universe of material, he does recognize the need for some focus to N.F.D.'s national energies. The year 1987 was the year of the Holiday Inn boycott. Wildmon accused Holiday Inn of promoting pornography through its in-room adult-movie service. It is irrelevant to Wildmon that a visiting preacher will not see one of the films unless he orders it, or that said preacher can make sure his family doesn't order them by simply having the service disconnected by a call to the desk.

Wildmon encouraged his followers to complain by calling the 800 reservation number of Holiday Inn (a number that he has published incorrectly on several occasions), to picket and, of course, to boycott.

Robert Brannon, Holiday Inn vice-president, said, "We will continue to show the films. We see no reason why we should not. Obviously, there are some people who disagree with the shows . . . but the [N.F.D.] argument is not with us; it is with the American people."

Wildmon claims that his efforts have generated 100,000 letters and telephone calls. Brannon says that the chain has received only 19,000, many of which are duplicates. He believes that the boycott had no effect. "We're having a great year, with both earnings and ocupancy up."

To support his boycott tactics, Wildmon is quick to invoke the liberal examples of civil rights and of lettuce boycotts. Of course, when Martin Luther King, Jr., took on Montgomery, Alabama businesses and Cesar Chavez took on lettuce, they asked for highly specific boycotts so that fuller rights would be accorded to deprived minorities. Wildmon's boycotts, on the other hand, would deny the opportunity of all to exercise their constitutional rights as readers or viewers.

Books and magazines are central to public discourse. They are clearly different from lettuce leaves, which cannot be read, even by fortunetellers. It makes about as much sense for Wildmon to picket Joe's Market, which carries *Playboy,* as it does for the village atheists to band together to drive a Christian bookstores out of a shopping mall.

Nor is it possible ever to satisfy Wildmon in his quest to eradicate evil. He sees it everywhere. In 1986, when one convenience-store chain stopped displaying *Playboy* on their magazine racks, they lost their N.F.D. pickets. But they picked them up again when N.F.D.ers decided to protest *Mad* and *National Lampoon,* because, according to one picketer, they promote "rebellion against parental authority."

Wildmon's *NFD Journal* repeatedly details the success that half a dozen phone calls, or even a single letter, has had in causing a local company to stop selling a magazine or other N.F.D.-condemned product. It is hard to believe that these merchants had a sudden awakening of morality, or that they had simply failed to take a hard look at the product. Invariably, the reason for curtailing sales was the unwillingness to put up a fight. Wildmon has been a catalyst for cowardice, not conscience. So it will remain until more of us realize that any society that allows itself to become homogenized by political pressure masquerading as moral suasion is one at risk of losing its direction, if not its national soul.

Why Reverend Wildmon wants to ban what you watch, hear and play

The Reverend Donald Wildmon is the quintessential advocate of the "If it affects anyone, ban it for everyone" school of regulation. The National Federation of Decency criticized the USA network for airing *Friday the 13th: Part III*, because an 11-year-old in Madison, Wisconsin hanged himself, allegedly trying to duplicate a stunt in the film. Similarly, the N.F.D. blamed the producers of *Rambo*, because Anthony James Jenkins went on a sniping spree in Mississippi shortly after he saw the film. Wildmon regularly blames the game Dungeons and Dragons for assorted teenage murders and reports on every suicide of heavy-metal fans who might have been influenced by AC/DC or Ozzy Osbourne songs.

There is no question that messages in films, TV and even games can occasionally contribute to terrible acts; the question is whether a free society should prevent their dissemination based on a possible effect on the most impressionable viewer. First, it is nearly impossible to anticipate what will set someone off. The behavior of one British mass murderer who killed women and drank their blood through straws was reportedly "triggered" by his attendance at Anglican High Mass. Second, even news coverage would be affected if Wildmon had his way. In Japan, the 1986 suicide of a pop singer led to at least a dozen apparent copycat suicides by teenagers.

Surely, news organizations cannot be held liable for reporting the truth. In fact, Wildmon should know that courts have consistently rejected imposing legal sanctions on publishers and broadcasters for the unintended effects of their published or broadcasted material.

Wildmon has also adopted a peculiarly simplistic understanding of social psychology. For example, he accepts the claims of child molesters and rapists that pornography led them to their crimes. One would think he would recognize the frequently self-serving nature of such claims. Pornography sounds a bit more contemporary than claiming that comic books made you a criminal and a bit more inherently reasonable than maintaining that the Devil made you do it.

Wildmon is also a big fan of mentioning that pornography is found in the homes of many sex offenders, as if that demonstrated some causal link between rape and reading. Surely, he would not attribute the same link to the presence of milk in the refrigerator or attendance at church as a child. Criminals who are obsessed with sex or violence are expected to be attracted to the depiction of the same things. That is a far cry from demonstrating that, but for pornography, these same people would have been Sunday school teachers.

Wildmon has some additional analytic quirks. In his *NFD Journal*, he regularly reports on violence, but only of a certain kind. He discusses violence only when he can make one of his fatuous arguments linking its occurrence to its representation in the media. Indeed, Wildmon has no apparent interest in "structural" violence. He has published scathing criticism of such programs as *The Day After* and *NBC Reports* for being "propaganda" for disarmament and anti-gun lobbyists. Nobody who looks at the data objectively can possibly conclude that *Rambo* has been responsible for a greater number of fatalities than have handguns left lying around in people's homes. One might not wish to restrict either, but clearly, restricting the latter would have a more direct effect on actual violence.

Wildmon has his own skewed vision of "sexual exploitation." The man who had his followers count the number of times women's breasts jiggled in an episode of *Charlie's Angels* in order to condemn the show views the Miss Universe pageant as "wholesome" and says that it is one of his children's "favorite shows." Wildmon explained that "we never counted [pageants] as jiggle television," because cameras don't "zoom in on women's breasts." Wildmon's endorsement of the pageant stressed the competitiveness of the event and its demonstration of the contestants' ability to answer questions under pressure.

Clearly, Wildmon is not a reasonable man, but reasonable or not, he remains a force to be reckoned with by reasonable people.

Barry Lynn is the American Civil Liberties Union's legislative counsel.

Media Regulation
Worksheet

1. Where do you stand on the Fairness Doctrine? Is the government's enforcement of every citizen's freedom of speech in opposition to the free speech guaranteed broadcasters? Does owning the station take precedence over the notion that the airwaves belong on the public?

2. The Fairness Doctrine was eliminated on August 4, 1987. Should it be brought back? In your view, is broadcast and narrowcast (cable) content "fair"? Are all perspectives on controversial issues being heard from? Support your answer.

3. The "Aladdin's Lamp" essay reflects upon the government's deregulation of children's programming, allowing for more commercials and commercialization of programs. In your opinion, should the government get more or less actively involved in the regulation of children's television? Is your answer consistent or inconsistent with hour belief about government intervention in general? Explain.

4. Which do you believe to be most harmful for freedom of speech: (a) the form of government intervention described in the essay "End of an Era"; or (b) the form of citizen group intervention described in the essay "How to Separate the Men From the Boycotts?" Explain.

V

Media Economics

In 1989, at 8 pm (eastern standard time), on NBC, *The Cosby Show* was watched by 27.9 percent of the total U.S. viewing audience. The star of this top rated TV program—Bill Cosby—earned $10 million for his efforts. By 1989, *The Cosby Show* had also accumulated enough episodes during its four previous years of production that it went into national syndication. Each episode of the program, which cost $150,000 to make, earned the producers $3 million in total syndication sales. That same year Michael J. Fox, who had become a movie star in *Back to the Future*, was offered a $1 million signing bonus just for coming back to his successful television series "Family Ties." In between these programs, the "Bo Knows" Nike sports shoe commercial depicting super athlete Bo Jackson (along with Michael Jordan ("Bo knows basketball"), Kirk Gibson ("Bo knows baseball"), John McEnroe ("Bo knows tennis?"), Curtis Strange ("Bo knows weightlifting"), and hockey star Wayne Gretzky ("No.")) lifted the company to first place in the $4.8 billion athletic shoe industry.

There is little doubt that the business of mass media is big business. Just *how* big is the subject of the first essay. This essay introduces the concept known in the media world as "Global Synergy," where international mergers of print and broadcast industries lead to the consolidation of the mass media and formation of large media conglomerates. These conglomerates posture for position, control, clout, and the large profits to be made or lost in international media ownership.

The second essay is the perfect counterpoint to the first, reducing the world of international media economics to the most basic of questions: "Does Advertising Work?" This essay presents arguments against and in defense of television advertising. Critics of commercials feel that advertising creates the need in consumers to purchase products; members of the advertising industry argue that advertising is relatively ineffective in this regard and simply influences consumers' product brand choice. Either way, it is made clear that the consumer, not the advertised product, is the consumed commodity in the world of media advertising, whether advertising is effective or not.

The third essay, "Free 'Plugs' Supply Ad Power" describes the latest trend in television advertising: the "casual" display or mention of commercial products or company names in regular

TV programming. Despite network policy to minimize these unpaid ads, or "plugs," viewers are exposed to more corporate ad product logos in programming than paid commercial ads between programs. This strategy gives new meaning to "commercial television."

The final essay, "The Serious Business of Movie Merchandising," examines how big-budget films exist not only as entertainment but also as promotional concepts for foods, games, clothes, souvenirs, and collectibles. Often, it is hard to know which came first—a popular motion picture spawning commercial products or a product needing a motion picture to launch it into the marketplace.

The Myth of Global Synergy
Joshua Hammer, NEWSWEEK

Richard Snyder, the chairman and CEO of Simon & Schuster, is a firm believer that bigger is better in the media world. When Eddie Murphy, the star of Paramount movies like *Coming to America,* decided to write his autobiography last year, S&S—Paramount Pictures' sister publisher—was able to sign Murphy to a lucrative book contract.

In the communications business, the concept is called synergy, and it's a major rationale behind the proposed Time-Warner and Time-Paramount mergers. Proponents say that consolidation makes sense in an era when foreign rivals like West Germany's Bertelsmann AG are gobbling up American properties from book publishers to movie studios. By growing bigger, they say, the American megafirm can control both content and distribution throughout the world. For instance, Time-Warner or Time-Paramount could produce an article that could be spun off into a book, movie and a TV show, and then sold abroad through Warner's or Paramount's international distribution network.

But the notion that bigness will lead to profitable synergies may rest more on hype than reality. Analysts say that merging assets can give a company more clout domestically. For instance, "you could sell ad space at discount in *Time* in conjunction with [the Time-Warner] cable network," says Dennis McAlpine, an analyst with Oppenheimer & Co. But such synergies are hard to pull off—and may be even harder in the international market. McAlpine suggests that the cry for global competitiveness is little more than "PR meanderings" to disguise the drive for dominance in America. "[Global] synergy looks great on paper, but it's almost impossible to execute," insists Larry Gerbrandt, senior analyst for Paul Kagan Associates.

Indeed, the promises of synergy remain largely unfulfilled. Rupert Murdoch turned News Corp. from an Australian publishing company into a worldwide media conglomerate. Murdoch now owns American newspapers and magazines, the Fox movie studio and TV network, and Sky Television, a Pan-European satellite-TV network. It's an impressive array of properties, but any global synergies are still to come. Despite a potential flow of programming from Fox, Murdoch's Sky Television has proven a tough sell in Europe and may lose $250 million in its first year.

For its part, Time Inc. repackaged its hot-selling *Sports Illustrated* swimsuit issue into a Home Box Office special and video. But many analysts say it has otherwise done little to exploit potential synergies. "Time's divisions have been notorious for [lack of initiative]," says Gerbrandt. "If you don't have someone who's fully committed to making these things work, you just wind up with divisions that are off doing their own thing."

Even where the possibility for synergy exists, heads of subsidiaries often find it more profitable to strike deals outside the company. Bertelsmann AG owns printing plants around the world and the Literary Guild book club, but continues to print books at competitors' plants and sell them through the Time-owned Book-of-the-Month Club. "It's strictly an economic, efficiency and service decision," says Alberto Vitale, president of the Bertelsmann-owned Bantam Doubleday Dell Publishing Group.

The search for synergy has seen some successes, particularly in the United States. Warner has spun off characters from its DC Comics division into *Superman* movies, the *Batman* and *Wonder Woman* TV series, the new *Batman* film and a best-selling *Batman* paperback tied to the movie. Paramount has earned tens of millions from its *Star Trek* films and a series of best-selling *Star Trek* books, published by Simon & Schuster. The Fox studio spun off its movie *Alien Nation* into a TV series, while the Fox's broadcasting group produces the tabloid show *A Current Affair* for the Fox network.

Quest for profits: If nothing else, a merger between two media giants might help revitalize sagging enterprises. Double-day, the publishing house, was struggling before Bertelsmann bought it in 1986 and merged it with Bantam; last year it had 17 best sellers, including Joseph Campbell's *The Power of Myth.* "Doubleday got an infusion of creative and financial resources," says Stuart Applebaum, a Bantam vice president. But in the unpredictable communications business, the quest for synergy can lead to disaster as often as profits: in one classic example, Frank Herbert's scifi novel *Dune* was a huge best seller for G.P. Putnam's Sons, owned by MCA Inc., which also owns Universal Studios. The $42 million movie version turned into one of Universal's biggest bombs.

Does Advertising Work?

Michael Schudson, ADVERTISING: THE UNEASY PERSUASION

I have grave doubts about the conviction shared by both the critics of advertising and its most enthusiastic promoters that advertising is highly effective in manipulating the minds of consumers and so in promoting a consumer culture. Critics of advertising contend, in one form or another, that advertising powerfully shapes consumer values and choices. While some critics point simply to a global consumer mentality as advertising's creation, most blame advertising for the sale of specific consumer goods, notably luxury goods (designer jeans), frivolous goods (pet rocks), dangerous goods (cigarettes), shoddy goods (some toys for children), expensive goods that do not differ at all from cheap goods (nongeneric over-the-counter drugs), marginally differentiated products that do not differ *significantly* from one another (laundry soaps), and wasteful goods (various unecological throw-away convenience goods). Advertising, it is often claimed, persuades people to buy these things that they do not need or should not have. Advertising shapes consumers' desires and makes them feel a yearning for things they do not really need.

The response of advertisers and marketers to this criticism would be comical were it not so serious. Advertising, they say, cannot do any of these dastardly things because advertising is ineffective or only modestly effective in changing people's habits of consumption. The reason advertisers advertise is not to change people's product choices but to change their *brand* choices. Advertising is not a war on consumers' minds but a competitive war against commercial rivals for a share of a market whose size is either constant or, if changing, changing for reasons far beyond the power of advertising to affect. The marketer with any sense tries not to persuade people to gamble on a new product but to find consumers who already use a product or are already predisposed to a product by their situation in life and to *remind* them that a certain brand of the product is available and attractive.

This argument may at first sound very dubious. Certainly it is self-serving. It is the kind of argument that marketers regularly take before federal agencies that seek to regulate advertising. But the marketers have a point. Despite the saturation of print and air waves with advertisements, few businesses invest great percentages of their budgets in advertising, and most businesses organize their advertising so as to rely as little as possible on its persuasive powers.

Nevertheless, the marketing ideology that advertising does not have great power (and so can do society little harm) is disingenuous. There are conditions under which advertising has a significant impact on sales. Beyond this, advertising may influence cultural life in the large even when it is not doing much to sell goods piece by piece. Whatever advertising's direct effect in stimulating sales and making people buy more goods, it fully merits its reputation as the emblem of fraudulence. I do not mean fraudulence in a sense the Federal Trade Commission would recognize. The vast majority of ads are not "unfair" or "deceptive." A great many are positively informational. But there is a persistent, underlying bad faith in nonprice advertising. I take as emblematic the old McDonald's slogan, "We do it all for you." That, of course, is a lie. McDonald's does it all for McDonald's. It may be that what's good for General Motors is good for the country, but that is not why General Motors takes the actions it does. Even if, as is generally the case, everything that the ad says about the product is scrupulously honest, or at any rate scrupulously avoids outright dishonesty; the implication of the direct address of most commercials—that the announcer speaks with the viewer's welfare at heart—is fraudulent. The advertisement seeks to promote sales, it does not seek to improve the lives of consumers except as a means to the end of sales.

Apologists are wrong that advertising is simply information that makes the market work more efficiently—but so too are the critics of advertising who believe in its overwhelming power to deceive and to deflect human minds to its ends. Evaluating its impact is more difficult than these simplicities of apology and critique will acknowledge.

Free "Plugs" Supply Ad Power
Scott Hume, ADVERTISING AGE

Film critic Gene Siskel followed his review of *The Little Mermaid* Dec. 19 on the *CBS Morning News* with the observation that his daughter immediately wanted to go to McDonald's and get a *Little Mermaid* Happy Meal.

That was a plug for McDonald's Corp., a free mention for an advertiser that spends $250 million annually on network TV advertising.

TV programming is constantly interrupted by paid ads, but increasingly, the programs themselves are also peppered with what really are unpaid ads: mentions of products by talk show guests, corporate logos superimposed behind newscasters' heads to illustrate a news story, signage or labels visible during dramas.

According to a study commissioned by *Advertising Age,* brand names get a significant amount of visibility free, through regular TV programming, compared with what they get through paid advertising.

To find out how many plugs occur during the average broadcast day, *Ad Age* joined with the Department of Advertising at Northwestern University's Medill School of Journalism.

A complete 24-hour broadcast day for each of the Big 3 TV networks was videotaped, one network a day for three consecutive days.

Those tapes were then viewed by 28 graduate students—with at least two students viewing each tape—who watched for and recorded every plug they believed they heard or saw.

The definition of a plug used was purposely broad and subjective. Basically, any mention of or appearance by a commercial product or company was counted as long as it was not judged to be a paid placement.

The subjectivity was factored in because *Ad Age* wanted to learn how many product names and logos a group of college-age people would spot.

When director Ron Howard mentioned on *The Arsenio Hall Show* that he lives in a Winnebago on the movie set, that counted as a plug for the motor home company.

When an actor on *General Hospital* bought an ice cream cone from a street vendor and the Drumsticks label was clearly visible, that counted. So did the ad for Marlboro 25's visible in the magazine another character on that show leafed through.

If the students thought the watch on a person's wrist clearly looked to be a Rolex, even if the name wasn't visible, or if someone in a program was wearing Levi's jeans, those appearances counted.

Prizes on game shows didn't count. Brand names or products that students differed in identifying also were weeded out.

In a single day of programming on the three major networks, this study found 818 instances of a recognizable product or mention of a brand or corporate name.

News programs No. 1 in plugs

News programs led the pack when it came to including such plugs, accounting for 44% of the brand-name inclusions.

Next were the talk/variety shows (accounting for 14.5% of the total).

For example, comedian Rich Hall's routine on NBC's *Late Night With David Letterman* included mentions of Exxon, Mickey's malt liquor, Milk-Bone dog biscuits, Milk Duds candy, Pop Tarts, Safeway stores and the *Village Voice,* as well as Mr. Hall's series of "Sniglets" books.

All plugs.

But the record was set earlier in the evening by comic Jay Leno, the guest host of NBC's *Tonight Show Starring Johnny Carson.* Mr. Leno managed to include in his routine mentions of the *ABC Evening News With Peter Jennings*, Adidas aftershave, Cycle 4 pet food, Eastern Airlines, 40-Plus Bran Flakes, the film *Friday the 13th, Part 7*, Garfield plush toys, Mary Kay cosmetics, the board game Monopoly, Toyota, *USA Today* and more.

Consumers have been conditioned to recognize corporate and product logos, and most people from 3 to 50 own at least one article of clothing bearing a product name or logo.

So it doesn't take a trained eye to notice that the bad guys are wearing Reebok shoes during CBS' *Jake & the Fatman.*

And during a late-night showing of an old episode of *Family Medical Center*, most viewers probably noticed the Johnson & Johnson logo on products above the hospital patient's head.

In a culture and economy where few things are as valued as the brand name, each of those mentions constituted a valuable—and free—piece of advertising.

The argument also could be made that they undercut advertisers by increasing the clutter of brand names on the medium.

Plugs can be negative, too, and these were counted. It happened, for example, that most newscasts on one of the days carried a story about new data gained from the cockpit flight recorder from a Delta Air Lines crash earlier in the year. Each mention of Delta constituted a plug, though not necessarily a positive one.

The broadcasts for the three networks (taped Wednesday through Friday, Aug. 2 to 4, 1989) were regarded, in total, to represent the equivalent of a single network day.

Among the results of the study:

- The networks carried roughly an equal amount of plugs in their programming. The students counted 297 plugs over 24 hours on NBC's WMAQ-TV, 270 on CBS' WBBM-TV and 251 on ABC's WLS-TV. All three Chicago stations are owned and operated by their networks.

- Most free mentions of company and product names come during news programming.

WMAQ's 6 a.m. *News at Sunrise* program included stories about possible buyers for Avon Products, trading activity by Drexel Burnham Lambert, the death of a woman when a train collided with the 1985 Mercury she was driving, an emergency landing made by a Piedmont Airlines pilot and a review of the film *Parenthood.*

The sports segment on WBBM's 10 pm news program included a short item on the Boston Celtics' Larry Bird. The Nike logo was visible on players' shoes and so was the Adidas name on an onlooker's T-shirt.

- News/feature programs such as NBC's *Today* ranked third, with 14.3% of total plugs.

Some of these plugs were for the books or films or TV programs with which guests were associated. But not all. For example, a *Today* feature on Jackson Hole, Wyo., included mention of Miller beer and Calvin Klein jeans.

Brand names visible or mentioned in news stories aired during *CBS This Morning* included Coca-Cola, Corona and Miller beers, Ford, Heinz ketchup and NutraSweet.

- Daytime dramas also had their share of plugs. The Bell symbol was prominent on the phone booths used by characters on ABC's *All My Children* and *General Hospital.* A character on CBS' *The Bold & the Beautiful* read *Elle* magazine. To signal the wealth of a character on NBC's *Another World*, the camera zoomed in on his Rolex.

All three networks said their policy is to eliminate or at least minimize the number of plugs in programming.

ABC's policy states that "identification of products [or services] by brand name or the use of brand-name products as props should be kept to a minimum and must be specifically approved in each case by Broadcast Standards & Practices. Approval will be given only when the product reference or prop is important to sustaining the dramatic and production value of the program."

But dozens of plugs still manage to slip through this net, especially on news and variety programs where content can't be pre-screened.

If there's a conclusion to be drawn from this study, it's one many of the students noted in their written evaluations: that product names confront us everywhere on TV, in programming perhaps more than through commercials.

Student Karen Davis wrote: "While I had always been aware that there were a good number of products appearing in today's TV programs, I did not realize the extent of the product appearances. . . . There is an almost blatant attempt to display the product names without hesitation."

The Serious Business of Movie Merchandising
Stephen Schaefer, PROFILES

Scarlett O'Hara china plates. *Teenage Mutant Ninja Turtles* sheets. *Batman* T-shirts, posters, telephones, and coffee mugs. *Robin Hood* cereal. A *Star-Trek* postage stamp.

Welcome to the amazing world of movie merchandising, where films exist not only as entertainment but also as promotional concepts for food, games, clothes, souvenirs. And postage stamps. Now comes *Hook*. With a Christmas movie season plum-filled with big budget pictures and ever ripe for tie-ins, *Hook* will be, in the words of *Advertising Age,* the industry weekly, "the season's marketing phenomenon."

TriStar Pictures has made one of this Christmas' brightest baubles, an all-star Steven Spielberg fantasy with Dustin Hoffman as the hook-handed pirate captain, Robin Williams as Peter Pan, and Julia Roberts to dart and dazzle as the seven-inch tall Tinkerbelle.

Since TriStar is a division of the expanded, globe-encircling Sony Entertainment, *Hook* is being viewed as the first test case of the much-vaunted synergy theory, which reasons why electronics giants like Sony bought entertainment companies like Columbia Records and Columbia/TriStar Pictures. The theory decreed that "software," namely movies, records, and electronic games, was needed by the companies that make Walkmans and Watch, the "hardware."

Hook has hooked huge toymaker Mattel, Inc. to make *Hook* action figures and other playthings. In addition to a Lost Boys Attack Raft and a Lost Boys Strike Tank, there will be seven action figures, a "life-size " Peter Pan battle sword and, most spectacularly, Captain Hook's hook. It's a fabulous toy, kind of a Swiss Army version of his hook," says Rob Hudnut, Mattel's director of marketing for boys' toys. "We can't make enough of them."

Sony will also synergistically promote *Hook* as the basis for its first major game since that division was reorganized earlier this year. And in the not-to-far-distant future, the sets from *Hook* along with the characters, could end up in Sonyland, a proposed theme park the company hopes to open in a still top-secret location somewhere in the world sometime in the mid-1990s.

But *Hook* is hardly alone. Paramount Pictures not only has *Star Trek VI: The Undiscovered Country* as the highlight of its year-long 25th anniversary Star Trek celebration, but the campy special effects fantasy, *The Addams Family*. A pair of years-in-the-making animated musicals also are here this season: Walt Disney Pictures' *Beauty and the Beast,* with songs by *The Little Mermaid*'s Oscar-winning team of Howard Ashman and Alan Menken, and the Universal Pictures-Spielberg production, *An American Tail: Fievel Goes West*. These, too, boast all kinds of tie-ins. The bottom line, of course, is exposure and more exposure, which translates into sales and more sales.

"As a promotional trend, movie merchandising is something you've been seeing for years," notes *Advertising Age* reporter March Magiera, because studios are looking for cross-promotion partners to offset their costs. It's another revenue generator."

By allowing a picture to be used as a promotional come-on for burgers, pizzas, and toys, a studio in return may generate as much as $40 million in Saturday morning TV commercials during the three-to-six month run of the film. Most movies, of course, are R-rated. Therefore, these merchandising programs are aimed at the family market.

That's why *Hook* has a planned tie-in with both McDonald's and Coca-Cola. For *Fievel,* there's a partnership with Pizza Hut; for *Beauty* and her *Beast,* a Burger King promotion. And for *The Addams Family,* there will be a cereal.

For all the Christmas films, there are also toys, video games, calendars, storybooks, recordings, and clothing.

What worked wondrously for *Batman*, probably the most successfully merchandised movie of recent times, isn't necessarily right for all other movies. And the fear now is that too much merchandising will make the movie seem almost secondary. Spielberg, for example, is sensitive about tarnishing his films' luster with commercialism.

"They definitely thought that the merchandising distracted from the artistic merit of *E.T.*," recalls Anne Thompson, a motion picture industry analyst for *The L.A. Weekly* and *Variety.* "But that realization came long after the film had opened. The current trend is to blitz [all markets] in advance of an opening."

"Today," Thompson explains, "the studios figure the only way they can make money [on a film] is to spend as much as they can in order to guarantee that it's a big hit. They need a big opening and they do that by a blitz of the airways, radio, and print media."

Just as Spielberg has his finger on what *Hook* promotions will fly, other big names can exert control, too.

Consumers didn't see Kevin Costner's face, for instance, on *Robin Hood* cereal. Costner is sensitive about that sort of merchandising.

Stars aren't the only influential factor. Attention to the calendar is essential. The general rule is that it takes at least six, and more likely 12 to 18, months to put together a merchandising campaign, especially if toys are involved. McDonald's is reportedly the only major promotions partner that can put together a campaign in less than six months.

Luckily, when studio executives are spending anywhere from $40 to $80 million to make a movie (*Hook* cost an estimated $70 million), they know enough to plan the ancillary sales far in advance. But the unexpected can happen, as it did in the case of *The Addams Family.* As filming was in progress, the big-screen version of the 1960s series suddenly switched studios. This limited the product development that could be engendered prior to the release.

Movie merchandising is almost as old as the industry itself. During the 1930s, movie theaters promoted chinaware with admissions, and Shirley Temple, the tot who reigned as box-office queen, make a fortune licensing dolls and other merchandise.

By 1938 when Disney's first full-length animated feature, *Snow White and the Seven Dwarf,* was released to universal acclaim, the studio that Walt built was already doing big business marketing its cartoon characters to children of all ages. That business has continued ever since, with *Pinocchio, Peter Pan, 101 Dalmations,* and other animated classics, not to mention the Davy Crockett coonskin cap craze of the 1950s.

Disney's domination of movie merchandising to children ended with the arrival of the landmark sci-fi *Star Wars* trilogy. George Lucas's innovative saga flipped the eternal battle between the forces of good and evil into a new realm of pop culture and a merchandising boom of epic proportions.

"*Star Wars* totally rewrote the rules," says Rob Hudnut of Mattel, the nation's second-largest toy manufacturer. The company is most famous for its Barbie doll—which generated $740 million in revenues last year alone—and in addition to *Hook*, it has done tie-ins with TV shows like the *Simpsons* as well as other films.

"*Star Wars* character figures, made by Kenner, provided the first really big, male action line. The best known figure before that time was G.I. Joe. What *Star Wars* did was shrink the figures to just four inches. When you make the figures smaller, the vehicles become more affordable; the Millenium Falcon [spaceship] was $15 instead of $50. Kids love to collect things, and at that price, they can buy lots of different figures."

If you're wondering just what "a male action figure" is, Hudnut has the answer: "Essentially, they're dolls for boys. But they're not called that; boys don't play with dolls."

He-Man and Masters of the Universe actually started as a toyline. "We were the first to put a television show behind an already successful toy line," says Hudnut. "The line was the biggest of anything to that point."

Ghostbusters was another big movie-based toyline that became a TV series. Ninja Turtles began as a comic book, was transformed into a toyline, then became a hit animated TV show and after that, two monstrously successful movies.

"Every major toy company turned the Turtles down." Hudnut recalls. "A little company called Playmates bet the farm on the Turtles. That was a very good bet."

Marcy Magiera says, "*Batman* is probably the most successful movie to be merchandised outside of ongoing Disney favorites or *Star Wars*. In fact, Lucas is bringing back the original movie this Christmas to promote some new *Star Wars* videogames."

Merchandising was behind the making of *Star Trek VI*, the Trekkie adventure that people thought would never be made. That's because *Star Trek V* "did not do well," admits George Takei who has played Mr. Sulu for 25 years. Takei is known, along with William Shatner, Leonard Nimoy, and four other original cast members as "The Magnificent Seven."

"According to Paramount's calculations, *Trek V* lost $30 million," Takei reveals. Then somebody noticed that since the series started on September 6, 1966, this year, 1991, would be the 25th anniversary.

"While Paramount could have had all kinds of promotions, they needed a movie to do it well. So, we're back." For the next millenium, probably. And may the merchandise, just like George Lucas's elusive Force, be with them all.

Stephen Schaefer is a New York-based theater and film writer who contributes regularly to USA Today *and* Entertainment Weekly.

VI

News

The reporting of news and information is not the oldest use of mass media; most media were initially used for some selling or business purposes. Nor is it the most widespread; most of us use the media primarily for entertainment. In fact, the reporting of news and information in the past was often an incidental function of mass media. Indeed, during the early days of television, network evening news was limited to 15 minutes and was only able to increase to 30 minutes after much negotiation between TV stations and networks. Local news was produced largely to satisfy license requirements. People spent time and money on mass media as part of their leisure activity, and if they got some news in the process, that was merely a side benefit.

Over the years, however, news because vital to the sustenance of nearly every mass medium. Network television in particular built up its news divisions to the point where the news program became the symbol and status of the organization. Ratings escalated to the level where one rating point represented a gain or loss of $10 million. However, rising costs of program production and a decrease in the number of viewers watching network television (despite an overall increase in television consumption) has placed a greater burden on news programming for revenue. Yet, the networks have initiated budget and personnel cuts in their news divisions to save costs. The result is presented in the four essays presented in this section. The first two essays, "Network News at the Crossroads" and "Days of Turbulence, Days of Change," offer insight into the specific problems network news programming is facing from local news, syndicators and cable. They suggest that a restructuring is in order to keep pace with the competition to increase audience share and rejuvenate advertising revenue. The third essay, "Dangerous Liaisons," presents the views of journalists, writers and editors regarding their associations with news sources. Given the high financial stakes associated with bringing in the story before the competition, and the need to offer the type of story that will generate an audience, has the give-and-take relationship between a news source and news correspondent become a dangerous liaison? The final essay, "Who Decides What is News," examines the give and take relationship between the press and the government and concludes that reporters are essentially puppets for the powers that be. Written by one of the country's keenest political observers, this article makes a devastating case for how incompetent and cowardly the American media really are.

Network News at the Crossroads
Burton Benjamin, GANNETT CENTER JOURNAL

A decade ago some observers of the press speculated that television news, with its speed, immediacy and huge audience, would make newspapers, as we knew them, obsolete. In 1982, Leo Bogart expressed a more moderate view in the *Wilson Quarterly:* "The real question is not whether newspapers will survive into the 21st century but rather *what kind* of newspapers they will be."

If you take Mr. Bogart's quotation, and substitute network news for newspapers, you have a striking parallel with the situation in television today. Increasing numbers of people are asking how long network news can survive its declining ratings and increased competition from local stations, syndicators and cable.

Will declining ratings affect the way the networks package their news? Is it all a ratings game? Are the networks beholden to the same forces that drive those on the entertainment side of television?

If you asked those kinds of questions a decade ago, in the halcyon days of network-news pre-eminence, the answer you were likely to get was this: "We're in the *news* business [the emphasis was always there]. Ratings have little or nothing to do with the way we present the news. We have a simple mandate—to present today's news today. We don't let popularity charts dictate what we do."

I heard that view a lot when I was producing the *CBS Evening News with Walter Cronkite,* and it was understandable in a way. We were so far ahead in the ratings that it wasn't too difficult to be a purist. I must say, the view sounds rather innocent today.

The Lesson In Newspapers

Perhaps there is a lesson for network news in how one newspaper responded to rising costs and flat circulation. (It is interesting, by the way, how "circulation" is regarded as an honorable, straightforward business objective while there seems to be something unworthy about its television counterpart, "ratings.") In the 1970s, the *New York Times's* future was such that, according to one executive, one more rise in the cost of newsprint would have put the paper into the red.

In 1976, the paper added a "Weekend" section, followed by "Living," "Home," "Sports Monday," "Business Day," and "Science Times." Since the introduction of these "theme sections," the *Times's* daily circulation has risen from 828,000 to more than 1,000,000. The *Times* faced its problem by enhancing its newsproduct in an innovative way.

Not all staffers were pleased. I remember one saying to me: "The only way to get a piece in the goddam paper is to hook a menu onto it." He was fortunate he didn't work for one of the networks whose response to falling ratings and rising costs is not to increase productivity but to run a scythe through the newsroom.

The restructuring of news reports already is taking place at the networks. As Tom Brokaw, anchor of the *NBC Nightly News,* said in a recent speech at the Gannett Center for Media Studies: "We are now in the process of redefining our place in the information spectrum. We are now less of a daily news diary and more of a daily news magazine, offering in addition to a capsule of the daily news, a broader and deeper view of some of the big stories. We are slowly conceding the breaking stories to local news stations."

Therein lies the major change. The networks have lost their exclusivity, especially their picture exclusivity. New technology has given the larger local stations and CNN a reach comparable to ABC, CBS and NBC. Local stations, or one of the syndication services to which they subscribe, will bring you the latest satellite pictures from Montana to Mali, just as the networks have done for years. It is this encroachment, along with the competition from other program sources (independent stations love to play hardball and program game shows opposite network news; even WABC-TV in New York has followed suit), that have cut into the numbers and dictated a new look for network news.

The networks even contributed to the revolution themselves. When I produced the Cronkite News, we held back our best footage from the syndication news feed that went to our more than 200 affiliated stations at 5 p.m. each day. We did not want the same stories running on local news before we go on the air. Roone Arledge broke that embargo when he became president of ABC News. He began sending everything down the line to the local stations, and we had to do the same. Our fiercely competitive affiliates no longer would tolerate an embargo. Today, the networks give their affiliates virtually everything they have, and even set up regional newsfeeds to sweeten the pot. By the time network news hits the local market (after two hours and more of news in the larger cities), the audience often has seen most of the stories already.

Some former colleagues of mine at CBS News were startled last year when the network news broadcast originated in Los Angeles. They fed to the eastern and central time zones at 3:30 p.m., local time, and then went back to their hotel to watch the Rather News on the air. They watched the local news while waiting. "We never get a chance to see local news when we're in New York," a writer told me, "and it was a revelation to us. By the time we came on the air, we looked so *stale*."

None of this has come as a surprise to the network news executives. It didn't suddenly happen. The erosion has been slow but steady. In 1980, the three network news broadcasts had a combined audience share of 72 percent (sets in use). Today, that share hovers around 63 percent. In the ratings (percentage of all TV homes), NBC and CBS are in a virtual tie, and ABC is not far behind. One rating point equals 874,000 households, and a one-point rating lead for the evening news time period is worth $19 million in advertising revenue annually. So we need not belabor the fact that this is a very high-stakes game.

All three networks are seeking to come up with a new mix that will bring back the viewers they have lost. Considerable groping is going on. Some nights the network evening news looks like *McNeil-Lehrer*, other nights like *60 Minutes*. Both Roone Arledge at ABC and Howard Stringer at CBS have used the same words to describe what they're up to. "We are going to start from scratch," they say.

The last time Arledge started from scratch was in 1977, when he became president of ABC News. He went on a talent-raiding spree marked by sharply escalating salaries. Using production techniques he had pioneered at ABC Sports, he gave ABC News a modern and classy look, which the other networks and many local stations have cloned today. He was helped by the network's strong entertainment schedule, and by the switch to ABC of some attractive local affiliates. The journalism improved and the ratings headed north, which is what the game is all about.

No one can expect a "repeat" of that success in network news. Industry circumstances have changed, probably irrevocably, and given the imperatives of the day, the networks will clearly have to change the way they do business. No one has suggested—at least, not lately—that they take the low road and go the *New York Post* route. But it is really quite naive to ask whether ratings-circulation will affect how the network news product is packaged in the future. That would be like asking what yardstick Knight-Ridder or any other responsible news organization uses to determine its success.

It is to be fervently hoped that the networks will succeed, if for no other purpose than to remove the specter of "lean and mean" from the newsrooms. Those Wall Street-inspired buzzwords are making this the worst of times for network journalists. If left alone, they have the imagination and wit to develop a network news for the 1990s. To many of us, the best way for them to go is to lead with strength, with probing, insightful *journalism*. Otherwise, they will be faced with the same lower ratings and reduced advertising revenues that beset them today. They will continue to be savaged by bean-counters and non-journalists, and they might lose the whole ball game.

Burton Benjamin, a senior fellow at the Gannett Center for Media Studies in 1986 and 1987, was executive producer of the CBS Evening News *from 1975 to 1978, and a senior vice president of CBS News.*

Days of Turbulence, Days of Change
James Kelly, TIME

Television has always been a land of flux, a place where few programs last beyond two seasons and yesterday's top-rated star is today's trivia question. But for more than 30 years, all three networks have aired evening news shows that reach more people than any single newspaper or magazine. Turning on the TV set around dinnertime to watch the news has become a sort of flickering ritual that unifies much of the country for 30 minutes a day.

Now, however, the producers of the three broadcasts—CBS *Evening News with Dan Rather*, NBC *Nightly News with Tom Brokaw* and ABC's *World News Tonight with Peter Jennings*—fear they may be losing some of that hold. Besieged by budget cuts and competition, the news departments are going through a period of turmoil that is urgently forcing them to re-examine how they go about keeping Americans informed. Though most executives insist the quality of their flagship news programs will not be affected, many are not so sure. Says a CBS *Evening News* producer: "There comes a point when a worldwide newsgathering operation stops being a worldwide newsgathering operation."

Anxieties are running highest at CBS, where the sharpest knife is being wielded. Over the past 18 months, some 150 of the CBS News division's 1,400 employees have lost their jobs. In January, Chief Executive Officer Laurence Tisch asked News President Howard Stringer to cut up to $50 million from this year's nearly $300 million budget. Stringer presented a plan to Tisch last week that called for about $30 million in savings. Within two days, he began firing more than 200 staffers, including about 20 of the division's 75 or so full-time correspondents. "We can survive it," says Rather, "but not happily."

As names of the casualties filtered through the division's headquarters on Manhattan's West 57th Street, a mixture of anger and shock gripped employees. Rather refused to help pick those who should be laid off, and an anonymous letter circulated through the building urging a walkout to protest the cutbacks—and to show support for the news writers, who struck CBS and ABC last week. (NBC's employees belong to another union.) Negotiations for a new contract collapsed when the networks insisted on greater flexibility in firing workers and hiring more temporary employees; during the walkout, news scripts are being written by managers and producers on the broadcasts. Rather, Jennings and 85 other sympathetic employees signed a letter saying they were "appalled" by management's demands. Says a CBS producer: "I've been here a long time, and I've never seen morale this bad."

At ABC, which pared 200 from its news staff of 1,470 before Capital Cities Communications took control in early 1986 and eliminated 75 more positions last year, News President Roone Arledge has ordered a re-examination of the division and its $275 million budget. Arledge's request for suggestions has already claimed a victim: Av Westin, vice president for program development, who distributed to Capital Cities/ABC executives an unpublished magazine article he wrote. Titled "Days of Penury, Days of Affluence," Westin's 18-page memo argued that ABC's producers were more efficient 18 years ago, when he produced the network's nightly news show and funds were scarcer, than they are today. Arledge, who interpreted the memo as a bid for his job, has temporarily relieved Westin of his duties, which include producing the newsmagazine show *20/20*.

At NBC, whose parent company, RCA, was bought by General Electric in June, News President Lawrence Grossman insists there are no plans to cut his $230 million budget or 1,330-member staff. Nonetheless, NBC News has hired McKinsey & Co. management consultants to study the newsgathering operations. and rumors persist that next year will bring a 10% slash.

The budget pressures come at a time when the three networks are already contending with a growing challenge to their onetime dominance of international and national TV coverage. The competitors—Cable News Network, syndicated newsfeed services and local stations—all use the same satellite technology the networks do to bring live pictures from around the world. Though the number of people watching Rather, Brokaw and Jennings has remained steady at about 44 million, the networks' share of the overall audience has gradually declined. In 1980 the three broadcasts attracted 72% of the viewers; so far this season the proportion is 63%.

The straitened circumstances have only intensified the ratings war, in which a single point translates into $19 million in advertising revenues a year. For nearly two decades CBS *Evening News* held the top slot, but it tumbled into second place during the last three months of 1986, when Brokaw narrowly beat Rather and NBC earned its first quarterly victory since the heady days of Huntley and Brinkley in 1967.* So far this year Brokaw has won six out of nine weeks.

Rather, Brokaw and Jennings compete directly in only 112 of the nation's 205 TV markets; in many instances affiliates have shifted the programs to make room for more profitable game shows. In December, for example, WABC in New York switched the Jennings broadcast from 7 p.m., where it finished third against Rather and Brokaw, to 6:30 and replaced it with *Jeopardy*. The popular game show beats the two news programs, thus allowing WABC to charge more for commercials in that time period. *World News Tonight* achieves better ratings at 6:30 than it did at 7, but Jennings complains, "I did not like the move at all. I want to compete head to head."

The assault on network news dates from 1980, when Ted Turner started Cable News Network. Based in Atlanta and available 24 hours a day, CNN reaches 38.5 million homes, or 44% of all U.S. households with TV sets. Though an average of only about 600,000 households watch CNN daily, viewer levels are highest in the early evening. An even more serious threat to Rather and his rivals comes from news-feed services like Conus Communications, a Minneapolis-based cooperative that distributes footage via satellite. Founded in 1984, Conus comprises some 50 stations—network affiliates and independents—that operate as a sort of video wire service. Stations share stories by beaming them to Conus headquarters, which relays them to other members.

What makes Conus possible is the Newstar, a van equipped with an editing facility and a 90-inch satellite dish mounted on the rear. The $210,000 vehicle has supplanted the helicopter as the most prized piece of technology in a station's newsgathering arsenal. At WCVB, the ABC affiliate in Boston, for example, News Director Phil Balboni has replaced the network's Saturday-evening news show with an expanded local program that includes national and international coverage provided by Conus and other news services. Some stations have grown even more ambitious; more than a dozen sent their own anchors to Geneva in 1985 to cover the U.S.-Soviet summit via satellite.

Thus the evening shows increasingly try to distinguish themselves from local programs. "The syndication services are going to cover the snowfall in Colorado and the Amtrak train crash," says Brokaw. "We have to provide the context and look ahead."

The quest to be different can be rocky. In 1982 Van Gordon Sauter, then president of CBS News, turned the *Evening News* away from Washington and toward emotion-laden stories about how government policies affect citizens. But by 1985 the broadcast had softened too much into what one CBS correspondent calls "touchy-feely stuff." In May, when Tom Bettag became executive producer, Rather took him for a walk at the Cloisters, a museum of medieval art in upper Manhattan. "I told him I wanted the broadcast to be harder, to run more reports out of Washington," recalls Rather. The administration of the Washington bureau was beefed up, writers were instructed to avoid the cute prose that sometimes curdled Rather's delivery, and correspon-

---

* NBC had a quarterly rating of 11.8. CBS 11.56 and ABC 10.6. That translates into 10.3 million sets tuned to Brokaw, 10.1 million to Rather and 9.2 million to Jennings.

dents in the field were told, as one put it, "to make sure we do stories with the word today in them."

At ABC, Jennings stresses international news, a tactic that capitalizes on his 15 years of experience as a foreign correspondent. He professes not to feel pressured by his third-place finish, partly because he has steadily increased his audience. Yet ratings influenced the decision a year ago to run a segment every Friday called "Person of the Week." which profiles a key newsmaker. "We have a younger audience than the other two broadcasts, and they tend to go out early Friday nights, missing the show," explains Executive Producer William Lord. The feature, which News President Arledge helped conceive, has indeed lured viewers, but Jennings found the promotional ads so embarrassing that he persuaded Arledge to drop them.

At NBC, News President Grossman added correspondents to the White House and Pentagon beat and emphasized the broadcast's "Special Segment," an investigative report or a background piece tied to the news that runs four or five minutes. Studies commissioned by NBC indicated that viewers thought Brokaw was the least experienced of the three anchormen, so the network ran TV and newspaper ads that showed him meeting with world leaders. Sometimes, however, the line between news and show business blurs. Last year Brokaw interviewed President Reagan during the Super Bowl, and in January he delivered a news update from the Fiesta Bowl. "It is in my interest to do promotion," insists Brokaw. "No one is breaking away from the pack, so we are looking for every advantage we can get."

Over the past year, the three shows have shaved costs through shrewder management: satellite time is scheduled more carefully, control rooms are booked for fewer hours, and tape is sent by plane instead of satellite whenever possible. Network executives acknowledge, however, that budgets have grown so dramatically that only a redesign of the newsgathering operation will produce lasting savings. CBS News' budget, for example, totaled only $89 million in 1978. "I approached this [budget-cutting] process as if we were starting CBS News from scratch," says Stringer, the division president. "It is an anxious time, but it is also an opportunity to apply a creative mind and rethink everything we do."

Cost consciousness has already had a subtle effect on coverage. Last year a CBS producer wanted to examine the impact of U.S. sugar quotas by focusing on a Caribbean country where the restrictive policies had forced some farmers to give up sugar production and turn to growing marijuana. After Bettag calculated that the story would take two weeks to film, he suggested the producer concentrate instead on how Washington's policies had bolstered sugar growers in Louisiana. "What the belt tightening affects are those stories that might be good but that we don't *have* to do," Bettag maintains.

Though some observers believe the evening news shows are in danger of extinction, most disagree. "Day in and day out, the local stations are not going to cover the events the network does," says William Small, who served as senior vice president of CBS News from 1974 to 1978 before holding the job of president of NBC News from 1979 to 1982. "If the Pope returns to Poland, a station in Chicago, which has a high Polish population, may cover it. But if something happens in Thailand, it's highly unlikely."

Many executives do acknowledge that the format needs to be rethought, partly because the three shows are so similar. ABC seems furthest ahead in this process. Paul Friedman, director of overseas news for *World News Tonight*, is currently in New York City revamping the program. If Arledge approves a major overhaul, it may be unveiled as early as May; if only minor changes are okayed, they will be introduced gradually. One plan calls for the program to begin with a quick rundown of the news, with Jennings narrating some of the film clips. Then the bulk of the show would be devoted to analysis, either a round-table discussion of the day's biggest news event or a lengthy filmed report by a top correspondent.

If audience share continues to decline, one or more of the networks could conceivably decide to drop anchor and have the correspondents introduce their own segments. Though that scenario is remote, there is an increasing sense at all three networks that nothing is sacrosanct about the nightly news show. Asked if he would still like to be anchoring the CBS *Evening News* five years from now, Rather, 55, answers quickly, "If God is good to me and with a little luck, yes." Ten years from now? Hesitation. "Gee, I don't know. It's a young person's game." On the chair next to him in his office is a small needlepoint pillow with the saying Always is Not Forever.

Dangerous Liaisons:
Journalists and Their Sources
Martin Gottlieb, COLUMBIA JOURNALISM REVIEW

Few articles on the subject of journalism have triggered more newsroom and cocktail-party debate, more belligerent editorializing, and more honest soul-searching than Janet Malcolm's New Yorker *series called "Reflections: The Journalist and The Murderer." The articles, appearing last March 13 and 20, focused on the relationship between Joe McGinniss, author of the nonfiction bestseller* Fatal Vision, *and his subject and business partner, Jeffrey MacDonald, an ex-Green Beret who was convicted of murdering his wife and two daughters.*

But Malcolm went beyond the particulars to make the case that all journalism, by its nature, is "morally indefensible." In her memorable lead she describes the journalist as "a kind of confidence man, preying on people's vanity, ignorance, or loneliness, gaining their trust and betraying them without remorse."

To many journalists, these assertions seemed simply ridiculous. Yet it seems unlikely that they would have reacted as they did—often furiously—had there not been some truth in what Malcolm wrote.

No hard and fast rules define the relationship that should, ideally, be maintained between a journalist and a source. Most journalists have, accordingly, worked out their own rules. Over the years, writers like James Agee, Tom Wolfe, and Joan Didion have provided impetus for journalistic self-questioning; none of these writers, however, attacked the craft of journalism in such a vigorous and sweeping—and, in the view of many, overly broad—fashion as Malcolm.

Malcolm's articles, and also the unusual nature of the McGinniss-MacDonald relationship, raise some specific questions: Should McGinniss have entered into a business partnership with a controversial figure whose story he sought to tell—and, indeed, should any journalist enter into such a relationship? Did MacDonald's subsequent lawsuit against McGinniss, by compelling the author to reveal his state of mind while writing, constitute a dangerous new threat to First Amendment rights? Was McGinniss's behavior in writing sympathetic letters to MacDonald while preparing a devastating book about him morally defensible? Were William Buckley and Joseph Wambaugh correct when, in testifying at the McGinniss-MacDonald trial, they stated that it is accepted journalistic practice to either imply agreement or overtly agree with a subject' assertions in order to keep him talking—even when the journalist privately disagrees with those opinions?

One question raised—but not addressed—by Malcolm's article was: Should she have disclosed her own legal battle with Jeffrey Masson, the subject of a New Yorker *profile who accused her deceptions in some ways similar to those MacDonald claimed McGinniss practiced on him, and of fabricating quotes that were injurious to him?*

In an attempt to focus on Malcolm's essential charge, the Review *asked a number of prominent journalists—including Malcolm and McGinniss, who declined to be interviewed—whether they had qualms about their work, whether they thought their attempts to elicit information from subjects and sources could fairly be called "seduction," and whether Malcolm's charge that journalists betray their subjects was legitimate. While these taped and condensed responses occasionally veer away from the questions, they are, we believe, enlightening.*

Ken Auletta

'In journalism your loyalty is to the truth as you perceive it, not necessarily to your subject'

When I am doing a book and I hope to see a person many times in the course of several years, I don't, on the first meeting, ask my most charged questions. In the first five minutes of my first interview, I do not confront the subject. I will ask softer questions. Because I am trying to get the subject to relax, just as you do with someone you are interviewing for a job, right? That's the nature of human intercourse, so it seems a legitimate act of seduction, if you want to call it that. And I think Malcolm rightly calls it that.

To move from "seduction" to "betrayal," the question arises, How do you determine whether the subject was betrayed? And here key questions are, Did you say anything to the source to mislead him into thinking you were sympathetic? Did you figuratively lie, steal, or cheat? It seems to me there's a difference between expressions of support and simply nodding when the source makes what he thinks is an interesting point. But it also seems to me that there are some lines responsible journalists don't cross. We don't give advice to people we write about. We don't say, "I agree with you." We don't suggest people they might hire. We don't ask them for favors.

It is natural for a source or subject to feel betrayed when the story comes out and the subject doesn't like everything in it. But that doesn't mean the accusation of betrayal is justified. In journalism your loyalty is to the truth as you perceive it, not necessarily to your subject. Forgetting that is exactly the failure of insider journalism.

When I wrote a profile of Mayor Koch for *The New Yorker* in 1979, Koch felt "betrayed" by the piece. We went through this whole argument and my side of it was this: "Yes, I did spend nine months with you and, yes, I laughed at your jokes and, yes, I went to lunch a lot with you—it was Dutch treat—and, yes, you allowed me to read your mail and, yes, you allowed me to read your phone messages. But you always knew—or should have known—that when I got to the typewriter I was going to forget about you in one sense, and that can seem a brutal thing to do."

In this sense, Janet Malcolm has a point: journalism can be ruthless and brutal. And though there are no codified journalistic rules of conduct there are commonly accepted values. If that were not so we wouldn't deserve to call ourselves a profession.

Ken Auletta is a columnist for the New York Daily News *and the author of* Greed *and* Glory on Wall Street.

Nora Ephron

'The world is full of people who honestly don't know that journalists are not their friends'

What Janet Malcolm was saying was so reasonable I was astonished anyone took issue with it. Joan Didion wrote twenty years ago that a writer is always selling someone out. This was exactly what I knew to be true about journalism, and I felt the same way about Janet's pieces.

I believe that to be a good journalist you have to be willing to complete the transaction Janet describes as betrayal. Do you always have to betray someone to write a piece? On some level, yes. A profile has got to be written from your point of view, not from the subject's. Part of what you are trying to do as a journalist when you are writing about other people is to sort of wave at the readers through whatever you're writing about; you are trying to get them to notice *you*, the writer, to notice *your* way of looking at things, to notice your own peculiar, particular voice. So even if you are just talking about a minor betrayal, you have to do that—you have to make the material your own. And there is no question but that you have to have a certain lust for blood to do this. Some of the best journalism I've read happened after what Janet is describing as a "betrayal" or as "immoral."

One of my friends who was disturbed by the points in Janet Malcolm's pieces said she worried that if people read them, they wouldn't give interviews to journalists. I don't see anything wrong with this. The world is full of people who honestly don't know that journalists are not their friends. They honestly have no idea how awful it is to be misquoted or to be quoted out of context or to have what they said quoted but used to make a point they never intended—all of which, I'm sorry to say, is standard operating procedure among the majority of journalists. So if people read Janet's pieces on Joe McGinniss and Jeffrey MacDonald and learn to be wary of journalists, they've learned a valuable lesson.

Nora Ephron is a screenwriter and the author of Heartburn, *among other books.*

Mike Wallace

'Early on we used a variety of techniques, among them the famed, notorious—or whatever—ambush interview'

As a journalist you do some role playing. You don't turn all your cards face up. But let me give you a real-life example. I had a telephone conversation this morning with a prosecuting attorney. We know from some records that we obtained that the background of one of his major contributors is questionable—to put it euphemistically.

Now this prosecutor has told the producer of our piece that he has "consulted the Lord" and decided not to participate. I have never talked to him, so I call and say, "Look, the producer and I are working separately on this," which is true. "I have information from one side, he has information from the other side, and let me tell you what some of that information is." Then, in a friendly, straightforward way, I let him know a couple of the things that we know, thinking that may persuade him. Finally, though, I failed, so we are just going to do without his appearance.

What I'm trying to say is that you certainly don't come on hard when you are trying to persuade somebody who is reluctant to come on the broadcast. On the other hand, there are times when you'll say, "Look, you'd better do this. It's in your own damn self-interest to do this," because you believe that approach will be more effective.

In a sense it's pointless to try to make distinctions between seduction and persuasion or urging or whatever. In each case what you're trying to do is to get cooperation. And as long as it's done honestly, as long as no promises are made which are broken, then it seems to me perfectly reasonable to quote sell unquote the object of your scrutiny on the wisdom of cooperation.

Early on in the development of *60 Minutes* we used a variety of techniques, among them the famed, notorious—or whatever—ambush interview. It was only when every other means failed and we wanted to get the person on camera that we resorted to the ambush. It generated a certain amount of drama. But after a while it became obvious that it was self-conscious drama, that you could do just as well by saying on camera that we had sent telegrams and got no response.

The kind of people we talk to are, by and large, people who are not unused to public colloquy, and they often have public relations people to advise them. I find that more and more public relations people, particularly the younger crowd, are suggesting to their clients that the most useful thing that they can do—once they've been properly coached by their media advisers—is to come on and put the best face they can on whatever it is that we are talking about.

Mike Wallace is senior correspondent for CBS News's 60 Minutes.

J. Anthony Lukas

'It is very much more likely to be the man in power who is manipulating the reporter'

There can scarcely be a reporter, a writer, an editor, or, for that matter, a reader, in America who is not arrested by Malcolm's startling opening sentence. I must say, however, that the beginning seems to me a profoundly silly one.

I am certainly not denying that reporters do their share of manipulation. Of course they do. But the relationship is *mutually* manipulative. And that's because human relationships are mutually manipulative. We all manipulate each other: husbands manipulate wives, wives manipulate husbands, friends manipulate friends. I mean life is complicated, after all. And therefore the relationship between a source and reporter is complicated and Malcolm thunderously oversimplifies it.

In my experience, the relationship between reporter and source, particularly one of long term, is filled with collaboration and manipulation, with affection and distrust, with a yearning for communion and a yearning to flee.

Malcolm's opening sentence, arresting though it may be, is utterly without necessary distinctions. Many newspaper reporters spend their lives largely reporting the doings of more or less public figures who are quite sophisticated about the press—and who manipulate the press as much as they are in turn manipulated.

The road to advancement in American journalism is, it seems to me, inexorably a road that involves covering politics. You may start covering city hall and crown your career by covering the White House. Well, in that world I think Malcolm's sweeping statement is utterly *not* true. It is very much more likely to be the man in power who is manipulating the reporter.

Some years ago when I was doing two full issues of *The New York Times Magazine* on Watergate, I got an interview with Elliot Richardson. He was out of office at the time, so he received me, very shrewdly, at his northern Virginia home—a lovely, rambling old farmhouse—and it was winter, as I recall, and he seated us in front of a roaring fire. There were beautiful prints on the wall and it was, oh, just very cozy and pleasant. And seated across from me was this enormously handsome, articulate man who had recently come through the "Saturday night massacre" looking very heroic indeed. And about halfway through this interview I remember thinking to myself, He likes me. Elliot Richardson likes me. And he trusts me and he is speaking to me not as a subordinate, not as a mere reporter, but as a literate and perceptive man who can understand. He probably can't talk this way to most Washington reporters. He is really opening up to me.

It wasn't until I was in the cab on my way back to Washington that I thought, Schmuck, you've been had. You've just been treated to the treatment that this guy is exceptionally good at, and you fell for it—and may have taken a little sting off some of your questions in return.

This isn't to say that I wasn't trying to manipulate Elliot Richardson; I was. I was trying to get information out of him which he didn't want to give me.

I think that one would certainly have to say that, when one moves on to the nonpublic person, Malcolm's opening assertion is somewhat more on target. There are subjects/sources who know very little about the way the press works and they are therefore subject to a kind of seduction.

But, by and large, in the seven and half years I spent writing *Common Ground* [a book about three Boston families and the ways they were affected by Boston's school desegregation plan], I did not have to use my seducer's skills to get my subjects to talk to me. They wanted to talk to me for reasons of their own, often very complex.

I devised with them, and with Knopf, a technique which I freely admit is unorthodox and which may strike some reporters or some editors as not justified. I devised releases in which they promised not to sue me for invasion of privacy and, in a couple of cases, not to sue me for libel, and, in the cases where they wouldn't agree not to sue for libel, they agreed not to sue me for libel except on specific items which were identified prior to publication. They were given the right to read the chapters about themselves, not the entire book, prior to publication. Further, they were invited to identify not only those points they felt were libelous but any verifiable matter of fact they thought was inaccurate.

With regard to matters of interpretation, the release said, You may argue with me and I will listen—as long as you fully understand that I make no promise to make changes. And, finally, there was a paragraph that explicitly said, You are going to have all these interviews with me, most of them are going to be on tape, you can withdraw nothing. One family did urge me to withdraw material and, on reflection, I declined to do so.

But the fact of the matter is that the three families did not feel I seduced and betrayed them. On my birthday following the publication of the book they gave me a party.

Although this was *my* story, *my* vision of what happened in Boston, I think I went to considerable lengths to make sure that the members of these three families were treated in such a way that they would recognize themselves. And I think that Malcolm does me and many of my colleagues a great disservice to suggest that we are cynical and manipulative.

There is one rather important point I wish Malcolm had explored at greater length, which is that a source has to face up to the fact that the journalist who seemed so friendly and sympathetic, so remarkably attuned to the source's vision of things, never had the slightest intention of collaborating with him; that the journalist always intended to write a story of his own. I think that is true.

When I went to Boston I set out to in effect cast by book as if I were a theatrical director. I was looking for a black family, an Irish family, and a Yankee family who would play almost theatrical roles in my drama—and it was *my* drama. Are we, to use Malcolm's words, appropriating their lives for our stories? Yes, we are. And does that raise problems? Yes, it does. And does the craft of literary nonfiction, with all its excitement and the wonderful books that it has produced, create problems? Yes, it does.

But I would say, with due respect to Malcolm, that we ought not to be turning this into a question of moral culpability. We are, I think, honest craftsmen by and large, working at an evolving craft, trying to tell our stories, and if we make mistakes it is not moral culpability we are talking about, but mistakes—sometimes serious ones—that are the mistakes of craftsmen.

J. Anthony Lukas is the author of Common Ground: A Turbulent Decade in the Lives of Three American Families, *and has won two Pulitzer Prizes.*

Joseph Wambaugh

'I think the seducer is the one who is doing the talking'

Those ivory-tower arguments of Malcolm's were just so much crap to me. That opening sentence just blew me away. If anything, I think many of the people I have interviewed as a policeman and as a journalist were trying to con *me* all the time. I never felt that I was conning anybody.

It is hard to con a con, you know, and the folks I dealt with as a cop were cons themselves. So I felt it was my job to keep from getting conned. And I think reporters feel the same way. I mean, after all, when they write about people aren't those people trying to be seen in their best light? Don't they want reporters to love them? Don't they want reporters to report them in a way that they see themselves? So I think that the seducer is the one who is doing the talking. In testifying on journalistic procedure at the McGinniss-MacDonald trial, my point was that there is something between truth and lie, as we all know. I don't think Malcolm quoted me fairly. I think that because large portions of my testimony were not quoted, she didn't fairly convey my meaning or what I was talking about.

As a journalist, I would say you don't lie to anybody. You don't lie to anybody in life, why would you lie to people you are interviewing? But are there times in life when I don't tell the exact truth? If my wife comes home and says, "How do you like my new dress that just cost five-hundred dollars?"—that sort of thing. As I said in my testimony, you go to a thirty-year reunion and everybody is saying things that aren't true. But nobody is lying. There is a hell of a difference. My idea of a lie is an untruth that is told with ill will, malice, or bad intent, or that is uttered with knowledge that it could harm the person.

Another thing absent from her article: I was limiting my testimony as an expert witness to my dealings in life as a policeman and as an author with sociopathic killers, who will manipulate you. I was trained as an investigator to interview this kind of person—the most heinous kind of horrendous person. And when one of these people who has just raped a defenseless woman says to the investigator, "You know what you feel like sometimes, you get this urge and they ask for it, don't they?" you react a certain way. You are trying to get this guy to confess so you can put the bastard behind bars so he can't rape anybody else. I was trained that you are supposed to say something like, "Oh sure, Charlie, I know how you feel. Jesus, I mean I can't quit smoking and drinking. How can I criticize you?"

Malcolm quoted me as testifying that even though I didn't believe one of the murderers in *The Onion Field*, I said I did when he asked me if I agreed that he didn't shoot the police officer. I don't know if I said the word "said" or if a court reporter wrote down "said" or if Malcolm misquoted me. But if I had to be precisely correct now as a result of this debate I would say I would *imply* understanding. I would say to the guy something noncommittal, something like, "Well, I haven't really thought it all out completely." That is no more true than it is not true because obviously I had come to a conclusion.

But is it a lie? If it's a lie, tell me where there is malice, ill will, or bad intent.

I am limiting this to dealing with sociopathic murderers. I am not talking about my interviews with victims, witnesses, or ordinary people. I am talking specifically about a Jeffrey MacDonald who must manipulate his interviewer as he must manipulate everyone in his life. At those precise moments I think it is fair play to give him a vague and noncommittal answer which is not exactly the truth.

I think Joe McGinniss's behavior was very unusual. It was very unusual to have that sort of an arrangement with MacDonald. I would never give anyone a percentage of my royalties, I don't care who it was. To me that sort of taints a relationship to begin with. But, on the otherhand, Joe was very naive about sociopaths. I, on the other hand, am not naive about people like that and I know how their m.o. works, and I would never ever get involved in a relationship with one of them or one who could be such a person by the very nature of what he is being accused of.

Joseph Wambaugh is the author of novels and nonfiction books.

Joe McGinniss

The sense of obligation I felt toward Jeffrey MacDonald changed at the point where I discovered he had been lying to me, trying to manipulate me, trying to use me to tell a false story. For many months after that jury verdict in his case, while intellectually I found myself persuaded he was guilty, emotionally I found myself unable to accept that. And during that period of—well, ambivalence is too mild a word—of real conflict, I tried hard to give him the benefit of every doubt that I could, and did indeed behave toward him in compassionate fashion without, however, telling him that the book I was going to write would say this or this or this. I didn't *know* what the book would say, so there would be no way I could make a promise to anyone about what the book would ultimately say.

I think that as you proceed with any extended writing project, your understanding of your subject depends, broadens, intensifies, or evaporates. Something happens. It's not a static process and therefore the personal concommitant to this professional relationship also goes through a variety of modulations, and I don't think that a writer should ever be bound in his finished work to reflect an opinion that he might have held three years earlier . . . . The only control the subject has is the right to say no to begin with. If you don't want to be written about, just say no and then the writer goes away. . . . [The] project is in the sole editorial control of the person doing the interviewing and once that understanding is established as the basis for the relationship, whatever personal relationship grows out of it is . . . secondary. It just doesn't matter in the end. In the end, the obligation of the writer, be it a newspaper writer, a magazine writer, or a book writer, is to his or her own perception of the truth and it is to the reader. . . .

Joe McGinniss declined to be interviewed by the Review. *These remarks were excerpted from comments made by McGinniss at a panel discussion on the Art of Nonfiction at the University of Massachusetts at Amherst in April.*

Wendell Rawls, Jr.

'Too many reporters play fairly fast and loose with what somebody said'

As reporters, we generally deal with adults, grown people, who should understand that we are seeking what we hope is the truth. To call this process indefensible is ludicrous. Without sounding too high-minded about it, we are in the business of informing the public, and that's more important than the feelings of the person being interviewed.

Yes, there are times when I feel uncomfortable reporting facts that I imagine will cause a source some pain. I deal with it by calling up the source and telling him what I'm going to do. I don't let the source get ambushed.

But what concerns me most is sloppy reporting. Having been an editor for two and a half years and also having been the subject of several interviews by supposedly first-rate journalists, I am very concerned at how inaccurate the reporting is. I've found that reporters are very selective about which quotes they're going to use and also rearrange quotes to prove a point. And too many reporters play fairly fast and loose with what somebody said. They don't take good notes. They are listening to only half the quote, then get back to the office and can't remember what the other half was and are embarrassed to call the person back to ask for a clarification. I think that's a much more severe problem in American journalism and a severe test of our credibility. It has nothing to do with betraying anybody; it's simply a matter of craftsmanship.

One more point: I think Malcolm is a little off base in the way she uses the term "journalist." To me a journalist is a person who writes for newspapers and magazines and when he starts writing books he's an author, not a journalist. I know it's convenient to talk about book-length journalism but that's really just general nonfiction. A newspaper or magazine reporter generally doesn't spend enough time with a source to develop an emotional relationship that can lead to betrayal. The reporter is seeking information and moving on. Book writers come to a subject with a point of view. As an author you sell that point of view in order to make money. You sell access, you sell insider information, you sell, sell, sell. The journalist doesn't do that. He puts together facts for a story on a given day and his salary doesn't change. To me there's a big difference between an author telling a publisher how this or that is going to improve his book and a reporter telling his editor, "This is the truth."

Wendell Rawls, Jr. is assistant managing editor of The Atlanta Journal *and* Constitution.

Barbara Walters

'I think everyone worries about being the victim of a hatchet job'

I think most of the time reporters come in and say, "Look, I want to do a piece on you and I believe that I will be fair and that it will be a balanced piece. Do you want to do it?" Still, there is a kernel or truth in what Malcolm says. It's not that the reporter comes on and lies; it's that there is a tendency in doing articles, especially magazine profiles, to look for what's sensational.

At the moment two different authors whom I don't know are writing books about me. From what comes back to me from the people they have called, the intent of one of them clearly seems to be to write something critical, derogatory, scathing, because that's what sells. Scathing profiles seem to sell more than flattering ones. I myself don't like to be interviewed for a magazine article. I feel much more comfortable being interviewed by television people because even if the interview is edited, some of what you said gets on. And there isn't the same opportunity to work in things like "she said sarcastically" or "she said, with a grin" or "with a smirk," I think everyone worries about being the victim of a hatchet job.

One of the reasons my specials with celebrities have been a success as long as they have been is that these people know that after I've talked to them I'm not going to go behind their back and talk to their ex-husband or the manager they fired or whatever. I mean, what you see is what you get. And that's one of the reasons they do these interviews. Nobody has been tricked, nobody has been deceived.

There are times when you're editing an interview when you think, Oh, I know he's not going to like this, but I'm going to leave it in. I *have* to leave it in. That's why you try not to do interviews with friends. But this just isn't the same as what Malcolm is talking about. I mean I never lead someone to think I'm going to do a flattering piece and then do something very different. For example, I was invited to do an interview with the Duvaliers. My feeling is that they probably thought they were going to come out very well. But I had a lot of cancelled checks that showed thousands of dollars on their government expense accounts for personal jewelry, for example.

Now the interview did the Duvaliers absolutely no good; if anything, it did them harm. But I didn't come on and say to the Duvaliers, "Look, I'm your greatest admirer. I promise you, you're going to look good."

There was something Mrs. Duvalier said. She's very articulate, very attractive, but she came on and she said—you know, you just can't live in Port au Prince without air conditioning, which in that poverty-stricken country certainly didn't make her look very good. Well, so do you cut that out? Of course you don't. You don't even have to make a comment.

Barbara Walters is co-host of ABC News's 20/20 *and host of* The Barbara Walters Specials.

Kitty Kelley

'If you measured betrayal by a subject's disappointment you are engaging in a useless activity'

I can identify with Joe McGinniss's situation because I was in a similar one. My reputation, whatever it is, is built on unauthorized biographies. But I did a piece with Judith Campbell Exner for *People* magazine. We shared the payment fifty-fifty. I did the opposite of what McGinniss did with *his* subject—I didn't ingratiate myself with Mrs. Exner. I challenged her. I stood up to her. I fought her. I had editorial control and, when I turned that piece in, Mrs. Exner called *People* magazine and complained that I refused to put in things about her coming from a wonderful background and about her being a painter and living in this pretty house in Newport.

People magazine called me, and asked, "Why won't you say this just to make her feel better?" And I said, "Because I didn't see any pretty house in Newport and because she didn't show me any paintings."

Exner had a right to read what I wrote about her but she couldn't change it. The point of the piece was to say what the relationship was between this woman and the president of the United States and what his relationship was with the Mafia. That was the historic aspect of the story, as far as I was concerned. And I made that clear to Mrs. Exner. But when I would say, "I have to ask you this question," she would get angry and wouldn't answer it. But I don't think there was anything like betrayal in my dealings with Mrs. Exner. I made my position clear from the start.

Often, you know, the things that as a journalist you think might bring discomfort to a subject, nine times out of ten that isn't the thing at all; it's something you haven't even thought about. For instance, I wrote a piece for *The Washingtonian* about the wife of Jack Kent Cooke [the billionaire real estate man, publisher, and sports team owner]. She gave me taped interviews over seventeen months and provided all the pictures. And when the piece was published she was very upset. And the things that bothered her were things the editor and I were stunned about.

We thought she would object to seeing herself revealed in print as a woman who talks about going off to have abortions at her husband's insistence. But, no, those weren't the things that bothered her: What bothered her was being quoted directly, saying, "Yeah," The word "yeah." She said it wasn't ladylike.

So if you measured betrayal by a subject's disappointment in the way he's presented, I think you are engaging in a useless activity.

Kitty Kelly is a contributing editor of The Washingtonian *and the author of unauthorized biographies of Jacqueline Kennedy Onassis and Frank Sinatra.*

Thomas B. Morgan

'The whole issue of integrity centers on what a journalist puts on paper'

When I have defended McGinniss, because I basically feel McGinniss has won this argument, a lot of people say, "Oh, you're one of those people who believes the end justifies the means," and I say "No, I believe some ends justify some means. He wrote an honest book, he got his story." I think the means were justified by the end. Because to me the whole issue of integrity centers on what a journalist puts on paper, what he publishes in a magazine or a book.

As for my own journalistic means—and I don't say this with any pride—I have many times pretended to be amused by people who are not amusing, have nodded in agreement when I do not really agree, have asked ten irrelevant questions, knowing that the eleventh question is going to be a karate chop. I feel that morally defensible journalism is rarely, to paraphrase Hemingway, what you feel good about afterward; it is only that which makes you feel better than you would otherwise.

As a rule, the people I wrote about—and I must have written some forty or fifty profiles—were all in the public eye. Now people who present themselves to the public consciously project a certain image, and I always felt it was my job to deconstruct that image, so to speak. The whole thrust of most of my articles was: now we will test this or that person's image against reality. That's really what the New Journalism was all about.

The older form was typified by one of my favorite profiles, the one Lillian Ross did of Hemingway in *The New Yorker*. You don't feel her presence in that article. Then in the late fifties we nobodies, representing all the other nobodies, got access to the great, the famous, and the beautiful, and, as I say, we went into the business of deconstruction. The people we were writing about were people of power, people of substance, people of great fame, and some of them turned out to be, *in our opinion*—quite unworthy of it.

There were limits, self-imposed limits. For instance, I never wrote about a subject's sex life. As a matter of fact, I usually didn't write about a subject's married life at all. I felt that was private. I had a strong sense of what was private and what was public in a public person.

Thomas B. Morgan is a novelist and journalist whose profiles written in the late 1950s and early '60s are considered precursors of the New Journalism.

Lawrence Weschler

'The rhetorical tone of Malcolm's piece is straight out of *Les Liaisons Dangereuses*'

You know about all the weird JM business in this story, with Janet Malcolm writing about Joe McGinniss writing about Jeffrey MacDonald and herself having written about Jeffrey Masson and the piece being called "The Journalist and the Murderer"? Well, I was telling someone you could have called the piece *Les Jouissances Meurtrieres*—Deadly Pleasures or Murderous Orgasms—because the rhetorical tone of the piece is straight out of *Les Liaisons Dangereuses*. It is out of the Age of Reason, when people took perverse situations and derived from them immutable laws of human nature. Freud, of course, comes out of that tradition and Janet in turns gets a lot of her rhetorical tone from Freud.

The marquise in *Les Liaisons Dangereuses* has all these elaborate theories about the complicated power relationships in love, and she looks down on the ordinary people who think of love as something really quite simple. Janet's piece, in a way, is the sort of piece about journalism the marquise might have written.

The marquise's analysis is spellbinding. But in *Les Liaisons Dangereuses* it falls apart the minute real love enters the scene. Janet's thesis is spellbinding, too, and I want to emphasize that I think it's a remarkable piece of writing. But it falls apart in the same way. While the dynamic she describes is potential everywhere in journalism, it doesn't inevitably have to materialize. There are journalistic equivalents of love—compassion, engagement, conscience.

I am still on far more than talking terms with all the people that I have done profiles of. And I think I have portrayed some fairly complicated individuals, and portrayed them as both admirable and also demonical and all sorts of other things. My ideal for a profile is that I want it to be as if you were meeting this person. The highest thing that I aspire to is fairness and transparency. Even when I do a profile of somebody I am critical of I aspire to do it so fairly that he or she will say, "Yes, that's me."

I mean, I don't want to sound Pollyannaish. I'm all for doing devastating pieces, but I prefer to devastate institutions rather than people.

Now some people might feel that if you portray somebody transparently, you're betraying him. The marquise might feel that way, but I don't.

Let's say, for example, that I am describing someone who, as I get to know him, I realize is an alcoholic. I don't think I need to say the guy is an alcoholic. I can portray him in bars, talking about being thirsty, or do other things that will provide a kind of feeling about that, but not a label. Later on, if somebody says, "God, you know he is an alcoholic. You didn't say that.' I can say, "Well, go back and read the piece. It is there."

To label is in some cases to betray. Whereas if you show things I think you are being fair.

By the way, sometimes in my political reporting I get into situations directly analogous to what Janet was talking about. In fact, there was one particular incident during my reporting recently in Uruguay when I dealt with these issues in the body of the text, but ironically the paragraph was taken out in part because the editors at *The New Yorker* did not want to call further attention to the Janet drama. My article ran only two weeks after hers.

I was interviewing General Hugo Medina, the former junta head who was now the defense minister. He said that sometimes when they were interrogating people during the military dictatorship, they would do so "energetically."

And I said, "Energetically?"

And the way I originally wrote it is as follows: "He was silent for a moment, his smile steady. For him, this was clearly a game of cat and mouse. His smile horrified me, but presently I realized I'd begun smiling back (it seemed clear the interview had reached a crisis: either I was going to smile back, showing that I was the sort of man who understood these things or the interview was going to be abruptly over). So I smiled, and now I was doubly horrified that I was smiling. I'm sure he realized this, because he now smiled all the more, precisely at the way he'd gotten me to smile and how obviously horrified I was to be doing so. He swallowed me whole."

But, of course, when I write, "He swallowed me whole," I swallow *him* whole. So I have the last word. I get to have the Cheshire-cat grin.

Lawrence Weschler, a New Yorker *staff writer, is the author of* Shapinsky's Karma, Bogg's Bills, *and* Other True-Life Tales.

Tom Wolfe

If a reporter stays with a person or group long enough, they—reporter and subject—will develop a personal relationship of some sort, even if it is hostility. More often it will be friendship of some sort. For many reporters this presents a more formidable problem than penetrating the particular scene in the first place. They become stricken with a sense of guilt, responsibility, obligation. "I hold this man's reputation, his future, in my hands"—that becomes the frame of mind. They may begin to feel like voyeurs—"I have preyed upon this man's life, devoured it with my eyes, made no commitment myself, etc." People who become overly sensitive on this score should never take up the new style of journalism. They inevitably turn out second-rate work, biased in such banal ways that they embarrass even the subjects they think they are "protecting." A writer needs at least enough ego to believe that what he is doing as a writer is as important as what anyone he is writing about is doing and that therefore he shouldn't compromise his own work. If he doesn't believe that his own writing is one of the most important activities going on in contemporary civilization, then he ought to move on to something else he thinks is . . . become a welfare eligibility worker or a clean-investment counselor for the Unitarian Church or a noise abatement surveyor . . . .

From The New Journalism, *by Tom Wolfe*

Sara Davidson

'Sometimes your subject is horrified and it is just at one tiny little detail'

The way I read her, Malcolm was finally airing the dirty little secrets of journalism. What she describes is something all of us are aware of and struggle with and come to terms with. It's something I first encountered as a very young journalist, in my early twenties. I was always very uncomfortable when I would go to interview someone.

Everyone has a different style of setting their subjects at ease, so that they will then tell you what, as Tom Wolfe said, in their own best interest they should never tell you. My style was to be very sympathetic, to make the person feel that I was a friend—not by saying anything false but by smiling or laughing at jokes, by seeming to agree with what they said. When you spend enough time with someone a relationship develops; whether it is a relationship of trust or humor or liking each other or being wary of each other, something develops. Then you go back to your room and everything that developed in that relationship is set aside while you sit down to write the truth as you see it. And you kind of go into a different space, a different mind set. You are looking at it as a piece of writing—whether it is coherent, whether the paragraphs work, whether it flows. And of course you are interested in its accuracy. Then you finish the piece and it's printed. And your subject calls you up and is offended or horrified, and sometimes it is just at one tiny little detail.

A real turning point in my career as a reporter came when *Harper's Magazine* asked me to write a piece about Jacqueline Susann. I knew going into it that I had no particular respect for her writing or her way of promoting books. But it was interesting; she was the first person who made promoting a book into a big-time operation, and she did it like a science. She was very suspicious at the beginning because I was with *Harper's*. I said, "Well, my editor feels that what you have done is a really important publishing phenomenon and we would like to do a piece on it," and I basically convinced her to let me come along for a week on the promotion trail.

Then I wrote the piece. It wasn't my finest hour because she was such an easy target. Everything about her was mockable—from her false Korean hairpieces to the fact that when she sat next to me on the plane she would take these various pills, she called them wake-up pills, just like her characters in *Valley of the Dolls*. And her husband was making inane remarks and I wrote everything down and I wrote the article and I was hesitant about turning it in. I didn't feel very good about it.

Then the magazine sent Diane Arbus to take pictures of her. And she didn't know who Diane was, so she let her into her suite at the Beverly Hills Hotel and Diane took her usual kind of pictures, where everyone comes out looking like freaks. And everybody loved the piece—my agent, the editors—everybody thought it was wonderful, and I felt about two inches tall.

I made a decision at that point that I was not going to write about people and subjects toward whom I felt so negative at the outset. I was afraid, as a result, that my journalistic career might be over, because so much of my early work and so much of the journalistic work that was being done in the sixties was tinged with sarcasm, with the sense that the author was superior to the subject. I wanted to see if I could write an interesting, vibrant journalism that did not have that sarcastic, mocking base, and that also wasn't a sugary puff piece.

My first attempt to do this was a long piece I was commissioned to do for *Esquire* about Richard Alpert, who was calling himself Baba Ram Dass. I was very interested in Eastern mysticism and I thought the piece I finally wrote was the best thing I had done in my entire career. I turned it in and it became the first piece I had every written for a magazine that was rejected. The editor told me, "You will thank me for not publishing it. This guy's ideas are absolutely unintelligible and your willingness to embrace them makes you look foolish."

That's when I started thinking my career in journalism was over because here was this piece that wasn't sarcastic but an exploration of this phenomenon and what its appeal was, and the only magazine that liked it was *Ramparts*.

Very shortly after than I started writing *Loose Change*, and it was about friends, about people I loved and still do love. So, again, I was writing in the way I had decided I wanted to write—about people for whom I felt admiration or sympathy or took great interest in. And when *Loose Change* came out it was enormously painful for the two women who, along with me, were the focus of the book. We were able to remain friends, but there was a year in which it was really touch and go.

Those were the days when the women's movement was in full flower and the heart of the movement was personal confession. Women were writing for publication about very intimate parts of their lives. And it was in that spirit that I wrote *Loose Change*. When I sat with the women to do those interviews, even though the tape recorder was running, it felt like hanging out with a friend.

There was an unreality about it. I had never published a book, neither of the other women had ever been interviewed for a book, and then three years later the book comes out and there's this vast audience that none of us had anticipated. I had gone to considerable lengths to disguise the identities of my two friends, but anybody who knew them and knew that they knew me could figure out who they were. And people would stop them on the street and say, "God, I didn't know you got pregnant when you were sixteen." Or, "I didn't know you could never have an orgasm." Suddenly this very private material shared with a friend was on the pages of a book for everybody to read. And former husbands and former boyfriends of theirs were absolutely livid.

One of the women said to me, "I kind of see why they're so angry. I didn't ask [my former husband] for permission to talk about the years we spent together, and here it is for anybody to read." She felt she had betrayed her responsibility to the privacy of people who had been in her life.

Later I wrote a novel called *Friends of the Opposite Sex*, which was inspired by a work project I did with a friend. I created a fictional character who was completely different from this person and I created a dozen other fictional characters. Nobody in the book had a personal history similar to the personal histories of any of the people I knew.

And *still* people got furious. One didn't speak to me for four years. And the people who got angriest were writers themselves, which stunned me. So at this point, frankly, I have just come to feel, as one of my friends said to me, you write it as you see it, then publish and be damned.

Sara Davidson, whose books include Loose Change *and* Friends of the Opposite Sex, *is working on a book about baby boomers raising their children.*

Barry Michael Cooper

'Sometimes I'll shut off the tape when I think subjects could be hurting themselves inadvertently'

There is a bit of the con man in the journalist. You have to console, you have to empathize, you have to plead, to get to the truth. And if you don't, if you are just blunt, you can say something that totally turns your subject off and he won't talk to you again. It's happened to me.

But I don't consider that malicious lying. I'd call it slanted empathy—empathy with a purpose. And that purpose is that you are trying to get to a larger truth. You are trying to establish what the real story is.

A lot of times reporting is war; you have to do what you have to do to get a truth. Once you are adept at getting someone off guard, I think you become a good interviewer.

Because I am always open to having my mind changed, I am not being two-faced. Essentially, what I am trying to do is to gather information. I will give you a case in point. In my interview with Larry Davis [who was charged with injuring six police officers in a shootout in the Bronx, but acquitted of the most serious charges], I knew I wasn't betraying him, even though my story was very critical in the end. I didn't know what I was going to write when I spoke with him. And he was spinning *me* around. I was just trying to get information from the guy. And I empathized with him in a few instances and in others I came right out and said, "I don't believe you."

I think a lot of times when you are honest with your subject you can get a reaction that tells the truth about him. Davis got impatient with me because I kept saying, "Tell me details you haven't told anybody else. Tell me the real truth." He got mad at first and then he started laughing and he said, "Wait for the movie." And that was a telling remark and an important part of the story because it was Davis seeing himself as what he had become: a media image.

This doesn't mean that I will print anything—particularly when the subject might not realize what he's saying. Sometimes, whether with Arsenio Hall or with Latinos who lived near the kids accused of raping the jogger in Central Park, I'll shut off the tape when I think they could be hurting themselves inadvertently. I'll say something like, "I want you to understand that this tape isn't running. What was recorded is on the record, as we agreed, but are you sure you want to continue with this conversation?"

In almost every case they say yes. In black and Latino neighborhoods in particular, I feel I have to do this. I hate to say it, but to be very honest, a lot of white journalists and reporters come to the black neighborhoods and never explain these things to people and the people wind up getting hurt. I find that when you are very honest with your subject—about what you know and what you think you are going to do—nine times out of ten people in the inner city are very honest in response and they respect you in the end.

Barry Michael Cooper is a staff writer for The Village Voice *who has written about teenage drug gangs in Detroit and Baltimore and about the youths accused of the gang rape of a jogger in New York's Central Park this spring.*

David Halberstam

'Reporters by dint of their training project a kind of pseudo-intimacy'

Malcolm really hit on something germane but she has gone after it with a sledgehammer. I think "betrayal" is a very, very strong and ugly word. And to say that journalists, as a matter of course, do this is particularly offensive to anybody who was a reporter in the South, where many sources were very vulnerable to the white power structure, and reporters kept their trust; to anyone who was a reporter in Vietnam, where we often had sources who were enormously vulnerable to a powerful military machine, and where we kept the trust; or to colleagues of mine who worked with dissidents in the Soviet Union and kept the trust.

Now I think you can practice journalism well and do your job and be straight. But I also think there is the potential for an imbalance here. The reporter has dealt with hundreds of people in all kinds of situations. And reporters by dint of their training have a considerable amount of charm and grace and the ability to get people to talk—to project a kind of pseudo-intimacy. By contrast, in many cases far from public-domain journalism they are dealing with ordinary people who have never dealt with a reporter before. Perhaps the way to confront this is to think of members of your own family: How would you want them to be treated?

When I was in Vietnam, Horst Faas of the AP and I got these little name tags that we sewed on our fatigue jackets that said, "Halberstam, New York Times," and "Faas, AP." Most of the reporters began to do this. We didn't want anyone to speak to us with any misimpression of who we were.

I think the relationship is much easier with sources in the traditional public domain. Both sides tend to know the rules of the game and how to play it. Neil Sheehan tells a very accurate story in *A Bright Shining Lie* about John Vann, the lieutenant colonel who was certainly in the great tradition of sources in that he was using us to disseminate information and we were relying on him for what we believed was his realistic appraisal of what was happening.

There was a moment when he virtually got court martialed because of his relationship with me. He was being sent home and we gave him a small silver cigarette box at the airport and he and I walked across the tarmac to his plane and I said, "You know, I was always scared that when I was writing about you I would hurt you."

He gave me a quite cold, steely look and said, "You never hurt me any more than I wanted to be hurt."

I think Malcolm is writing about a new and important and contemporary phenomenon, a change in nonfiction letters, where the book is show-business driven and the reporter is not so much a reporter in the classic sense but an agent of Hollywood. I would call this mini-series journalism, where the journalist covers a murder in no small part because it has a potential mini-series in it.

The networks like these mini-series done off real life stories. And, of course, they want releases from the subjects. In this area Malcolm is quite right: the writer wants to ingratiate himself or herself with X or Y in order to get not just the story, but the release.

I think this leads to all kinds of abuses. Instead of normal access you need a new level of intimacy and a legal relationship. The murderer may be your literary partner.

McGinniss's relationship with MacDonald was bizarre, and I think it was unnecessary. Joe McGinniss is so talented he could have written a wonderful book without MacDonald being his best pal, roommate, and literary partner. Whether he could have gotten a legal agreement which released the mini-series is another thing. I am terribly bothered by a contract that gives a man like MacDonald 30 or 35 percent. I think Joe should be ashamed of himself.

David Halberstam, who won a Pulitzer Prize for his reporting from Vietnam in 1964 for The New York Times, *is the author of several books of nonfiction.*

Joan Didion

My only advantage as a reporter is that I am so physically small, so temperamentally unobtrusive, and so neurotically inarticulate that people tend to forget that my presence runs counter to their best interests. And it always does. That is one last thing to remember: *writers are always selling somebody out.*

From Slouching Toward Bethlehem, *by Joan Didion*

A.M. Rosenthal

'When people write about other people, they are really writing about themselves'

Malcolm is absolutely right when she says that the relationship between subject and reporter can very easily lead to shading the truth, even to falsehood, in order to draw people out. But when she says that this in *inevitable*, I don't think it is true. It may very well be true about *her*, because—it's a fascinating thing—I've found that very often when people talk or write about other people they are really talking or writing about themselves. They are looking at themselves. They are holding up a mirror.

The world of journalism is more complicated than she makes out. Nowadays we all tend to reduce journalism to cops-and-robbers stories or scandal stories or corruption stories. The purpose of journalism has come to be seen as to hit somebody hard. But there are other purposes—namely, to find out and inform. We've had our share of those destructive stories at the *Times*, but they are not, to my thinking, the be-all and end-all.

I know of occasions when the *Times* wouldn't print stories because we couldn't get them our way—honestly, through careful interviewing and fact-checking. The *Times* doesn't permit masquerading. You can get a lot of good stories by pretending to be a cop, but that isn't what journalism is supposed to do. Journalism is not a license to lie, steal, cheat. Quite the contrary.

If you have a story and you know it is going to hurt the person about whom you are writing, first you simply have to sit down and write the story as you think you ought to. Then, I have always said to people, including myself, reread the story and mentally substitute your own name in place of the subject's. If you do that you may think to yourself, This is a hell of a mean, tough story. It is going to make that person's wife or husband cry. Or the person will be severely damaged. But if you can say, still thinking as if you're the subject, "It's a fair story. He quoted me accurately. He didn't read thoughts into my head. He didn't pretend he knew more than he could know. He didn't use any anonymous pejorative quotes"—if you can say all this, then you say, "Well, okay. That is my story. Too bad for him"

A lot of things in Malcolm's articles were terribly interesting to me as a person who has been interviewed rather than as an interviewer. She makes it clear, she describes it—the person being interviewed almost always talks too much, says too much. I myself always say, "Well, I'll give you thirty minutes and that's it." I never stick to it though. And if you go on, sooner or later you will say things you probably didn't want to. And the interviewer just nods. So I recognize that: I have a tendency to rattle on when I am being interviewed.

She also explains very well how the interviewee wants the interviewer to see him as he sees himself. Which just doesn't happen, or seldom happens. I've found that if a person is hostile when he enters the room, he'll leave hostile. I've learned this, but I still don't quite believe it, so, for instance, I still agree to talk to people, or most people, who want to interview me, not just because I feel I have an obligation to, but also because I still believe I can persuade that person, make him see things as I do.

A.M. Rosenthal, the former executive editor of The New York Times, *is now a columnist for the* Times.

John Taylor

'A portrait could be done of us that is nothing more than an accumulation of our failings'

Malcolm's main assertion is so overly broad as to be ridiculous. But there are aspects of what she says that are worth considering seriously.

I think the journalist has a responsibility not to take advantage, for the sake of his own article, of the kind of human, weak, foolish things that we all do and say in the course of our lives. To make merciless fun of someone who has agreed to be profiled is, I think, very unfair. To me that is like breaching the sort of social contract you have entered into.

It's a different matter if you are doing a story about a person who hasn't cooperated; the same sort of social contract doesn't exist. This doesn't mean, however, that you are required to be totally ruthless and exploit every weakness and slip up on the part of your subject. After all, the point of writing a profile is to capture the spirit of the person and what that person is all about in unguarded moments. We are all vain and pompous and ridiculous and a portrait could be done of us that is nothing more than an accumulation of our failings. But that isn't what we are all about; there is more to all of use than the sum of our flaws.

John Taylor writes for New York *magazine; his article "Holier Than Thou," published in* New York *in March, explored Jeffrey Masson's libel suit against Janet Malcolm.*

Emily Yoffe

'A little part of me wanted to see if she could vindicate herself'

When I want people to talk to me I am sincerely interested. That's not my false self. That's me. I take notes with a notebook, so I'm always writing down everything the source is saying and, if I get behind, I will say, "Hold on a second. Let me get that," or "Say that again?" So there are constant reminders that what I am doing is going into print.

I do think we journalists have a lot of power and I don't think we can be careless about it. For example, I was working on this story about a doctor who was accused of causing the deaths of or permanent injury to several people. Everything I looked into led me to believe that she was dangerous and that the medical profession had abdicated its responsibility to stop her. Still, when I spent a day talking to her and listening to her side of the story, even though I didn't feel it held up, part of me identified with her. Here was a professional woman about my age—a little bit older so she had experienced more discrimination—and part of her defense was that this is a sexist world and these professional men don't want to see professional women as equals. I felt her humanity and I knew what the effect of my story would be.

During the negotiation to get her to agree to talk, I said I wanted to tell her side of the story. And I did, and it's there. I didn't say, "Talk to me because I will show how you've been mistreated."

Now, all the time she was talking to me, I thought, Boy, everything I have heard indicates to me that nothing you can possibly say is going to vindicate you. So why didn't I say this to her? Because, for one thing, a little part of me wanted to see if she *could* vindicate herself. And, for another, because if I started out with that, I probably wouldn't get her side of the story. But my questions to her made it very clear what I had discovered about her.

Once I did a story about congressional press secretaries. And one of the press secretaries I interviewed lost his job over the story. I felt absolutely awful; it was never my intention to have anyone lose his job and, in fact, he lost his job because he was being too honest about what it was he did and because it made his boss look like the publicity hound he was. It was a case where I was sitting there interviewing him, thinking, "I can't believe you are telling me this stuff." And he was very young and I was very young. I don't know if I'd warn him—through the tone of my questions—

about what he was saying. But then again, what he did was describe his job and I just wrote down what he told me. It was his boss who fired him—simply for telling the truth—not me.

Emily Yoffe is a senior editor of Texas Monthly.

Clarence Page

'It would be very sobering for journalists to put themselves in the shoes of the newsmaker'

I have been in the situation myself where I have been the subject of interviews and found my words being subjected to the interpretation of somebody else's journalism.

I think it would be very sobering for all journalists to go through that experience so they can put themselves in the shoes of the newsmaker. My personal experience had to do with my former wife's suicide two years after we were divorced. Her name was Leanita McLain; she was an editorial writer and columnist here at the *Chicago Tribune.*

It was quite a remarkable story—very sad and very shocking to a lot of people. I was interviewed by broadcast and print journalists locally and nationally. In some cases I kind of gritted my teeth as I was being interviewed because I did not have much trust in the reporter's abilities to tell the story straight. For example, some journalists really felt a crying need to find a reason why Leanita committed suicide. The fact is nobody knows; I don't think anybody knows why anybody commits suicide. All you can do is speculate. And journalists aren't supposed to speculate. Journalists are supposed to report.

One broadcast journalist said, "Friends attributed her suicide to the pressure of being a role model for other young blacks." I have yet to find a friend who said that. I think that sounded so good that the journalist just couldn't resist saying it.

The way the reporters conducted the interviews telegraphed to me the point they were trying to make. For example, the ones who just kept asking, "But didn't she feel real anger about white folks? Didn't she feel real depression about the state of Black America?" I just had to give answers that were honestly ambivalent like, "She may have said or written this or that, but as far as whether or not that contributed to her actual depression, I have no way of being able to say that." And, in fact, a good case could be made that her ability to express that in print may have eased her depression.

A candid journalist would accept those answers at face value and report them that way. Others would ignore the ambivalence and just use the part that supported their point. That is the sort of thing I could see some people interpreting as betrayal. I feel that it was just sloppy journalism.

Sometimes, though, you are in situations where you think, Boy, somebody just cooked his goose, I should be judicious with this. I am thinking about Jesse Jackson and the Hymietown quote. Evidently, Jesse thought it was off the record and the reporter interviewing him did not. That became a point of controversy. Other reporters told me afterwards that Jesse had talked that way to them or in their presence and they understood it was off the record so they didn't report it. I think it is a gray area.

If it had happened to me, I will tell you quite frankly—and this is Monday morning quarterbacking—I would ask Reverend Jackson for clarification. I would simply say, "Excuse me, Reverend. When you refer to Jews as 'Hymies' and to New York as 'Hymietown,' just exactly what do you mean by that?" In general, though, to tell you the truth, I have always been troubled by the notion that we should not run quotes past the newsmaker after we have interviewed them. But I always end up sticking by the idea that we should not.

Clarence Page is an editorial writer at the Chicago Tribune *and winner of a 1989 Pulitzer Prize for commentary.*

Dan Wakefield

'There is no way a reporter does not react personally to a subject'

Janet Malcolm raised important questions about issues that rightly make journalists uncomfortable, because there isn't any set of rules dealing with the ambiguous area of the personal interaction between journalist and subject. We try to adhere to fairness and objectivity but there is no way a reporter does not react personally to a subject, and this is bound to influence what is written. The recognition of this is really a taboo subject—as the overheated attacks on Ms. Malcolm seem to indicate.

Despite the purity of my own intentions, I probably have seduced people. I don't think I ever knowingly said to somebody, "Well, I really like you," and then did that person in. What I did was just not say anything at all. When I went to the South for the *Nation* and somebody asked me, "What is the *Nation*?" I didn't say, "It's a liberal magazine that thinks segregation is evil and is out to get you." What I said was, "It's a weekly and it's published in New York," and I remember that several people asked, "Is it anything like *Nation's Business*?" and I said, "I guess so, because they're both weeklies and they're both published in New York." That certainly wasn't playing straight.

When I think back to that period, to the business of reporting in the South, there was only one journalist I ever heard who played it straight and this was in a courthouse in the Mississippi delta.

Somebody in New York who wanted to get Murray Kempton in trouble had sent one of his columns to the sheriff and this guy with his gun belt strapped on comes over to Kempton and says, "Boy, are you the fellow who wrote this?" and Kempton said something like, "Yes, sir, I have been sent here to do you in. I have been sent here to make you look bad."

I was shocked. I had never before, and I have never since, heard anything like that and it was great.

There was a point where I stopped hedging around, even in the South, and here is what happened. I was down there on one of those segregation stories and I was staying at the local motel and I called up the guy who was the head of the White Citizens Council. He knew what the *Nation* was, so he said, "Why should I talk to you? That's like Gimbels talking to Macy's," and I said, "I'm going to write about this anyway, so you might as well talk to me. I would really like to know what you have to say." We talked on the phone for about ten minutes and he said. "Why don't you come on out here right now and we'll have a beer."

I went out to his house and I spent the whole afternoon talking to the guy. At certain points I would be listening and I would be writing things down, and sometimes I would use a seduction technique I had developed: if people were saying something I thought was really embarrassing I would try not to be writing at that moment, because I didn't want them to see my hand moving and clam up. I would wait until they said something kind of innocuous and that's when I would write down the awful thing they had said. So I would be there pausing and the Citizens Council guy would say, "Write that down, boy!" And he would be making what I considered outrageous statements about blacks, and I would say to myself, Oh, he wouldn't want this in print. But he would say, "Write that down, boy."

At any rate, my lesson from that and also from writing profiles was that basically everybody wants to be interviewed, no matter who you are or what your position is. Somehow there is some kind of honor or prestige involved in being interviewed. My experience was that everybody in the world was willing to talk and I was always amazed.

I honestly feel that if I were to go out to do a piece of journalism right now, I would do it better as a result of having read Malcolm's article. I think I could do my job with greater integrity, because the issues are staring you in the face and you can't just kind of let the ethical issue slide by. If I was interviewing the head of some White Citizens Council somewhere, for instance, I think I would really try to come closer to the Murray Kempton technique.

Dan Wakefield is a novelist, a journalist, and a screenwriter. His most recent book is Returning: A Spiritual Journey.

Jessica Mitford

'I make up ethics according to the situation'

I thought Malcolm's articles were marvelous. What came through was the whole awful business of McGinniss leading the convict to believe that he was absolutely on his side. I thought that was rotten, particularly while McGinniss was partaking of his hospitality. Which doesn't mean that I am against certain tactics. I make up ethics according to the situation. In fact, when I was teaching journalism and students would come to ask me about ethics, I would say, "Well, ethics have never been my strong point, so let's skip it."

A couple of examples: Is it ethical to ring up an undertaker and, when it isn't so say your mother is dying and you want to make some arrangements for the funeral? I did that quite a bit in gathering material for *The American Way of Death*. I don't see anything wrong in that at all.

Another example has to do with a story I was assigned but then decided not to write. This was years ago when Julie Andrews was making a film called *Hawaii*.

Anyway, I had met Julie Andrews when I was down in L.A. working on the film *The Loved One*. We used to have dinner together and I thought she was the most charming, unspoiled girl. Then *Redbook* asked me to stay with her in Hawaii for a week or so and do a profile.

George Roy Hill, the director of *Hawaii*, had recruited a lot of extras who were Fiji Islanders. At one point the company wanted to fire Hill because he had exceeded the budget by who knows how many million dollars. Well, the Fijians banded together and said they wouldn't work for any other director because Hill was the only person who had been decent to them and had not behaved like a racist. And, of course, the company had to capitulate.

I thought that was marvelous, but Julie was absolutely on the side of the company. Well, to me that was a very important issue. That was one thing; the other was that she told me a lot of very confidential things about her childhood and her psychoanalysis. She'd gone all Hollywood.

So I didn't do that profile. I didn't want to make it all rosy, especially because of this business with the Fiji Islanders. And yet I felt that, since I had accepted her hospitality, I couldn't really bad-mouth her.

You make decisions based on the importance of what you're doing weighed against the feelings of the person you are dealing with.

Jessica Mitford is the author of The American Way of Death *and* Poison Penmanship: The Gentle Art of Muckraking.

Mark Singer

'I struggle more with my own peculiar need to omit than with the idea that I could mug somebody.'

The thing I most resent about this whole controversy is that, by forcing us to defend ourselves against the charge that journalism is morally indefensible, it makes those of us who practice journalism sound like self-righteous jerks. And that's regrettable, because the issue in the abstract is really important and it is not one that I had ever seen discussed.

Here is how I relate to it. I get an actual, physical symptom when I go out to do reporting—a kind of butterflies-in-the-stomach feeling. And that's because I have to sort of barge in on somebody's life. Why I do it? Because, for me, it's fun to find something out. I don't see the process as heartless or cold-blooded but as an act of discovery. Whenever I write about someone at length, something approximating friendship arises. I get to know them, and I have learned things about them. I happen to be the sort of person who feels compelled—I hope not in a narcissistic way but out of a sense of fairness—to reveal part of myself to the person I am writing about. This comes in part from a genuine feeling that I am an invader, an intruder. Ultimately, with most of my subjects I come to feel that they have revealed too much of themselves. Let's say a person reveals that he or she is having an extramarital affair, and adds, "But please don't print that." What happens with me is that I wouldn't print it anyway. It bothers me that the subject even raises the issue.

My point is that, as a journalist, you're given a lot of responsibility. I'm aware that there are some people out there who abuse it. But I just don't believe that it is done universally. That notion is ridiculous.

As for myself, I am more bothered by my own peculiar need to omit and I struggle with that more than I do with the idea that I could mug somebody. Perhaps I could be accused of betraying the truth by protecting the subject, but as far as I'm concerned the word "betrayal" isn't relevant to what most journalists do.

Mark Singer is a staff writer at The New Yorker *and the author of* Funny Money *and* Mr. Personality.

Martin Gottlieb is Gannet Visiting Professor at Columbia's Graduate School of Journalism. Gottlieb has been editor-in-chief of The Village Voice *and a reporter at* The New York Times, *The New York Daily News and* The Record *of Hackensack, New Jersey.*

Who Decides What is News?
(Hint: It's not journalists)
Walter Karp, HARPER'S

Who decides what is news in America? The answer lies right on the surface, as obvious as Edgar Allen Poe's purloined letter. Reporters themselves know the answer, and talk of it candidly enough in their memoirs. Newspapers carry the answer in almost every news story they publish. What keeps us looking in the wrong direction, as I recently discovered while wading through an ample supply of media studies and books by working journalists, is a deep-seated linguistic habit. Instead of speaking of news, we speak of "the press" and "the media"—corporate entities with wealthy owners, paid employees, profits, holdings, forests in Canada, and, thinking of these, it is almost impossible not to speak of "the press" doing this or that—which is exactly what hides the purloined letter. For to say the press *does* things conceals the fundamental truth that the press, strictly speaking, can scarcely be said to do anything. It does not act, it is acted upon.

But wait. Is the American press not powerful and autonomous, famously accountable to no one? Is it not, as we so often hear, a "shadow government," a "second adversarial government," that exercises, in the words of former publisher Walter H. Annenberg, "at least as much power in determining the course of the republic as the executive, legislative, and judicial branches set forth in the Constitution"? Virtually every media study says so; the entire political spectrum says so. Our press is "imperial," says William Rusher, publisher of the *National Review*, a voice of the right. It exercises "perhaps the greatest power there [is] in politics: the power to define reality," says Mark Hertsgaard, a voice of the left. The leading media moguls are America's "powers that be," says David Halberstam, a voice of the center.

Yet a more accurate picture of the American press immediately becomes clear when one considers how and where reporters find the news. Very few newspaper stories are the result of reporters digging through files; poring over documents; or interviewing experts, dissenters, or ordinary people. The overwhelming majority of stories are based on official sources—on information provided by members of Congress, presidential aides, and other political insiders. A media critic named Leon V. Sigal discovered as much after analyzing 2,850 news stories that appeared in the *New York Times* and the *Washington Post* between 1949 and 1969. Nearly four out of five of these stories, he found, involved official sources. The first fact of American journalism is its overwhelming dependence on sources, mostly official, usually powerful. "Sources supply the sense and substance of the day's news. Sources provide the arguments, the rebuttals, the explanations, the criticism," as Theodore L. Glasser, a professor of journalism at the University of Minnesota, wrote in a 1984 issue of *Quill*, a journalist's journal. Powerful people not only make news by their deeds but also tell reporters what to think of those deeds, and the reporters then tell us. The dean of the Washington press corps, *Washington Post* columnist David Broder, notes that for many years the Associated Press covered the House of Representatives for scores of millions of Americans through daily chats with Rep. Howard W. Smith, a conservative Virginia Democrat who chaired the powerful Rules Committee.

Covering the White House means dancing daily attendance on the president's aides and spokesmen. "We're in small quarters with access to only a small number of official people, getting the same information. So we write similar stories and move on the same issues," says a White House correspondent interviewed in the book *The Washington Reporters* by Brookings Institute scholar Stephen Hess. A dozen great venues of power and policy—Defense Department, State Department, Justice Department, Central Intelligence, FBI, and so on—form the daily beats of small cliques of Washington reporters "whose primary exercise is collecting handout from those informational soup kitchens," as Alan Abelson once put it in *Barron's*.

Sources are nearly everything; journalists are nearly nothing. "Reporters are puppets. They simply respond to the pull of the most powerful strings," Lyndon Johnson once said. So pervasive is the passivity of the press that when a reporter actually looks for news on his or her own it is given a special name, "investigative journalism," to distinguish it from routine, passive "source journalism." It is investigative journalism that wins the professional honors, that makes what little history the American press ever makes, and that provides the misleading exception that proves the rule: The American press seldom investigates anything unless it is urged to by powerful sources.

"Exclusive" stories are less a sign of enterprise than a passive service to the powerful. When Reagan's State Department wanted to turn its latest policy line into news, department officials would make it an "exclusive" for Bernard Gwertzman of the *New York Times*, former State Department spokesman John Hughes recently recalled in the pages of *TV Guide*. Hughes could then count on "television's follow-up during the day," since TV news reporters commonly used the *Times* reporter as *their* source, knowing that he was the trusted vessel of the highest officials. It is a bitter irony of source journalism that the most esteemed journalists are actually the most servile. For it is by making themselves useful to the powerful that they gain access to the "best" sources.

So passive is the press that even seemingly bold "adversarial" stories often have the sanction of the highest officials. In December 1982, *Time* questioned President Reagan's queer mental equipment in a cover story entitled "How Reagan Decides." This was the first such story given prominence in a major news outlet. Yet the story's source, it turned out, was none other than the president's own White House aides, who thought it would help them club Reagan awake. Without White House approval the story would never have run, as the *Time* editor involved, Steve Smith, told Mark Hertsgaard, author of *On Bended Knee*, a book looking at the press's relationship with Reagan. Then, just five months later, with an economic summit conference scheduled for Colonial Williamsburg, the same White House aides set about repairing any damage to Reagan's image they might have inflicted in December. To make sure that the president's fictional competence would be the media's line at the conference, Reagan aid Michael Deaver invited Hedrick Smith, a star reporter at the *New York Times*, to lunch at the White House in order to press home a point. "A few days later the *Times* ran a page-one story on President Reagan's vigorous preparations for the summit," *The Wall Street Journal* reported. "But the real payoff was how Mr. Smith's piece set the tone for the television network' coverage of the summit. All of the TV broadcasts conveyed the image of a president firmly in charge." As Lyndon Johnson once remarked, "There is no such thing as an objective news story. There is always a private story behind the public story."

The private story behind our national news is usually found in Congress. The powerful sources generally are congressional leaders telling the press what to think and say about anything that happens in the capital and anyone who matters in the capital—excluding themselves. "This is a well-known 'secret' in the press corps: *Washington news is funneled through Capitol Hill*," notes Hess, rightly italicizing a secret well worth knowing: that congressional leaders make and unmake the nation's news.

As long as Congress made aid to El Salvador contingent on improvement in human rights, Salvadoran death squads and political crimes were news in America. To keep well supplied, the *New York Times* put an El Salvador-based investigative reporter on its staff. As soon as Congress lost interest in El Salvador, in 1982, the murderous regime virtually ceased to be news; the *Times* investigative reporter—Raymond Bonner—was promptly replaced by a reporter more amenable to the new congressional line. On matters of public consequence, it is not news editors but the powerful leaders of Congress who decide what is news and how it will be played.

Do Americans harbor a clear and distinct impression about national affairs? If we do, quite likely it comes from congressional leaders. "To a large extent, the reputations of presidents and their top political appointees—cabinet members, agency heads, etc.—are made or broken on Capitol Hill," David Broder notes in his memoirs. The preposterous "news" last spring that

President Bush was haplessly "adrift" six weeks after his inauguration was whispered to reporters by congressional Democrats and "Republican insiders"—leading politicians of both parties. That is surely an example of what Hertsgaard calls "the power to define reality," and just as surely, that power is not in the hands of the press. The myth of media power is nothing more than a political orthodoxy that conveniently masks the purloined truth: the professional politicians of Washington quietly shape our national news to suit their interests.

The passivity of the press is commonly—and mistakenly—called "objectivity," the ruling principle of American journalism ever since World War I put an end to the Progressive movement's revolt against oligarchy, monopoly, and privilege. The code of "objective journalism" is simplicity itself. In writing a news story a reporter is forbidden to comment on his or her own, or draw inferences on his or her own, or arrange facts too suggestively on his or her own. Yet even in the most "objective" story, as *New York Times* columnist Tom Wicker notes in his book *On Press*, nothing can be said, "unless some official-enough spokesman could be found to say so."

In 1984, the president and Congress were in agreement that a large voter turnout in El Salvador's presidential election would prove that "a step toward democracy" (as the *New York Times* would later characterize it) had been made, justifying massive aid to the ruling regime. The turnout proved large; the results were hailed and Congress voted increased military aid at once. In the vast farrago of El Salvador news, one fact was missing: voting in El Salvador is compulsory. What rule of objectivity kept the American press from telling us the simple, salient, objective fact that gave the lie to the whole futile policy? None.

On February 25, 1986, the *New York Times* reported, a presidential panel investigating the crash of the space shuttle *Challenger* proved incapable of explaining "the cause of the National Aeronautics and Space Administration's apparent insistence that the liftoff proceed on Jan. 28." According to the *Times*, the panel was baffled by NASA's "changed philosophy" of launch safety and puzzled by its sudden decision to put engineers "in the position of proving it was unsafe [to launch], instead of the other way around." What went unmentioned in the *Times* story of official bafflement was a fact formerly known to all—that on the night of the ill-fated launch President Reagan had planned to deliver a State of the Union paean to "America moving ahead" (in the words of a Reagan aide explaining why the speech was postponed). What rule of objectivity required the *Times* to omit mention of this "coincidence" and so shield its readers from the blatant dithering of a presidential panel? None, of course.

There is no public information more objective than an official government document, yet "few Washington news operations have their own facilities for serious documents research," notes Stephen Hess. Even when there is time, there is a "shunning of documents research." What rule of objectivity accounts for the shunning of unimpeachably objective sources? None, yet even the most newsworthy documents disappear into journalistic oblivion at the mere behest of the powerful.

On February 26, 1987, Reagan's "special review board," known as the Tower Commission, issued its long-awaited report on the Iran-contra scandal. An hour's reading revealed a president obsessively concerned with and intensely curious about Iran-contra matters, and determined to keep those matters in the hands of close personal advisers. To the press, however, the three members of the commission said exactly the opposite. In public statements, interviews, television appearances, and private meetings with leading editors, they insisted that Reagan was victimized by a "management style" that kept him in complete ignorance of everything blameworthy. That disgraceful lie, which in effect accused the president of his own defense, was endorsed at once by Democratic leaders and duly became the day's news, as if the report had never been written.

When the Iran-contra committees of Congress issued *their* report on the scandal, congressional leaders told the press at once that the whole sordid chapter was closed. The press did as instructed and closed the books at once on the most extraordinary abuse of power in presidential history. The report itself was ignored; a wealth of newsworthy information, with an impeccable source, sank into journalistic limbo. The report termed Reagan's private war against Nicaragua "a flagrant violation of the Appropriations Clause of the Constitution." But that grave charge, worthy of blazing head-lines, was scarcely noticed in the press and ignored entirely by the *New York Times*. What rule of journalism dictates such base servility to the powerful? No rule save the rule of the whip, which political powers crack over the press' head.

"Aggressive challenges to the official version of things" arouse what Tom Wicker calls "Establishment disapproval" and thus bring down the Establishment lash: "lost access, complaints to editors and publishers, social penalties, leaks to competitors, a variety of responses no one wants."

Punishments need not be severe. "Manipulating access," says Wicker, "is the most standard means of stroking and threatening, and by all odds the most effective, even against bold and inde-pendent reporters." If draconian methods are needed, political leaders do not scruple to use them. When David Halberstam's Vietnam reporting for the *New York Times* angered President Kennedy, his White House henchmen whispered to Wicker "the slander that Halberstam was a Saigon bar-hopper who had never been to the front." Twenty years later, Robert Parry's Central America re-porting for the Associated Press ran afoul of Reagan's State Department, which launched a whisper campaign against him, accusing Parry of being a Sandinista sympathizer disguised as a journalist. Slandered by State Department hatchet men, Parry discovered that, as he told Hertsgaard, "if you don't succumb to all that, you get the line from your editors that maybe they should take you off the story, since you seem to be pursuing a political agenda. When the government attacks you, even your colleagues begin to doubt your credibility."

Fearful of losing access, "beat reporters must often practice self-censorship," notes Herbert J. Gans, a sociologist who studied the media in his book *Deciding What's News*, "keeping their most sensational stories to themselves." For nearly 20 years reporters covered the FBI beat without re-porting that the bureau was engaged in massive domestic spying under the transparent guise of "counterintelligence." For 10 years reporters covered the CIA without reporting on the agency's own illicit domestic spying operation, although they surely had wind of it. Were the power of the media anything more than a shabby fiction, there might be some hope. In fact, there is none.

Self-serving politicians routinely bully and threaten the journalists employed by American publishers, hinder their work, and weaken their stories, yet almost no audible protest comes from the rich and powerful businessmen who ultimately control the U.S. media. The political whip that falls on reporters also falls on the media "powers that be." The publisher or broadcaster who allows his reporter to delve into the forbidden secrets of government or to challenge the official version of things, says Wicker, "is likely to be denounced for 'irresponsibility.'" His patriotism may be questioned, his advertisers roused against him. He can be held up to the public as a prime example of unelected elitist power. What effect all this would have on profits, the powers that be do not wait to find out. "All too many of [them] are fundamentally businessmen," says Wicker, and nothing scares more easily than a billion dollars.

CBS was the protagonist in one of the most telltale stories of political power and the national news media. On October 27, 1972, CBS News carried a 14-minute survey of the Watergate scan-dal as it stood after four months of brilliant investigative reporting by the *Washington Post*, which had dared treat the break-in as a crime to be solved, even *without official approval*. Elsewhere in the media, however, the story had been "bottled" up," notes Halberstam in his account of the episode. The rest of the press treated it as mere partisan bickering. Now, millions of CBS viewers heard Walter Cronkite describe in detail "charges of a high-level campaign of political sabotage and espionage apparently unparalleled in American history." A second installment on laundered money was scheduled to follow. At the White House, a coarse-minded scoundrel named Charles Colson was in charge of intimidating the press on behalf of the president. The day after the broadcast he telephoned the great power-that-be William S. Paley, board chairman of CBS, to hector and berate him. If Paley did not stop the second program, warned Colson, CBS would be stripped of the licenses to operate its five lucrative television stations. A frightened Paley tried his best to carry out the White House order. His newspeople, to their credit, resisted, and a compromise was reached: the second story on Watergate was cut nearly in half and substantially weakened.

That was not compliant enough for the White House, however. A few days after Nixon's re-election, Colson called up Paley's longtime lieutenant, Frank Stanton, to issue a still more sweeping threat: If CBS persisted in broadcasting hostile news about the president, the White House would ruin CBS on Wall Street and Madison Avenue, "We'll break your network," said tyranny's little henchman. Stanton suppressed his rage. Paley, deeply ashamed, told no one of Colson's threats. Why didn't these two media magnates turn those threats into news? What else is a free press for if not to hold powerful interests accountable to the people? Yet here was a president grossly abusing the power of his office (which was newsworthy in itself) in order to censor the news (which was doubly newsworthy) so that the electorate might not hold him accountable at the polls—which was newsworthy three times over.

In John Adams' thunderous words, a free people has "an indisputable, unalienable, indefeasible, divine right to that most dreaded and envied kind of knowledge, I mean, of the characters and conduct of their rulers." In this case, a ruler—Richard Nixon—was subverting our inalienable right to dreaded knowledge of him. Surely that was newsworthy, yet it didn't become news. It rarely does. The news media in America do not tell the American people that a political whip hangs over their head. That is *because* a political whip hangs over their head.

Why would Washington politicians want us to know that our knowledge of them comes from them? That is the kind of knowledge that awakens a sleeping people, that dissolves political myths and penetrates political disguises. To keep all such dreaded knowledge from the rest of us is the "information policy" of those who rule us. And so it is we hear, from the left as well as the right, the steady drone about the immense power of the media.

From the Salvadoran elections to the impeachable offenses documented in the shunned Iran-contra report, the private story behind every major non-story during the Reagan administration was the Democrats' tacit alliance with Reagan. It is this complicity, and not the Reagan administration's deft "management" of the news we hear so much about, that explains the press' submissiveness during the Reagan years. As usual, it was Congress that was managing the news.

"It was very hard to write stories raising questions about Reagan's policy, because the Democrats weren't playing the role of an opposition party," said AP's Parry, explaining to Hertsgaard why the press seemed to be "on bended knee" during the Reagan years. Members of Congress, said Leslie Stahl of CBS News, "don't want to criticize this beloved man." Even good stories fell flat, said Jonathan Kwitny, a *Wall Street Journal* reporter at the time, because "there is no opposition within the political system."

Even stories with eminent sources "just went nowhere" during the Reagan administration, because the political leadership in Congress, unwilling to challenge the president, refused to license them. For nearly six years New York Sen. Daniel Patrick Moynihan charged in numerous speeches and op-ed articles that our paralyzing budget deficits were deliberately created by President Reagan and his supporters. By slashing taxes, (not to mention doubling military spending), they planned from the start to "create a fiscal crisis," Moynihan said, and use that crisis to force the country against its will to reduce "social spending" for years to come. This indictment was truly grave: an American president conspiring to deceive the American people in order to achieve goals he would never have dared avow. The would-be source was impeccable: a prominent senator, respected, reflective, and uncommonly eloquent. Yet Moynihan's indictment never became news, not even in the spring of 1986, when David Stockman's astonishing memoirs substantiated that indictment in dense and vivid detail. Instead of turning the former budget director's memoirs into momentous news, Washington's press corps attacked Stockman for writing them. "In all this torrent of comment about the book," noted James Reston of the *New York Times*, "there is very little analysis of his indictment of the methods and men who are still deciding the nation's policies." Against a political establishment resolved to keep dreaded knowledge from the country, not even an eminent senator can make that knowledge news on his own.

For eight years the Democratic opposition had shielded from the public a feckless, lawless president with an appalling appetite for private power. That was *the* story of the Reagan years, and Washington journalists evidently knew it. Yet they never turned the collusive politics of the Democratic party into news. Incapable of enlightening the ruled without the consent of the rulers, the working press, the "star" reporters, the pundits, the sages, the columnists passed on to us, instead, the Democrats' mendacious drivel about the president's "Teflon shield." For eight years we saw the effects of a bipartisan political class in action, but the press did not show us that political class exercising its collective power, making things happen, contriving the appearances that were reported as news. It rarely does.

On May 8, 1969, the *New York Times* reported, none too conspicuously, that President Nixon was bombing a neutral country in Southeast Asia (Cambodia) and making elaborate efforts to conceal the fact from the American people. The Democratic Congress ignored the story completely, and without a congressional news license, it "dropped out of sight," as Wicker notes. The entire party establishment had tacitly rallied around a president who harbored dangerous ambitions. That was what happened, but it wasn't news. Instead of revealing a would-be tyrant in the White House and his congressional allies, the news showed the American people nothing. Think of it: nothing. Our divine right to dreaded knowledge of our rulers, far from being indefeasible, could scarcely have been said to exist.

Three and a half years later, the same congressional leaders decided to delve into the Watergate scandal, almost certainly to check Nixon's careening ambitions. Yet how many Americans know that a bipartisan political establishment had actually made such a decision, wise and prudent though it was? All too few. How many Americans believe instead that an "imperial press" had taken it upon itself to drive a president from office? All too many. And how many Americans have the faintest idea that "the earliest and most serious blow to Jimmy Carter's credibility as president," as Broder recently recalled, "came from the way Democrats in Congress had described to reporters their early disillusionment with the president"? This *fact* would have been dreaded knowledge, indeed, at the time: an "outsider" president, newly inaugurated, is assailed at once by his own party's "insiders." But that, too, never became news. Instead, the press reported the hostile jibes of Democratic leaders as if they were impartial judgments rather than blows struck in a political struggle. These Democratic party "insiders" probably altered the course of our history, but thanks to a servile and subjugated press, we scarcely knew they existed.

So it has continued day after day, decade after decade. Our rulers make the news, but they do not appear in the news, at least, not as they really are—not as a political class, a governing establishment, a body of leaders with great and pervasive powers, with deep, often dark, ambitions. By their subjugation of the press, the political powers in America have left the American people more deeply baffled by their own country's politics than any people on earth. Our public realm lies steeped in twilight, and we call that twilight news.

Editors' note: Walter Karp, who died unexpectedly at the age of 55 following surgery last summer in New York, was a Harper's Magazine *contributing editor. His articles and essays on politics, the press, and civil liberties appeared in many magazines. His* Harper's Magazine *article on the Reagan administration's efforts to undermine constitutional powers of Congress and the courts was selected as one of the Top Ten Censored Stories of 1985. He was also the author of* Liberty Under Siege: American Politics, 1976–1988 *and* The Politics of War. *He lived in New York with his wife and two children, and was a Phi Beta Kappa graduate of Columbia University.*

VII

Politics and Media

The instruments of mass communication in the modern world have an enormous potential for shaping politics. This is particularly obvious in totalitarian countries, where the media are under direct political control. Misuses in our own society are less obvious but real enough, and in recent years public concern has grown over such issues as political bias and control, the effect of media on campaigns and voting behavior, and the long-range implications for the political system.

The influence of media on politics need not be the result of misuse and abuse, however. The 1960 Kennedy/Nixon presidential debate, for example, demonstrated that political information relayed through different media may well result in different interpretations by the audience (Kennedy was perceived the winner by those watching the debate on television and Nixon was proclaimed the victor by those listening to radio). The type and quality of political coverage may also be influenced by the relationship between politicians and the press. For instance, much depends on the personality of the president and his underlying feelings about the press. Kennedy maintained good relations wit the press. Lyndon Johnson lost their trust. Nixon brought a longtime fear and distrust of the press into the White House and was treated accordingly. Reagan and the press had a long and substantial love affair.

The first two essays in this section examine how media influence politics as well as how politicians use the media. "Q/A: Walter Cronkite," reflects on the views of television's definitive anchorman and examines the impact of television on presidential politics over the past 30 years. According to Cronkite, conventions are now staged events for the television audience, and the presidents are selected based on their television appearances and media demeanor. This essay is complemented by the second piece in this section, "Campaign '88: TV Overdoses on the Inside Dope." This piece implies that contemporary politicians are all too familiar with how the press has transformed the political arena. Politicians have developed strategies to best take advantage of the form and forum of contemporary press coverage (and the free television air time and print exposure) without getting into issues or committing themselves to any particular stance. The final essay, "The President and the Press," examines the relationship between the press and President Bush and their respective efforts to control the flow of information. It points to the fact that a reporter's functions, and how well she or he serves those functions, is largely dependent on dancing to the President's tune.

Question/Answer, Walter Cronkite
Peter Ross Range, PANORAMA

The biggest news in television this year was not sitcom ratings, a new mini-series or corporate profits. It was an event that in ordinary circumstances would be noted merely with the awarding of a gold watch. It was the announced retirement of a 63-year-old man to take up lighter duties within his company.

But the departure from the *CBS Evening News* of Walter Cronkite, anchorman *extraordinaire* and national uncle, was no ordinary retirement. Among the affairs of state, it ranks closer to the abdication of a reigning but aging monarch in favor of the crown prince than to the election of a President, which, after all, occurs every four years. Cronkite first joined CBS in 1950, after nearly a decade of reporting from Europe for the United Press, and he has occupied the *CBS Evening News* anchor chair for 18 years. Since 1970, when CBS began outdrawing the other evening-news shows, Walter Cronkite has sat unchallenged on the throne of American newscasting. His retirement was not a matter of corporate change, but of national succession.

Yet before he passes the swivel anchor chair to Dan Rather, Cronkite still has a lot of news to cover, including the Republican and Democratic National Conventions scheduled in July and August. If Walter Cronkite's special place in the history of American television is rooted in re- membered moments—Presidential inaugurals, a Presidential assassination, the space program, the war in Vietnam—none stands out more than his coverage of the national political conventions for the last 28 years.

When the conventions open this summer in Detroit and New York, Cronkite for the last time will put in long hours at the anchor desk of our national political circuses (his endurance has earned him the nickname "Old Iron Pants" among his network colleagues). It will be Cronkite's eighth summer as convention anchorman—more than anyone else in the business. And, except for election night in November and, possibly, the inaugural in January, the conventions will be Cronkite's final marathon appearance before he goes into a semiretirement combination of news analysis, science reporting and a schedule that will leave a lot more time for his favorite pastime, sailing.

In his windowless, book-filled, cozy office in a corner of the *Evening News* studio at the CBS Broadcast Center in New York, Cronkite looks and sounds exactly like the man who shows up on the television screen every weeknight—except that his eyebrows have an unusually thick, bushy flare. His office is pleasantly professional: reference materials on the shelves, yachting memorabilia on the walls and some mild disorder on his desk. Yet beneath his unflappable appearance, Uncle Walter is obviously a hard-driving man who knows his role in American life.

To obtain his assessment of the impact of television on Presidential politics during the past three decades, Panorama sent free-lance writer Peter Ross Range to interview Cronkite. Their edited conversation:

Panorama: *Well, we're there again—1980, another quadrennial political circus lies ahead. Are you excited or does it seem kind of old hat?*

Cronkite: No, I can't say it's old hat. Each campaign and election has its own dynamics. I enjoy it more than almost anything else I have done in my journalism career. The political campaign is so basic to the vitality of the Nation that it is the most enjoyable thing I do. Nothing is more important to whether we survive and how we survive. It also has the human drama of winning and losing. You can hardly beat it for a long-running story.

Panorama: *What changes have you seen over the years?*

Cronkite: Between 1952 and 1960, there was a great deal of change. 1952 was really the last convention that was *not* organized for television. It was an old-fashioned convention. The first convention covered by television was in 1948 [in Philadelphia], but only in three markets, as I remember, and a very primitive kind of coverage. So it didn't make much impact.

But 1952 made an impact. The political parties realized how much of their workings they exposed to the camera. They realized that the lack of decorum of the convention was upsetting to many people who believed that these were serious delegates doing serious business. And while there were some serious delegates, there were a lot of people just along for the free ride and as a lark. This was perfectly clear when you saw them on the floor of the [Chicago] convention hall.

A lot of people weren't there during important speeches—you could see all the empty seats. Others virtually never went home. People were in their shirt sleeves or with their shirts off in that rather hot hall. The floor of the convention hall was filthy dirty, littered with papers. In fact, a fire was set in those papers.

It couldn't happen today because they don't stay in session that long. They try to pace the proceedings so they hit prime time at their best moments—they hope. And they have swept a lot of the functioning of the convention off the floor and into closed rooms. The conventions today are not really anything like they were in 1952.

Panorama: *It sounds like the difference between blood and guts and antiseptic politics.*

Cronkite: Yeah, but it's coming back a little bit. Participatory democracy has returned to the primary process with more primaries and caucuses this year. And I would expect to see an increase in the number of people pursuing special causes, who are not beholden in any way to the political organization, who are going to have their say on the convention floor. We saw this in the Democratic convention in 1976 [in New York]—and to a certain extent in their conventions in 1968 and 1972 [in Chicago and Miami].

What we have not seen since 1952 is a real wide-open convention in the sense of the candidate choice emerging from the convention itself. By the time of the first ballot, we're pretty sure who is going to win.

Panorama: *Some people say that television has replaced the political parties as a kind of preselector of candidates, that by convention time there is no selection role left.*

Cronkite: I don't accept that. What television has done is increase the number of primaries. This means there is less opportunity to manipulate the delegates once they're in the convention city. They're committed by law and by vote before they get there, so there isn't much chance for horse-trading.

Panorama: *If television's impact has been to increase the impact of the primaries, it has in turn made the conventions less dramatic and gripping. In that case, what's the need for gavel-to-gavel coverage?*

Cronkite: I would agree that some of the drama is gone. You don't have that human confrontation—a winner and a loser determined right there in front of your eyes. But the importance of having gavel-to-gavel coverage is that this is commercial television's one great opportunity—and once every four years is surely not too often—to present the public with one great civics lesson. This is the root, the core of our democratic process. Why not show it to the people? The mere exposure of it forces it into the public consciousness.

Panorama: *How does having so much coverage affect the role of the anchorman who has to sit there the whole time and make it go?*

Cronkite: Since the parties began sweeping as much as they could under the rug and behind closed doors, our role has changed. It used to be that you could pretty well tell the story with floor coverage.

Panorama: *You mean be the voice-over of an ongoing drama?*

Cronkite: Yeah. The main role was interpretive. What is meant by this motion just put to the floor? That was a matter of good reporters finding out what happened behind closed doors and being ready to reveal it when the moment broke.

Now our role is to get out where those meetings are taking place. We can be outside the closed door. We've been able to do that partly because of better equipment—we've got minicams. We don't have to depend simply on the reporters' eyes. And people appreciate the importance of television, so they are ready to talk, to get their side told.

And the more they have put behind closed doors, the more the parties have tried to dress up the open part of the convention. We have had to try to avoid being sucked into that. So when we get to this dull series of speeches on the American way, we just cut away to where the real action is—behind those closed doors.

Panorama: *To what extent, then, has a reporter's convention coverage become, like war to a military man, a star-maker or a star-breaker in the television business?*

Cronkite: Well, I suppose it certainly is a testing ground of a reporter's ability to work under fire and to be bright and attentive. And since there is a high viewing audience over the entire course of the event, it exposes people who can capture the public's imagination. But I don't think that anybody is going to be *made* a star who doesn't have the capability in the first place.

Panorama: *What about the time when you announced the promotion, on the air, of Michele Clark to full correspondent during the 1972 convention? Wasn't that choice of timing an example of star-making?*

Cronkite: She was a marvelous black reporter out of Chicago who was later killed in an airplane crash. Certainly if she hadn't made it on the convention floor, we would not have made a point of doing that.

Panorama: *It seemed a bit like making an MVP award at the World Series.*

Cronkite: I guess so, but I hate this line of reasoning and questioning. I don't like the comparison of a serious news-gathering effort to a show-business or sports event. It just really shouldn't be that way. We're trying to cover the darn story. We're trying to get the news out of it. I admit that in television we've got this problem of stars. I guess there's no way to beat that.

Panorama: *Speaking of your distaste for show-business comparisons, to what extent do you fulfill an entertainment function as a convention anchorman, especially during the dead time?*

Cronkite: I don't think we ever think of it as entertainment. Now, of course, we must throughout the convention—or any news broadcast—do what we can to make it interesting. But there's a difference between being interesting and being entertaining, as far as I am concerned.

Panorama: *Technically speaking, what are some of the special burdens on the anchorman, especially when he comes up against dead time? And how do you get through them?*

Cronkite: Well, it hasn't been nearly as much of a problem in the last several conventions as it certainly was in 1952 and 1956. By 1960, we were getting our organization together and understanding what it really took to do the convention properly. Before then, the burden was really on the anchorperson.

Now, you have all this support machinery. You have hundreds of people out there gathering news and information. We're loaded with reports from around town, from our correspondents in the field, with background reports, old film and so forth. We have more than we can ever get on the air. The anchorperson isn't stuck with long fill periods.

I still want to be ready in case they don't have something—and there are occasions when we suddenly don't have anything that is appropriate or won't fit the time, sometimes just a minute and a half or two minutes.

So I study—and have ever since I got into this business—the history of American politics. And because it is such a habit, I rewrite a book-length thing for myself each year because that's the way I remember things best.

Panorama: *What is it called?*

Cronkite: My desk book. It is thick with loose-leaf pages, some of them are yellow with age now. I scarcely ever turn to it, except maybe for some past dates, but that's very rare. What happens is, in doing the homework, the information is planted in my mind and items come to me without needing to go to the book.

Panorama: *In the matter of pacing and flow, of inserting items and staying with the floor, how much of this is decided by you and how much by the producers and directors?*

Cronkite: I think I probably participate a great deal more in that than my colleagues at the other networks do. I always have. I've got a kind of managing-editor mentality. I think I see things and detect trends about as fast as anybody in our shop. I suspect that the anchorperson knows more about what's going on throughout the operation, and particularly on the floor of the convention, than anybody else in all of CBS. Everybody else is concerned with other things and they're not listening at all times to the program, even in the control room. They're discussing things taking place in the control room, where they're going next, setting up another camera.

Panorama: *You concentrate on the incoming reports?*

Cronkite: I'm hearing every word, because I may want to refer to it. Simultaneously I'm listening to the floor, to the podium. Now, of course, I don't listen very carefully to a speech about how we ought to observe Mother's Day next year. But I'm following the thread throughout. Frequently I'm the one who alerts them in the control room: "Did you just hear that? We ought to get something on such-and-such."

Panorama: *Do they try to keep the chatter in your earplugs down?*

Cronkite: They don't chatter to me. I got rid of that a few years ago. In the early days I wore double earphones with the on-the-air program coming in one and the podium speaker—whether he was on the air or not—coming in the other. I also had an interrupt line so the producer could tell me what to do next.

But that's not the way it ought to be done. So instead, I've got a guy whose hand sometimes appears on television putting something on my desk. He is usually buried in a little hole down at my right knee. He passes me notes from the producer as to where they'd like to go next. Rather than get it in the ear, I get a little note so I can concentrate on what's coming in and don't have to hear chatter and interruptions.

Panorama: *Speaking historically for a moment, do you regret commenting during the tumultuous 1968 Democratic convention in Chicago that perhaps CBS ought to pack up its gear and go home?*

Cronkite: No. I don't regret it. I don't regret my visceral reaction when they punched Dan Rather and I said, "We've got a bunch of thugs down here." I think there are times when you're permitted to drop your cool.

Panorama: *Do you feel that 1968 convention was a turning point for political conventions as well as TV?*

Cronkite: No, not really. Chicago in 1968 was a rather perfect reflection of the mood of the people and the times. The violent reaction of Mayor Richard Daley's police wasn't because of the politicians. It was Daley's operation of a convention. That became a marvelous demonstration of what political machines can't get by with in the days of television. That brought an end, I would think, forever to that kind of operation. Even the galleries had been trucked in there a couple hours before the convention session with signs saying "We Love Daley." They were rather obvious when you put them on television.

Panorama: *Another point of history: in 1964, you suffered the humiliation of being removed from the anchor seat after the Republican convention in favor of Roger Mudd and Robert Trout for the Democratic convention. They were supposed to challenge Chet Huntley and David Brinkley over at NBC for the ratings. How do you look back on that experience?*

Cronkite: Well, it wasn't all that humiliating, to tell you the truth. I said then and I say now, "It's their candy store." I think they ought to be entitled to fire somebody if they want to.

Panorama: *But what does it tell us about television news and the ratings game?*

Cronkite: Well, undoubtedly, it was all due to ratings. But, again, if you can't appeal to the public with your reporting, I suppose you ought to make a change. That's the most instantaneous vote I know—acceptance. In the case of the 1964 Democratic convention, however, I always felt that I was something of a scapegoat for a disaster. It was the result of Fred Friendly coming in at the last minute and overturning all of our previous procedures in the belief that he alone knew how it should be run. But that was his prerogative—he was head of the news department. It just turned out that none of those things worked.

I do not doubt for one minute that my performance in '64 was the worst I've ever given in that kind of role, because I was totally handicapped. Nothing was working the way it should. The camera setup was impossible. The information flow to me was poor. They separated me from the person I had giving me the information as to where we should go next.

Panorama: *Returning to this year's election, how has television changed the Presidential candidates and the way a campaign is covered?*

Cronkite: Now we demand, of course, that a person make a good appearance on television. I don't think that's bad. Television is the most powerful force we've ever known to reach the people, to rally the people, to move the people. We ought to select a President partially on the ground that he is able to use this medium to do that. That's being a leader today. It's being able to reach out to every home in America through this magnificent box.

Panorama: *The box has replaced the campaign stumps of, say, Lincoln and Douglas in 1858 and 1860?*

Cronkite: Yes, it has. The number of persons, the percentage of the electorate that heard the Lincoln-Douglas debates or saw any candidate before radio and television was really infinitesimal. People were mostly there for the historical reason of saying, "I was there that day." They couldn't really see or hear them.

I saw that myself with whistle stops when I was a press reporter. You'd run to the back of the train, but you were so far away, even as a reporter, you couldn't see the guy, let alone hear him. Even with a P.A. system.

I think one of the advantages of this terrible burden of so many primaries is that the candidate does learn an awful lot about the country. Not just the people, but the issues within each state. I would think that rather than less use of television, more use of television would be a good way to conduct our campaigns in the future. Maybe with cable TV and the increased number of channels available, candidates can spend more time on television and less time in buses and automobile motorcades and airplanes.

I think a better mix might be productive. If television could cover an open-forum question-and-answer period in a school auditorium, a candidate could do two or three of those a day instead of going to the factory gate to shake hands or to a tea party to talk nothings. I would think there would be an improvement in his ability to talk issues.

Panorama: *As it is, by going to the factory gate or the farmer's corncrib, the candidate is doing symbolic acts for the television audience. Did the print medium ever quite function this way?*

Cronkite: Oh, sure it did! Remember the front-page picture of the guy at the corncrib or the guy wearing the funny hat? Television has not done a damned thing that has not been done by print. It's just a higher impact medium, that's all. National television replaces the local newspaper, local news decisions. Where before you had 1700 editors and that picture might make it onto 20 or 30 front pages, today you try to get on the network newscast of that local station.

Panorama: *Thereby reducing the 1700 editors to three networks?*

Cronkite: That's Spiro Agnew's "handful of willful men."

Panorama: *Is it true?*

Cronkite: Certainly it's a handful. Less than a handful. But I don't know any other way to do it. You can't have a plebiscite as to what ought to be on the newscast each night. Of course, it goes to a vote of the people in a sense. If they don't approve, they'll turn you off.

Panorama: *What are the implications for the politician who then has a much smaller number of editorial judgments to satisfy?*

Cronkite: But, remember, he's seeking delegates state by state. During the primaries, he's still got to appeal to the local station. Maybe that's one reason the primary system has become so popular over the last few years.

Panorama: *It has been argued that television has transformed all our politicians into media creatures. One visitor to Congress recently characterized them as "a roomful of local anchormen." Does this suggestion offend you?*

Cronkite: I don't know if that's bad. To pick a person who is able to reach the people better seems to me a rather good test of who ought eventually to be in the job. It's unfortunate if it means that you lose some real thinkers who just do not have the ability to communicate. But then they shouldn't be in positions where communication is important. Let them be back-room boys.

Panorama: *Or maybe they just don't have the ability to communicate in 45 seconds, which is as long as most news clips go.*

Cronkite: Well, that's probably a fair criticism. It's worrisome, too. That's why I'd like to see an expanded use of television rather than cutting it back.

Panorama: *Returning to the conventions, can you recall any special triumphs or botch-ups over the years?*

Cronkite: Oh, gosh, there are some every hour, some little thing that you don't anticipate.

I remember one during the 1972 McGovern convention in Miami. The South Carolina delegation had begun a very complicated political maneuver regarding women's representation. It had become a major vote because the outcome looked like it might influence whether McGovern got nominated or not. And we were really a little behind on it. Our reporter at the hotel had never gotten through to me—a blockage that was unfortunate.

Panorama: *What was the problem?*

Cronkite: Well, Mike Wallace got Gloria Steinem on the floor of the convention to try to explain what was going on. And we were using these hip-flask mikes that were cutting in and out, [their transmissions] breaking up in some parts of the hall. Mike and Gloria were surrounded by a lot of people making a lot of noise and Gloria was declaiming in great detail. It was just a ridiculous scene. And I wasn't able to understand it.

When they cut back to me, I was kind of laughing and said "Mike, did you understand that?" And Mike said, "Boy, I don't think I did. Well, thank you, Gloria."

Then some male reporter for The Washington Post who was trying to make points as a feminist wrote a piece about the chauvinism of Walter Cronkite and Mike Wallace. And none of the hothead feminists had complained until they read his piece. Then the mail just besieged us. Gloria wasn't speaking to me. I had to take her to lunch in New York to try to convince her that I wasn't a male chauvinist pig.

Panorama: *Finally, can you give us a more detailed idea of your plans after you retire from the CBS Evening News anchor desk next spring?*

Cronkite: Listen, I'm a guy who is opposed to these "media events." I don't believe in that phrase. And this story of my retirement is a media event.

Panorama: *It's more than that, isn't it? With 12 million households watching you every night, you know why they're interested.*

Cronkite: Oh, sure, I understand the interest. In any case, I'm going to stay with CBS. And I'll definitely do the science series, *Universe.*

And I hope to appear on the *Evening News* quite a lot. I'd like to be available either at my suggestion or theirs, when the big story breaks, to scoot out on it and do a kind of on-the-scene analysis. Not an in-office thing. I don't want to be a pundit. But I'm pretty good at doing first-person impressions of stories. Three Mile Island, for instance. What's it really like to be there? Let somebody else handle the news conference, the hard stuff. I'll do the old sidebar bit, you know.

Panorama: *And the idea of joining the U.S. Senate is on ice?*

Cronkite: Yes. I'll go if appointed . . . and nobody's going to appoint me.

Campaign '88: TV Overdoses
on the Inside Dope
William Boot, COLUMBIA JOURNALISM REVIEW

The Bush era is nearly upon us and the shoal of political correspondents is migrating rapidly toward the feeding grounds of a new administration. All eyes are on the future, but I'm going to ask you to cast your mind back several months to October 5, 1988. That evening the networks aired live from Omaha, the Dan Quayle-Lloyd Bentsen debate. Quayle, you may recall, faltered repeatedly when asked what he would do if he had to take over as president; he spewed out his programmed answers and, after Bentsen hit him with "You're no Jack Kennedy," just seemed to deflate. Even some loyal Republicans were made queasy by his performance—and so, evidently, was the public. By a margin of 51 to 27 percent, 600 people whom ABC polled that night deemed Quayle the loser and about half said he was unfit to assume the presidency.

Curiously enough, here's what some prominent TV commentators told the nation, just after the debate ended but before the poll results were announced, about Quayle's performance:
- "He did a credible job . . . Most of the time he performed well"—Jeff Greenfield, ABC.
- "The bar over which Senator Dan Quayle had to get was pretty low. It seemed to me that he did that. He was calm. He marshaled his arguments rather well"—Dan Rather
- "No one tonight scored a decisive victory"—Tom Brokaw, NBC.
- "No, but I think Dan Quayle did himself a little bit of good. . . . If you were undecided . . . I think you might feel that Dan Quayle is not the kind of hopeless lightweight the Democrats have said he is"— John Chancellor, NBC, responding to Brokaw.

What is astonishing is not so much the networks' stretching to be charitable. It's that these were the same news organizations that just a few weeks earlier had been in frenzied pursuit of Quayle, sharply questioning his record and qualifications. They never got satisfactory answers, but, for reasons I'll touch on shortly, they called off the chase.

And this was by no means the only sharp turn of 1988. As I was monitoring the campaign coverage last fall, with a focus on the networks, news organizations often darted in tandem, first one way, then another; they turned suddenly toward George Bush's Dukakis-bashing rhetoric and away from Michael Dukakis's blander message; toward the idea that Bush had locked up the presidency (e.g., ABC ran a lengthy lead story on October 12 showing Bush with a colossal electoral lead, and the *Houston Chronicle* wrote on October 15 of a "growing perception that . . . Bush will be the inevitable victor "), then away from it (e.g., ABC, on October 30, reported that Bush aides were nervous because of an apparent Dukakis surge, and *Time*, on October 31, cited arguments that Dukakis "has the longshot chance to win"), then toward it again (e.g., GOP THOUGHTS TURN TO LANDSLIDE—*Richmond Times–Dispatch*, November 3; "*What might have been . . . .* should be the Democrats' song of lamentation for this year's campaign"—*Time*, November 7).

Most intriguingly, they turned away from tough scrutiny of candidates' conduct (Gary Hart and Joe Biden must have wondered why it didn't happen sooner) and toward "inside dope" stories on candidates' strategies for prevailing on the all-important TV screen. This last topic, television, led the networks into a hall of mirrors where they lost their bearings and began darting toward their own reflections. More about this hall of mirrors a little later.

How can one account for all these sudden shots in direction? Seeking some scholarly insight, I turned to Dr. Richard Rosenblatt. He is an ichthyologist at the Scripps Institution of Oceanography in La Jolla, California, and knows a lot about group behavior ("schooling") in fish. Why was it, I asked him, that when schools change direction they seem to do so as one organism, each fish turning almost simultaneously? Rosenblatt explained that the creatures are "oriented on one another"—they use their eyes and a special organ sensitive to water movement (the lateral line) to keep tabs on their fellows and copy their every movement reflexively. "If the first fish turns, everybody turns," he said. "Any fish that gets out of the school is vulnerable prey. There's safety in numbers." For those of us who have covered national presidential campaigns, Rosenblatt's account may sound a bit like a job description.

The top ichthyologists of the 1988 campaign were, of course, Bush's men—campaign chiefs James Baker, Lee Atwater, and media guru Roger Ailes. These three were far more effective than Dukakis's team in exploiting the reporters' safety-in-numbers instinct. They used negative reinforcement and other behavior modification techniques to entice the schooling journalists into their corner. They stirred the water and sprinkled food in just the right way to make the fish turn in useful directions at strategic moments.

Negative reinforcement included the notorious "Huntington massacre," just after the Republican convention, in which reporters clamoring to question Quayle finally were permitted to do so—in his home town, over a live microphone, before a loudly booing pro-Quayle crowd—and were made to look like bullies. After Huntington, reporters faced booing crowds frequently at stops along the Bush-Quayle campaign trail. The pursuit of Quayle slackened, perhaps not coincidentally, and by the time of the debate with Bentsen he was being given the benefit of a great many doubts. (For the record, James Baker denied that Huntington was an anti-press setup.)

Among other techniques employed by Ailes and Baker were tricks perfected by Michael Deaver & Co. in the Reagan campaigns of 1980 and 1984. Here (encapsulated in a sound-bite, as is only fitting) is the Deaver approach—"Read my lips: No access. Daily visuals. Simple message. See Dick clap. See Jane cheer. See Dick and Jane vote Republican." Adhering religiously to that credo, Bush's handlers kept reporters at such a distance from the candidate that some resorted to binoculars and megaphones. And at least once a day they cast their bait—carefully staged visuals concocted to exploit TV's hunger for lively pictures. With the bait came a hook, the so-called message of the day, usually a barbed one-line about Dukakis. With astonishing frequency, the networks bit, the hook was set, and TV was running with the Republican message.

Here's an example of just how well the Republican technique worked:

Labor Day, September 5. NBC's Lisa Myers reports on Bush campaigning in Disneyland. We see Bush surrounded by U.S. Olympic athletes and folks dressed up like Disney cartoon characters. He awards gold medals in the shape of Mickey Mouse heads to the Seoul-bound athletes. Cut to scene of Bush at lectern, with Mickey Mouse dressed in red-white-and-blue Uncle Sam garb standing beside him.

Myers (voice-over): "Sometimes it pays to be vice-president!"

Bush (to athletes): "You're representing the country of the little guy. No matter what the circumstances of your birth and background, you can go anywhere and do anything."

Cut to the Andover-Yale-Skull-and-Bones man, sleeves rolled up, unloading fish at a San Diego cannery. (Myers: "To identify with the little guy.") They cut to Bush at lectern, San Diego Harbor as a backdrop, firing a salvo at Dukakis: "I wouldn't be surprised if he thinks that a naval exercise is something you find in Jane Fonda's workout book."

Note: No press conference, no access, yet Bush images compliantly mongered, along with the scripted messages: Bush is no elitist but Dukakis is an exotic lefty.

The Dukakis people were simply no match in this contest to reel in "free media." Dukakis's incredible slowness in responding to Bush's attacks left him mauled in the battle of the sound-bites. Ultimately, Dukakis did hit back and even emulated Bush's p.r. approach to some extent, cutting back on press conferences, staging more events purely to be photographed (e.g., he staged a cross-country trip for the sole purpose of being photographed viewing Yellowstone Part forest fires), and pounding home a simple-minded slogan: "We're on your side." But the Democrat never put himself totally off limits to reporters, even when he was politically wounded. This openness drew some hungry predators, as illustrated rather poignantly by the following case, courtesy of ABC:

October 19. We see the governor in shirt sleeves speaking at an outdoor rally in Illinois. He de-nounces the Bush people for purveying "garbage . . . political garbage"—referring to a brochure declaring that criminals such as the notorious Massachusetts rapist-on-furlough Willie Horton would be voting for Dukakis.

Cut to scene on a campaign motorcade bus, where we see Dukakis struggling ineffectually to close his window. It seems that Sam Donaldson and crew have been given access to the candidate's own bus. (That alone would have constituted news had it occurred on the Bush campaign.) Donaldson: "Did you see in the paper that Willie Horton said if he could vote he would vote for you?" Dukakis (face impas-sive, eyes averted from Donaldson, still struggling with window): "He can't vote, Sam."

Dukakis had tried to go on the attack at his rally, but by responding to Donaldson he slumped back on the defensive. He had "stepped on his message," as they say in today's politics.

This was a mistake that Roger Ailes had coached Bush to avoid like poison. During Bush's fa-mous foray to Boston Harbor to blast Dukakis as a pollution-coddler, reporters sought to question the vice-president on his own environmental record. Bush brushed them off with a frankness border-ing on gall: "We're not taking any question. . . . We want the message to be on what I got to say later." He felt confident he could get away with it, and he did.

One can't blame Donaldson for asking Dukakis the Willie Horton question. But more broadly speaking one has to question the perverse pattern of rewarding candidates who refuse to answer questions, while circling the more accessible ones like sharks. Should the networks have been airing Bush's visuals and sound-bites, which were tantamount to free campaign commercials, while he was hiding from reporters? It isn't as if television was unprepared for the likes of Baker and Ailes in 1988. There had been a great deal of soul-searching in the news business following 1984, when the insulated Reagan team had spun its hallucinations so easily. There were, in fact, some major im-provements in 1988. Among other things, the networks seemed to devote a little more airtime to campaign issues of substance such as the deficit; they painstakingly, if sometimes belatedly, cor-rected misstatements made by the candidates during the debates; by the end of the race, they were even running point-by-point rebuttals of the most egregiously misleading campaign ads. CNN, for its part, transcended television's traditional superficiality, at least for a half-hour a day, with its *Inside Politics '88* program. But these improvements, welcome though they were, came through rather faintly in the daily din of sound-bites and visuals. As Garrick Utley put it in an October 23 NBC *Sunday Today* report on campaign coverage: "It is the candidate's message, visually and ver-bally, which has the greatest impact."

The most astonishing thing about campaign coverage in 1988 was that so much of it was *about* media manipulation—highly introspective and self-critical. "Is TV doing its job. . . . What is hap-pening here? Is it reporting or a political commercial or both?" asked Utley. Tom Brokaw, in a November 6 special, asked whether the Republican media chieftains had been exploiting the net-works. ABC's Ted Koppel devoted a full hour to press performance a day after the election, etc. (Major newspapers also weighed in: TV MANIPULATION IN THE '88 CAMPAIGN, POLITICS GETS THE UPPER HAND—*Boston Globe*, October 24; FRUSTRATED REPORTERS ADD MEGAPHONES, BINOCULARS TO NOTEPADS—*Washington Post*, November 2; etc.)

This news-media hand-wringing ran in cycles: staged events were compliantly aired, then they were exposed as manipulative, then a new round of reports on visuals was aired, and then these, too, were picked apart or derided on the air. Frequently this bizarre cycle was repeated in a single rep, with the correspondent mongering a campaign's concocted images but at the same time stressing such terms as "backdrop," "choreographed," and "staged." Consider Brit Hume's October 28 ABC report on a Bush visit to a California Highway Patrol Academy:

We see a police car skidding dramatically in a demonstration of high-speed-chase training. Cut to a watchful Bush. We see patrol cars driving in formation. Cut to Bush. Then cut to new scene of candi-date surrounded by cheering uniformed cops, receiving plaque from beefy officer. Officer: "America's number one crimefighter award!" Finally, we hear Bush's attack line: "The [Democratic] leadership, much of it, is a remnant of the sixties, the New Left, those campus radicals. . . ."

Meanwhile, in his voice-over, Hume all but mocks the contrived proceedings: "Bush didn't get to go to Disneyland today, but, given the enthusiasm he's shown for law enforcement in this campaign, he probably thought the place he did go was even better . . . . Bush didn't go on the rides they have here, but he watched with the obvious interest and later he got some prizes—a jacket and a cap, which he didn't put on, and a plaque with a billy club on it."

Hume was evidently trying to function as a kind of consumer's warning label (Caution: what you're seeing is a setup), but as an old TV pro he must know that verbal disclaimers of this sort are close to futile. Mark Crispin Miller of Johns Hopkins University said recently (*Sunday Today*, October 23): "A visual image is always going to overwhelm a mere voice that accompanies it—the pictures will win out, and that's something that the most adept handlers really understand. I'm afraid not enough TV reporters understand. . . ." Miller later told me, "These correspondents seem to think that their discussion is so articulate that it will erase the effects of the footage." He appears to be right about the impact of visuals. After my first viewing of the Bush-cops broadcast, the main thing that stayed in my mind was not Hume's sarcasm; it was the image of a speeding police car and a quick cut to the vice-president—an almost subliminal linkage between the candidate and the forces of justice. "Poppy" Bush and Don Johnson.

On the whole, network correspondents seemed to have few serious objections to taking what they were given each day by the image mongers. CBS's Bob Schieffer told Utley in the *Sunday Today* report: "It is not our business to make the agenda or to make the debate." Lisa Myers of NBC seemed to think Deaver/Ailes-style campaigning was a pillar of American democracy: "From a reporter's point of view this kind of campaign is frustrating. But from a politician's point of view it's absolutely necessary. Because it's only by hammering away at the same message day after day that the message gets through to the American people." As if sound-bite politics were an institution, something to include in a civics text.

Others in the TV news business made more radical noises, vowing to shake themselves free of the grip of the demon visual. *The New York Times* reported on October 4:

"If the photo opportunity of the day is simply a visual with no substantive core we should walk away from it," said the NBC news correspondent Andrea Mitchell. . . .

Brian M. Healy [of] CBS News, said the [Bush] flag factory [event] was really the last straw. "They're going to have to earn their way onto the air," he said.

Brave talk, but of course nothing really changed. On Sunday, October 30, for instance, Bush went to Pennsylvania on a trip laid on at the last minute to demonstrate that he was not complacent about his lead. He performed a few stunts for the camera—catching a football on the tarmac at Andrews Air Force Base, bellowing to crowds through a bullhorn in Pennsylvania, and posing with a Catholic prelate decked out in photogenic red trappings. He said nothing of consequence, even by the special standards of his own campaign, yet he made it onto the networks, getting heavy coverage on ABC. The "substantive core" of ABC's story can be summarized as follows: "George Bush wanted some free TV advertising. We gave it to him." Correspondent Mike von Fremd's only complaint was that Bush, less well-choreographed than usual," often [had] his back to the cameras."

Often had his back to the cameras? That comment suggests the depths to which TV news had descended—faulting the candidate's competency at manipulating TV news itself. More broadly, it points up the networks' preoccupation with politics as performance, with the mechanics and strategies of political persuasion and all the little details of life in the campaign fishbowl. As Tom Brokaw said self-consciously of the tight circle of politicians, campaign aides, pollsters, and political reporters who run together in a presidential election year: "We kind of speak our own language, live in our own universe, have our own culture." He can say that again—and note the word "we."

After both of the Bush-Dukakis debates (September 25 and October 13), the network correspondents dwelt heavily on the candidates' skills as television actors. In their new role as drama critics, the correspondents seemed to be telling viewers that what was really important was how well a would-be president could project qualities such as:

- Nonchalance, when he was probably quite nervous. ("I think it was [Bush'] body language throughout. He seemed more confident and relaxed. . . . I saw a comparable change in Dukakis, but I thought Bush did it in a more believable way"—NBC's John Chancellor, October 13.)
- Likeability, when it may not come naturally. ("[Dukakis] . . . wanted to show he was a sympathetic figure. He smiled a lot . . . but I'm not sure that in that ninety minutes he came across as anybody's idea of their favorite uncle"—NBC's Chris Wallace, September 25.)
- A mature understanding of TV camera angles. ("I noticed . . . how Dukakis played to the camera. . . . When he answered a question . . . he looked straight into the camera"—ABC's Jim Wooten, September 15.)

You may be thinking that there are other, more important considerations in choosing a president. Well, the networks agreed. They heavily stressed two other vital factors, sound-bites and spin doctors, and virtually made them into household words.

No sooner did each debate end than the networks were harping on which candidate had produced the most memorable bites. After the second debate, for example, NBC's Ken Bode told viewers: "[An] exchange you are liable to see tomorrow on the instant television replays had to do with labels . . . and this is how it looked." (Cut to sound-bites.)

Is it just me, or is there something downright daft about predicting on the air which snippets you are likely to broadcast the next day? Over on CBS, sound-bites kept coming up like King Charles's head when Dan Rather had the floor. "Senator Bradley?" Dan inquired after the September 25 debate. "If you were putting together a campaign commercial for Michael Dukakis and you wanted to use a George Bush sound-bite out of this, what would you use?" He then asked New Hampshire Governor John Sununu: "What Dukakis sound-bite would you use in a George Bush commercial?" A few minutes later, his intensity building, Rather asked Republican pollster David Keene: "Now, Dave, let's turn it around. You're making a George Bush commercial and you're looking for a sound-bite of George Bush. . . . What's his best shot?" etc.

Sadly, two weeks later, shortly after the close of the second Bush-Dukakis debate, a perplexed-sounding Rather broke this news to viewers: "There weren't many, I didn't hear or see many *sound-bites*." But correspondent Bruce Morton jumped to his rescue with a key insight: "One of [Dukakis's] problems in this whole campaign is that his message doesn't sound-bite as easily." Yes, ladies and gentlemen, it's official—"sound-bite" is now a verb.

Then there were the spin doctors, the partisans for each candidate who besieged the pressroom after the debates and became another 1988 network obsession. On the one hand, the networks treated them as figures of fun, so predictable and biased that correspondents could not keep straight faces. On the other hand, they were regarded in a strange, convoluted way as campaign soothsayers. If you interpreted correctly what their utterances *really* signified, you had discovered the ultimate inside dope.

Consider this exchange, following the October 13 debate:

Dan Rather (lightheartedly): Their handlers—and don't they have a lot of them?—have been nonstop on what's called spin patrol, descending on the assembled reporters, trying to influence press accounts. Lesley Stahl joins us now from the eye of the spin storm. Lesley?

Stahl (smiling): Frankly, it's getting a bit like a broken record. We're spinning round and round and round . . . All the handlers standing right up next to each other, Republicans and Democrats, with hordes of reporters crowing in to hear a good sound-bite. . . . And standing next to me, Dan, are three reporters who have been spun. . . . This is Mark Nelson, first, of The Dallas Morning News. . . . Let's ask him first what the Bush spinners are saying.

Nelson: The Bush people are very happy. They think the vice-president did exactly what he had to do . . . .

Stahl: You gonna write that in your paper tomorrow?

Nelson: I don't know. . . . We don't believe everything we hear from these guys.

Stahl, still in a joking mood, then asks Bob Drogin of the Los Angeles Times *what the Dukakis spinners are saying.*

Drogin (smiling): Even before [the debate] started, one of the Dukakis aides came up to me and said, "In case I don't catch you later, we're elated." And they're trying to keep that up. . . .

At this point, the banter stops as Stahl turns to Linda Breakstone of the Los Angeles Herald Examiner *and asks the touchstone question.*

Stahl: What's the difference between the two spinning teams? Do you feel one side is genuinely more elated than the other?

Breakstone (earnestly): I think the Bush people are happier. They're calmer about their spin. The Dukakis people are a little afraid of their own spin. . . . Lee Atwater [the Bush campaign leader] . . . is very calm about it, secure about it.

The Stahl-Breakstone exchange illustrates one of the real innovations in campaign reporting last year—the quest for what one might call "genuine spin." Through appraisal of the posture, voice, tone, and facial expressions of the spin doctors after a major campaign event, you make a judgment as to which candidate's quacks are lying least. That's the candidate who "won." Oh, I forgot—another criterion is the speed at which the spin doctors reach the press area from the debate arena, as in: "Tonight the Bush people were literally bounding into this room" (Lisa Myers, NBC, October 13). The campaign that wins the post-debate 200–yard dash to the press room also wins the debate. Perhaps the Federal Election Commission should begin testing for steroids in 1992.

Speaking of sports, political reporters assumed a role akin to sportswriters in 1988. This was in keeping with a long tradition of "value-free" political reporting. But in '88 the limitations of that tradition became more painfully apparent than ever before. For much of the race, journalists discussed an unprecedented flood of inaccurate charges and misleading television campaign ads in terms of the effectiveness of a candidate's "game plan." The focus was on strategy, not content or legitimacy—to wit: HOW THE FURLOUGH ISSUE BECAME A STRATEGEM OF THE BUSH FORCES (*Washington Post*, October 28); or, again "Bush . . . moved early to offset a major potential negative, casting Dukakis as the polluter with his dramatic 'raid' on polluted Boston Harbor . . ." (*Boston Globe*, October 23).

It was not until the Bush camp ran its notoriously inaccurate "tank ad" attacking Dukakis that TV news saw fit to correct the record. The ad—which appropriated footage of an ill-conceived Democratic visual in which Dukakis rode in a tank, grinning goofily—claimed he opposed several weapons that he, in fact, supported. On October 19, ABC ran a point-by-point rebuttal of the Republican ad and other networks followed suit (as did a number of newspapers). By then, unfortunately, several factually dubious Bush ads had been running for weeks, all but unchallenged in the press, among them the "furlough" spot showing prisoners going through a revolving door and implying falsely that, under Dukakis, 268 Willie Horton clones had been released.

Not only were news organizations late in zeroing in on the inaccuracies; they were overly cautious in what they said, bending so far backward to appear balanced and nonpartisan that they gave the impression both candidates were equally at fault in the distortion game. The Dukakis camp did claim misleadingly in one ad that Bush had voted to cut Social Security (in fact, he had votes to cut a cost-of-living raise—a cut that would have weakened a pensioner's buying power). But University of Texas professor Kathleen Hall Jamieson, who has written books on the history of campaign advertising and who studied the 1988 TV commercials closely, says the Bush campaign was the more flagrant offender by far, perpetrating the most blatantly distorted TV spots ever aired in a presidential race.

Jamieson told me that, when she was invited to appear on network talk shows (*Good Morning America, Sunday Morning*, etc.) to discuss distorted ads, an equal number of cuts from Bush and Dukakis spots would be shown, giving the false impression that the two sides were "equally sleazy and unfair." Jamieson added, "It was very difficult, given that visual structure, to make the point that Bush's ads were, one, effective and, two, lies, and that Dukakis's ads were, one, ineffective and, two, truthful."

That impression of equal culpability was widely circulated, in print as well as on the air. *Newsweek,* in a cover article illustrated with a Garry Trudeau cartoon showing Dukakis and Bush hurling mud at each other, declared: "There was blame enough to spare for the flying mud" (October 31). In an October 10 report—2 SIDES ESCALATE AIRWAVES WAR OF NEGATIVE ADS—*The New York Times* equated Dukakis's efforts to counter distorted ad attacks ("Do you believe it when George Bush tells you he's going to be the environmentalist president?") with Bush's original attacks.

There are limits to what news organizations can do to correct lies and distortions during a presidential campaign. "Single news segments cannot erase dozens of exposures to a sludge-clotted Boston Harbor," as Jamieson put it. When a candidate fails to carry the burden of rebuttal, as Dukakis failed to do for much of the race, that makes it all the harder for reporters to patrol as accuracy cops, because they might be accused of serving as surrogates for the silent candidate.

Nevertheless, commercial television had a special obligation to counter the distortions. For one thing, commercial TV was the original breeding ground for sound-bite politics. For another, it carried Bush's allegations, unchallenged, to millions of homes. TV's obligation is even more compelling given its role in creating what *The Washington Post*'s Lloyd Grove has termed the "perpetual fusion" of news and advertising. News broadcasts have borrowed techniques from TV commercials (shorter bites, quicker cuts, flashier graphics, more attention to camera angles), while campaign commercials have aped the style of news and exploited impressions created on the TV news. All of this causes public confusion—an *Adweek* study in early September showed that a number of viewers mistook news reports for commercials.

Confusion was compounded in 1988 by a proliferation of television news reports about commercials, of commercials inspired by news reports, and of commercials about commercials. Consider Dukakis's "tank" event: in the beginning was a campaign visual, and the visual begat news reports making light of the stunt ("Biff! Bang! Powie!" was how Bruce Morton of CBS summed it up); and these begat a Republican attack commercial ridiculing Dukakis, and the Republican attack commercial begat more news reports, and all of the above begat a Dukakis ad attacking the Republican attack commercial. The Dukakis spot spawned even more news reports. These generally showed the correspondent standing beside a TV set on which could be seen an angry Dukakis, himself standing beside a TV set, on which could be seen footage of Dukakis on the tank in the Republican ad. The paragraph you are now reading is, as nearly as I can calculate, at least four (or is it five?) times removed from the original visual, a phony event to begin with.

There are several things television could have done in 1988 to break us free from this crazy world and restore some reality to the campaign. Initiatives along the following lines might have been especially interesting:

Dan Rather: Seven days after the Labor Day campaign kickoff, and the two presidential candidates are still ducking major issues. Nothing from either on what programs they would cut to fight the deficit. . . . (Cut to end of broadcast.) And that's the way it is, Monday, September 12, the seventh day of general-election waffling by the two major party candidates for president. (This closing line would be repeated daily unless or until the candidates grappled with the substantive issues.)

Peter Jennings: ABC can report tonight that the major networks have invited George Bush and Michael Dukakis to participate in a series of weekly debates. One on one. Specific topics, starting with the deficit. If one may agree and the other declines, the first will be given an hour of prime time per week to use in any way he sees fit.

Tom Brokaw: George Bush spent the day in his campaign cocoon again, avoiding reporters. He appeared as usual at a carefully choreographed event before a friendly audience, in this case an Orthodontists for Bush rally in Sarasota, Florida. You won't be seeing any film of that visit. The reason: NBC has imposed the following conditions on our campaign coverage: film of candidates' staged events will be shown only on days when they hold press conferences. Bush did not hold one today.

Of course, in reality, the networks are petrified at the idea of using their maximum power to improve electioneering. (Yes, ABC invited the candidates to debate on the Ted Koppel show, but that was a one-time shot, late in the campaign, on October 25. Dukakis had to submit to Koppel's tough interrogation, solo, for ninety minutes. This in itself might have persuaded Bush to stay off the air, letting his rival be the one to writhe alone.) The networks' fear stems in part from questions about their own identity: Is network TV the playing field on which candidates contend, making it inappropriate for the networks to redraw the boundaries during the game and compelling them to assume a *totally* passive role? Is it a detached interpreter of the campaign, thus *largely* passive? Is is an active player—a character cop, accuracy policeman, arbiter of what the issues should be? Most of the time the networks don't seem to know which role to emphasize and uncertainty breeds weakness. The more passive roles held sway for much of the fall.

In any event, it's all over now and we ended up with George Herbert Walker Bush. Within a short time of inauguration, God willing, he will hold his first press conference as president. I can already imagine the big evening. It is 8:45 and Bush and his wife sit contentedly before a roaring fire in the family living quarters, a dog at their feet. At length Bush yawns, stretches, sets down his teacup, and gets to his feet. "Well, Barbara," he says, "Tension City. I've got to go and feed the fish."

William Boot is a contributing editor of CJR. *Research for this article was underwritten by the Fund for Investigative Journalism.*

President and the Press
Jonathan Alter, NEWSWEEK

George Bush has had a puffy press of late, but it probably won't last. After eight years of feeling manipulated by Ronald Reagan, the White House press corps is primed to work out its frustrations on his successor. To forestall that, Bush has begun to change the rules. Reporters were dumbfounded last week to find they could actually enjoy frequent give-and-take with the president. That will no doubt change. But even when the news is bad, Bush is unlikely to hide as much as Reagan.

For news organizations, revising the terms of engagement is harder. How to chart a middle course between the harshness of the Carter coverage and the pliancy of the Reagan era? Everyone seems to want a new kind of Washington reportage in the Bush years, but no one knows exactly what it should be. What it *shouldn't* be—the traps to avoid—are easier to identify:

The popularity trap: Mr. Dooley, the famous turn-of-the-century fictional character, once said that the Supreme Court follows the election returns. The same can be said for the press. "If [the president] is highly popular, he will be treated with kid gloves, and vice versa," Jimmy Carter said recently at a forum sponsored by Columbia University's Gannett Center for Media Studies. The "Carter Curve," as the forum's moderator, Robert MacNeil of PBS, quickly dubbed it, suggests that presidential-popularity polls and the tone of press coverage track almost perfectly. This is the Washington press corps at its conformist worst, hewing to power as defined by the whims of the public. There's an older and more noble press tradition that argues that when a public figure is riding high he needs more tough scrutiny, and when he's in trouble it's sometimes because he has done something commendable but politically offensive. Avoiding the pack judgment—writing against the tide—is so rare that it almost constitutes an exclusive.

The good-visuals trap: This is a TV problem that prompts much hand wringing but little action. Last week, at another Columbia forum (this one sponsored by the journalism school), ABC News president Roone Arledge said: "Somehow we have to cut through the wall of phoniness and camouflage" built by media advisers who want their pretty pictures on the air. If public officials deny access, Arledge threatens, ABC News might say, "Either you talk to us—and let us see some meat—or we're not going to show you in a cowboy hat." These are welcome threats. The only problem is that Arledge also made them last year, *before* the empty 1988 campaign. Will good pictures—the lifeblood of TV—again speak louder than good intentions?

The prestige trap: The best way to reduce coverage of colorful-but-empty visuals is to change the status system of Washington reporters and to rethink assumptions of what constitutes news. When he left his White House beat last month, Sam Donaldson said, "I'm walking away, kid, no one's carrying me out or shifting me to the ecology beat." Of course, ecology is of far more enduring importance than some of what Donaldson and the rest of the pack covered in the Rose Garden. It is just not recognized as a "power" beat worthy of sustained attention. The environment is covered full time by fewer than a half-dozen Washington reporters, none from TV. In the "The Power Game," a 793-page book by former *New York Times* reporter Hendrick Smith, the issue appears not once. The debut of "American Agenda" on ABC and some longer analytical features on other evening news programs marks a move toward such real issues and away from transitory news-of-the-day stories. "We've go to cover ideas and documents instead of buildings," says NBC News president Michael Gartner. But in TV, anyway, the White House beat has disproportionate prestige.

The briefing trap: This is what keeps reporters chained to the White House press room waiting for public-relations handouts when they might be elsewhere digging up stories. The need for sound bites from briefers keeps the TV folks, in particular, on short leashes. Scheduling frequent, useless briefings is a time-honored way of distracting reporters from the real stories; the Soviets have even picked up on the technique. Then there's the related "body watch" problem. Despite "pool" arrangements, many news organizations devote thousands of man-hours making sure they don't miss an assassination attempt—or Bush's jogging. That time could be spent exploring real stories instead of playing defense.

The match trap: *Oakland Tribune* Editor Robert Maynard, a former *Washington Post* White House correspondent, notes that enterprise reporting from the White House is difficult because so much time is spent "matching" often inconsequential stories printed by the competition. Editors and producers often insist on such coverage; perhaps they imagine someone is keeping score. The reporters themselves, in turn, fret that they have "missed" something, even when there is little to miss.

Given these traps and more, is it any wonder that huge stories like Watergate and Iran-contra are uncovered by people who are not assigned to the White House? To break the old patterns, reporters would do well to keep in mind John Mitchell's advice at the beginning of the Nixon administration: "Watch what we do, not what we say." In practice, that means worrying less about every comment from the new president and his men, and more about what they are doing to the country.

Politics and Media
Worksheet

1. In the essay "Q/A: Walter Cronkite," it was noted that some people say that television has replaced the political parties as a kind of preselector of candidates, that by convention time there is no selection role left. Cronkite disagreed with this. Do you? Explain.

2. Cronkite also noted that "television is the most powerful force we've ever known to reach the people, to rally the people. We ought to select a president partially on the grounds that he is able to use this medium." Do you believe that style (e.g., coming across well on television) has replaced substance among our presidents? Do presidents need style *and* substance to survive in modern day politics?

3. Commercial network coverage of the political conventions has diminished from three hours a night in 1984 to two hours a night in 1988 to several hours to be shared with public television in 1992. Did you watch any of the convention coverage on television during the 1992 election year? If yes, why and was it an important source of political information? Was it good television, and is that an important criteria? If you did not watch any of the last convention, why and where do you get your political information?

4. Do journalists have an ethical obligation to paint the President of the United States and his activities in the most positive light? Is it unpatriotic not to do so?

VIII

Stereotyping in the Media

The relation of mass media to sexism, racism, and ageism in American Society is a complex issue. It can be approached by asking, first, how various groups should be treated by the media industries if the media are to build a less discriminatory society? That is, are the industry's hiring practices contributing to or fighting against discrimination. The first essay in this section, "Discrimination in Hollywood," addresses this question by providing the findings of a special report on the struggles of minorities and women attempting to make a living in television.

Stereotyping in media can also be approached by asking how the media cover or portray different racial and ethnic minorities, the sexes, and people of different ages? The assumption behind this question is that media confer the status of those individuals and groups it selects for placement in the public eye, telling the viewer who and what is important to know about, think about, and have feelings about. Those who are made visible through mass media become worthy of attention and concern; those whom media ignores remain invisible. The remaining essays attempt to answer this question. "TV's Killer Businessmen" examines the portrayal of the American businessman in primetime television—a portrayal that the author claims differs sharply from reality. "Moving Beyond Ethnic Stereotypes: Latino Americans" reviews how Latinos have been presented in media in the past and offers a prescription for more accurate portrayals in the future. Both essays wonder if these images are more the result of the mediamakers projecting their own biases and ignorance than sound and accurate reflections of reality. "Covering Racial Tensions" reflects back to the 1960s to determine whether the news media have learned anything from covering the racial tensions of the day. This essay examines both the "hits" and "misses" of contemporary TV coverage of blacks in America through news programming primarily produced by whites, via a medium more accepting of visual drama than unseen, underlying problems.

Discrimination in Hollywood: How Bad is It?
Michael Leahy and Wallis Annenberg, TV GUIDE

A woman director, a victim herself, agrees to talk about discrimination in the television industry only on the condition that her name not be used. "If you use my name . . ., you might as well bury my career," she says softly. Hers is a familiar name to some in Hollywood's inner circles, a name that inspires comments like "enormous potential" and "a nice touch."

She worries about being blackballed even more than she agonizes over a personal nightmare of three years before, when a producer suddenly broke his promise to hire her to direct an episode of his hit action-adventure series. "He had seen some of my work for which I had won [an award], and he was really excited to have me," she recalls. The producer informed neither his cast nor crew of the identity of his new director. Later, the star of the series, hearing that a woman was slated to direct an episode stormed into the office of the producer. "I won't do it," said the star, an adamant man. "Women can't write or direct action-adventure. You know it." The producer cajoled his star, the star would not yield. Finally, the producer sheepishly called the woman to tell her she could not be hired.

The woman director says she will not reveal the name of the series, producer or star. "If it gets out, they'll know who it came from," she says. Long ago, she resigned herself to silence, believing that eventually the phone would ring and another producer would say that he wanted her to direct a series. Three years later, she is still waiting. "I hope and expect that sometime soon I will get a nice opportunity," she says. "I have to think that judging by all the people who are always talking about equality."

There is always talk about equality in Hollywood from producers and studio executives. They pride themselves on being pioneers, on creating shows that bring positive images of minority groups into millions of American homes where none might enter otherwise.

Those producers were all the more shocked, then, when the Federal Equal Employment Opportunity Commission opened an inquiry recently into alleged discrimination against ethnic minorities and women in the entertainment industry.

As other investigations and threatened legal actions followed—a suit by the Directors Guild against Columbia and Warner Bros. studios, and a Writers Guild complaint to be filed with the EEOC—some in Hollywood's "creative community" were outraged.

"I just can't believe that the Federal Government or anyone else would go after an industry that has generated such positive images of women, blacks and other minorities," one producer fumed.

"This is absolutely appalling. We have helped other people to understand changes in America, to see what is right and wrong—bigotry, war, all those things. We've been forerunners."

Of course, such portrayals have always been largely written, directed and produced by white males. There has always been a certain irony in that, a paternalism that could not be missed, and ultimately, women, blacks, Hispanics and Asian-Pacifics began to attack a tokenism that effectively excluded them from key positions in television writing, production and management, an exclusion that came to affect even the roles they played.

Minority actors were generally cast in less than five per cent of all dramatic prime-time television and motion-picture roles, a reflection, in part, of producers' and studio executives' conviction that series with minority themes and minority leads would result in low Nielsen ratings and, therefore, disaster. Moreover, in the 1983-84 season, only a scant number of shows employed black staff writers, and these were, predictably, series with black stars or largely black casts—*Diff'rent Strokes, The Jeffersons, Webster, Just Our Luck* and *Benson*, which hired two black writers. No Asian staff writer could be found on television during the season, nor any Hispanic staff writer after the demise of a short-lived ABC series, *a.k.a. Pablo*.

Women fared better than ethnic minorities in some sectors of television, worse in others. In no season, however, did they receive representation proportionate to their numbers. And, like ethnic minorities, they were underrepresented in the most important creative sectors of television. In a recent year, women directed only 10 percent of all television production and wrote only 17 percent of all prime-time network programming (and less than 15 per cent of all theatrical movies). Only six per cent of the writers at Paramount Television were women, and at Universal Television, only one of six episodic series had women on its writing staff. Among the independent television producers, MTM Enterprises employed the fewest women writers, less than eight percent. There were no women on the staffs of MTM's *St. Elsewhere* and *Remington Steele*, two series with major female characters.

And the statistics do not begin to convey a sense of personal stories, of careers impeded and, in a few cases, derailed by discrimination. They do not tell you, for instance, about a director and writer named Beth Brickell, who won a 1981 Houston International Film Festival award for "A Rainy Day," a film about a mother-daughter relationship starring Mariette Hartley. But, aside from an aborted episode for a canceled series, Brickell received no offers from network television for the next three and a half years.

The statistics do not begin to tell you about LeVar Burton, who, after exploding into the pubic eye with his searing portrayal of Kunta Kinte in *Roots*, played, in the next two years, a sullen street kid who ends up in jail; an inmate who becomes a baseball player; a wife beater and an imprisoned deaf mute. He had been type-cast, and his personal manager, Dolores Robinson, knew it. "They couldn't see LeVar playing some character who was a positive symbol, like some professional person," says Robinson. "They have him playing criminals or misfits. . . . He hasn't worked on ABC since *Roots*, except for one *Fantasy Island*. One *Fantasy Island!* The most dispensable actor in the business is a black dramatic actor. Look at *Roots*: [the black actors] were struggling to find work after they had done the most successful TV show of all time."

The statistics tell you nothing about Karen Hall. In 1983, at 26, already considered to be one of television's finest young writers, Hall accepted an offer from MTM Enterprises to join the writing staff of *Hill Street Blues*, fresh from *M*A*S*H*, where she had served as the series' executive story consultant. At the end of her second season, Karen Hall resigned from *Hill Street's* writing staff. (This season, independently, she will write three episodes for *Hill Street)* "Women and minorities are vastly outnumbered, especially at *Hill Street*," says Hall. "I was the only one. I'd say something like, 'I think this scene might be offensive to women'. . . and someone would roll his eyes and say, 'Here comes the women's lib crap' . . . . I know that talking about this might make it difficult for me."

Or as LeVar Burton says, "It is important to be judicious when talking in this town."

One who has not been judicious enough is Julie Johnson, a stunt coordinator for *Charlie's Angels*, who, four years ago, openly complained that studios and production companies all over town were taking away work from minority and women stuntpeople by putting wigs on stuntmen so that they could do women's stunts, and "painting down" white stuntmen so that they could look black. She filed a class-action suit against the Association of Motion Picture and Television Producers, the Screen Actors Guild and three stunt associations. Julie Johnson has not worked since.

Typical of Hollywood's defense against such allegations is this reaction by one leading producer: "Understand, people fall through the holes all the time in this business," he says. "Discrimination? This town has always fought bigots. How could anyone question the good intentions of an industry that has created shows like *The Jeffersons, Good Times, St. Elsewhere* and *Hill Street Blues?*"

Like others in the TV establishment, he talks a great deal about *St. Elsewhere* and *Hill Street Blues*. But on the sets of those shows, there is an uneasiness, a suspicion that some of the minority portrayals are facile, stereotypical. Rene Enriquez, a Hispanic who stars as a police lieutenant on *Hill Street*, complains bitterly that his character has been undercut. "I was one of the original eight stars," he says. "Now the cast is at 15. My character hasn't been developed at all. Everyone else's has grown, but not mine . . . It's very depressing."

Things are worse in the offices of *St. Elsewhere*. In late March, producers Tom Fontana and John Masius called in Kim Miyori, an Asian actress who starred as Dr. Wendy Armstrong. The series' original script had called for Wendy Armstrong to be played by a "pert redhead," but then the producers had listened to Miyori read for the role and minds changed. "Pert redhead" was stricken in favor of "young Asian woman," and Miyori suddenly had a regular role in a prime-time television series. Virtually overnight, she became a potent symbol in the country's Asian communities, which for years had endured Asians in roles as obsequious butlers and menservants, the kind of characters that Miyori calls "F.O.B,"—Asian slang for "Fresh Off the Boat." It is precisely the kind of role played in *AfterMASH* by actress Rosalind Chao, who stars as a Korean immigrant, able to speak only halting English and married to a returning United States serviceman.

Miyori represented something quite different, and wherever she went, Asians stopped her to say how proud they felt. "Most of them had always thought they had no place in this business," she says. "I was a symbol that things were different." Yet, privately, Miyori felt dissatisfied. Her part had not grown in months; Wendy Armstrong had been given no life outside the hospital, and so she wondered now, sitting in the room with the producers, what Fontana and Masius could possibly want.

Fontana broke the news: Wendy Armstrong commits suicide in the next episode.

For a moment, Miyori thought he was joking, but Fontana began talking about details of the suicide. Miyori realized he was serious. "Why?" she asked. "He told me that they couldn't write as well for my character," Miyori recalls Fontana saying. "He said my character hadn't developed like the others, wasn't as interesting. . . . How could it be? You never saw Wendy Armstrong out of St. Eligius Hospital, not with her family or friends. And you don't see any Asian writers involved, obviously."

The number of minority writers on *St. Elsewhere* and *Hill Street Blues* is, to be precise, zero. "Sometimes," says black actor J. D. Hall, who has been a guest star in three *Hill Street* episodes, "you get a sense of how not having any minority writers limits a show's perspective. . . . In two episodes of *Hill Street*, I was a criminal. The third time, I was the friend of a welfare mother. . . . It's as though those are the only roles there are for blacks, the only things those writers can envision." MTM executives and such producers as Bruce Paltrow of *St. Elsewhere* will not comment on the absence of minority writers on their shows.

It is not much different at the other production companies and studios. Robert Harris, president of Universal Television pauses when asked how many minority television writers Universal has on staff. "I don't think we have any," he admits finally. "It is very hard," he says. "There are not many."

The membership roles of the Writers Guild of America, West include just over 100 blacks, 45 Hispanics and six Asian-Pacifics among its 6300 members—numbers destined to be low because, before anyone can become a member, he has to have sold a property or been hired as a writer by one of the studios bound by a Writers Guild agreement.

Minorities, then, usually find themselves confronting a second barrier. "There is a feeling that the black writer can only write 'black'," insists Naomi Gurian, a representative of the Writers Guild, West. "Producers don't feel that a black or a Hispanic can write, for instance, about whites in a sitcom."

Studio executives publicly deny this, but a former producer of a hit detective series concedes privately that you "regularly hear talk of how this 'new guy' which is sometimes shorthand for some black or Chicano—thinks he can write a certain thing, but the producers doubt whether he understands what is funny in Beverly Hills. Of course, you never hear anybody saying the white guy can't write 'black.' . . . It can be a very tight little club."

But there is another, even larger problem: "Lots of white producers and executives just don't believe a program written by black people about black people can make it," says Topper Carew, one of the few successful black producers. "They look at the Nielsen ratings, and that's it."

"It's hard to argue with the numbers," says Universal's Robert Harris, smiling. ". . . *Simon & Simon* couldn't have been a top-10 show if the leads were black," he declares. "Just couldn't be. There's evidence in the Nielsens for that." It seems an extreme write-off of all black actors, and so a visitor asks him if he thinks any dramatic TV series with a minority lead will ever succeed.

"I'll tell you what the facts and figures are," he says. "Aside from comedy shows, there has never been a long-running hit series with an all-black cast or a single black lead . . . *Harris and Company*, a show about a black middle-class family, didn't work. Neither did *Get Christie Love!*, about a black [woman detective]. All fell through. What does that tell you? In one way or another, it is what executives always ask: how can they urge a network to take a chance on a show that no one will watch? And they are quite convinced of that: no one will watch. Some of these men want very much to see a minority series succeed, but, as with Robert Harris, their jobs hinge on making shows that attract huge audiences. So they will quickly tell you how bad the Nielsens were when black actor James Earl Jones starred in the 1979-80 CBS series *Paris* and shrug.

Maybe Leonard Goldberg, one of Hollywood's most successful producers, sees the truth most clearly. Through the '70's, Goldberg produced *Charlie's Angels* and a string of other hits with Aaron Spelling. "Listen, this business has nothing to do with social consciousness, unless it sells," he says. "If Aztec human sacrifices sell, then that's what we'll make."

Out of this fealty to the Nielsens has been born a kind of self-fulfilling prophecy: black dramas have not succeeded; therefore they will not be attempted, insuring that none ever will succeed. Minorities have virtually no mentors in positions of power, no studio presidents or executive producers to push their projects. You can find a handful of respected black directors and line producers in television, men like Ivan Dixon, George Stanford Brown, Charles Johnson—and Bill Duke, who directed episodes of *Cagney & Lacey, Dallas, Knots Landing* and *Falcon Crest*. But you rarely see blacks as writer-producers, those who create shows and write the scripts.

Many black actors and their agents now accept whatever roles come their way, feeling fortunate, on the one hand, to be working, but disturbed, on the other, that their opportunities seem limited to playing cultural stereotypes—a black pimp, an Asian house-boy—"the only part of the minority existence," insists producer Topper Carew, "that white producers find in their *Times* and *Newsweeks*."

Hearing about problems like these every day, Bill Duke sees only one solution to the exclusion of minorities. "We need to get black producers who can hire other people. In other words, we need financial and artistic power and control. We need people to take charge and begin doing it for themselves."

That sounds good to Peter Kwong at SAG, but Kwong has heard the same lines for years. "Power is pretty much in the same hands," says Kwong. "I mean, nobody is giving up, but the problems are worse today for everybody—blacks, Hispanics, Asian-Pacifics and women."

You rarely hear women mentioned in discussions with minority representatives. They keep the focus on ethnic discrimination, just as women's representatives usually confine their attacks to issues of the gender gap, the two groups' problems not always being similar.

Women directors have to fight a suspicion that they cannot preside over a band of males unaccustomed to seeing a woman in charge; that they cannot be, in short, tough. "There is an idea out there that some can only write and direct certain things; that they can't do car crashes, football games or bar brawls," says Carol Roper, who has done scripts for series on NBC and CBS.

"You'll find resistance from producers who say crews won't listen to a woman director," adds Leonard Goldberg, whose production company has hired a long list of woman directors, producers and writers in recent years. "They wonder whether a woman can kick butt, handle stunt-men, do chase scenes, scream 'Cut!' When a woman is unsuccessful, these guys say, 'I told you so.' Of course, they don't ever say that when a man fails."

At the networks, you can find a few women executives—according to a recent survey by *Entertainment Tonight*, four of 22 at ABC, and seven of 21 over at CBS (NBC declined to supply figures). But no network, aside from cable's USA Network, whose president is Kay Koplovitz, has a woman executive in top management. "Women don't have any real power at the three networks," insists Koplovitz. "There is not one woman VP. There's no one among them who can say yes to a project. No one with final say."

Those most helpful to women have not been crusaders, but cool Hollywood executives like Dick Rosenbloom, president of Orion Television, which has hired women to write 37 per cent of its projects, a record no other production company comes close to equaling. At Orion, women have written the hit series *Cagney & Lacey* and a score of TV-movies. Terry Louise Fisher has become *Cagney & Lacey*'s producer-story editor. Rosenbloom sees what Orion has done as strictly good business. "You want the most talented people." he explains. "I think you'll see women receiving more acceptance as producers see how much they can help them."

With problems so pervasive in all the guilds, and no signs indicating that women or ethnic minorities will soon gain the kind of power that can effect change, more women and minorities are looking to the courts for redress. Last month, the Equal Employment Opportunity Commission's attorney in Los Angeles presented her report to the commission's Washington officials, who would soon decide whether to pursue a formal investigation. Sumi Haru and other officials at SAG fear that the EEOC will do nothing. "You know they are counting on nothing happening." says Naomi Gurian at the Writers Guild. "They are sitting tight at the networks and studios, waiting for it to pass."

They are. "You know, there they are, ensconced in their big offices, trying to keep minorities off their TV schedules so that Americans won't have to feel guilty looking at something," a black director declares one afternoon. The words always evoke images of moguls conspiring in private projection rooms. But in the real Hollywood, admen do studies to see which audiences have disposable income for cars and cleansers, and 30-year-old programming executives, pointing assuredly at the Nielsens, speak solemnly about which shows will not be watched. In the real Hollywood, there are production schedules, budgets and numbers to be feared: that is all.

"Aside from a few jobs, does it really matter to anyone outside Hollywood?" a producer demands one evening. Maybe he should have spoken with George Gerbner, a man who has never programmed a TV show in his life, who labors in a cluttered office. A continuing study by Gerbner, dean of the Annenberg School of Communications at the University of Pennsylvania and one of the Nation's leading social scientists, has concluded that television cultivates indelible attitudes of sexism and racism. Heavy television viewers, Gerbner has reported, are more likely than light ones to believe that "women should take care of the home and leave the running of the country to men," and to support the proposition that "white people [should] have the right to keep blacks out of their neighborhoods." George Gerbner has an ominous thought on what all this means. "If you can write a nation's stories, you needn't worry about who makes its laws," he writes.

Gerbner has numbers to support his conclusions, too. Everyone in this business has numbers, but Gerbner's numbers speak of a cost that all the Nielsens and other indices cannot measure. They speak, indirectly, of the cost of the numbers themselves. In the end, it is their force that will have to yield if television is to change. For the EEOC and anyone else involved in lawsuits, investigations, or "studies," it promises to be a long and, perhaps, a sadly quixotic battle.

TV's Killer Businessmen
Peter Brimelow, FORBES

It's no use a visiting journalist hoping to interview Robert Lichter in one of K Street's famous expense-account lobbyists' luncheries. The 43-year-old codirector of the Washington D.C.-based Center for Media & Public Affairs recently developed a lactose intolerance and prefers to discourse happily about the media's peculiarities over an austere cafeteria muffin.

The fare Lichter serves up, however, is rich. Since 1987, with his wife and fellow codirector, Linda, he has worked full time applying the social science technique called "content analysis" to network television and the national press. The result is food for thought—and some heartburn.

Thus, the Lichters recently pointed out that opinion polls showed women supporting Supreme Court nominee Clarence Thomas by about two to one, little different from men. Yet this fact was not reflected in media coverage, where the issue became a battle of the sexes. Network newscasts had women interviewees favoring Anita Hill three out of four and opposing Thomas two out of three.

One reason for this anomaly, suggest the Lichters: Surveys of media professions have revealed that the increasing numbers of women journalists are even more disproportionately liberal, relative to the general population, than the men. Significantly, the Center's *Media Monitor* newsletter has noted that abortion stories by women journalists typically quote a majority of pro-abortion sources. Men are more balanced.

Statistics are the core of the Lichter's method. Both Ph.D.s (his, government from Harvard; hers, sociology from Columbia), they met while working on a massive study of elites and social change. The study was initiated by Stanley Rothman, director of the Center for the Study of Social & Political Change at Massachusetts' Smith College.

Rothman had a theory, which he traces back to Joseph Schumpeter (*Forbes*, May 23, 1983) and beyond, that key elite groups in the U.S., such as educators and civil servants, were becoming systematically hostile to the very economic system that pays them. These groups are sometimes described as the "New Class," although Rothman has scholarly scruples about the term. He also surmised that the mass media play a vital role in coordinating the groups in this class. And he thought this could be measured.

It could. The first Rothman-Lichter elite study, *The Media Elite* (Adler & Adler, 1986), demonstrated through polling that the American major media were run by a surprisingly homogeneous group: upper-middle-class, northeastern urbanites who professed no religion except a political liberalism sharply more intense than in the population at large. (From 1964 to 1976, for example, the proportion of media leaders voting for Democratic presidential candidates never dropped below 80%, 30 to 45 percentage points above the overall electorate.) Through content analysis, the Rothman-Lichter team was then able to trace the effect of these values in the coverage of issues like nuclear power and the oil crisis.

This year the Lichters have again collaborated with Rothman to produce *Watching America: What Television Tells Us About Our Lives* (Prentice Hall, 1991). Again, a poll of key television writers, producers and executives revealed a tightly educated, secularized urbanites. (They were also virtually all white males, over half Jewish.) Again, their political attitudes were sharply to the left of Americans generally but strikingly similar to the rest of the New Class.

To trace the effect of all this on programming, the authors then analyzed a cross-section comprising some 620 TV entertainment shows aired between 1955 and 1986 and now stored in the Library of Congress video archive.

The results are, perhaps, predictable—with some twists. "Television's America may once have looked like Los Angeles' Orange County writ large—Waspish, businesslike, religious, patriotic and middle class," write the authors. "Today it better resembles San Francisco's Marin County—trendy, self-expressive, culturally diverse and cosmopolitan."

But the new vision of America is at least as unreal as the old. Thus 71% of shows supported feminist arguments and only 7% were critical. But, despite this lip service to feminism, the actual practice of television is virtually unchanged over three decades: Female adult characters are twice as likely as men to be under 30; women supply only one in five of television's "mature" (and hence "authoritative") 30-to-59-year-old adults.

Similarly, it is perhaps unsurprising that whereas FBI statistics indicate that about half of America's murders are committed by blacks, in TV-land the proportion is around 3%. Instead, 90% of TV murderers are white, with seven out of ten from "a generic northern European background."

But why does one out of every four TV Hispanics commit a crime, including twice as many murders as any other identified ethnicity?

Which is still better than businessmen. Although they make up only about 8% of TV characters, businessmen are responsible for about a fifth of all TV crimes and a third of murders—considerably more murders, in fact, than TV's professional criminals. And an extraordinary one in three of the crimes committed by TV businessmen are violent.

The TV elite clearly thinks FORBES readers are a pretty desperate crew. Only 37% of businessmen on TV in the period surveyed played positive roles, compared with 45% negative and the rest neutral. Characters in all other occupations came out 2-to-1 positive.

A common industry excuse is that TV is merely continuing popular art's long-standing hostility to business—witness novelists like Upton Sinclair and Sinclair Lewis. But this can't explain why TV's bad businessmen have been getting badder each decade.

Business bashing is also sometimes rationalized on the grounds that Americans are traditionally inclined to question authority figures. But the most obvious establishment figures, corporate executives, have been treated (relatively) kindly compared with small businessmen, although both finished the period in bad shape.

The specific allegations TV makes about business unmistakably reflect a fundamental aversion: greed (businessmen began the period three times as greedy as others and finished it ten times as greedy), corruption (occurring more in the last decade studied than in the previous two combined) and abusive power over government (over 60% of occurrences since 1975).

The implication, write the authors: "Business at best serves no useful social function and at worst is a threat to humane social order."

Whence comes this business-bashing bias? Perhaps the television elite just naturally assumes that all businessmen behave like Hollywood studio executives—or TV types and their agents at contract time.

But Rothman and the Lichters suspect these values are sociologically derived. Thus, in dramatic contrast to its treatment of businessmen, television gives overwhelmingly positive coverage to professionals like doctors, lawyers, teachers and social workers.

Stanley Rothman is now completing the concluding volume of the series, *Elites in Conflict: Social Change in America Today.* He believes that, as his elite groups increasingly collide with other Americans, serious trouble is inevitable.

But Robert Lichter thinks the media may be "ripe for change." They are so far out of line with general public values and attitudes that competitive pressures might cause something to give.

Meanwhile, he plans to apply content analysis to media treatment of issues like global warming and cancer. He also intends to use it to help clients understand their public relations problems and how to affect them.

And his favorite show is *Northern Exposure.* At least, he says, it manipulates you in a sophisticated way.

Moving Beyond Ethnic Stereotypes: Latino Americans

Felix Gutierrez, TELEVISION AND CHILDREN

Since the title of this presentation is Moving Beyond Ethnic Stereotypes, there are some historical points I'm not going to mention. I'm not going to talk about Ricky Ricardo, Pepino on *The Real McCoy's,* or Frank the gardener on *Father Knows Best.* I won't mention Pancho in *The Cisco Kid* or Sargeant Garcia in *Zorro.* Nor will I mention the Mexican banditos, sexy senioritas or fat mamacitas that populated many westerns. These were the Latino role models on television when I was a child in the 1950s, but I'm not going to mention them!

I'm also not going to mention the 1960s, with Jose Jiminez and his short-lived TV show, or *The Flying Nun* with all its Latino secondary characters who couldn't get their lives straight, or Bob Hope's battles with the Mexican consul over his portrayals of Latin Americans, or the Frito bandito. I won't mention them, either.

I'm not going to mention the 1970s with *Chico and The Man,* and tell you why it's not funny to have a young aggressive Latino work for a racist—too many of our people have faced the barrier and have not been able to get ahead. I won't mention Viva Valdez or *Condo* or the Mexican maids played by the multi-talented Carmen Zapata, or the gang leaders played by Pepe Serna. Nor will I mention the plots in too many fine series, such as *Lou Grant,* who, when they want to treat a serious Latino theme, turn predictably to illegal aliens, farm labor, or Latino youth gangs. Nor will I remind you of stories that come up very often of young Latinos trying to make it despite their own environment, Latinos who can't cope with their own reality without help from Lou Grant, Barretta, or some other Anglo lead.

And since not all stereotypes are negative, I won't dwell on the super-Mex heroes that we see on TV; people in *Chips* and other shows who are portrayed in a positive light because they are Latinos who have been processed and certified by the Anglo system. They wear uniforms. They have been educated. They are so far to the positive extreme that somehow their Latino identity has been processed or changed so that they now serve enforcement functions in our society as police officers, social workers and even college professors. These sanitized Latinos often do have very positive roles, but there's a clear class bias in these portrayals. So I'm not going to mention any of those things.

Our goal is to look ahead. We must go beyond what we know and have seen in the past. The creative people in this industry have begun to make sincere efforts at portraying Latino reality within the constraints of commercial television; trying to address a heterogeneous mass audience, a national and international audience with programs that will work across the board. It is both a hard task and a heavy responsibility.

Now in order to understand Latinos, I'd also like to talk a little bit about my people. We're not just lighter skinned versions of the black minority who sometimes speak Spanish. Latinos in the United States are a heterogeneous population including substantial numbers from families originating in Mexico, Puerto Rico and Cuba. More recently, Central Americans have become a major force in the immigrant pool because of turmoil in their homelands. We have been in this area oftentimes longer than you. My family settled here in Southern California out in San Gabriel in the year 1812. You're the newcomer to some of us. But on the other hand there are others who are just as recently arrived as those who came in last night from Tijuana. We are a heterogeneous population that reflects that diversity of populations that have been here for a long time and those who have just arrived.

There are untrue stereotypes about Latinos that the media often perpetuate. For instance, we are an urban, not a rural population. The Latino population is more concentrated in cities than the U.S. population overall. Those of you who write for network television know the importance of major markets. Most people don't know that the market with the largest Latino population is not Los Angeles, Miami or San Antonio, but New York. Because we're more heavily urbanized we are not concentrated in farm labor. As a matter of fact, we have a lower percentage of our work force working in farm labor than the U.S. work force overall.

We are younger, with the median age of 22, versus the national average of almost 30. This means we are more desirable target for advertisers and networks who want younger demographics. This also means that about half of our population is under 22, and that their most productive child bearing years are still ahead of them. So, you're looking at a population that will continue to experience a faster growth rate than the U.S. population overall.

We have a population of about 20 million in this country, which is 9 to 10% of the population. If all the Latinos in the United States decided to secede from our own country, we would be the fifth largest Latino country in the world. We have larger families, again making us a more desirable advertising target and, contrary to many stereotypes, we learn English. Seventy-eight percent of the Latinos surveyed by the Census Bureau report the ability to understand English. The difference is that we do not feel you have to forget one language in order to learn another. My family has lived here for many years. I am more conversant in English than I am in Spanish, but I do have the ability to speak Spanish. My children have the ability that has not left us, and it's not because of any intensive effort but because of the geographic reality of where the United States is and the immigrant pool that comes to this country.

But numbers do not necessarily equal power. We are also poorer in terms of economic wealth, less educated, less comfortably housed, further from the levers of power, and less well-served by the medical system. We still experience discrimination in employment and education. We work hard, but often our hard work is not rewarded by more than a glimpse of the American dream. Yet we have collective wealth, and the Latino market in the United States is estimated as having a purchasing power in excess of $70 billion a year. This is a tremendous amount of money for advertisers to reach. So we cannot be ignored. We are a permanent fixture in American life, both as an audience on television programs (ABC consistently comes up as the favorite among Latinos in audience surveys) and as a group that must be included, portrayed and characterized for others in this society.

Most studies, including the most recent by the League of United Latin American Citizens, document that despite the numbers, Latinos are still the "barely visible" minority on television. We are scattered all too infrequently as secondary characters in only a few shows, and, perhaps, featured only once a season in token Latino episodes in a major series. Unlike blacks, we have not yet received the unenviable and dubious honor of being stereotyped or typecast. We simply are not cast at all. And when we are included, the chances are that our women are under represented. Five Latino male characters appear for every women character. So our women are even more discriminated against than our men. We exist everywhere but on television, and for us television is still the vast wasteland that Newton Minnow described 22 years ago.

I have a few recommendations to make to you. First, don't shy away from us. We belong on television, and you have the power to put us there. You may need to broaden your own awareness, but that's what creative genius is all about. We aren't so complex that you can't come up with ways to put us on television with accuracy and impact.

Look for ways to integrate Latinos identifiable by name or appearance in both speaking and non-speaking roles across the board. We don't have to be central to the plot in order to be on the show. Our problems do not have to be central to what is going on for us to be part of the action. We're there every day in society. There's no reason why we can't be there in different roles in television. Make it a habit to call for scenes that reflect us and do this by specifying us in your scripts. Don't try to make profound statements on undocumented immigration, youth gangs, drug dealings and other issues everytime you include a Latino in the show. These elements do occur in our society, but they aren't our only characteristics. We have roles and responsibilities that are not always intertwined with our ethnicity. Our background may provide us with a different perspective on the issue that has not been identified solely with our community. So give us a chance to show who we are.

Allow Latinos who do not have Anglo-certified credentials as law enforcement officers, teachers or social workers to come across as credible, serious, admirable characters. Too often there is an unintentional, but very obvious, class bias in the way we are portrayed. Most of our people are working class and they do quite well in this society; raising and supporting their families, going to church, and keeping their own lives under control. A television character should not have to possess middle class credentials to be taken seriously.

Don't characterize all of us by the obvious symbols that have become so handy in movies and television—thick accents, styles of dress, mustaches, listening to loud music. These may be handy stage mechanisms that instantly identify a character for an audience, but they also end up stereotyping the people who are portrayed. Use these devices when they may be appropriate, but remember that by introducing them you also have the responsibility to counterbalance them.

Broaden your own personal range of contacts and involvements. Consult with knowledgeable individuals. Help integrate the staffs of the companies you work with. Do some reading in our own literature. Enhance your own ability to write effective television programs for an increasingly racially diverse population in this country. Here in Los Angeles, you have the opportunity to become aware of groups that you're not a part of but who do exist and should be portrayed.

Don't be afraid of dealing with us creatively. Don't be bound by the stereotypes of the past, but think in bold and experimental terms that will effectively communicate the plot and the story to your audience. Bilingual dialogue, telling the story through the eyes of one of the Latino characters, showing the hero in a situation that must be explained by Latinos, showcasing Latino comedians, exposing our music, affording our actors and our actresses a wider range of roles are all part of this.

You may not always be applauded, but you're used to that. Not everything you try will be successful, but you're used to that too. You may be criticized, and you're used to that also. But we will all have gained ground by the fact that something new has been tried, someone has tried to break out of the stereotypes and do something different to communicate to a wide and diverse audience.

Finally, see racial diversity as an opportunity to be taken advantage of, not a problem to be solved. An opportunity presents many avenues for development and exploitation; a problem begs for only one single solution. An opportunity creates; a problem confronts. An opportunity develops your abilities; a problem taxes them. An opportunity continues to afford new opportunities; a problem is forgotten and discarded once it is solved. Latinos are an opportunity you can take advantage of, not a problem you have to solve.

Felix Gutierrez, Ph.D., is past Executive Director of the California Chicano News Media Association. He is Chairperson of Graduate Studies and Associate Professor, School of Journalism, at USC.

Covering Racial Tensions: Has TV Learned Anything From the 1960s?
Edward Tivnan, PANORAMA

"Black folks live with racial violence day to day. That story needs to be told until white folks understand, until they can't run or hide from it, but have to deal with it."
> —Rev. Charles Stith, Boston black leader.

Nothing, but nothing, makes for more shocking, more riveting, more visual television than an American race riot, and for three days last May viewers of the evening news sat in their comfortable living rooms watching yet another one in action. This time Miami was burning, and cameras from ABC, NBC and CBS were there documenting it all; police sirens screamed through the night, black billows of smoke filled the television screen, and then, on ABC, the camera picked out a gun, a lonely pistol, lying on the street . . . followed quickly by pictures of black looters running out of stores, cars ablaze, bleeding men, more smoke erupting from burning buildings and an angry black face shouting: "I wanted to believe in the American system. No more. Never again." And then a picture of a trigger, then the rifle, an M-16 cradled by a National Guardsman standing warily at a street barricade.

All these startling images flashing across the TV screen seem to tell the story about racial violence. But from what the networks were reporting, did "white folks" understand what those pictures were really saying about the status of race relations in 1980?

On CBS, Dan Rather called the explosion in Miami "the Nation's worst outbreak of urban disorder in a single city since the riots in Detroit and Newark in the so-called long hot summer of 1967." The television images from Miami jolted the country into the realization that black rage had not disappeared with the Sixties. Angry blacks had taken to the streets within hours after an all-white jury acquitted four Dade County policemen charged with the fatal beating of a black insurance man named Arthur McDuffie.

"We despise that verdict," said McDuffie's sister Dorothy, who was not alone. The evening news programs covered the results of that hatred, just as they had done 13 years before when similar instances of what blacks saw as police brutality and a double standard of justice triggered riots in Newark and Detroit. The pictures of violence, the interviews with black leaders and government officials, the reports of casualties, were much the same. So was their major defect.

In 1968, after examining 955 network and local television reports on the previous summer's riots, the National Advisory Commission on Civil Disorders, also known as the Kerner Commission, criticized television for spending too much time covering the visual drama of police trying to control riots rather than examining the tensions and grievances in the black community that caused them. The commission bluntly concluded that newspapers, radio and "especially television" had "thus far failed to report adequately on the causes . . . of civil disorders and the underlying problems of race relations."

For television "thus far" is now 1980. Miami certainly did not jolt any black leaders or ghetto residents across the country of even black newsmen. That anyone was surprised by this most recent example of black rage only confirmed to them that the Kerner Commission's 12-year-old indictment of television news coverage still holds. "Unless there is burning or raping, the black story is yesterday's story," says Roger Sims, a CBS news producer who is black. "There is still no commitment on the part of the networks to shed additional light on the problems of blacks."

Pleading time limitations and pressure to beat the other guys, the men who run the evening news programs prefer their stories short and punchy, pegged to breaking news. They're inclined to leave the sociologizing to the pipe-smoking chaps in documentaries. And to be fair to the networks, during the Seventies ABC, NBC, and CBS did do their share of creditable documentaries on issues that affect black America, such as juvenile crime, drugs, prisons and unemployment.

Even now it seems that it takes a riot as furious and bloody as Miami's to rate national television coverage. In 1980, sparks flew, bottles were thrown, angry blacks hit the streets and many were injured in racial flare-ups in Philadelphia; Orlando, Fla. Chattanooga, Tenn.; Flint, Mich.; and Wrightsville, Ga. Most Americans never knew they happened because those stories got either no or minimal network coverage. When the Ku Klux Klan burned a cross at a rally in rural Connecticut last September and several people were injured when 400 demonstrators protested the presence of the Klan, NBC decided not to run the story—on its weekend report, usually a slow news time—although the network had news footage from the rally. The reason, according to NBC's vice president of news coverage Ed Planer: "It's not a big enough story now."

Even the violence in Miami was treated only as a breaking news story. ABC, NBC and CBS treated the riot as just another disaster. Indeed, on the second day of the riot, NBC preceded its coverage with *three* other disaster stories: the eruption of the Mount St. Helens volcano, a helicopter crash in Hawaii and a follow-up from the chemically poisoned Love Canal area of New York. On the final day of coverage, both ABC and CBS decided to pair the Mount St. Helens and Miami disasters—"natural and man-made," a description used by both networks.

There was no effort to connect the violence in Miami to black problems elsewhere in the country or to place it in the context of persistent racism throughout the Seventies. Each network offered separate reports on the causes of violence in Miami, which were portrayed as local causes. NBC's analysis was typical: the McDuffie verdict was, as one black official interviewed put it, "the last straw" in a series of frustrations for Miami's 223,000 blacks, including other cases of police brutality, the conviction of a prominent local black for second-degree theft in diverting school funds, and the influx of Cuban immigrants who threatened to take away the few jobs left in that high-unemployment area.

What was missing in all this coverage was any effort to tell "white folks" that big-city ghettos across the country were only a few straws away from another long hot summer. Friction between the police and blacks is an especially high-charged, national phenomenon; the Justice Department has actually received more complaints of police abuses from cities such as Philadelphia, Houston and Memphis than it has from Miami. Boston has had so many racial incidents—approximately 200 in the first half of 1979 alone—that the police have created a special unit to handle "community disorders." Miami was the perfect "news peg" to examine the continuing struggle of blacks to grab their share of American democracy, but not one network took advantage of it. After three days, as the fires smoldered, the cameras left the riot zone; the next intensive evening-news installment of the black story would have to wait for the fire next time.

Why? The answer lies in the nature of television news and its obsession with striking pictures, beating the competition and holding its audience. That it takes a riot for the cameras to focus on black faces also has plenty to do with the news judgment of the men—virtually all of them white—who decide what gets on the air. "News directors have been very irresponsible and insensitive about covering news in the black community," charges Pluria Marshall, chairman of the Washington-based National Black Media Coalition. "It's mainly because very few have the ability to decide what's important in the black community, what ought to be covered."

At some mysterious moment during the past decade the black story went out of fashion. "It's not the overriding story it was in the Sixties," says Stan Opotowsky, director of news coverage at ABC, who covered his first civil-rights story in Little Rock for the *New York Post* 23 years ago. "It's now an economic study, a broader social story." Laws have been changed, rights affirmed and blacks have entered schools, neighborhoods and jobs never before open to them. Many whites, including news directors, seem to believe that blacks have finally gotten the chance to share the problems nagging the rest of the country.

"It's no longer exclusively a black story," says NBC's Ed Planer. "The story is now about housing, unemployment, inflation, public hospitals, all sorts of issues that affect everybody."

Black leaders, even black newsmen, beg to differ with such conclusions. "Nothing has changed since the Sixties," says Claude Matthews, a black news producer in NBC's Washington bureau. "That's the story." Matthews and others point to problems whites don't share with blacks: black income has dropped relative to white income; black unemployment is twice that of whites; back teen-age unemployment—also twice that of whites—has approached 40 percent; the number of blacks below the poverty line remains steady between 25 and 30 percent; blacks have shorter life expectancies; and budgets of the Federal programs that had once helped blacks cope with all those grim statistics have been cut drastically. Some blacks, of course, have made progress, but for most the facts confirm what Vernon Jordan, the executive director of the National Urban League, recently concluded: "The Seventies were not a time of progress within the black community.

And the reason, according to black leaders, is the same one that has kept blacks stymied since the end of the Civil War. "De Tocqueville said it in the 19th century," points out Rev. Charles Stith, a Boston minister who has played a central role in keeping things cool in that racially hot city. "William E. B. Dubois said it at the turn of the 20th century, Gunnar Myrdal said it in the Fifties—that the biggest problem America faces is the problem of racism. And each step along the way it gets worse."

It also gets more difficult to detect, especially with a television camera. Television news remains a reactive medium, dead air waiting for a live story to fill it—preferably a story with great pictures. The civil-rights story of the Sixties was made to order for television news; massive demonstrations, charismatic black leaders, Pleistocene politicians, redneck sheriffs, snarling dogs, flailing truncheons, burning cities—great drama, great pictures.

"It's a fact of life in television news that what makes good audio and good video gets on TV," says Fred Friendly, who learned his television facts of life producing programs for Edward R. Murrow in the Fifties and running CBS News in the early Sixties. "Some of the most important minority stories are ho-hum stories. The deadly serious story is more important than the spectacular unimportant story. But the spectacular story will win out every time because the news editor knows it will get the ratings."

The spectacular and downright gruesome brought the network cameras back to the black community twice last fall. "Slaughter of Blacks Veils Buffalo in Fear" screamed the *New York Daily News* headline, and soon network correspondents were in Buffalo where six blacks had been brutally murdered; two of the victims had had their hearts ripped out. Somebody had also erected a burning cross in the middle of the black community, and black leaders were trying to keep the city from blowing up.

Then, within days, a boiler exploded in an Atlanta nursery school, killing four black children and focusing attention on the fact that 14 black children had disappeared from that same neighborhood during the previous 15 months; 10 bodies had been found. The networks rushed in again to cover the story—and stayed with it for *more than a week*, interviewing puzzled police, angry critics of the police, weeping mothers and a New Jersey psychic who declared to the cameras that she wouldn't give up until she found the murderer of "my little angels."

Great stuff. But neither story did anything to advance the Nation's understanding of what was happening in the black community. Buffalo and Atlanta merely provided juicy old-fashioned tabloid stories, the sort that glut local news programs every day. Clearly both stories had national TV coverage only because they were so utterly shocking. Yet the fact remained that 14 black children had been missing in Atlanta for 15 months before the cameras arrived.

Meantime, important stories about discrimination in banking, jobs, housing, insurance and government go unreported (or worse, get reported but don't get on the air) because evening news producers decide they need a "news peg" or the stories are judged to be boring.

"There's too much concern about getting great pictures in this business," says Shad Northshield, senior executive producer of CBS's much acclaimed magazine show *Sunday Morning* and the former producer of the Huntley-Brinkley news of NBC during the late Sixties. "My own experience has taught me that a black teen-ager back-lit, sitting on a stoop in a Baltimore ghetto saying he is unemployed because of his color, can be an enormously moving symbol of anger and despair—as heart-wrenching as a kid bleeding in the streets of Birmingham."

"We've done all those stories," contends ABC's Opotowsky. "We've informed people that problems exist. We're journalists, not reformers." Though newspapers and magazines never seem to worry about how many times they do the same story, television news programs live in constant fear that viewers will brand a report "an old story" and switch the dial for more fireworks on another network. "Saying 'We've done that story' is a disease peculiar to television news," explains Fred Friendly. "But doing stories over and over again is the only journalism that really works. If Murrow had said, 'We've done the McCarthy story,' what would have happened? Instead, he did eight to 10 programs on McCarthyism, and he followed McCarthy's activities night after night on his radio show."

Some news executives, however, worry that too much repetition will come across to the audience as "preaching" or "sociology." In Shad Northshield's opinion, "That's a cop out. It's like saying, 'I'm a journalist, not a human being.' Some stories just don't have two points of view. Racism is one of them, and I don't think there is a more significant news story today than the story of race. It's a uniquely American story."

For that reason, Northshield has never been worried about doing stories about black problems over and over, raising the question to his audience, as he puts it, "Are we serious about democracy?" He contends his CBS *Sunday Morning* magazine show tries to do "between 10 to 20 percent" of its stories about blacks. In the past year, *Sunday Morning* did several in-depth reports on black problems, including a Miami follow-up, a story on black teen-age unemployment, a look at how historical preservation in Savannah, Ga., was not disrupting the black community and, just last September, a splendid story on how local black leaders in Philadelphia averted a near riot last summer and decided to give city officials a chance to carry out their promise to check police brutality.

That piece even began with a stab at Northshield's colleagues in the network evening news departments. Opening with a shot of a Jimmy Carter campaign speech last August in a Philadelphia black church, the camera then cut to CBS correspondent Richard Threlkeld standing on a ghetto street in North Philadelphia, saying, "There was another Philadelphia story that didn't make as much news as the Carter speech, and that's why it bears repeating . . ." Threlkeld then went on to tell the story of how the killing of a black teen-ager by a white cop stirred up three days of demonstrating and rock-throwing in North Philadelphia, which would have turned into another Miami if community leaders had not managed to calm things down.

Last August, more than three months after the Miami riots, CBS returned to that subject with an hour-long documentary about the McDuffie case ("Miami: The Trial That Sparked the Riots") narrated by Ed Bradley, a top CBS correspondent who is black. Though this report was an unusual look inside the workings of the criminal justice system, it was largely a complex legal story and touched only briefly on the fact that reports of police brutality and a double standard of justice have blacks on the verge of violence all over the country. But more important, this CBS documentary, no matter how admirable, was watched by only about eight million households, compared with the approximately 51 million households that tune in the evening news an average of three times a week. For most of these viewers, if the story doesn't appear on the network news programs, it hasn't happened.

More and more directors of network news coverage are perceiving the black story as a local story. "Our bureau was aware of what was going on in Miami before the riot," says ABC's Opotowsky. "There were economic problems, high unemployment. But we reported the story not in its racial context but as part of our general national economic roundup stories. The tension between Miami blacks and Hispanics was a local story; we touch on that when it blows up."

The argument has some merit. The networks can't be expected to cover every story in the country that involves blacks; blacks themselves now claim that there is no need for national black leaders because only local leaders really understand the problems of each community. Besides, the network newsmen point out, local news shows have more time to examine these problems with formats that are an hour, even two hours long in some cities.

Trouble is, local stations are not covering the black story any better than the networks. "On a scale of one to 10," says Pluria Marshall, whose Black Media Coalition and its 65 affiliates nation-wide monitor local coverage of black issues, "I'd give them a two. Local news directors still have the attitude that an issue or incident has to be explosive or exciting or scandalous before it's covered."

Worse, Marshall points out that the four black-owned stations in the country (in Rochester, N.Y.; Detroit; Rhinelander, Wisc. and Jackson, Miss.) are only doing "just a tad" better covering black issues, mainly because they're either underfinanced or dependent on the white community for their advertising profits.

There are definitely plenty of stories to go around, but Marshall and others charge that local newsmen tend to be so "insensitive" to an important black story that they miss even the potentially great ones right under their noses.

Consider Boston, "the local media capital of America," according to a Black Media Coalition analysis of the top 50 markets, which rated Boston as number one in local-news and public-affairs programming. During the Seventies, Boston stations instituted special shows on black issues—black magazineprograms, even a news show called *Black News*. But critics of those shows claim that such "ghetto programming" is viewed only by blacks; whites remain ignorant of what's happening in the black community.

Meantime, regular news programs were giving the impression that things had calmed down in Boston since the bloody racial clashes following court-ordered desegregation of the city's school system in the mid-Seventies. Nothing could have been further from the facts. A Justice Department director of community relations believes the Department has received more reports of racial incidents from Boston than from any other city, although no comparative statistics are kept. In fact, Boston may be the only major urban area in the country where *blacks* fear whites. No black in that city dares to visit South Boston beaches or even the grandstand of Fenway Park, home of the Red Sox—unless he enjoys getting beat up by white thugs. In the first half of 1979, blacks accounted for 71 percent of the victims of racially motivated crimes, though they make up only 20 percent of the city's population.

That racial tension finally broke in 1979 when a black teen-ager named Darryl Williams was shot in the neck while huddling with his coach on the Charlestown High football field; three white teen-agers were charged with the sniping—and the city blew up with demonstrations, stonings, beatings, the works.

"The average television viewer was led to believe that Boston was calm, Darryl Williams was shot, and then there was a riot," recalls Howard Husock, reporter for Boston's public-television station. Husock put together a four-part series on the black victims of Boston's racial violence, complete with a shocking interview with three white Boston teen-agers nonchalantly discussing how they "rocked houses" owned by blacks and beat up black kids for kicks. Notes Husock, whose report beat out several network contenders for a national award for minority reporting: "Racial incidents had been going on all the time, and nobody was covering them. I just picked up the crumbs that were there for everybody to see."

Such "crumbs" would have made a terrific special report on one of the network news programs, but there is little pressure on them to look for stories not connected with a major breaking news event—like a riot. "Sure the networks ought to be doing more black stories," concedes James Walker, an ABC correspondent who covered Miami. "But unless you get a riot, those stories won't get on the air or won't get done at all. The competition is fierce inside and outside the networks. It's wrong, but that's the way the news business works."

Not even national black organizations are pressuring the networks for more coverage. Complains Pluria Marshall: "Most black groups—the Urban League, the NAACP, PUSH, the Southern Christian Leadership Conference—don't even have the media on their agenda." Similarly, black newsmen, still a token force at the networks, bemoan their own ineffectiveness in getting their bosses to do more black stories. "You meet and talk," says one, "but your impotence is the unspoken constant. You make suggestions, maybe even bang your fists on somebody's desk. The execs say, 'We agree'—then usher you out the door, and that's it."

What will it take to change this attitude of benign neglect toward the plight of black America? "Blacks should use their consumer economic power." suggests Pluria Marshall. "If we could pick up a phone and say to Oldsmobile, 'Look, we're getting ready to put a picket line around your place because we talked to you about sponsoring that racist news and you're still doing it, so we're going to cut off your 25 percent black patronage,' you'd have some changes in the news." Marshall concedes that such action might stir up a wrangle over the First Amendment; he also notes that the black leadership does not seem eager to adopt an economic-boycott strategy. In 1977, when Benjamin Hooks took over as executive director of the NAACP, he criticized television for not reporting "the totality of black life in America" and threatened to picket stations if coverage did not improve. Coverage has not improved, but there have been no pickets.

The shocking fact is, as one network executive quite frankly put it, "few people really care any more" about the problems of blacks. White Americans are caught up in their own problems—inflation, unemployment, energy—and feel that blacks have got plenty of help; it's now time to aid the financially strapped middle class.

That message of white indifference already has reached big-city ghettos across the country, and many black leaders fear that the fury in Miami last May was the first reply from their frustrated and bitter constituents. The message from the ghettos: one proven way to get people to care, to put the problems of blacks back into fashion, is the way it happened in the Sixties—with riots.

Yet there is a more peaceful alternative. By refocusing its cameras again and again on the black community, television can help inform and educate viewers that racism is not yesterday's story but today's story, tomorrow's story, every day's story for as long as "white folks" continue not to care.

Edward Tivnan is a free-lance magazine writer and former writer for ABC's 20/20.

Stereotyping in the Media
Worksheet

1. "Covering Racial Tensions: Has TV Learned Anything from the 1960s" compares 1960s news coverage of racial unrest to the era when the essay was written in 1981. More than a decade has passed since this essay was published. In your opinion, how has television coverage of racial tensions in this country and abroad improved? Give at least one example (If you don't typically watch the news, do so for one evening for this assignment).

2. In your opinion, how has television coverage of racial tensions in this country and abroad decayed? In the past twenty years, have we forgotten lessons learned during the '60s? Give an example or, if you recall TV coverage of the 1992 beating of Rodney King by L.A. police and the resultant public reaction, use this as a case study to support your answer.

3. "Moving Beyond Ethnic Stereotypes" reminds the reader that Latinos make up 10% of the total U.S. population and, as a result, should be more accurately portrayed and portrayed more often in the popular media. Do you believe that popular media have an obligation to present a certain number of characters in their entertainment programming in accordance with their real-world representation? That is, should 10% of all media characters be Latino? Should 10% of all media drama focus on issues directly pertinent to Latino Americans? Explain your answers.

4. There are very few physically and/or psychologically challenged/handicapped individuals acting or portrayed in primetime television and major motion pictures. Why do you think this is?

IX

Media Violence

You people and 62 million other Americans are listening to me right now. Because less than three percent of you read books. Because less than fifteen percent of you read newspapers. Because the only truth you know is what you get over this tube. Right now there is a whole, an entire generation that never knew anything that didn't come out of this tube. . . . But man, you're never going to get any truth from us. We'll tell you anything you want to hear; we lie like hell. We'll tell you that Kojak always gets the killer. That nobody ever gets cancer at Archie Bunker's house. And no matter how much trouble the hero is in, don't worry. Just look at your watch. At the end of the hour he's going to win.

This brilliant monologue by Howard Beale, the anchorman-gone-mad from the movie *Network*, reflects media critics' greatest fear—that viewers replace real world experience with media and that the world of media becomes their reality. This fear is particularly strong with regard to media violence and largely directed at young children who, during their first 15 years of life, spend more time watching television than going to school.

The first essay, "Violence in Our Culture," adds fuel to the fear that media violence may have major and detrimental effects on our youth. After doing a detailed body count from the most popular movies over the past few years, the author argues that it is not *whether* an effect is likely to occur but rather *what kind* of effect—catharsis, desensitization, or inspiration? The second essay shares the concern that media violence may lead to real life aggression. However, "Public Enemy's Rap War" argues that the most powerful messages about violence and revenge are not in films. Rather, mediated violence is reaching the nation's youth directly through the popular media of Rap music and their accompanying videos. The third essay, "Does Bloody Footage Lose Wars?" examines the possible emotional impact of real life violence portrayed on television. Finally, *Parents* magazine offers insight into "How TV Violence Affects Kids," as well as a prescription for how parents can help.

Violence in Our Culture
Peter Plagens, NEWSWEEK

If artists, as Ezra Pound said, are "the antennae of the race," they're picking up some plenty bad vibes these days. A few years ago, who would have imagined that one of this season's top-grossing films (no pun intended) would be about a psychopath who not only murders women but also skins them? Or that the actor who plays the film's helpful psychopath—his quirk is cannibalism, but he finally helps track down the nasty psychopath—would be introduced by Jay Leno on *The Tonight Show* to a studio audience whose female contingent oohed and aahed as if he were Mel Gibson? Or that meanwhile, over in the world of letters, a young novelist would describe, in revolting detail, women (and, less notoriously, men, children and dogs) being tortured and butchered? Or that his novel, suppressed by its original publisher, boycotted by feminists, and savaged by critics, would become a best seller? Or that the best mind in American musical theater would conceive a snappy show about the assassins of American presidents? Or that MTV would still be blaring last year's hit song about a teen incest victim pumping a bullet into her daddy's brain.

Sure, ultraviolent fare has always been out there—but up until now, it's always been *out there* on the fringes of mass culture. Nowadays it's the station-wagon set, bumper to bumper at the local Cinema 1-2-3-4-5, that yearns to be titillated by the latest schlocky horror show. And the conglomerated, amalgamated media corporation obligingly churn out increasingly vicious movies, books and records. Mayhem has gone mainstream.

American's addiction to make-believe violence is like any other addiction: it takes more and more to accomplish less and less. Thirty-two people get offed in *RoboCop* (1987); the 1990 sequel serves up 81 corpses. The makers of *Die Hard 2* (1990) really outdo themselves: up from the original's 18 to a body count of 264 (this, of course, includes a plane crash that takes out more than 200 in one fell swoop). *Die Hard 2* makes *The Wild Bunch,* a stomach-churner back in 1969, look, in retrospect, like *National Velvet.* In his horrifying *Silence of the Lambs,* director Jonathan Demme straddles the old and the new, taking a gruesome plot and filming it with Hitchcockian discretion and taste. "We wanted to exploit people's endless fascination with scary stories, and provide them with a tremendously powerful version of a scary story, but we didn't want to upset their lives," he explains.

But people *are* upset by the assault of brutal imagery on radio, TV, in the theaters, in best-selling books. It is not any one film or program that is singularly disturbing, it is the appalling accretion of violent entertainment. It is the sense that things have gotten out of control. And there is legitimate alarm at what all this imaginary violence might be contributing to in an increasingly dangerous real life. According to a NEWSWEEK Poll conducted by The Gallup Organization in mid-March, 40 percent think movie violence is a "very great" cause of the real kind and an additional 28 percent see it as a "considerable" factor (only 11 percent answered "very little").

American martyr: Even as we express such heartfelt concerns, we are packing into the multiplexes, lapping up the fictive blood, renting $1.5 billion worth of "action" videos a year and eagerly awaiting the next Stephen King novel. "Like most Americans, I get off on make-believe violence to some appreciable degree," says King. "I was raised to think Audie Murphy and Sergeant York and Davy Crockett were great American heroes, that George Armstrong Custer was a great American martyr, and that Saddam Hussein needed to have his butt kicked. . . In a violent world, where violence continues to be perceived as a solution, violent make-believe will continue to be a part of that world's imaginative diet."

"Maybe," says *GoodFellas* director Martin Scorsese, "we need the catharsis of bloodletting and decapitation like the ancient Romans needed it, a ritual but not real like the Roman circus." The Roman analogy is somewhat terrifying. What kind of people find it fun to drop a Vio-lence cassette into the tape deck? (*Break your knee caps, left then the right/Next your eyeballs, lose your sight.*) What kind of people cheer lustily when Bruce Willis pokes an icicle through an eye socket into a baddie's brain? Or, to elevate the level of discussion, what value is it to have as talented a writer as Paul Theroux write *Chicago Loop*, about a man who ties up a woman and literally gnaws her to death: "[He] snapped at the ragged flesh like a mastiff."

To be fair, violent narratives go back a lot further than the Steadicam—or even the Marquis de Sade. But the amount of explicit carnage in both serious and popular fiction has exploded, and there's a similar trend in detective novels, whose villains have become increasingly psychotic and whose medical examiners must find it increasingly hard to act blasé. Victims in James Ellroy's *The Big Nowhere*—praised even in the culturally conservative *Wall Street Journal*—have their eyes poked out, genitals mutilated, and (ho hum) their flesh chewed. And worst of all is detective *fact*. Rex Miller's "Chaingang" Bunkowski isn't as compelling a monster as the real-life serial killer Randy Kraft, subject of *L.A. Times* reporter Dennis McDougal's forthcoming *Angel of Darkness*. Kraft tortured and murdered 67 people, snapping Polaroids throughout. Our fascination with such material is older than Lizzie Borden. What's new is the obsessively detailed description of all 40 whacks, with their attendant shrieks and splatters.

Movie violence these days is likewise clearer, louder, more anatomically precise and a lot sexier. When a gunslinger got shot in some black-and-white potboiler, all we saw was a white puff of smoke and a dab of fake blood. When Jamie Lee Curtis takes one in the arm in the protracted climax to Kathryn Bigelow's *Blue Steel* (1990), there's a slo-mo eruption of ersatz fabric, gristle and blood that ends up looking as pretty as a nature film's blooming desert rose. And the claret of Curtis's precious bodily fluid is nicely set off against the light blue of her uniform, which is melded subtly with the gray Wall Street façade. This movie isn't so much directed as it is designed.

Ammo clips: In the past decade, a growing number of feature directors (Ridley Scott and Adrian Lyne, among them) got their training in TV advertising. They are masters of seduction. They can make a soda pop glisten and crackle so you can almost feel it on your tongue. Give them 30 seconds and they can make you feel the wind in your hair as a car takes a curve on the screen. This new breed of director has been bringing ad techniques to the larger screen. But where, on the small screen, one hears a pop can hiss, on the large screen one hears black matte ammo clips clackering like castanets. Or bones being cracked. "Today we have the technology to do sequences that are louder and bigger and more effective than before," says *Die Hard 2* director Renny Harlin. But it's not simply that the special effects are more sophisticated than before, it's the way in which—and the purpose to which—directors use them. In Harlin's film, Bruce Willis seems to be constantly rolling across the floor, blasting away at several neo-Nazi ninjas at once, making plate-glass partitions swell and break and sparkle like lovely surfers' waves. It's all so insidiously yummy that you lean forward to get closer to the action. Our ability to feel compassion is brutalized by excessive brutality, especially when it's given that Hollywood sheen.

In all of pop culture (as in most of society) women are the victims of choice. "Consider this a divorce!" Arnold Schwarzenegger bellows just before he blows his wife away in *Total Recall*. Audiences love it: she got hers! Just like Lara Palmer, *Twin Peaks*'s homecoming queen, who was actually a *slut*, got hers. (And judging from the latest teaser, another one of those *Twin Peaks* girls has something coming, too.) An awful lot of hostility against women is being played out in popular culture these days, and it's not pretty.

> *She begged me not to kill her, I gave*
> > *her a rose*
> *Then slit her throat, watched her*
> > *shake till her eyes closed*
> *Had sex with the corpse before I left her*
> > *And drew my name on the wall like*
> > *Helter Skelter*

That's from the Geto Boys' recent *Mind of a Lunatic*, a sort of *American Psycho* with a bass line. It sold about half a million copies. Maybe that was 500,000 too many.

Playwright Steve Tesich (whose currently running *The Speed of Darkness* has its own moments of stunning violence) notes, "I haven't seen a single anti-rape movie that doesn't promote rape. The very manner in which sexual scenes are shot causes rape to look like an activity that is energizing."

There are those who argue that none of this means much. That no one, except perhaps a lone sicko, listens to the Geto Boys and then jumps the next woman who passes by. That healthy American families don't rush out to buy Uzis just because Schwarzenegger seems so cool wielding one. But the psychological road between real life and make-believe doesn't run only one way. In this society, mass-produced and mass-consumed movies, books, records and TV programs are a considerable part of our real lives; they contribute greatly to making us behave the way we do. To argue otherwise is to consign the arts to a total passivity—always mere reflections, never real influences. The popular arts are certainly quick enough to claim allegedly *positive* effects of their noble-farmer movies, triumph-of-the-spirit novels and anti-drug rock records; they ought to accept some blame for the negative ones.

Pop a cassette: When it comes to the impact media violence has on children, well, moviemakers are quick to insist these flicks are not for kids. At the same time, they will market an unnecessarily violent film like the Arnold Schwarzenegger vehicle *Kindergarten Cop* as if it were meant for kindergartners (it isn't), and they hide behind the Motion Pictures Association of America's ratings system, as if an R rating means much anymore. When was the last time a kid was turned away from a theater for being underage? Any child can catch a movie on cable or pop a cassette into a VCR. Five years ago Purdue University researcher Glenn Sparks surveyed 5- to 7-year-old kids in suburban Cleveland. Twenty percent said they'd seen "Friday the 13th," 48 percent had seen *Poltergeist*—in almost all cases they'd watched them on cable.

By the age of 18, the average American child will have seen 200,000 violent acts on television, including 40,000 murders, according to Thomas Radecki, research director for the National Coalition on Television Violence. (The average 2- to 11-year-old watches TV 25 hours a week). University of Illinois psychologists Leonard Eron and L. Rowell Huesmann studied one set of children for more than 20 years. They found that kids who watched significant amounts of TV violence at the age of 8 were consistently more likely to commit violent crimes or engage in child or spouse abuse at 30. "We believe . . . that heavy exposure to televised violence is one of the causes of aggressive behavior, crime and violence in society," they wrote in 1984. "Television violence affects youngsters of all ages, of both genders, at all socioeconomic levels and all levels of intelligence. . . . It cannot be denied or explained away."

Seven years later, Huesmann remains convinced: "Serious aggression never occurs unless there is a convergence of large numbers of causes," he says, "but one of the very important factors we have identified is exposure to media violence . . . If we don't do something, we are contributing to a society that will be more and more violent."

As disturbing and repellent as its subject was, Demme carefully considered what to show and not to show when transferring Thomas Harris's best-selling *The Silence of the Lambs* to the screen—a book so horrifyingly graphic that some Hollywood honchos deemed it unfilmable. It's the story of FBI trainee Clarice Starling (Jodie Foster), whose assignment is to crack the case of a serial killer who skins his female victims. She turns for guidance to a brilliant but violently psychopathic psychiatrist, Dr. Hannibal (the Cannibal) Lecter (Anthony Hopkins).

Terrifying ideas: Much of the movie's power comes from Demme's delicate, masterful use of suspense—planting terrifying ideas in our heads but leaving out a lot of potentially horrific images. "For a two-hour movie, there are very few minutes devoted to anything that would be described as a scene of violence or gore," the director says. "It makes you think about awful things and tries to stimulate the audience to use their imagination as much as possible."

The movie has topped the box-office heap for five consecutive weekends. There are morguesful of recent films with more hurtling bodies, more blood, more slo-mo sundering of flesh and more preening self-satisfaction when, toward the end, good guys start dishing out punishment. But none are more successful in turning an extraordinary cast, literate screenplay and arty cinematography into an ode to the subtleties of violence. In one harrowing sequence, when Lecter does attack his keepers, Demme used a classic Hitchcockian trick: just as the Master of Suspense never showed the knife actually piercing Janet Leigh in the shower scene in *Psycho*, we never see Hannibal so much as nibble somebody's ear. But for the aftermath of that sequence, Demme decided the scene of carnage was so tame—a long shot that pulled away from any detail—that the audience was cheated. "We were beginning to betray the book and more importantly we weren't giving the viewer the elements with which to react with appropriate horror to the idea of someone doing this to other people," he says. So in the editing room, Demme added one brief, graphic close-up of one victim. "We slam in there for a just a split second," he explains, "so either you've looked away or you're going to get the relief of the pullback, but we're not going to rub the audience's face in it."

'Dirty reality': Brief as it is, Demme didn't flinch at showing "real" carnage—nor did he back off from an autopsy scene that shows glimpses of a partly skinned female corpse. More than two decades ago, in praising the landmark gore of *Bonnie and Clyde* critic Pauline Kael wrote, "The dirty reality of death—not suggestions but blood and holes—is necessary. . . . It is a kind of violence that says something to us; it is something that movies must be free to use."

It's an important point, the key to the somewhat elusive distinction between "good" violence and "bad" violence; what is art and what is gratuitous. Few movies are as raw or vicious as Martin Scorsese's extraordinary *GoodFellas*. The blood and bullet holes in his true-life tale of modern gangsters have a brutal immediacy. "I know that violence personally," Scorsese says. "Growing up I had a sense that it could erupt at any moment, over nothing. It is really frightening." To critics who've charged he went overboard on the gore in a scene where a Mafia Lieutenant is executed, he admits, "I never intended the scene to be so bloody," but says he felt it was necessary to "engrave on the minds" the real cost of the mob lifestyle. Forget engrave; Scorsese shatters. There is nothing seductive about violence in *GoodFellas*.

At the same time, because we are being so inundated with violent images—both artful and manipulative—it is almost impossible to resist growing numb. We risk becoming insensitive to the horror of suffering, and that is probably what worries social scientists most. "Sadly enough, that [numbing] is normal," says Edward Donnerstein, a professor at the University of California, Santa Barbara. "Think of the tape of the Los Angeles police beating Rodney King. Everyone was initially horrified, but now, when you've seen it several times, you've become desensitized. Your outrage is moral, intellectual, not visceral."

Last winter, following the massive box-office success of the comparatively benign *Ghost* and *Pretty Woman*, the press was quick to predict the doom of violent biggies. "People were saying, 'You've got to make romantic comedies and lighter fare'," says Joe Roth, chairman of Twentieth Century Fox, studio to both the very violent *Predator 2* and the cozy comedy *Home Alone* (the third biggest hit of 1990, with that charming tyke still blow-torching the burglars). "But it was just a combination of studio execs who think it makes their job easier to follow trends, and journalists who have their own biases. They think they can wish [violent movies] away quickly. But there's no monolithic response against movies like these. *Total Recall* grossed $117.5 million and *Die Hard 2* grossed $112.7 million—those movies delivered. And now here comes *New Jack City*, and it's a hit and it's hardly an upbeat, romantic little movie."

Roth ain't seen nothin' yet. "On the escalator of violence, no sooner has some movie established itself as the new standard, the pressure mounts in Hollywood to outdo it," says Todd Gitlin, professor of sociology at the University of California, Berkeley. Lurking just offshore, waiting to hit the beach on July 3, is a real monster: the $88 million (and still spending) *Terminator 2: Judgment Day*. This bulging Schwarzenegger epic, whose plot is still swathed in secrecy, indicates not only where Hollywood will continue to put its serious money, but its ethical rationale as well. James Cameron, director of both *Terminator* films, explains: "If you're making films for mass-audience consumption, there is a fine line between action, which is good, and violence, which is bad. Now, basically action and violence are the same thing. The question is a matter of style, a matter of degree, a matter of the kind of moral stance taken by the film, the contextualization of the violence."

And what, you may well ask, is the moral context of the sequel to the film in which our Arnold strolled into a police station and mowed down 17 cops? "I think of *T2* as a violent movie about peace," Cameron says with a laugh. "And I'm perfectly comfortable with these ambiguities. It's an action film about the value of human life." Such a have-it-both-ways attitude is not confined to Hollywood: Bret Ellis maintains that *American Psycho* is an anti-greed tract; Eazy-E, of the rap group famous for *F— the Police*, joined a $2,500-a-pop GOP club for a luncheon with President Bush, and the same public that complains about too much violence in its entertainment lines up to shell out for more. For time being there's no light—just more fright—at the end of the tunnel.

Public Enemy's Rap War
Linda Sanders, ENTERTAINMENT WEEKLY

That violent new video by Public Enemy—you know, the one in which the group blows up the governor of Arizona, poisons a state senator, and guns down a few lesser officials in retaliation for the state's rescinding its Martin Luther King holiday—is that actually meant to *condone* bloodshed?

Ask the band, the most politically militant and controversial in all rap, and you get this: "Scientific counterviolence always remains an optional response . . . to racist violence." That is a statement from Public Enemy's "Director of Enemy Relations," Harry Allen, who is speaking—as he hasn't always in the past—for the group, as its more orthodox publicist affirms. Translation: Yes, the video does condone bloodshed.

As for how King, that apostle of nonviolence, might have felt about the stance of "By the Time I Get to Arizona" taken in his name, Public Enemy has addressed that question too, also through Allen: "While Dr. King may have stood for nonviolence," the band tells us, "we wonder what he would have stood for, if he had been *able* to stand after that bullet ripped violently through his neck. Being assassinated, it's been said, will often change your political viewpoint." The civil rights leader's widow, Coretta Scott King, doesn't quite see it that way. "We do not subscribe to violence as a way to achieve any social or economical ends; we condemn violence in any form," she said recently in response to the video. In Arizona, the Rev. Warren Steward, leader of a coalition working to reinstate the holiday and pastor of a black Phoenix church, has said that the video "does a disservice to the legacy of Dr. King."

MTV, after a few showings, has decided not to air the video in regular rotation. And back in the group's home territory, New York City, the Urban League's Dennis Walcott is still wondering why Public Enemy invited him to bring a group of children to its press conference about the video without telling him what the kids were in for. How did Walcott get to know Public Enemy? Two years ago, the group raised money for a campaign implemented to benefit the Urban League. Its name? "Stop the Violence."

Welcome to political science, Public Enemy–style.

It's important to get one thing straight early on in what is a very tangled subject: As controversial and seemingly pro-violence as they may be, the members of Public Enemy aren't "gansta" rappers, like N.W.A., the Geto Boys, or Ice Cube, whose records can be a stew of inner-city street mayhem, foul language, and twisted machismo. Public Enemy directs its rage into politics, presenting itself less as a group of entertainers than as rapping revolutionaries committed to unifying, educating, and inspiring black youth in what they call a war waged against blacks by a racist society.

PE's three central performers are Chuck D (Carlton Ridenhour), 31, who does most of the rapping; his clock-wearing sidekick Flavor Flav (William Drayton), 32, who cuts Chuck D's purposefulness with manic riffs; and the group's DJ, Terminator X (Norman Rogers), 25. This hard-core trio is backed, both onstage and off, by a uniformed, paramilitary-style unit called the Security of the First World, or S1Ws. Other ancillary members come and go as needed, bearing menacing titles like "Czar of Education" and "Lyrical Terrorist."

Yet for all the group's cartoonist posturing, Public Enemy is the real thing when it comes to making music. Its current album, *Apocalypse 91 . . . The Enemy Strikes Black* (from which "Arizona" comes), debuted at No. 4 on the pop album chart last October and sold a million copies the first week it was out. *Apocalypse* has been nominated for a Grammy for best rap performance, and the group's three previous records are consistently cited by critics as among the best rap albums ever made. Public Enemy has been called, by the *Chicago Tribune's* Greg Kot, "not just a great rap group, but one of the best rock bands on the planet"; its sound, says *The New York Times'* John Pareles, is "as insurrectionary as its words."

Designed by Chuck D and a posse of producers called the Bomb Squad, that sound is a disso-
nant, clashing mix of street racket, snippets of speech and music, and the hardest beat around; it sum-
mons up an inner-city world torn to pieces by racism. Against this background, Chuck D and Flavor
Fav perform counterstrikes—more typically verbal ones than the kind they resort to on "Arizona"—
against any and every perceived assault on black life and dignity. Their targets have been wide-ranging. They have blasted malt liquor advertisers who prey on black communities ("1 Million
Bottlebags" on *Apocalypse 91*), black drug dealers who prey on their own kind, black lack of self-re-
spect ("I Don't Wanna Be Called Yo Niga"), and lack of respect from the culture at large ("Most of
my heroes don't appear on no stamps," says Chuck D in "Fight the Power," the group's 1989 anthem
heard in Spike Lee's *Do the Right Thing*).

But the prophet-of-rage trade is a far more complicated business in the '90s than it ever was in
the revolutionary '60s. Call Public Enemy the victim of the tyranny of political correctness or just of
simple decency, but when the band has strayed it's paid—and it's strayed with high-profile frequency,
often in a very ugly way.

In 1989, some three years after the members began appearing together, Public Enemy landed in
its first brouhaha, one of the biggest in recent music history: Professor Griff, Public Enemy's
"Minister of Information," made anti-Semitic remarks that almost broke up the group before Chuck
D fired him and—reluctantly—made a public apology. Public Enemy has also gone head-to-head
with a genuine issue like racism in the media, then made a mockery of its gutsiness by what Peter
Watrous in *The New York Times* has called the group's self-serving "martyrdom at the hands of the
press." In fact, no subject recurs more frequently in PE's recent songs than the supposed victimization
of PE itself, complaining that the members are mistreated by the media and don't get played enough
on the radio.

On an even less elevating note, there's the continuing saga of Flavor Flav, who missed the debut
of the "Arizona" video because he was in a Mineola, N.Y. jail, after being nabbed for a silly traffic
violation (illegal lights around his license plate) but held under outstanding warrants for driving
without a license and for a family court matter involving a fight with Karen Ross, the mother of his
three children; last May Flax spent 20 days in the slammer after pleading guilty to punching her in
the face.

Ironically, the Public Enemy story seemed to be taking a more consistently positive turn last fall
when *Apocalypse 91* was released to a chorus of critical praise for the band's new "maturity."
Moreover, PE embarked on a national tour with the all-white heavy-metal band Anthrax, a move interpreted as an effort by PE to reach out to the surprisingly large part of its audience—PE's record
company, Columbia, estimates around 40 percent—that is white. At the end of October, Public
Enemy was even scheduled to give a concert in Boise, Idaho—a state whose entire black population
wouldn't fill the bottom tiers of New York's Madison Square Garden, and where this band that so
many adults consider the last word in divisiveness was inspiring passionate testimonials from white
kids.

"I didn't know hardly anything about black history," said Joe Merkel, 14, of Boise. "But then I
started listening to Public Enemy, and got really into it, and started reading books about Martin
Luther King, and Malcolm X and all that."

Surrounded by ancient looming turbines and rusting debris in the vast, sinister building called
the Power House in the old Brooklyn Navy Yard (where the group was shooting a video of the album's forthcoming single, "Nighttrain," a stark and disturbing meditation on the limits of black solidarity), Chuck D sat down to talk.

The self-described Public Enemy Number One wouldn't make a bad wanted poster. His face is
menacing, set with a hard, sullen expression that doesn't soften much even when he laughs. Only his
hands, graceful and classically artistic, offset his air of contained belligerence. They serve as a reminder that Carlton Ridenhour, child of middle-class parents and native of Roosevelt, N.Y., didn't
start out as a revolutionary. He was politicized in his teens at a summer school on Long Island run by
the Black Panthers, and was a graphic-arts major at Long Island's Adelphi University when he started

working at the campus radio station—where he met fellow student Flavor Flav—and getting into hip-hop.

Chuck D is surprisingly cooperative about going through the cat-and-mouse game of responding to questions on the controversies he has addressed dozens of times before. Asked about the lingering fallout from the Professor Griff affair, he says, "I think it's cool for Jews to be screamin' anti-Semitism; it makes their community strong. We've got to start doing that, screaming racism, racism!" And he comes off as an articulate radical theorist when he lays out what he thinks can turn things around for black Americans. "I'm a firm believer in reparation," he says. "Until reparation comes along, we're all wasting our time. We don't have control of the media, which is my No. 1 goal, to get as many black points of view heard at the same time." He doesn't waste much time coddling well-meaning white folks, but he seems genuinely sympathetic to white kids when he talks about their lowered expectations ("They're finding out their backs are getting closer up against the wall just like black people's") and why they've gone so mad for rap ("White leaders have failed white society and people are gettin' fed up with it. They're excited about hearing a story they're not used to hearing").

And no one is sharper at answering critics who say rappers's lyrics have gone over the top, but here the message begins to grow rougher.

"Make a long story short on all that shit," he says. "I think any rapper's view should be respected, whether it's PE, Ice Cube, anybody. Because black people have had clamps and vises and tape over our mouths for 500 years, and now everything should be put on the table! I don't care if they talk about killin' all white people yesterday! That should be taken, listened to and analyzed, not everybody just go AAAAGH!"

Then, protectively flanked by a pair of S1Ws, Chuck D settles into an ominous rumble, punctuated by freestyle rants ("If anything happens to me or mine, you know, I could go off, the mutha's gonna straight-out die, and . . .") and prophecies of doom ("If the racial situation isn't turned around you'll see mayhem in 5 or 10 years, you'll start seein' Presidents, their heads bein' chopped off, you know, congressmen bein' slain . . ."). And when asked whether he thinks white kids' interest in black culture represents any kind of improvement in the world, there are indications that he's begun to believe his own hype.

"I think it's an improvement," he says, suddenly cautious. "But I also think the next couple of years are gonna be a test for black men, who've ended up bein' looked up to by white kids more than their parents, or doctors and lawyers, or whatever."

Meaning . . .

"Meaning I think we're gonna catch hell for it," he says. "I think right now we're seein' a lot of strange things happen, especially to black leaders, people of importance, you know, Muhammad Ali, the speech problem; Richard Pryor, multiple sclerosis; the Magic Johnson incident. All the way down to Bo Jackson's hip injury. Who's to say, we're next or what?"

And the diabolic nemesis in all this would be. . . . ?

"It just seems like one big government conspiracy," Chuck D continues, with a shrug that says to hell with how it'll look in print. "That's my personal opinion; I'm sorry if I've offended anybody but f— it."

Chuck D has been described as a man who never met a conspiracy theory he didn't like (he believes, for example, that AIDS is part of an antiblack plot), and paranoia and martyrdom have been part of the PE mystique since day one ("Uh-oh, Chuck, they're out to get us!" were Flavor's first words on their first album). But this conspiracy, offered without invoking any evidence except general malevolence, seems out of the park, even for Chuck. Does he really *believe* that?

Well, he canceled his Boise concert, pleading illness, then in a speech he gave a few days later at the University of Vermont, derided Idaho as a state with virtually no black people, and said he'd really canceled because it has too many white supremacists. It's true that the notorious group Aryan Nations makes its home in Hayden Lake, Idaho, 400 miles from Boise. But was Chuck D—the man who, in "By the Time I Get to Arizona," leads a paramilitary force "to head off a white suprema-

scene"—really nervous about going into Boise because there might be a nut group within a day's drive?

"I wasn't nervous!" he snaps. "I just said I wasn't going! It was the end of the tour, I wasn't feeling well, and I saw no reason to go. The people, you know, they interested in seein' Public Enemy in Boise, they need to take all them Aryan Nations kids outta there!"

Insulted on behalf of the young white fans I met there, I try to disabuse him about who's living in Boise, but his mind is not on white kids. "Anywhere else," he says heatedly, "where I know that there's black people, there can be KKK down South, they not jumpin' off 'cause I know I got thousands of motherf—ers ready to do damage. Idaho! I don't know motherf—ers ready to go to war!" He's pounding on the table now. "I don't go in no lion's den!" he mutters angrily, looking round at his S1Ws. "Lessen I know I got *tigers* around"

Even paranoids, of course, face real lions. The day PE didn't come to Idaho, the *Idaho Statesman* ran an item about the sheriff of Owyhee County, south of Boise, who had to apologize for a poster he had displayed in his office. Titled "Run Nigger Run," it featured an echo of Public Enemy's famous logo, the silhouette of a black man in the cross hairs of a rifle. There's no doubt that when Chuck D talks about a war against blacks, he's not speaking metaphorically: He means a war people die in.

But never has Chuck D's compulsion to embroider reality taken a more slippery turn than with "By the Time I Get to Arizona.' You'd never know from the video, for example, that the current Arizona governor, Fife Symington, is in favor of reinstating the King holiday, or that Evan Mecham, the former governor who rescinded it, hasn't held office since he was impeached in 1988. As the new video and previous controversies have demonstrated, about the last thing this band inspires is constructive public discussion: It has an uncanny ability to bring out the worst in practically everybody.

So the fight grows more bitter and the list of recriminations longer, with Chuck D the only noticeable beneficiary. Says another militant rapper, KRS-One, "It's the ultimate way to sell a record: Kill a few politicians. I bet all the white kids in Arizona are running out and buying PE.' Chuck D and Public Enemy are champs, but maybe it's time they found a new style of play.

Does Bloody Footage Lose Wars?
Jonathan Alter, NEWSWEEK

In TV newsrooms last week, producers were asking one another that familiar question: "Will he (or she) cry on camera? With a dozen Marines dead, it was time for interviews with grieving buddies and families. Over time, such stories strike fear into the heart of any administration trying to prosecute a war. But do weepy or bloody pictures really sap the will to fight? Contrary to the mythology growing out of Vietnam's "living-room war," the answer may be no.

Saddam Hussein and George Bush agree on one thing: the voracious American media will use human-interest stories to prey on the sensibilities of the American people, who are extremely sensitive to casualties. Saddam said as much in meetings with visiting Americans last year; the Bush administration, determined to present as antiseptic a war as possible, has designed its censorship program around preventing access to such stories. Even some reporters agree that an unfettered press would prevent the United States from sustaining a war. Steve Kroft, a *60 Minutes* correspondent, admits to feeling "relieved" by the Pentagon's decision to close Dover Air Force Base to coverage of the arrival of body bags from the gulf. "We can't help ourselves," he says, referring to TV's addiction to emotional pictures.

But if TV can't help itself, perhaps the public can. It doesn't take extraordinary faith in people to believe that they will make their decision about support for a war independent of any pornography of grief they might see on TV. By that standard, the government should be allowed to censor only stories affecting military security, not those that might be inconveniently affecting.

Historically, it has censored both. In World War I, according to Phillip Knightley's "The First Casualty," censorship was so tight that even reports of a gift of wine cases to American troops by the French were deleted for fear of making the Americans look unsavory. In World War II, not only was any negative reporting censored, but no photographs of dead American soldiers were allowed to be published until 1943, more than a year after Pearl Harbor. Reporters covering the Korean War, still very much on the team, actually requested censorship to help them stay on the right side of the authorities. Only the undeclared Vietnam War lacked censorship, though the networks voluntarily avoided airing the goriest shots.

Does that help explain why Vietnam was also the only war the United States lost? Not really. Traditionally, Americans initial reaction to damage inflicted by the other side is anger, not defeatism. A 1967 NEWSWEEK survey, for instance, found that the vast majority of viewers said the televised images of death actually made them more hawkish on Vietnam. A similar dynamic was at work when the Iraqis displayed mistreated American pilots.

Obviously, large-scale casualties eventually diminish public appetite for war. In the gulf conflict, the deaths may generate reminders of Vietnam that are unhelpful to the war effort. But low tolerance for casualties in fact predates both Vietnam and bloody TV pictures. The popularity of the Korean War dropped in half in just one week after the heavy casualties—in an era before TV. Clearly it is the results of war, not the esthetics, that in the long run sway public opinion.

D-Day: Whatever TV's true power, the perception of that power carries great weight. That's why the gulf war restrictions on access to combat (as distinct from censorship as such) are greater than in any previous major war. The military says it cannot accommodate a horde of reporters, but it did during World War II. On D-Day, 558 journalists were accredited to travel with the invasion forces. In all major wars until this one, reporters like Richard Harding Davis and Ernie Pyle mingled freely with troops, who mostly liked the attention.

It may be, as author David Halberstam says, that this country is "extraordinarily ill-prepared emotionally for this war." But if it is—if doubts about the war's purpose, length and human cost come bubbling forth—the explanation will lie a lot deeper than the airing of maudlin, exploitive footage on television.

How TV Violence Affects Kids
Lilian G. Katz, PARENTS

For more than a quarter of a century, evidence has been mounting that children's exposure to violence on television has long-lasting effects on their behavior. Between 1982 and 1986, the amount of television time allocated each week to violent cartoons increased significantly. And the number of violent acts on television in the past decade has increased from about 19 to 27 per hour. Given the amount of time that children watch television, its has become one of their most powerful behavioral models.

The Position Statement on Media Violence in Children's Lives, recently adopted by the National Association for the Education of Young Children, points that preschoolers are particularly vulnerable to the negative influences of the media because they are not yet fully able to distinguish fantasy from reality, and their grasp of the underlying motives for behavior and the subtleties of moral conflicts is not yet well developed. For example, the rapid recoveries of people on TV from violent attacks give children an unrealistic picture of the injuries that have been sustained.

Effects on play. Children naturally often want the toys shown on and advertised during these programs. And with these toys, their play tends to be more imitative than imaginative. Children simply mimic the behavior observed during the program, thus undermining both the imaginative and the expressive functions of play. The narrow range of most violence-related toys advertised on television jeopardizes the role of play in helping children make better sense of their own feelings and interpret their world. Some research even suggests that children apply the behaviors observed on TV programs to their real-life situations.

Parents can help. It is a good idea for parents to monitor the amount as well as the kind of television their preschooler watches. If your child appears to be obsessed by war play and weapons, it would be a good idea to restrict his viewing. Controlling viewing is easier to do during the preschool years than during the school years, so you should initiate a pattern of restricted television watching now.

Help your child to interpret what she sees—to think of explanations for the events depicted and to imagine how the show is put together. Make simple critiques of a show without implying that her fascination with the drama and the weaponry makes her guilty by association.

Ask the staff of your child's preschool about their policy on war play and toy weapons. Many preschool teachers prefer not to have commercially made toy weapons brought into the classroom and welcome hearing your concerns about this matter. Look for other parents who share your views. Work together to limit the amount of violent programs watched, and the number of violent toys found, in the home. Try to arrange play dates for the children as an alternative to TV viewing. Or look for videos of wholesome, nonviolent programs for preschoolers, and encourage their use as an engaging alternative to violent television programs.

Lilian G. Katz, Ph.D., is a professor of early-childhood education at the University of Illinois at Urbana-Champaign and director of the ERIC Clearinghouse on Elementary and Early Childhood Education.

X

SEX IN MEDIA/ PORNOGRAPHY

Sex sells. That notion seems to have become axiomatic in modern American society. The mass media are business enterprises not supported by taxpayers or subsidized by government. They need to sell to make a profit to stay in business. Sex and sensationalism have therefore become staple ingredients in much popular mass communication in order to gain and hold an audience and earn a profit. Pornography has become a thriving business all its own.

In truth, however, American newspapers on the whole are not nearly so sexually blatant or sensationalistic as the tabloids of London's Fleet Street. Our television is titillating and teasing, but far from graphic in its sexual reference. Our pornography industry is not nearly as large as other developed nations, and many pornographic magazines sold or generated in this country have more explicit versions that are sold overseas. A recent survey by *USA Today* revealed that X-rated movie houses are closing down at a rate of fifteen a month.

Nonetheless, sex in media continues to be one of the most hotly debated, emotion-laden, and highly controversial areas of discussion regarding mass communication, and appears to have generated renewed attention in recent years. The reason can be traced to four developments beginning in the 1970s. First, the nature of hard-core pornography has evolved from nonviolent depictions of sex to violent and degrading images of sexual conduct, including rape, sadomasochism, and other acts generally demeaning to women. This has generated much outcry from feminists, social scientists and lawmakers, among others. A second development is the role new technologies (e.g., cable, VCRs) have played in making sexually explicit materials more accessible. Third, in 1970 the Commission on Obscenity and Pornography reported that erotic materials do not cause sex crimes. This stirred interest among religious fundamentalists and political conservatives, who joined forces in an effort to eradicate pornography despite the Commission's findings. And fourth, in 1985 The Attorney General's Commission on Pornography reported that pornography *does* contribute to sexual crimes and antisocial attitudes toward sexuality. This renewed interest among those same fundamentalists and conservatives, who now have documentation to support their nation-wide anti-pornography campaign.

"The Awkward Embrace," the first essay in this section, reviews the long-running debate over obscenity and pornography in the federal government and public reaction to the resultant legal actions. The second essay, "He Who Laughs Last," focuses on the Attorney General's Commission on Pornography and examines how its findings have been interpreted and enforcement by the law. The essay suggests that the Commission has "elevated obscenity to a top criminal justice priority" and added fuel to the fire of anti-pornography groups. The next essay, "Censorship and the First Amendment," is written by Kurt Vonnegut (whose books were frequently banned by right-wing activists). Written immediately before the Commission generated its report, the author informs the Commission that the root of all pornographic evil is . . . the freedom of speech and of the press as granted by the First Amendment. The final essay suggests that we need go no further than our own livingrooms to find sexual content in our media. "Is TV Too Sexy?" argues that commercial television is the nation's most prominent pornographer, exposing Americans to more than 9,000 scenes of suggested sexual intercourse, sexual comment, and sexual innuendo per year.

The Awkward Embrace:
The Legal Battle Over Obscenity
Frank Beaver, GANNETT CENTER JOURNAL

From the *Kama Sutra* and the poems of Sappho to *Fanny Hill* and Boswell's *Journal,* men and women of every culture and epoch have been fascinated by sex and its various representations.

"So I began to write tongue-in-cheek, to become outlandish, inventive, and so exaggerated that I thought he would realize I was caricaturing sexuality," wrote Anais Nin in the preface to *Delta of Venus.* "But there was no protest. I spent the day in the library studying the *Kama Sutra,* listened to friends' most extreme adventures."

"'Less poetry,' said the voice over the telephone. "Be specific.'"

Where does one draw the line between the bawdy and the socially pernicious tale? Should the line be drawn at all? And if so, by whom? Pornography is perhaps the thorniest problem in the sacred realm of free speech and First Amendment rights, and the perennial dilemma, legally and interpretatively is how to define it. "What is pornography to one man is the laughter of genius to another," said the novelist D.H. Lawrence. "There is no such thing legally as obscenity because obscenity is a matter of individual interpretation," argued Supreme Court Justice Hugo Black. "Obscenity cases are a dangerous hodge-podge," Justice William O. Douglas concurred, "They have no business in the courts."

Federal Precedents

But obscenity and pornography—the two terms are interchangeable for the purposes of this essay—have been very much debated in the courts in America and in other arenas too, especially since 1957, when the Supreme Court decision in *Roth* determined that "obscenity is not within the area of constitutionally protected speech."

The *Roth* decision upheld a lower court ruling that convicted a New York man of sending pornographic materials through the mails and of advertising them, and set off a complicated struggle that shows no signs of abating. The main lines of the legal battle have been drawn at the Supreme Court, and the general trend has been away from the nationally applied standards in the liberal-minded Warren Court to locally applied standards in the more conservative Burger court, whose 1973 *Miller v. California* decision was a second landmark ruling after *Roth.* The pornography battle today is being fought primarily in local settings.

Since 1970, the executive branch has also attempted to clarify the issue with two presidential commissions whose reports have confounded more than informed the debate. The presidential commissions tried to examine obscenity data objectively and scientifically, and at bottom viewed the potential behavioral consequences in terms of the "clear and present danger" test that Justice Holmes once proposed as a reason for limiting free speech.

If a person falsely shouts "Fire!" in a crowded theater, the act of speech presents a clear and present danger of inciting a stampede. While words themselves do not constitute criminal liability, their consequences under certain circumstances can. To change the context while keeping the principle, if pornography should he linked directly to criminal behavior—pedophilia, racketeering, or rape—it could be banned not as speech but as incitement to criminal activity. Stronger laws beyond those implied by Roth and Miller could then be enacted to prohibit it.

The first presidential panel, appointed during the Johnson administration, reported no significant causal relationship between pornography and sex crimes, and recommended the repeal of restrictions against adults buying, reading, and viewing obscene material. The commission's findings received little credence when the first report was presented to President Nixon in 1970 and then-Attorney General John Mitchell, Nixon's top law-and-order man, promptly shelved it. Not surprisingly, Mitchell's counterpart in a more recent Republican Administration decided to revisit the issue.

The Meese Commission report, released in 1986, reached an exactly opposite conclusion. Exposure to pornography does contribute to the incidence of sex crimes and to organized crime, this second panel found. Its report urged that censorship efforts be renewed and stepped up through increasing prosecution and the buttressing of existing laws. However, many experts questioned the scientific evidence on which the Meese Commission based its findings, and the 11 members in the group were unable to agree on a single definition of what they were investigating.

In the absence of a strong constitutional reason for banning pornography outright, independent critics and government censors have had to work within the legal framework provided by the 1973 *Miller v. California* decision. A work can be banned as obscene if it is found, in whole not in part, to have 1) appealed to the prurient interest; 2) depicted or described sexual conduct in a patently offensive manner; and 3) lacked any serious literary, artistic, political, or social value. The "trier of fact" in this three-pronged test, the Court said, should be "the average person, applying contemporary community standards."

Who is the "average person?" What are "contemporary community standards?" The landmark aspect of Miller was that it shifted responsibility for interpreting the three criteria to local citizens and judges, instead of presumably more lenient federal ones.

Pornography Law in Middle America

Since 1973, local authorities have had broad leeway to persecute authors and distributors of pornography, but the results have often been more comic than successful. The right to make "local norms" has proven to be a costly, case-by-case proposition, and, while many state and local ordinances have offered their own definitions, few have lasted long. In 1984, in one of the more inventive efforts, the city of Indianapolis passed a local ordinance that defined and penalized the distribution of sexually explicit material on the grounds that it systematically exploited and violated the civil rights of women. This attempt at censorship would have warmed the hearts of Meese Commission members, but its feminist backers were odd bedfellows alongside right-wing conservatives in the fight against pornography. Other cities, including Minneapolis and Cambridge, joined this effort to move the obscenity issue into this new legal arena, but in early 1986 the Supreme Court struck down the Indianapolis law. The First Amendment decision, issued without opinion, upheld a lower court ruling that the law discriminated "on the ground of the content of speech" and sought to promote "an 'approved' view of women."

Another local anti-pornography measure that worked more directly within the guidelines of the 1973 Miller decision was signed into law in late 1984 by Governor James Blanchard of Michigan. Senate Bill 899 defined the community standard criterion as the entire state, and sought to "upgrade" the state's obscenity laws through a two-tier legal mechanism. Obscenity in the second degree, with a fine up to $10,000, was defined as the distribution of obscene materials by establishments whose primary business was other than pornographic trade, like shopping malls and supermarkets. Michigan State Senator Alan Cropsey, who helped write the bill, told the *Detroit Free Press*, "Out intention was to get rid of adult bookstores and X-rated movie houses and also to get this pornography off the book shelves of the grocery store." The law also provided that individuals or establishments found guilty of distributing pornographic material as a predominant part of their business would be charged with obscenity in the first degree, with first-time offenders subject to a fine of up to $100,000 and/or one year in jail, and second convictions resulting in a minimum fine of $50,000, a maximum fine as high as $5,000,000 and a mandatory one-year jail term.

Senate Bill 899 offered adult bookstore dealers the option of taking adult books, magazines, files, or video tapes to the jurisdiction's prosecuting attorney for a prior obscenity opinion. If the material was judged not obscene, the distributor would then be protected from prosecution in that jurisdiction. Senator Cropsey maintained that this "safe harbor" provision was designed to prevent censorship by protecting materials which had been legally tested, but owners of adult bookstores and X-rated movie houses could only view it as some kind of legal joke, like cameras in bank teller windows and rental car outlets that videotape legitimate customers under the guise of protecting them from theft.

This portion of the bill quickly proved "unworkable" as Michigan's corps of prosecuting attorneys was quick to point out. "Material which is ruled obscene in one county may be marketable in an adjoining jurisdiction," Guy Sweet, assistant prosecutor in Michigan's Ingham County argued: Senate Bill 899 "will force each prosecutor to couple tried-and-true, precise legal analysis with unprecedented and subjective value judgments." Another prosecutor said, "We'll have 83 different obscenity laws"—one for each Michigan county.

There were other, equally unworkable sections to the bill. Exactly what, in terms of sales and rentals, constituted a "predominant or significant part of business?" Among home video dealers threatened with enormous fines and jail sentences, this became a nagging issue. Many began removing adult movies from their shelves. Video dealers also began to ask where to draw the line between "mainstream" files like *Emmanuelle* and *Last Tango in Paris* (both X-rated) and hard-core material like *Deep Throat* and *Behind the Green Door*. In either case, dealers believe they had the right to sell pornographic material publicly if their customers had the right to view it privately in their own homes.

Within months of its passage, Senate Bill 899 was challenged in the courts. In March, 1985, a U.S. district judge struck down the section on obscenity in the first degree as vague and unconstitutional. The Michigan Attorney General's office appealed, and a see-saw legal battle ensued. In December, 1985, the U.S. Court of Appeals for the 6th Circuit reversed the lower court decision, leaving the provisions and severe penalties of the bill intact. And in June, 1987, the U.S. Supreme Court stayed the 6th Circuit decision.

The Michigan anti-pornography bill appears to be on the books for good, but its impact on the pornography business in the state has thus far been almost negligible. Grocery stores and other "obscenity in the second degree" establishments still sell Playboy and Penthouse, bookstores and video dealers have put adult material back on their shelves, and ex-Senator Cropsey is now a lawyer in private practice.

The "Average Man in Kalamazoo"

In addition to writing a largely unworkable bill, the sponsors of the Michigan legislation appear to have over-estimated the public's appetite for striking back at pornography profiteers. In early 1987 an obscenity case came to trial under Senate Bill 899 and put the three criteria of the Supreme Court's *Miller* decision to a direct local test. Terry Whitman Shoultes of the Executive Arts Studio was charged with distributing material described by one reporter who covered the trial as "some of the most vile material available in Kalamazoo."

Was Shoultes' material a prurient and patently offensive representation of sexual conduct? Did it have any redeeming artistic, political, or social value? When the three key obscenity criteria were interpreted by a jury of peers, the "average individual" and "contemporary community standards" were put under a spotlight.

Michigan's law had sought to clarify the meaning of "contemporary community standards" by defining it as "the customary limits of candor and decency in this state at or near the time of the alleged violation of this act." Thus, 33 prospective jurors were questioned about their familiarity with pornography prior to the trial. All but one admitted to personal exposure to obscene materials or to having visited an adult bookstore. The Kalamazoo trial attorneys selected three men and three women to sit on the jury. After viewing Shoulte's material and hearing prosecution and defense arguments, the jury found the defendant and his business establishment not guilty.

Was the outcome in Kalamazoo a fluke? Was the jury atypical? Would the same material shown elsewhere in Michigan have brought different results? The Kalamazoo case offered just one legal window onto the obscenity issue but the jury profile and the not guilty verdict suggest that pornography is far more widespread in middle America than would-be censors would want to admit, and that Senate Bill 899 is a weak law that holds up poorly.

Pornography and New Technologies

New technologies, especially home video, are making pornography an accepted part of everyday home life. In a survey of 20 randomly-selected home video rental centers in Michigan conducted by this writer in November, 1987, all admitted to renting sexually-explicit adult videos and discussed this part of their business freely. A consistent pattern of consumption emerged from one store to the next.

Managers of home-entertainment video centers around the state estimated that adult rentals of hard-core pornography videos constitute 15 percent of all rentals, although on Fridays and Saturdays the percentage rises to 40 to 50 percent. One clerk in a suburban video center described late Friday night rentals of adult materials as "frenzied."

Who rents? "Everybody rents from time to time," said one manager. A second concurred, "every type, every adult age group, including a lot of senior citizens. Sometimes older women come in with their adult daughters and make a selection together." According to a third, it is common practice for parents and children to come in together, with the parents choosing material from the adult section while the children make a choice elsewhere in the store.

One manager in a large Michigan home entertainment chain emphasized the business importance of its approximately 200 adult tapes among 4,000 possible selections: "If we didn't offer the adult option our movie club subscriptions would suffer significantly. Most subscribers want adult material."

This nonchalant attitude toward the availability and private use of adult materials is more than just a Michigan phenomenon. In its September, 1987 issue, *Video Magazine*, a serious, nationally-marketed journal devoted to video technology, art and business, began to include a 12-page sealed cut-out section with advertisements for pornography. The idea behind the section, according to the magazine's publisher, was to preserve the family magazine image while serving general readers who wish to purchase adult entertainment privately through the mail. The November, 1987 issues contained articles in the magazine proper on new theatrical releases and technological and business topics, but the sealed section contained ads for videos with titles like "Oriental Orgasms," "Foreskin Foreplay," "Dildo Girls," "Men of Ft. Lauderdale," and "Wanda Whips Wall Street." Publisher Debra Halpert explained: "After new theatrical releases, interest in the adult video market is second highest, well ahead of the educational and instructional areas. Our readership responds enormously to this material."

Another arena where the privatized consumption of adult materials is increasing is in hotels. The *New York Times* reports that adult pay-as-you-view movies are now available in 47 percent of America's hotels with 300 or more rooms, an estimated 40 percent increase since 1980. Within 10 years, it is predicted, nearly all hotels will offer the adult video option. In the hotel industry such service is regarded as simply another amenity. "It's a little thing. But if you don't have it, people will ask for it," says Serge Denis, general manager of the Hotel Parker Meridien in New York.

Many large hotels offer two or more adult channels. Ann McCracken, public relations director for Washington D.C.'s newly-renovated Willard Hotel, says her hotel's pay-as-you-view service provides only one adult option, but will not divulge what percentage of pay-as-you-view revenue it generates. A guest service representative of the Boston Sheraton estimates that one fifth of its pay-as-you-view revenue comes from two adult channels, adding "just about everybody watches the free 10-minute previews."

What impact will this pattern of increased consumption of obscene material have on the future regulation of pornography? The U.S. Supreme Court today is sharply divided on the issue. In May, 1987, a 5-4 decision again altered the guidelines for judging sexually explicit materials. On an appeal by two Illinois adult bookstore dealers charged with selling obscene magazines, the Supreme Court dropped the community standard and ruled that judges and juries should assess such material solely from the standpoint of a "reasonable person." In dissent, Justices Stevens, Brennan, and Marshall maintained that the "reasonable person" criterion was too vague and subject to the same questions of constitutionally as the community standards guideline, and went on to term unconstitutional all laws that "criminalize the sale of magazines to consenting adults who enjoy the constitutional right to read and possess them."

The constitutional right of private use of obscene materials in one's own home, as determined in *Stanley v. Georgia* in 1969 has not been followed with the protected right to sell and distribute such materials. Therein resides the division on the current Court. The law seems to be saying, "Read it, watch it, but don't sell it."

What the Future Holds

In *The Secret Museum*, a book which traces the history of pornography in modern culture, author Walter Kendrick maintains that technology may in fact help sustain pornography. "If the smut of 50 or even 20 years ago looks tame by comparison with today's," Kendrick argues, "the reason may have nothing to do with pornography itself. Every mode of representation has become explicit. It has become possible to photograph the earth from outer space, a fetus in the womb, and Vietnamese children in the process of dying. The only difference in the case of pornography is that it faces steady resistance, while other advances in explicitness win praise."

Perhaps the worst fear of obscenity critics is that human nature will combine with new technologies to foster a social and criminal problem blown all out of proportion with the bound of "normal' decency, and their response, predictably, is to mount new campaigns to blunt the viper's thrust.

"This will be a big year for obscenity prosecutions," said William Weld, the head of the Justice Department's criminal division in January, 1988. Attorney General Edwin Meese, acting on the findings of his 1986 commission, has vowed an "all-out campaign against the distribution of obscene material," relying on a broad interpretation of a 1970 federal anti-racketeering statute.

But some scholars who have studied the pornography "problem" believe that laws expressly written to make this social phenomenon disappear may in fact render it more acute.

"The problem people have with pornography," writes Lee C. Bollinger in his book on the First Amendment, "is in its attraction, or the fear of its attraction. The real social difficulty posed by obscene material, in other words, may lie in the potential for confusion about what toleration would mean . . . (Those) in the law cannot casually dismiss the claim that sexual instincts . . . lie at the core of an individual's, and presumably a community of individuals', identity."

Where does that leave the defenders—and the censors—of pornography? Locked in an awkward embrace, most probably. If obscenity laws do not work—and the evidence is that they don't—the final irony may be that those who seek to enforce them turn out to be the pornographer's best friend.

As one lawyer in the Michigan Attorney General's office bemusedly said of Senate Bill 899 and the Kalamazoo test case, "The surest way to get rid of a bad law is to try to enforce it."

Frank Beaver chairs the department of communications at the University of Michigan.

He Who Laughs Last. . .
Christopher M. Finan, PLAYBOY

In 1985, Attorney General Edwin Meese III started a joke that started the whole world laughing. Unfortunately, Meese may get the last laugh.

The joke? The Attorney General's Commission on Pornography, a.k.a. the Meese commission. And why was it so funny? Well, who could take seriously the titillating testimony, the erotic exhibits, the Keystone Cop quality of the proceedings—other than the prudish anti-pornographers? The *New York Times* didn't even see fit to publish reports of the New York hearings.

When the punch line was finally delivered in the form of The Final Report of the Attorney General's Commission on Pornography, the Meese commission was clearly on the defensive. Social scientists disputed its conclusion that pornography causes violence; indeed, two commissioners disputed the conclusion and severely criticized parts of the report. *Playboy* and others sued Meese and the commissioners for using a kind of official blackmail to try to get certain magazines off the shelves of convenience stores (The Playboy Forum, August 1986.)

In fact, once the commission issued its report, it dropped from the news—out of sight, out of mind, a dead subject.

It was far from dead, however. Quietly behind the scenes, the Justice Department was reviewing the commission's 92 recommendations—and preparing to act.

In October 1986, crusader Meese was ready; he outlined his plan of attack. He would create a National Obscenity Enforcement Unit (NOEU), headed by Robert Showers, a well-known anti-pornographer; he would open a Justice Department Center for Obscenity Prosecution; he would introduce a number of anti-obscenity bills in Congress; and he would urge the law-enforcement community to focus its attention on obscenity-law violations.

Oddly enough, after Meese's announcement, the commission gained respectability. Because skeptics refused to deal with it, the true believers were able to push their view of the Meese report as Gospel.

Those law enforcers who believed in Meese's program (or thought it was politic to do so) went into action. The National District Attorney Association, for example, issued a policy statement urging its 6000 members to vigorously enforce obscenity laws.

Legislators listened, too. Early in 1987, numerous obscenity bills were introduced in state legislatures. South Carolina enacted an obscenity law that mandated that any offense of publishing or selling an obscene book or magazine be a *felony* punishable by as much as three years in prison with a fine of as much as $10,000. Other states have anti-obscenity bills pending.

In February 1987, Meese ordered that one attorney in each of the 93 U.S. Attorneys' offices must specialize in obscenity prosecutions—and he put pressure on them to perform. The pressure paid off. Among other cases, a Missouri Federal prosecutor sent letters to St. Louis video retailers warning them not to rent or sell obscene tapes, and an Ohio U.S. Attorney joined a civil suit to prohibit the distribution of obscene video tapes in Columbus.

In April 1987, the Federal Communications Commission believed that the political climate was right to put into force a new generic definition of obscenity (*The Playboy Forum*, August). That was a direct attack on disc jockeys who specialize in "shock radio," and it also served to make all radio personnel more cautious about erring in what they aired. Meese followers expressed full support for the new FCC standard.

Meanwhile, the NOEU began its roll. It aided Federal prosecutors in the Traci Lords case; it wanted the producers of Lords's movies to be held liable for using a minor in pornographic films. (Lords had reportedly lied to them about her age.) The NOEU was also instrumental in the Dennis and Barbara Pryba case (*The Playboy Forum*, May). The Prybas, owners of a chain of video stores and adult bookstores, were convicted of obscenity under Federal racketeering laws. Convictions under those laws allow prosecutors to seize all the assets of a company, even those that have not been judged obscene, hence putting store owners out of business conceivably even if they had sold only two "obscene" tapes. Federal prosecutors have vowed to prosecute more obscenity cases under the racketeering laws.

NOEU was also involved in the conviction of two Los Angeles companies that provided dial-a-porn services in Utah.

"Mr. Meese elevated obscenity to a top criminal-justice priority," Showers explained. "We're not just prosecuting kiddie porn and violence."

A U.S. Attorney in Utah predicted, "I would expect that within the next 12 months, there will be literally an explosion of cases on the Federal level."

The Meese commission's influence didn't stop with Government agencies. It also had a serious impact on the fortunes of antipornography groups. Those groups believed that they had received a Government directive (via the commission report's encouragement of private action) to boycott places of business that offended their extreme right-wing views.

The members of the National Federation for Decency (N.F.D.), headed by Donald Wildmon, picket any store that displays adult magazines and any Holiday Inn that offers pay-per-view adult movies (*The Playboy Forum*, April). The Michigan N.F.D. fights dial-a-porn; the Baltimore group fights adult magazines and videos.

Another antiporn group, Citizens for Decency through Law (C.D.L.), acquired Alan Sears, executive director of the Meese commission, as its legal counsel. The C.D.L. gives state and local lawmakers models of obscenity laws and provides legal advice to prosecutors.

A similar organization, Morality in Media, planned an all-out campaign in Pennsylvania to urge law officers to increase their efforts in enforcing obscenity laws. If the drive is successful, Morality in Media will carry its campaign to other states.

The Reverend Jerry Kirk, head of the National Coalition Against Pornography, has worked hard to bring his fringe group to the "average American"—and the Meese commission helped bring him legitimacy. He also organized the Religious Alliance Against Pornography to add religion as a way to bolster the believability of antiporn groups.

Kirk now claims that the fight against pornography has become mainstreamed and, indeed, that is another legacy of the Meese commission.

The Meese commission has had another insidious effect. Retailers, knowing that Federal, state and local prosecutors are keeping an eagle eye out for obscene material, will censor their own stock in order to avoid legal hassles and prison sentences. Publishers and retailers of adult books, videos and magazines will shy away from dealing in material with sexual content. The Justice Department is in the process not only of *chilling* the distribution of books, magazines and videos with sexual content but of *freezing* it.

In two years, the Meese commission went from being a laughing matter to a serious matter. As a result of the commission, retailers and publishers are censoring themselves, antiporn groups are flourishing, the number of obscenity cases has increased, more antipornography laws are being considered in state legislatures and a major obscenity bill is before Congress.

Two years after the release of the Meese commission's report, the laughter has stopped.

Christopher M. Finan is director of Media Coalition, Inc.

Censorship and the First Amendment
Kurt Vonnegut, Jr., BRIEFING

I have read much of the heart-rendering testimony extracted from victims of sexual abuse at meetings of the Attorney General's Commission on Pornography. It is clear to me that our government must be given the power to suppress the words and images which are the causes of sexually motivated insanity and crimes. As the Bible says, "In the beginning was the word."

I myself make my living with words, and I am now ashamed. In view of the terrible damage freely circulated ideas can do to a society, and particularly to innocent children, I beg my government to delete from my works all thoughts which might be dangerous. I want the help of our elected leaders in bringing my thoughts into harmony with their own and thus into harmony with the thoughts of those who elected them. That is democracy.

Attempting to make amends at this late date, I call to the attention of the Attorney General's Commission on Pornography, and God bless the attorney general, the fundamental piece of obscenity from which all others spring, the taproot of the deadly poisonous tree. Kill the taproot and the tree dies, and with it its deadly fruits, which are rape, sodomy, wife-beating, child abuse, divorce, abortion, adultery, gonorrhea, herpes, and AIDS.

I will read this most vile of all pieces of so-called literature aloud, so that those who dare can feel the full force of it. . . .

All right. Everybody ready? Tighten your G-strings. Here we go:

"Congress shall make no law respecting an establishment of religion, or prohibiting the free exercise thereof; or abridging the freedom of speech, or of the press, or the right of the people peaceably to assemble, and to petition the Government for a redress of grievances."

That godless loop of disgusting sexuality, friends and neighbors, happens to be a basic law of this country. How could this have happened? Some communistic, pederastic, wife-beating congressman, while we weren't watching, must have tacked it onto the Rivers and Harbors Bill. It should be expunged with all possible haste, in order that innocent children can be safe again. . . .

It is not enough that sex crimes of every sort are already against the law, and are punished with admirable severity. It is up to our leaders, and particularly to our attorney general, to persuade a large part of our citizenry that even the most awful sex crimes are perfectly legal, and even celebrated in some godless quarters, because of the permissiveness of our Constitution. Only then will an aroused and thoroughly misinformed citizenry rise up in righteous wrath to smash the First Amendment—and many other only slightly less offensive parts of the Bill of Rights.

Is TV Too Sexy?
Cynthia Crossen, McCALL'S

What was the most shocking scene you saw on television last season? Was it the lesbian kiss on *L.A.Law*? Was it Rachel Ward in soaked clothes on a tropical island on the CBS miniseries *And the Sea Will Tell*? Maybe it was Rebecca DeMornay wearing almost nothing when she greeted Jason Robards in another miniseries, *An Inconvenient Woman*. Or perhaps it was Rosie O'Neill wondering aloud whether or not to get her "tits" done.

Whichever one it was, there were hundreds more like it. These days Americans can hardly turn on their television sets without seeing or hearing something about sex. In an average year of television viewing, Planned Parenthood reported recently, Americans are exposed to more than 9,000 scenes of suggested sexual intercourse, sexual comment or innuendo. Even disregarding cable, with its nude talk shows and X-rated movies, plain old over-the-air television has literally become a boob tube.

The onslaught of television raunch is all the more remarkable because it comes at a time when AIDS has dampened the freewheeling sexuality that characterized much of the past two decades. Today television is a battlefield occupied by two passionate forces: those who believe that television only delivers what viewers want—and viewers want sex—and those who believe that television's subtle power to teach and influence must be tempered with moral responsibility.

"It's not that sex on television is bad," says Denise Vezey, a Californian with four children who has complained to the Federal Communications Commission. "But they only portray half the story"—failing to show "love and marriage and AIDS and pregnancy."

Many viewers and experts believe depictions of sex and violence on television are dangerous for children. "The destructive effect of degrading sexual themes" on television contributes to more "13- and 14-year-olds casually jumping into bed together these days," says Thomas Radecki, M.D., a psychiatrist and the research director of the National Coalition on Television Violence. Adds Terry Rakolta, a Michigan woman so outraged by an episode of Fox's *Married . . .With Children* that she launched a pressure group called Americans for Responsible Television, "By the time anyone can measure the long-term effects of children viewing such shows, it will be too late."

Yet critics of television sex have a hard time being heard when sexy themes and images are attracting millions of viewers. *Nightline* won its highest rating of 1990 when it broadcast an uncut version of Madonna's "Justify My Love" music video, the one even rocking MTV wouldn't run. Adultery and promiscuity are common themes on popular prime-time shows, and daytime soap operas are also awash with sex.

"The bare-breast barrier will soon be broken," says Tom Shales, a television critic for the *Washington Post*. "Breasts now seem about 80 percent revealable. The nipple is the new frontier."

With so much spirited and public debate, why is there more and more sex on television? Because in one way television is like democracy: People vote by turning on their sets. And despite the vocal minority of militant profamily groups, feminists and TV watchdogs, the vast majority of Americans are voting for sex. "Television is basically responsive to what the audience wants, and public tastes and standards have shifted," says Timothy Dyk, a Washington, D.C. attorney who argued against the FCC when it tried to extend its ban on indecency to 24 hours a day. "What might have been viewed as inappropriate 25 years ago is now appropriate."

So Long, Ozzie and Harriet

Indeed, the history of television includes a steady progression toward more sex, beginning in the early 1950s, when Ozzie and Harriet Nelson slept in twin beds. Larry Hagman never got too close to the half-naked Jeannie who moved in with him, and Superman, although he looked fabulous in tights, never got physical with Lois Lane.

But as American society began loosening up in the 1960s, so did television. Bland comedies like *The Brady Bunch* broke new ground by allowing married partners to share a bed, according to *Watching America*, a book by S. Robert Lichter, Linda S. Lichter and Stanley Rothman. *Laugh-In* featured, among other titillating scenes, Goldie Hawn frugging in a bikini.

The banner year was 1972. *M*A*S*H* burst onto the scene with Hot Lips Houlihan, and *The Sonny and Cher Comedy Hour* engaged in occasional ribaldry. Norman Lear launched *All in the Family* and *Maude*, which tackled social and sexual taboos. Each year, it seemed, a new standard was set. Cop shows like *Starsky & Hutch* and jiggle shows like *Charlie's Angels* introduced partial nudity and leering sexual banter. In 1985, *Watching America* reports, a character on *Hill Street Blues* died having sex with a sheep, and the silence was deafening.

But two years later *Married . . . With Children* provoked a new wave of angry debate. This sitcom, about a shoe salesman, his wife (who constantly talks about sex but never gets any) and their two obnoxious teenagers, so offended Rakolta that she organized a boycott of the show's sponsors.

She soon found many people sympathetic to her cause. The Reverend Donald Wildmon's American Family Association, based in Tupelo, Mississippi, entered the fray, claiming that television was shaping behavior in an alarming way. If television weren't such a powerful persuader, Wildmon argues, "advertisers wouldn't spend billions of dollars trying to sell products" on it.

Where Have All the Censors Gone?

People like Rakolta and Wildmon are patrolling the public airways partly because the government and the networks have backed away from their role as official censors. Although the FCC bans "indecent" programming between the hours of 6 A.M. and 8 P.M., indecency is so vaguely defined that it makes enforcement almost impossible. Meanwhile, cost cutting at the networks weakened their standards-and-practices departments, where decisions about what passes muster are made, while spicy cable shows and the freewheeling Fox network have started cutting into their viewers and revenues.

As a result American corporations have begun—usually unenthusiastically—to assume the role of national censors, voting for or against shows with their advertising dollars. Because of advertiser pressure, a controversial *thirtysomething* episode with two gay men in bed was never repeated, nor was a *China Beach* episode about abortion. ABC said that in the 1989-1990 season it had lost $14 million in advertising because of sponsors pulling out of controversial shows. Although no subject is supposed to be forbidden on network television, the networks say sponsors have a hit list of subjects, including child abuse, homosexuality and neo-Nazism.

Yet despite the vehement complaints advertisers hear when television crosses the line, sponsors have sometimes proven to be remarkably liberal. Despite their controversial nature, orgasms were discussed on *Sisters*, and a woman kissed a woman on *L.A. Law*.

Today profanities such as "you suck" and "piss off" routinely fly over the airwaves. In fact, last fall, when Jackie Collins's torrid *Lucky* aired on NBC, the author told a reporter for the *Montreal Gazette* that she had enjoyed a very smooth relationship with the network's standards-and-practices office. "There were trade-offs," Collins said. "Someone in the censor's department would say 'We'll sway you a bastard for a bitch ' or maybe it's the other way around." And even *Married . . . With Children* continues on the air, earning more than respectable ratings.

Yet the networks are oddly puritanical about the content of ads themselves. Until recently bra commercials couldn't show women actually wearing them. And even today, although condom jokes crop up on *Doogie Howser, M.D.*, none of the networks accept paid advertising for any kind of birth control. To Peggy Charren, president of Action for Children's Television, a Boston-based advocacy group with fierce First Amendment sympathies, that hypocrisy verges on the criminal. "In a world where inappropriate sex can kill you, you're giving teenagers a terrible message," she says. (In 1987 the networks decided to allow local stations to accept condom public-service announcements; few do.)

So What's a Mother to Do?

"Turn off your television set," says Martha Zornow, a New York mother of two small children. "Change the channel. Nobody's making you or your kids watch." Other television watchdogs, such as Charren, advise parents to think twice about using their television as a baby-sitter. "The television set is not a friend of the family all the time," she says. Charren suggests forgoing adult-oriented movies on network and cable television and using your videocassette recorder to show quality films. Later, when children are going to be exposed to television whether their parents like it or not, it's up to the adults to counter negative images with information and discussions about healthy sexual relationships. "We have to teach children about caring," says Charren. "Sex on television so often has nothing to do with love, and so much of it happens with violence."

But however long this battle rages, it's unlikely to be resolved. Some viewers will always want less sex on television and some will want more. After all, according to a new book, *The Day Americans Told the Truth: What People Really Believe About Everything That Matters*, 15 percent of Americans would rather watch television than have sex.

Cynthia Crossen covers lifestyles for a national business paper; Claire Mcintosh contributed to this story.

Sex in Media/Pornography
Worksheet

1. In "The Awkward Embrace," Supreme Court Justice Hugo Black is quoted as saying that "there is no such thing legally as obscenity because obscenity is a matter of individual interpretation." Do you also believe that obscenity and pornography are in the eye of the beholder? Explain.

2. In regard to your answer to Question 1, if you *do* believe that obscenity is in the eye of the beholder, would you go so far as to suggest that pornographic movies be shown at local movie theaters and that the rating system for mainstream movies be eliminated? If you *do not* agree with Justice Black, should the government become more involved in the censorship and regulation of mass media?

3. The report produced by the Attorney General's Commission on Pornography listed the most blatantly pornographic movies, books and magazines available on the market. Shortly after the report was issued, those movies, books and magazines were among the hottest selling/rented items in book and video stores. Explain this if you will. Does it suggest that the Commission is out of step with the tastes of contemporary society?

4. Is censorship of pornography a violation of the First Amendment, as Kurt Vonnegut implies in his essay "Censorship and the First Amendment"? Should pornographers be guaranteed free speech? Explain your answer.

XI

Religion in Media

Religion has been a part of mass media content since the birth of mass communication. The introduction of movable type to the western world in the 1400s is typically associated with Gutenberg's Bible. The first voice broadcast in history was a religious service sent to ships at sea in 1901; the first radio church service was broadcast just two months after the inauguration of our country's first commercial radio station in 1921. Religious programs have been available since the beginning of television in the late 1940s in the form of sustaining-time programs on the networks (with air time given free-of-charge to mainstream religious denominations), syndicated sustaining-time programs, programs produced by local television stations, and paid-time programs produced by largely independently, evangelical organizations and financed from viewer contributions.

This last type of program became a mainstay for religious broadcasters in the 1970s, after the commercial television networks severely reduced the free air time given to religious organizations. The evolution and nature of this form of religious expression is examined in the first two essays entitled "The New Awakening: Getting Religion in the Video Age" and "Ten Commandments of Religious Television." In the late 1980s, a revelation occurred with regard to the way viewer contributions were being used by one of the largest television ministries—PTL. On October 5, 1989, PTL founder and leader Jim Bakker was convicted of defrauding his followers of $3.7 million and is serving 15 years in jail. The trials and tribulations of Jim Bakker, and the resultant impact of his fall from grace on other televangelical leaders, is explored in the third essay "TV Preachers on the Rocks." The fourth essay, published in *People* magazine ("Unholy Roller Coaster") is both an in-depth look at the cast of characters associated with the PTL scandal and a classic example of how the popular media have exploited the demise of a television preacher. Together, these four essays offer insight into one of the most controversial forms of alternative media content.

The New Awakening:
Getting Religion in the Video Age
Margaret O'Brien Steinfels and Peter Steinfels, CHANNELS

He is the symbol of an explosive mixture of fundamentalist faith, right-wing politics, and modern technology. People who wouldn't know the difference between Rex Humbard and Mother Hubbard, people who might well assume that Oral Roberts was a tooth-brush manufacturer, are nonetheless worried about the power of the "prime-time preachers." Not even when Bishop Fulton J. Sheen scored a hit with his prime-time series in 1952 was there such a furor over religion and television.

The resources—and resourcefulness—of the so-called electronic church are indeed impressive. Not only have the fundamentalist evangelists on television created a single but effective TV message, they have mastered the means of delivering it. They produce their own shows in their own studios with their own production facilities. They own TV cameras and transmitting equipment, and have begun to acquire transporter time for satellite transmission, enabling their programs to run on a growing number of cable systems across the country. They pay for their own broadcast time, and they've developed extensive support organizations to build their "congregations" and raise funds.

Religious networks are springing up. Pat Robertson, one of the most successful of the TV preachers, has organized the Christian Broadcast Network (CBN), headquartered in Virginia Beach, Virginia, which used a twenty-four-hour-a-day transponder on Satcom IIIR and computerized production and transmitting facilities. CBN owns four UHF television stations and five FM radio stations, and keeps a staff of more than seven hundred busy. It operates seventy-one regional call-in centers staffed mainly with volunteers who follow up on financial pledges and provide prayerful counseling. CBN University offers graduate training in communications and theology. Recently Robertson has spun off a secular counterpart, the Continental Broadcasting Network, which will transmit general programming suitable for family viewing.

It is the political potential of establishments like Robertson's that has stirred so much controversy—at least since 1979, when Jerry Falwell used his *Old-Time Gospel Hour* television program as a base for organizing the Moral Majority, and even more so since 1980, when the Religious New Right not only contributed to Ronald Reagan's victory but was widely regarded as a decisive factor in the defeat of several leading liberal Senators. At the same time, the media success of the fundamentalists has posed a direct challenge to the other churches, giving a new urgency to long-standing questions about organized religion's approach to television.

Not that the churches have ever lacked individuals aware of television's power—critics who worry about the medium's destructive or trivializing impact on personal values, enthusiasts who hope to exploit its hold on mass audiences for explicitly religious purposes. But the success of the prime-time preachers, linked as it is to the advent of new technologies, has added fuel to old debates. To some, the electronic church is further evidence of television's distorting effect on authentic religion. To others, it is an implicit call to "go and do likewise."

Swaggart in the Morning

Getting perspective on the electronic church itself is not easy, in view of the political passions it has stirred. In an effort to raise funds to combat TV evangelists, Norman Lear has claimed, "The ability of moral majoritarians to shape public attitudes and to influence the climate of public debate is unprecedented and poses an enormous danger. The leading 'television preachers' alone have an audience approaching 40 million." In sum, says Lear, "The moral majoritarians have overpowered America's airwaves with their messages of hostility, fear, and distrust."

The casual viewer of these programs might be hard pressed to see why Lear was so incensed. For a start, few prime-time preachers actually appear during prime time. In most major markets, they are still likely to be found early in the morning, late at night, or in the Sunday-morning "religious ghetto." Lear also fails to acknowledge the sheer variety of the programming—everything from fire-and-brimstone preaching pitched to stir fear in the backsliding Christian, to staid Bible-study programs sending all but the truly devoted into a stupor.

In the morning, Jimmy Swaggart pedantically explains God's views on first and second marriages; in the evening, he paces the platform, conjuring up pathetic scenes of the alcoholic so wretched that he stole the shoes from his own child's corpse to buy liquor.

Jim Bakker, one of the born-again, gesture-for-gesture imitations of network talk-show hosts, publicly shares the domestic dramas of his marriage to gospel singer Tammy Fay.

Ben Kinchlew, Pat Robertson's athletic-looking black co-host, presides over a slickly produced edition of *The 700 Club*, featuring:

- the author of a book claiming that low liquidity among major corporations lies at the root of our economic troubles;
- a reformed workaholic who, but for seeing the light and being saved by Jesus, would have lost his wife and children;
- a clip of a conference on cable television and "narrowcasting," from which *Screw* magazine publisher Al Goldstein's remarks had to be deleted because of his language;
- a woman, once gay, who turned to Jesus and now offers a ministry to homosexuals.

Not to everyone's taste, certainly, and clearly laced with political conservatism. But have the TV evangelists truly "overpowered America's airwaves"?

If audience size is any measure, the evangelists have hardly been a resounding success. During the 1980 elections, normally skeptical journalists were reporting that Jerry Falwell reached anywhere from 18 million to 30 million people each week; by contrast, the Arbitron and Nielsen reports revealed that Falwell was actually reaching fewer than 1.5 million viewers. Contrary to Norman Lear's assertion that the "leading" preachers alone had an audience of 40 million, the 1980 Arbitron figures showed a combined audience of half that size for all sixty-six syndicated religious programs. Furthermore, as Jeffrey Hadden and Charles Swann reminded the readers of their book, *Prime Time Preachers*, not all the top syndicated religious programs were conservative, not all the conservative programs were political, and most of the religious and conservative programs, at least during the greatest public uproar, were losing rather than gaining audience. (More recently, the top programs have recouped their losses, although without any startling growth.)

None of these facts should lead one to underestimate the power of the Religious New Right, but they do suggest that the television component in that power is easily inflated. In this tendency to overrate the influence, critics like Lear mirror the attitude of the right-wingers themselves, who commonly attribute the successes of liberalism to the media power of a small number of established liberals—including Norman Lear. It is easier for all of us to believe that unpopular ideas prosper because their advocates hold some "unfair" technological advantage than it is to think they actually resonate with the experience of large numbers of people.

Quite apart from the appeal of their right-wing ideology, the evangelical programs have more going for them than their willingness to invoke the Lord's name. The talk, the accents, the clothes, the tragedies and comedies of God's people have a touchingly real quality about them—a quality they retain even amidst their studied imitations of "real" television. The electronic church is, if nothing else, one of the few places on television where you encounter genuinely homely people. Neither the stars nor the guests hold back: They exhort, they preach, they laugh, and they cry—oh, do they cry! Not for them the deep-chested authoritativeness of Dan Rather, the cool mien of Barbara Walters, or the impish savoir-faire of Johnny Carson and Dick Cavett. These programs remind viewers that most of the country is not, after all, so slick, so professional, so well-dressed, and so damnably *in control.*

Despite the claims of Falwell and others to a truly national audience, the TV congregants are still predominantly female, Southern, small-town or rural, and getting on in years, according to Hadden and Swann. To see people like themselves, or at least like someone they know, confirms their sense of reality. If the guests on some of the shows—ex-alcoholics, former drug addicts, widows with young children, victims of unhappy marriages and miserable childhoods—routinely strike a maudlin note, the viewers can nonetheless identify with these all-too-familiar casualties of ordinary life: this is something every successful soap-opera writer understands. And the casualties are always repaired, with the help of friends, of the church, and above all of Jesus. Though the world's problems can seem insoluble, viewers may take some small comfort in the apparent capacity of individuals and small groups to deal with their own problems.

Obviously the electronic church trades in a kind of unreality of its own. Indeed, it is commonly accused of misleading people about the true nature of the human condition. According to the Reverend James M. Dunn, "The quick, certain, black-and-white theologies so made to order for television are inadequate for life in the real world."

Dunn's criticism is especially interesting because he is a leading staff member of the Baptist Joint Committee on Public Affairs—an agency sponsored in part by churches that many Americans might fail to differentiate from the electronic church itself. Even Carl F. H. Henry, elder statesman of evangelical Protestantism, has echoed this criticism. The strongest reproof, of course, has come from the mainline Protestant churches, generally those belonging to the National Council of Churches (NCC). Their leading complaint is that electronic churches twist the Gospel into a quick fix, promising a painless life, and aping, rather than questioning, the values of secular culture. If you accept Jesus, you will enjoy immediate relief from suffering. Success, prosperity, and earthly happiness will be yours. This presents an odd contrast to Jesus' message, but it bears more than a faint resemblance to the run of TV commercials.

A Far-flung "Congregation"

The religious critics' second objection is that Jesus called people into a church community—a fellowship of worship and service. The electronic church, however, substitutes for this a pseudo-community of isolated viewers. Finally, TV evangelism fosters the cult-like following of a single leader. In 1979, a habitually measured and good-humored commentator on American Protestantism, University of Chicago church historian (and Lutheran pastor) Martin E. Marty warned that "the electronic church threatens to replace the living congregation with a far-flung clientele of devotees to this or that evangelist. This invisible religion is—or ought to be—the most feared contemporary rival to church religion."

But isn't that rivalry only the latest chapter in an old story? Religious "awakenings" have frequently been tied to new forms of communication—like the printed book in the sixteenth century or the open-air revival in the eighteenth and nineteenth—and on each occasion the established churches have warned that the new techniques were altering the character of the faith. In a sense the established churches were right. Certainly the Protestant emphasis on "scripture alone" derived from both Renaissance humanism and the new power of the printing press. Likewise, the simplified theology and emotional fervor of American Protestantism sprang from the needs of the faithful in the camp meeting. And church structures could no more escape alteration than church doctrine. When so many more people could read and own their own Bibles, the need for a teaching hierarchy diminished. Revivalism put a premium on showmanship and platform oratory, rather than theological training, as a path to religious leadership. The electronic church is not terribly sophisticated about answering the establishment's criticism, seeing it mainly as a reflection of the mainliners' lack of fervor and enterprise. But paradoxically, if it wanted to, it could defend its innovations as nothing new.

To the Electronic Collection Plate

But the tension between independent evangelists and the mainline churches is also part of a larger story—that of broadcasting in America. The early days of radio saw all kinds of religious groups not only buying time but frequently owning stations—which were often used as weapons against one another. By 1934, however, when the Federal Communications Act established a "public interest" obligation for licensees, a less chaotic pattern began to develop. Led by NBC, most major stations—and eventually the other networks—provided free time to broad, ecumenical groups, which in turn produced religious programming of a non-divisive kind. (NBC, for example, worked in partnership with the Protestant Federal Council of Churches [now the NCC], with the National Council of Catholic Men and with the Jewish Theological Seminary of America.) As they were providing free time to such mainline groups, NBC, CBS, and ABC actually refused to sell others any time for religious broadcasting, and many local stations followed suit. The Mutual Broadcasting System did sell time, but in 1944 it forbade soliciting funds on the air—a sharp blow to paid-time preachers. In short, the new arrangement left independent evangelicals to fend for themselves—buying time where they could, or owning and operating their own commercial stations.

With the advent of television, a consortium of Protestant, Catholic, and Jewish groups divided free network time on a 3, 2, 1 basis: Of every 6 hours the networks allotted, the Protestants would receive 3, the Catholics 2, and the Jews 1. The networks subsidized the programming, and local affiliates carried it free. This arrangement allowed the stations to meet their public-interest obligations and avoid sectarian strife, while the major religious groups controlled their allotted time (mostly on Sunday mornings, when audiences were small and advertisers few) and benefited from network expertise and technology.

Richard Walsh, former director of communications for the National Council of Catholic Men and producer of *The Catholic Hour* from 1953 to 1968, remembers the arrangement as highly practical and conducive to good relations between the churches and the networks, as well as among religious groups. "The purpose of network programming for the religious groups was not to convert, and they did little direct preaching *à la* today's electronic church," says Walsh. In his view, the point was to foster dialogue. "*The Catholic Hour,* though addressed to the Catholics, was on subjects that might be of interest to others." While financial support varied with each network, Walsh recalls enjoying great independence from the networks in producing a variety of programs—talk shows, operas, plays, documentaries.

Though generally comfortable, the relationship between the networks and mainline religious groups did have its share of ups and downs even before the electronic church hove onto the scene. Some Protestant groups continued to complain that the NCC did not represent the totality of Protestant views—and NBC, for one, provided time to the Southern Baptists. By the end of the sixties, network funds began to shrink and affiliates began to be more reluctant about providing free time. Some of this may have been due to a perception, perhaps exaggerated, that religion was no longer, in the cant term of the day, "relevant," a view that declining church attendance figures supported. Bill McClurkin, director of broadcast and film for the NCC, adds another factor: The increase in Sunday sports broadcasting narrowed the time boundaries of the Sunday-morning "religious ghetto." In any case, when enterprising evangelicals proposed to pay for air-time that affiliates had been giving away—why, that was an offer the affiliates could hardly refuse.

More than ideology, program content, or style, money may be the key to the electronic church's rise. As Hadden and Swann point out, 1970 to '75 were years when the costs of video production dropped. They were also the years when the evangelists' audiences doubled, often at the expense of the mainliners' programs. The fact is that mainline and evangelical programs have never gone head-to-head, on the same terms. Would the mainline shows have been dropped by so many stations if they, too, were paying their own way? The TV evangelists, having been forced to wander in the paid-time wilderness for so long, have simply played by the free-market rules and won.

Money may also prove to be the Achilles heel of the TV preachers. Secular critics dwell on the huge sums the electronic church rakes in: the "electronic collection plate," they call it. But the TV ministry not only draws in support; it has to pay it out as well. Television is an expensive habit to maintain, and the TV preachers are hooked. Also, large amounts of money flowing in and out of the coffers are a constant temptation, even to the righteous. With or without scandal, the moderately prosperous lifestyle of most TV evangelists sits uncomfortably with their constant solicitation of funds and the panoply of memberships, pins, study guides, and booklets that they dangle before their followers. Some preachers resolve the incongruity by emphasizing their own version of Save the Children campaigns—relief and missionary work in impoverished areas of the globe. But that appeal has provoked further demands for accurate accounting of how much money really goes where.

Jerry Falwell has joined with Billy Graham and some other evangelical ministers in establishing an Evangelical Council for Financial Accountability to insure financial self-regulation. Most of the other TV preachers have kept their distance.

Television's Calling

The success of the electronic church has given the established denominations the "feeling of being outflanked, threatened," according to Stewart M. Hoover, TV producer, lecturer on mass communications, and author of *The Electronic Giant,* published by the Church of the Brethren. Why, then, don't they simply start paying their own way too?

The question ignores the important *organizational* consequences of church involvement in television. With the electronic church, what you see is pretty much what there is. Television is at the heart of these ministries. "My specific calling from God," Jim Bakker has written, "is to be a television talk-show host. I love TV. I eat it. I sleep it." Most other church organizations are complex and their activities highly decentralized. Most of their personnel serve local congregations: most of their financial resources are invested in church buildings, community centers, schools, hospitals, and so on. The major churches all have skilled, respected individuals dealing with television. But enlarging their activities would mean switching substantial funds and energies from other areas.

For reasons of theology, propriety, and concern for the effect on other church activities, most of these churches object to soliciting funds on the air. Accordingly, they're not ready to give up on the free-time tradition. In the face of FCC deregulation policies, many church groups have defended the practice of free air-time for public-interest programming, and not just that of a religious nature either.

The cause is not lost. Free air-time does continue to be available. *Insight,* a drama program produced by the Paulists, a Catholic order of priests, is shown free by about a hundred stations. In 1980 it was among the top ten religious programs in the Arbitron ratings, and in 1981 it won three Daytime Emmy Awards. *Davey and Goliath,* a cartoon series for children produced by the Lutheran Church in America, continues to be re-run in free time slots—and to gain quite respectable ratings.

The networks, however, no longer seem interested in supporting these kinds of shows, so without giving up entirely on free time, the mainline churches know they have to explore other alternatives. Basically there are three:

1. to follow the lead of the electronic church by building their own production and distribution apparatus for religious programming;
2. to concentrate on influencing the effects of non-religious television on public and personal morals;
3. to reject using television entirely.

The last, most radical course has been proposed by Harvey Cox, a noted Harvard theologian. Suppose, he argues, that "all the mass media of all the countries of the world could be turned over to the churches for one whole week, or one whole month, exclusively for making the Gospel known. At the end of the month, do you really think the world would be much better off, or the Kingdom of God be appreciably closer?"

The problem, says Cox, is that the mass media are one-way, hierarchical systems inherently incapable of eliciting the profound belief the Gospel demands. The media "are controlled by the rich and powerful," while "God comes in vulnerability, and powerlessness. The message of the Gospel is essentially incompatible with any coercive form of communication. All 'mass media' are one-way and therefore inherently coercive."

Cox derides Christian "communicators" who want to infuse the networks with "a new and spiritually significant content. The churches should not be wasting their efforts trying to pilfer a few minutes of time from the reigning Caesars of the 'communications industry.'" Instead, "the Christian strategy *vis à vis* mass media is not to try to use them but to try to dismantle them. We need a real revolution in which the control of the media is returned to the people and the technical development of media is turned toward accessibility, two-way communication, and genuine conversation."

Less radical than Cox's approach, but still having something in common with it, are the efforts of some individuals concentrating on influencing non-religious television. Dr. Everett Parker, for example, is director of the United Church of Christ's Office of Communication, a veteran of religious broadcasting, and a leader in struggles to widen access to the airwaves. Under his leadership, the United Church of Christ has tried to influence the values communicated on television by insuring that all community groups are represented on the air. Parker's Office of Communication is a leading critic of FCC deregulation plans, and sponsor of educational efforts and consulting services. The church-launched Community Telecommunications Service, for instance, has developed a workshop curriculum to teach local churches how to produce cable programs, and another to teach community and church leaders how to negotiate cable contracts, assure public access to cable, and enforce fair employment practices.

Other church programs try to influence the impact of television on values by educating the viewers: The Media Action Research Center, a body sponsored by several denominations and headquartered in the National Council of Churches office in New York, developed television awareness training in the mid-seventies. Its *Viewer's Guide* shows "how we can take command, use TV intelligently and creatively, instead of mindlessly letting TV use us."

Finally there is the first option—getting into the TV business in a big way. There are three outstanding examples of this besides those of the electronic church.

The United States Catholic Conference (USCC) has taken two steps toward keeping its hand in the game. First, an annual Catholic Communications Campaign raises about $5 million a year, 50 percent of which remains in the local dioceses where it is collected; the other half is used to support the USCC Office of Communications and to award grants to a range of communications-related projects.

Second, the USCC has formed the independent, for-profit Catholic Telecommunications Network of America (CTNA) to provide local dioceses with a variety of satellite-transmitted services: news and photo services for diocesan newspapers, electronic mail, video conferencing for church leaders, administrative and educational materials, and TV program redistribution. The network, which began transmitting last fall, is supported by voluntary affiliation and maintenance fees from local dioceses—and by the sale of its services to commercial users. As of November 1982, 33 out of 172 local dioceses had signed affiliation contracts. Wassyl Lew, head of CTNA, expects that a number of religious orders, Catholic colleges, universities, and hospitals may eventually affiliate with it. Lew emphasizes the word "telecommunications" rather than "television" in describing the network: Its primary purpose is to provide a communications service for the bishops, though TV programming provided by the network will be available for redistribution to local TV stations or cable systems.

The fifteen hours of programming per week that CTNA currently plans to redistribute include programs on marriage counseling and enrichment; an interview program called *Christopher Close-Ups*; several Bible and theology programs; two Spanish-language programs; a missionary program produced by the Maryknoll religious order, and a variety of magazine-format and entertainment shows. All of this will be produced not by CTNA but largely by religious orders and local dioceses. Lew anticipates that as the system becomes fully operational, some of its downlinks will also serve as uplinks, thus allowing dioceses to be senders as well as receivers of TV programming. In the meantime, programs will go out from CTNA's New York transmitter.

CTNA is an attempt to meet the diverse needs of a decentralized church organization with the capacities of the satellite for coast-to-coast transmission. As such, the network might become a model for other church groups. Yet it is unlikely to increase the number of Catholic TV shows available to a large television audience.

One reason that telecommunications will always play a less important role for the Catholic church than for TV evangelists is that it "just doesn't fit with what Catholics think of as a church," argues Richard Hirsch, head of the USCC's Office of Communications. "The electronic church is not a church: it is a pulpit." The point applies to a number of other churches as well—those that consider sacrament and ritual as important to their worship as preaching, in particular the Episcopalians and Lutherans. It is interesting to recall that Bishop Sheen's famous programs had nothing of a church service about them. The bishop was dressed in resplendent episcopal garb, but *not* in his vestments for celebrating mass. The format was one of teaching, not preaching or prayer: a blackboard was the chief prop. Sheen's example suggests the distance that the "ritual" churches are apt to see between effective television and the central acts of their faith.

The Eternal World Network, another of the three noteworthy efforts by religious groups to build a television base, also depends on satellite technology. Mother Angelica, a Franciscan nun whose convent in Birmingham, Alabama specializes in preparing and printing religious pamphlets and other materials, made the leap from the printing press to a satellite transponder on Satcom IIIR with four hours of programming seven nights a week. From a converted garage, she produces her own show, *Mother Angelica Talks It Over,* makes time available to other religious programs, re-runs old favorites, and subleases unused transponder time to the First United Methodist Church in Shreveport, Louisiana. She reports that forty-two cable systems, reaching up to 800,000 homes, carry her programming. The network is supported by direct-mail donations, unsolicited contributions, and foundation grants.

The United Methodists tried a different approach: In 1980, they launched a fund-raising drive to buy a TV station. The church group planned to produce its own religious programs with the projected $1 million profit from the station. But ownership of a commercial station posed conflicts between the values of Methodism and the values the station would be communicating much of the time. The sheer expense of the project has also deterred some church members, who have asked, "How many hungry people can you feed with that money?"

The pitfalls encountered by the United Methodists illustrate the dangers for mainline churches that might be tempted to emulate the fundamentalists. According to Stewart M. Hoover, writing in *The Electronic Giant,* "The mainline churches could probably not 'beat the electronic church at its own game': they probably would not really want to."

But it should be remembered that the electronic church itself was not born yesterday—which is when it first began getting national attention. It was more than two decades ago that Pat Robertson managed to put back on the air the defunct UHF station he had bought. Jerry Falwell went on the air in Lynchburg, Virginia, six months after he started his church there—in 1956. Oral Roberts first appeared on television in 1954, and his current TV format dates from 1969. At that time, the other churches were comfortably ensconced on the networks; twenty-five years later, they are groping. The outcome of that groping may not be clear for another quarter-century.

Peter Steinfels, executive editor of Commonwealth *magazine, is the author of* The Neoconservatives *(Simon & Schuster). Margaret O'Brien Steinfels is an editor and writer, and is business manager of* Christianity and Crisis *magazine.*

Ten Commandments of the Electronic Church
Robert Abelman, CHANNELS

In the beginning, Vladimir Zworykin and other engineers created television. Now television was un-formed and void of programming; it was a resource untapped by the powers that be. And Bishop Fulton J. Sheen said, "Let there be religious fare so to spread the word of God to the multitudes." And he went on television as he did on the radio before it. And millions of viewers saw the image and thought it was good. And other religious leaders from other denominations said, "Let us explore this medium so to give our message to the masses." And so they did, and thought it was good.

And the broadcasters said, "Let us give free airtime to religious organizations in the public's in-terest, but only in accordance with their prevalence in the land—three parts Protestant, two parts Catholic, and one part Jewish." And it was so. And television brought forth tent revivals, fire-and-brimstone sermons, and solemn services on weekend early mornings and late evenings. But as televi-sion's popularity grew and secular programming flourished, religious fare took to the background, unable to compete with the appeal and budgets of network shows.

And a resurrection of the electronic church did occur, the result of the miracle of satellite com-munication and cable technology. And the availability of religious fare did grow a hundredfold and spread across the land to the north and south, east and west. And the face of religious fare did change accordingly to compete with secular programming for the attention of the masses. And religious lead-ers who once praised the medium now question its utility and wonder if it has not changed the face of religion as well. And the nonbelievers who once laughed and thought religious television folly now reflect and are humbled by its presence and power. And social critics sit and wonder if religious fare has not fallen to temptation by providing a collection plate for the millions or a forum for the chosen few of politics.

To seek the answers, two social scientists did journey to the electronic church and from it did bring forth 10 commandments that reflect the world of religion on television:

I. THOU SHALT MAKE UNTO THEE A SECULAR IMAGE.
Religious television programming is no longer limited to simple preaching and revival shows. Like its secular counterpart, religious TV is comprised of just about every popular programming format, in-cluding talk shows *(700 Club)*, game shows *(Bible Bowl)*, children's shows *(Davey and Goliath)*, soap operas *(Another Life)*, news-magazine shows *(Reel to Real)*, and music/variety shows *(PTL Club)*.

II. THOU SHALT BE LIKE BISHOP FULTON SHEEN BEFORE THEE.
Eve may have fallen before Adam from the land of Eden, but pioneers of the world of religious TV were men. Today, men continue to dominate religious programming, outnumbering women three to one. In addition, nonwhites constitute only 14 percent of the total religious television population. When women and ethnic minorities *are* presented, they are typically in subservient roles or positions of authority and control. Regarding contemporary televangelists, very little has been changed since Bishop Sheen took to the screen—televangelists are overwhelmingly male and white.

III. THOU SHALT NOT BEAR WITNESS TO ANY DENOMINATION.
The vast majority of nationally distributed religious programs do not specify an association with or financial support from any particular denomination. Nonetheless, these programs are highly consis-tent in their fundamental approach to Christianity and typically feature pentecostals and charismatics in evangelistic roles. The 3:2:1 ratio of denominational representation on television, as established by broadcasters during the birth of the medium, is no longer a reality. Together, Protestant and Catholic programs outnumber those representing all other religions by approximately 50 to 1.

IV. REMEMBER THE SABBATH DAY, BUT WEEKDAYS CAN BE JUST AS HOLY.

As a result of satellite communication, cable technology, and prospering religious TV networks, (e.g., PTL, CBN), many programs are received in all parts of the country, seven days a week, from early morning to late night. The myth that religious television is broadcast solely on Sunday mornings is just that—a myth. Religious programming is the fastest growing genre in American television.

V. IGNORE THY GRANDMOTHER AND THY GRANDFATHER.

The elderly are highly underrepresented on nationally distributed religious television, comprising only 5 percent of all persons appearing in these programs but constituting 13 percent of the American population. In addition, they are typically reduced to minor roles when they do appear. Based on these portrayals, religious programming suggests that the elderly do not serve as leaders in the church, are not prevalent or respected members of religious communities, and have no place in today's family life.

VI. THOU SHALT NOT STEAL, BUT DONATIONS ARE GLADLY ACCEPTED.

A viewer of religious fare can expect to be solicited for an average of $189.52 an hour for donations and $8.95 every five minutes for purchasable items. Consequently, a viewer watching only two hours of religious television a day will be solicited for a minimum average of $138,350 in the course of a year. The most frequently stated reason for requests for money was the need to pay for domestic educational activities, which included keeping the TV program on the air. Although figures reflecting how much money is actually collected through on-the-air solicitations are not readily available, the increasing frequency of these high-budget programs is testimony to the success of these appeals. As a result. . . .

VII. THOU SHALT NOT BITE THE HAND THAT FEEDS YOU.

The function, content, and impact of the broadcast media is one of the most referred-to social topics in religious programming, second only to death and dying. The role of mass media in this country has been criticized by various religious organizations and leaders. Within the confines of religious television programming, however, the mass media are referred to in either neutral or positive terms.

VIII. THOU SHALT DISCUSS ADULTERY, BUT NOT POLITICS.

Criticism of the electronic church itself has arisen, focusing primarily on the notion that it strays in the political arena. The most visible and vocal debate about the political ramifications of religious fare has been between TV producer-writer Norman Lear and Moral Majority leader Jerry Falwell, himself a televangelist. Criticism of this nature is unfounded, however, for although highly conservative in its political stance, religious programming is rarely political in content. For the most part, it concerns itself with issues of religious and social import, presenting God or the church as the primary solution to the world's problems.

IX. THOU SHALT COVET THY COMPETITION'S AUDIENCE.

The majority of religious programs are neither geared toward an exclusively "born again" audience nor an audience exclusively composed of candidates for conversion. Rather, these programs assume the same programming strategy as that employed by secular programming—gearing themselves to the lowest common denominator. Furthermore, in order to appeal to the greatest possible home viewership, no specific audience (i.e., shut-ins, non-believers, Catholics) is ever identified in religious programs. Consequently, these programs are aimed at the same general audience that NBC, CBS, and ABC seek.

X. THY MEDIUM IS THY MESSAGE.

Television is the ultimate pulpit. Because television reaches nearly 100 percent of American households, it can bring religion to those who would not ordinarily have access to it and to those who would not normally seek it out in their community. The Reverend Billy Graham hinted at the potential of television when he suggested that he could "preach to millions more than Christ did in his entire lifetime." Today, around 14 million Americans watch some form of religious programming every week. In addition, every month another television station devotes itself primarily to religious content.

In June 1984, yet another religious cable network, the American Christian Television System, began operation, thereby furthering the electronic church's ability to deliver the flock.

Poet T.S. Eliot's observation that "television is a medium whereby millions of people can listen to the same joke and still remain lonesome" has some relevance to religious programming. Television has depersonalized the religious experience by substituting a two-dimensional figure on a 19-inch screen for the local preacher, and by replacing the congregation's social interaction with the isolation of one's own apartment or hotel room. The community involvement that revolves around Sunday morning or Saturday evening services has been removed. Furthermore, one's "personal relationship with God," as it is often referred to in religious fare, has become a media event shared by millions. There is nothing personal about watching television.

And God created Man in His own image. Man created television in his, and television tried to reflect God in all his glory. But the limitations of Man and the limitations of the medium brought forth a portrait of God and His Word and that was more Man and medium than glory. And is it good?

Robert Abelman is a communications professor at Cleveland State University; he and Kimberly Neuendorf conducted the research reported here for UNDA—USA, a Catholic communications organization.

TV Preachers on the Rocks
Larry Martz, NEWSWEEK

At first it seemed like old times in televangelism's gaudiest empire. There was Tammy Faye Bakker, her lashes as spiky as ever and a smudge of lipstick on her right tooth, in royal progress through the faithful outside the PTL studio at Heritage USA. She bestowed hugs and smeared cheeks, posed for the Instamatics and cheered insistently. "We're coming home!" she exulted. "The sun's going to shine again!" And the crowd of two dozen took the cue. "Amen!" they shouted, and a white-haired woman pressed a money-filled envelope into Tammy's hand. "Take this to Jim," she whispered.

But it was all a fantasy, as empty as the stony silence of the other watching pilgrims whose faith in Jim and Tammy Bakker died with last year's sex-and-money scandal. The reality was taking form 75 miles away from PTL's rolling acres, in a bankruptcy courtroom in Columbia, S.C., where plans for the final liquidation of the ministry were being hammered out last week. And the Bakkers were not the only TV preachers facing—and denying—calamity. Jimmy Swaggert, defying his church's discipline after his own fall from grace, was also fending off financial collapse. "What you have seen here is the natural rise and fall of unchecked power," said sociologist William Martin of Rice University, a student of televangelists. Oral Roberts was struggling to stay solvent amid his follies. Pat Robertson, his presidential hopes a shambles, was trying to refloat his Christain Broadcasting Network. Jerry Falwell was back in Lynchburg, Va., healing the rifts in his flock created by his PTL misadventures. Even preachers untainted by the headlined scandals, like California's Robert Schuller, were losing viewers and revenues.

Nobody was writing the obituary of the electronic church. The hard-core faithful were still viewing, still sending money and still believing that the Lord's work must be done even if a few shepherds proved unworthy of their calling. But across the country, preachers were succumbing to improbable sins and rumors of further scandal were flying—and sources of new money were drying up. Even before the PTL and Swaggert sensations, the religious audience had stopped growing and competition for donations was fierce. The bad news cut deeper. Last week the Arbitron TV ratings service reported new losses for all the ministries in major markets. Swaggert, once the unchallenged leader in the field with 2.1 million households in February 1987, had lost more than half of his flock and dropped to third place with 923,000. Schuller was the new leader, with 1.4 million households, but even he had lost more than 50,000 in just over two years. Robert's audience, once more than 2 million, was only 635,000 in May. Robertson's *700 Club* had lost 45 percent of the 440,000 households watching in 1987, and PTL, with 105,000, had fallen off the charts of the Top 20.

The loss of money was harder to pin down, since TV ministries have no obligation to disclose their finances. Many routinely exaggerate their operations; others trumpet their crises, to help with fund-raising; some do both in quick succession. Robert Abelman, a communications professor at Cleveland State University, says his studies show that since the scandals, religious viewers are giving less often than before to fewer televangelists, but sending more money in each envelope. Other observers say local evangelical churches may be getting bigger donations, offsetting the TV loss. But there is no doubt that televangelists as a class are reaping less—or that they are hunkering down for what may be a long dry spell. Among the major players:

The End for PTL

In the bankruptcy court, the issue was no longer whether PTL should be broken up and sold, but how. M.C.(Red) Benton, latest in a string of court-appointed trustees for the ministry, said he hoped to sell the whole operation to someone who would operate Heritage USA as a Christian family retreat and lease the TV studio and other facilities to an independent ministry. But there was no guarantee of that. Benton said he had "a real serious offer" of a $200 million buyout; he set a deadline of July 19 for offers and said he would decide which one to recommend by mid-August.

Meanwhile, what was once a $172 million religious empire had become a shell. There was only a trickle of visitors to the Heritage USA theme park. Even after hundreds of layoffs and draconian budget cuts, Benton said PTL needed donations of about $60,000 a day to survive. The latest week's average was $21,600. At last week's hearing, the bankruptcy judge reluctantly approved dipping into escrow to keep PTL going and open the water park for the July 4 weekend.

Back from their exile in California, Jim and Tammy had not lost hope. They filed their own plan with the court, proposing to rent the whole operation on a monthly basis and use their own televised magic to raise enough money to buy PTL outright, bit by bit. Jim even waved an envelope that he said contained a $100 million letter of credit. But it had yet to be proved that they could raise enough for rent, let alone cover PTL's $130 million or more of debt, and court officials held out no hope to the dwindling core of Bakker fans.

The Odds Against Jimmy

The preacher's fall has been Satan's delight: *Penthouse* magazine's July issue sold out in five days with its raunchy photos of prostitute Debra Murphree, demonstrating the pornographic poses she said Swaggert paid her to perform. Swaggert himself, who has confessed only an unspecified "moral failure," was back in his pulpit, defying the Assemblies of God and its order that he spend at least a year doing penance. But the Jimmy Swaggert Ministries were hemorrhaging money. Donations that once flowed at a rate of $500,000 a day were estimated at less than one-third that level. A ministry spokesman admitted that the staff has been cut by almost a third. Swaggert's broadcasts, once heard in 120 nations, now play in only four or five.

And Swaggert's image was further tarnished by the staff exodus. His ministry was always more secretive than most. But after the scandal the Assemblies of God threatened to strip the credentials from Swaggert associates who stayed with him, and many chose to leave. Others who were willing to stay were fired when they questioned Swaggert's defiance of the mother church. Some of the defector's painted a picture of the ministry even more shocking in its fashion than the preacher's peccadilloes. As they told it, his wife, Frances, and son, Donnie, ran a virtual reign of terror at the ministry. To check for leaks, polygraph tests have been almost routine. All staffers, except the top ministers, must punch a time clock, and anyone found more than one minute late four times in six months can be docked or fired.

Swaggert's staffers maintain that the ministry is only "restructuring." But the rumors persist that more scandal is to come, this time on the financial front. A special task force of the Internal Revenue Service is known to be auditing the ministry. Swaggert's lifestyle has been a touchy topic for years. Though he has boasted that his salary is only $86,000, it was recently confirmed that he gets a housing allowance of about $10,000 a month. Nepotism is built into the ministry: at last count, Swaggert had at least 12 relatives on his payroll.

Oral's Giant Puzzle

Oral Roberts has always been the most flamboyant of the TV preachers. His followers swooned under his healing hand and swallowed his vision of Jesus, 900 feet tall, urging on construction of his elaborate hospital. True to form, when the Swaggert scandal erupted, Oral called Jimmy for a long-distance prayer session and said later he had cast out long-fingernailed demons who were tearing at Swaggert's flesh. But Oral tipped some fatal balance last year when he said God would "call me home" if the faithful didn't send in $8 million for medical missions. In a national wave of derision, his ratings and revenues plummeted disastrously. Donations fell 50 percent in the first three quarters of 1987, and Oral had to cancel his weekly show in 71 of his 220 national markets. Roberts has tried in vain to lease his hospital, which has never filled all its beds. His ministry sold four Mercedes cars and Oral's $3.25 million Beverly Hills mansion.

But Robert's credibility hit bottom early this year when he abruptly called off the medical-scholarship program he had been ready to die for. Then, after a hail of protests, he reversed himself again. "My faith wavered," he explained in a mass mailing to his "prayer partners" last month. "I saw the medical school like a giant puzzle that had been sitting on my shoulders, weighing me down and tearing me up." Now God had shown him "a beautiful plan," he said: 80,000 followers should give $100 each to raise $8 million a year for the missions.

That isn't likely to prove more effective than Oral's healing of Jimmy Swaggert. Roberts is now rumored to be shopping for loans to shore up his ministry, and his appeals for funds have grown strident even by his standards; he is so pinched, he told his viewers recently, that I "fell across the bed and I cried. . . . [But] we're not going under. We're going over!"

As always, he will go in style. Oral and his son, Richard, have taken some heat over their lavish houses but, as he explained to the flock last year, they need big houses for entertaining. Richard's wife, Lindsay, defending her costly watch, said she didn't want to insult the donor who had given it to her. Answering the question posed by a country-music ballad at the height of last year's scandal, Lindsay added that even Jesus might have worn a Rolex if somebody had given him one.

Pat Returns to the Fold

By most accounts, Pat Robertson came home to Virginia only reluctantly after his presidential foray: he would have preferred to stay in politics, building the state and local machinery for another run for the top, but felt duty-bound to rescue the Christian Broadcasting Network that was falling apart in his absence. Robertson released no figures and refused a NEWSWEEK interview, and the depth of CBN's problems remains unclear. Staffers tend to minimize the trouble, but Robertson himself told The Daily Press of Newport News that "We're in serious trouble here." By one account, the CBN budget is less than a third of its peak $200 million; there have been hundreds of layoffs, with whole departments decimated. The security-conscious Robertson didn't even have a man on duty recently at the guardhouse of the 200-acre compound in Virginia Beach.

As he has from the time the scandals broke, Robertson insists he is not a televangelist but a "Christian broadcaster." Nonetheless, says Clevleand State University's Abelman, "his viewers have found him guilty by association," and the label hurt him badly among voters. Robertson hasn't given up his political goals, just deferred them to restore his base at CBN. The consensus: CBN can probably survive. But as Robertson's son Tim told the viewers recently, it won't be easy, and the problem is money: "It is urgent, my friends."

Falwell's Retreat

Riding with Jerry Falwell in a Kansas City taxicab not long ago, a mischievous reporter asked the driver if he recognized his passenger. "Sure do," said the cabbie, eying Falwell in the rear-view mirror. "They've kinda got you in a jam with that chick, don't they?" Falwell used the story in a sermon to show how all TV preachers have been tarnished by the recent scandals. For his own part, however, Falwell insists that his troubles are past. His followers have forgiven him for taking over PTL and failing to save it from bankruptcy, he says; he is even welcome to preach these days to Baptist congregations that had shunned him for his charismatic associations. And thanks to some last-minute major gifts, Falwell said, his ministry ended fiscal 1988 in the black.

But even if that proves true—and Falwell's past figures have often been subject to revision—he is a long way from out of the woods. The May Arbitron ratings show his audience rebounding a bit from the year's low, to 410,000 households, but he is still down more than 30 percent from a year earlier. And he is bracing for a long pinch; the Falwell strategy is to depend less on donations and more on other revenues. He is restructuring his cable-TV operation, with a new satellite feed that can reach more cable networks and a new family-oriented set of programs. The fallout of the scandals could well continue, said his aide, Mark DeMoss, and "our attitude has been to assume things will not get better."

That assumption is safe enough for all the TV preachers. Scandal now seems endemic in the electronic church; rumors about one major preacher after another have kept evangelical circles buzzing all year. And lesser figures keep falling into bizarre sin, as a constant reminder of preacher fallibility. Two weeks ago Truman Dollar, pastor of Detroit's largest Baptist church, resigned his pulpit after confessing that he had made a series of sexually explicit phone calls to a woman in Kansas City.

Even without scandals, the TV church would have problems. Competition for the viewer's dollar is still growing, and demographics are at least temporarily unfavorable: low birthrates in the Depression have cut the population of viewers in their mid-60s, the preachers' prime prospects. In the long run of a decade or so, the maturing baby boomers may well take care of that problem. But to reach them, the preachers may have to change their message. "It's a fine line they have to walk," says Stewart Hoover, communications professor of Temple University, "between staying conventional enough to attract a broad audience and religious enough to attract a religious audience." Meanwhile, there's no lack of preachers ready to try. In Jimmy Swaggert's hometown of Baton Rouge, two defectors from his own ministry, Jerald Ogg and Glen Berteau, have already started ministries that attract several hundred followers every Sunday. "Given all the people who have been disillusioned, hurt and broken," says Berteau, "if there is any place for a church to be built, it's Baton Rouge."

Unholy Rollercoaster
Montgomery Brower, PEOPLE

Finally, sadly, there seemed nowhere new to run, no place to hide, no new crusade to announce. In a federal courtroom in Charlotte, N.C., disgraced televangelist Jim Bakker, 49, stood on trial for a long list of alleged sins, facing 120 years in prison and a $5 million fine on 24 counts of fraud and conspiracy. He's accused of siphoning $3.7 million from his PTL (Praise the Lord) ministry to live like Croesus while telling his flock to live like Jesus. Then, as has happened so often in the 30 months since disclosure of the Jessica Hahn affair shook Bakker's pulpit, a flood of tears and bathos washed away what has seemed the continuing tragicomedy of Bakker's life and left behind something closer to a theater of the absurd. Chapter and verse so far:

- Day One: The chipmunk-cheeked Bakker strolls into federal court, exuding confidence. However, he hears damaging testimony to the effect that he tacitly approved a $265,000 hush money payment to Jessica Hahn.

- Day Three: While testifying that some of Bakker's TV solicitations were deliberately misleading, prosecution witness Steve Nelson, a former aide, swoons on the witness stand and collapses unconscious in his chair. After a stage-whispered nudge from his lawyer—"Jim, Jim, *Jim*"—Bakker rushes to Nelson's side, kneels and prays for the witness. (Nelson later recovers in a hospital.)

- Day Four: Unholy hell breaks loose as Bakker crumbles to the floor of his lawyer's office and hides his head under a couch. He rolls into the fetal position and begins to weep. Judge Robert Potter suspends the trial and orders Bakker to the Federal Correctional Institution in Butner, N.C., for psychiatric evaluation. Bakker's psychiatrist, Dr. Basil Jackson, reports the preacher is suffering from a Goyaesque hallucination in which "suddenly people took the form of frightening animals, which he felt were intent on destroying him, attacking him and hurting him." As he's deposited in the backseat of a squad car after being led from his lawyer's office, Bakker once again assumes the fetal position.

- Day Five: Wife Tammy Faye Bakker arrives in North Carolina from their Orlando home and begins a not-very-lonely vigil outside of Butner. Near the gates of the prison, Tammy sobs and complains to the press about the treatment of her husband. "What Judge Potter has done to my husband is a disgrace to the Consitution," she insists. "Jim has been manhandled, strip-searched and paraded like a freak at a carnival show."

- Day Eight: Wearing a bright yellow shirt and looking glassy-eyed and emotionally vacant, a haggard and hunched-over Bakker is returned in manacles to court. Dr. Sally Johnson, a psychiatrist at Butner, declares him mentally competent for trial, despite his "panic attack" of the previous week, in which, she explains, Bakker saw the throng of newsmen as "giant ants with antennae waving." Meanwhile the wheels of justice begin to grind again as the trial is resumed.

If some saw a Christian being thrown to the lions, others took a more jaundiced view of the events. Courtroom skeptics say that the Bakker defense team had simply miscalculated. Angling for an insanity plea at best or a mistrial at worst, they hoped Bakker would be sent to a cushy private mental hospital. Instead he was sent to the prison facility at Butner, whose famous alumni include the likes of would-be presidential assassin John Hinckley and *Hustler* publisher Larry Flynt. There, some say, Jim got scared straight. Fast.

Yet others, even those who are normally deeply distrustful about Bakker, take the breakdown at face value. One of them is Charles Shepard, a reporter for the *Charlotte Observer,* who won a Pulitzer Prize for his investigation of the PTL and whose book about the Bakker scandals *(Forgiven)* will be published this month. "I'm convinced Bakker's breakdown was real," says Shepard, who watched as Bakker wobbled down the courthouse steps in handcuffs. "His pain appeared genuine. So genuine I couldn't even ask him questions. Neither did the TV reporters. He has this problem thinking people are always after him, out to get him. It is sort of a psychic nightmare of his. Now he is being dragged out in chains. He always felt like a victim, that people were after him. Now they really came and got him." Indeed, the "frightening animals" nipping at Bakker's heels are more than mere hallucinations. The 24 counts of fraud and conspiracy focus on his hawking $1000 "lifetime partnerships" in the PTL that supposedly allowed PTL members three free nights of lodging a year for life at his $200 million, 2,300-acre Heritage USA theme park—a sort of Christian Disneyland—in Fort Mill, S.C. Problem was, say the indictments, there was not nearly enough room at the inn. The Heritage park hotel wound up way overbooked, while Bakker lavished the $4 million he skimmed from the $158 million he raised on luxury cars, jewels, vacation junkets and cinnamon buns. One PTL aide would regularly purchase $100 worth of cinnamon buns for Bakker. Though the reverend never ate them, he loved the aroma.

But if Bakker's breakdown was a ploy, it was reputedly not the first time he had curled into the fetal position under stress. When the going gets tough, some who know him say, Bakker's reaction is often to hit the deck and curl up like a pill bug. One occasion came after his illicit 1980 tryst with Jessica Hahn—the former secretary who helped bring down the klieg-lite Church of Fund-raising known as the PTL. "When I got up this morning, it was the first thing I saw," says Hahn of the day that Bakker's courtroom collapse made the news, "and I just went, 'Oh, my God, here he goes again.'" Hahn says that after Bakker had his way with her in her Clearwater Beach hotel room, John Wesley Fletcher, the evangelist and middleman for the Bakker-Hahn liaison, rushed in and told her, "Jessica, you're not going to believe it, but Jim Bakker's in a fetal position right now, crying and hallucinating and having a fit and not knowing how to handle what just took place. He's just a mess and is saying how much you helped him because of the problems he's having with Tammy." Hahn believes Bakker opts for the fetal position whenever "there's been a very desperate situation where he needs people's sympathy. He's a master of manipulation."

Bakker reportedly hit the carpet again shortly after the affair, when he confessed his sexual misdeeds with Hahn to psychologist Fred Gross, a PTL counselor. Quickly, Gross joined him on the floor. "Within 10 minutes, we were prone on the floor," Gross once said in an account authorized by Bakker. "His face was buried in the carpet, sobbing. He was kicking the floor. He was writhing. He was retching." But Bakker could also adopt a more catatonic mode of collapse. Tammy Faye wrote that in 1978, when she and Bakker were having marital troubles over his refusal to have children, he had a breakdown. "He lay in bed for a month in the back bedroom with his Bible in his hand, begging God not to let him lose his mind totally," recounted Tammy in her autobiography, *I've Gotta Be Me.*

Others offer backhanded praise for what they see as Bakker's three-hankie tactics. Lawrence Bernstein, the former FCC attorney who investigated Bakker for alleged misappropriation of funds in a 1979–82 inquiry, says that Bakker often opened the spigots during 11 days of cross examination. "It takes him about 30 seconds to work it up, then he can't be stopped. He interrupts the proceedings, and it reached a point where we had to withdraw questions. We thought it was an act by a talented actor." In a controversial decision, the FCC decided not to bring Bakker to trial. Perhaps the go-with-the-flow emotionalism dates to one of Bakker's earliest successes as a novice televangelist. Soon after he got his first show on CBN in 1966, he performed at a telethon to raise funds for the fledgling network. Tears streaming down his face, he looked into the camera and announced, "We need $10,000 a month or we'll be off the air. . . . Christian television will be no more." The dollars came flooding in.

Despite his jittery emotional gyroscope, Bakker proved a genius at raising money, though former supporters and PTL members allege that Jim and Tammy's greed corrupted their ministry. Disillusioned followers have portrayed Bakker as a kind of Kewpie Caligula, ruling over the decadent imperial court of the PTL. "Bakker built a city where he would sit on the throne and have people pay him tribute," says Austin Miles, who gave up his career as a circus ringmaster two years after joining the PTL ministry in 1974 and who witnessed Jim and Tammy's theatrics for 10 years. "That's when the sex started to go wild."

Although Shepard's 635-page book is perhaps the most thorough and scholarly analysis of the rise and fall of the Bakker empire yet to be published, the author devotes an entire chapter of *Forgiven* to Tammy and Jim's many indiscretions. While Tammy played the role of the neglected wife, she became friendly with country musician Gary Paxton and later cozied up to married PTL executive Thurlow Spurr. So angry was Bakker over their crumbling marriage that he melted down his wedding ring and had it turned into a charm.

Meanwhile, Jim himself was no angel. "They put a Jacuzzi right in Jim's office which we called the Floozie Jacuzzi because of the gossip about what went on there," says Miles, whose own recently published book, *Don't Call Me Brother,* chronicles his life with and without Bakker. Before Jessica Hahn, Miles alleges, Bakker had an affair in the late 1970s with a born-again Christian beauty. Bakker reportedly did not limit his dalliances to women. In a 1989 *Penthouse* article, fellow PTL minister Fletcher alleged he caught Bakker in bed with his right-hand man, David Taggert. Fletcher said he himself had homosexual encounters with Bakker on three occasions. Their affair reportedly began when Bakker made advances to Fletcher as Fletcher was giving him a back rub in the ministry sauna at Heritage Village. Shepard recounts that one aide who traveled often with Bakker, a married man, used to give Bakker back rubs that Bakker took as a prelude to masturbation. Though upset and disgusted by his role as Bakker's geisha, the employee explained that Bakker compensated him for this arousal service with an unlimited budget, travel and his assurance that this was God's work.

Miles offers a more richly descriptive account of Bakker's homosexual cavorting. On Jan. 13, 1977, he walked into the steam room and found Bakker naked with three young men. "There they were, frolicking about, taking turns placing each other on the massage table. The hands started with the knees, working their way up the thighs into the intimate massages—accompanied by schoolgirl giggles and cries of 'Whooooee!' " he says. When Bakker realized someone was watching, a silence fell over the scene of good ol' boys at play. Then Bakker became businesslike, complimenting Miles on his performance on that day's show and telling one of the three men with him to "book Austin every month on this program." While retreating from the steam room, Miles heard footsteps and ducked into a corner. "It was Tammy Faye storming across the place," he says. "She banged on the door and said, 'Jim Bakker, I know you're in there. Now come out of there right now.' Then she broke down and started to cry."

Although such goings on took their toll on Jim and Tammy's marriage, they somehow managed to have an active sex life. Shepard reports that Bakker liked to boast about his and Tammy's sexual exploits, recounting a tryst in a park and how their screams of passion startled innocent strollers. Bakker also strongly touted PTL staffers on the marital benefits of vibrators. But sexual aids were no longer sufficient by 1980, the year of Bakker's fateful encounter with Jessica Hahn. At a PTL world prayer conference in Honolulu that year, reports Shepard, Tammy complained about her husband to other PTL wives and talked of divorce. Through failed attempts at reconciliation, they kept the marriage together for the sake of a profitable ministry, but Tammy took to drinking and popping pills, resulting in several nervous breakdowns of her own.

If Jim Bakker's reputed lust knocked the cornerstone out of his PTL edifice, it is his alleged corrupt financial dealings that toppled it. His and Tammy's rise from storefront TV preachers to famed televangelists had been a giddying, nonstop journey to success. "They are phenomenal, charismatic personalities," says Miles. "Even when you know they are lying through their teeth, there is something folksy and good about them. No one else could have pulled it off."

Miles says he saw the light when he flew from his home in Forest Hills, N.Y., to help raise money for a PTL telethon in 1982. "They said they were going to pull the plug out of the TV satellite if they didn't get so many millions of viewers by a certain date," he recalls. "Tammy was crying, mascara running—'We've sold everything we have. This is a real crisis.'" After the fund drive was over, Miles claims, Jim's brother, Norm Bakker, told him, "There's no crisis. We had the money all along. This gave us a tool to raise money and something for people to rally around." Miles asked about a plea made four months previously, in which the Bakkers claimed that Heritage USA was going to be dismantled. "That was just the same thing—just business," says Miles, who alleges that Bakker used a fund-raising firm that composed carefully timed pitch letters and planned each "crisis" in advance. The letters, says Miles, were sent "to arrive the same time that the welfare and Social Security checks come, the first week of every month." Miles says he told a PTL producer "little old ladies are eating cat food to send in their money for God" and walked out. He now suspects that the PTL's "overseas ministries" were nonexistent and that film clippings purporting to show the PTL in Brazil, Italy and Africa were shot in a corner of the Heritage Village studios.

Despite being accused of more machinations than a Renaissance pope, the Bakkers have launched a new ministry in Orlando. "We are fighting for our lives, literally," says Tammy Faye. "And I don't think we're just fighting for our lives. I feel that we are fighting for the life of Christianity the way we know it today. I think we're fighting for the right to preach the gospel in the United States of America. I think we're fighting for the right to have Christian television."

The new *Jim and Tammy Show* broadcasts from his New Covenant Church headquarters in a tacky, pink strip shopping mall just minutes from Disney World, in the heart of the city's factory outlet district. The Bakkers lease about a dozen of the empty storefronts for their church service, studio and offices. Two bars, the Oriental Bazaar and Designer Boutique, where Tammy has dress designs on sale, also occupy the mall. The look of their rust-and-blue studio set, filled with floral gifts from supporters, matches the opulence of their former Heritage USA studio set. A bank of nine phones stands ready to receive callers pledging donations, and they do occasionally ring during the show, which currently goes out to about a dozen stations compared with the 200 stations that broadcast the PTL show in its heyday.

These days Jim and Tammy live on a cul-de-sac in a wealthy lakefront section of Orlando. The word around town is that the neighbors aren't happy about having the Bakkers next door. The house includes a swimming pool and a three-car garage that can only park two. The rest is taken up by Tammy's 30-foot dress rack.

The Sunday of Labor Day weekend, Jim and Tammy's friend Orlando Pastor Roy Harthern preached the New Covenant service. He told an audience of 150 supporters and the curious that Tammy was planning to stay by Jim in his time of distress and that it was unclear when she would be able to return to Orlando. "But when she does," Harthern said, "let's show her how much we care by making offerings. Write out your checks to New Covenant Church. This will make her happy." Though their judgment day seems well nigh, Jim and Tammy are still in business.

XII

Cameras in the Court

In the 1920s, the famous Scopes "Monkey" trial was broadcast live on radio. Much of the nation was informed not only of the evolution v. creation controversy, but of our judiciary system. They were also entertained by the drama created by flamboyant attorneys Clarence Darrow and William Jennings Bryan. In the 1930s, the trial of the men accused of kidnapping the son of world famous flyer Charles Lindbergh was covered by 141 reporters and 125 telegraph operators. Once again, the nation was informed and entertained by the drama of human tragedy.

Today, in the 1990s, television viewers have more options. They can turn on *People's Court* or *Divorce Court* and watch a half hour of real human conflict set before a retired judge in an artificial court. Or, as described in our first essay "It's Court Time," they can watch *Court TV*—a 24 hours-a-day courtroom network. These are real trials of everyday people. While the drama of court proceedings cannot always keep pace with the Lindbergh trial, and the lawyers cannot possibly be as entertaining as those from the Scopes trial, the judiciary system in all its glory is certainly on display.

The second and third essays examine several recent high-profile instances of cable and broadcast cameras in the court. "Thomas Takes TV's Center Stage" describes the televised Senate confirmation hearings of Supreme Court Justice Clarence Thomas. What promised to be a glimpse of a boring democratic process layed before the general public turned into a made-for-television drama filled with allegations of sexual misconduct, racism, and deceit. "Cameras in the Court—Sort of," examines the televised trial of the accused rapist William Kennedy Smith and the huge audience it drew. The final essay puts the controversy of televising trials into proper perspective. "The Media: Old Circus, New Context," notes that the trial of international drug lord Manuel Noriega and other interesting and important court proceedings were not given airtime but rather the networks chose to air the most graphic sexual testimony imaginable. Could it be that this new wave of live coverage is not for public information and enlightenment but for entertainment and ratings?

It's Court Time
Scott Minerbrook, U.S. NEWS & WORLD REPORT

New York City—As seen on the monitors of a midtown Manhattan television studio, American courtrooms are scruffy places. Few attorneys boast Perry Mason eyes, Arnie Becker haircuts or the loony detachment of Judge Wapner. In these real halls of justice, life grinds a bit painfully, soaring only every so often. Innocent questions leave witnesses looking stricken. Examinations wander. Boredom often prevails. Cutting deals looks entirely possible.

This is Court TV, a cable venture that began broadcasting from here last week, relying on cameras in courtrooms across the country to provide the scripts. In a typical case, an elderly man accused of murdering his mother-in-law 25 years ago sat slumped in a chair, looking as if he wanted to jump out of his skin. For good reason: He was on trial because his son, a Fort Lauderdale, Fla., police detective, had the case reopened. Even the news correspondents imitate real life much more than in more controlled network settings: One got caught in a pouring rain and continued doing his job.

Steven Brill, the 40-year-old publisher of a far-flung barony of legal trade journals, says he got the idea for his 24-hours-a-day courtroom *vérité* network in a grimy New York taxicab, listening to reports about a gruesome child-murder trial. "The courts are supposed to be the most public of all branches of government," says Brill, "but on many levels they remain the most hidden and least understood." In his view, Court TV is as much an educational as a commercial venture, the electronic equivalent of the 19th-century courthouse where citizens watched trials to learn and to be entertained.

Presumably, the cameras are also intended as profit vehicles. Brill hopes that investments of $40 million from backers—including his own American Lawyer Media L.P., Time Warner Inc., NBC and Cablevision Systems Corp.—will put the venture in the black within four years. Last week, 450 systems in 38 states received middlebrow trial coverage of high-profile cases such as the Christian Brando murder trial and the Robert Mapplethorpe case. By the end of July, Brill hopes to have 5 million viewers. He says he plans to expand coverage to landlord-tenant and night court as well as to courts in the Soviet Union.

Judging by its first day of operations, the network has its work cut out for it. There were a few technical glitches, and Brill and his associates continued fine-tuning programming and style. Anchor Fred Graham, a former CBS correspondent, was sometimes given to breathless analyses, which the producers decided to cut back on, letting cameras tell more of the story. By week's end, the format wasn't seamless, but it wasn't clumsy either.

Reversing commercial television's sound bite tradition in favor of real life may take some time. The first few days, Brill says, were too commercial, with too much production and too little law. If anything, he wants to slow down the pace a notch or two—a risky proposition, given current mass appetites. Brill is betting there are viewers curious and mature enough to watch life as it really happens in one of the nation's most vital crossroads. If he's right, it could mean that people may yet learn why lawyers can't sum up their cases in 15 seconds and why 15 minutes of fame is barely enough time to seat a jury in its box.

Thomas Takes TV's Center Stage
Rich Brown, BROADCASTING

The Senate confirmation hearings on Supreme Court Justice Clarence Thomas swept through the broadcasting industry like a tornado starting 10 days ago, turning everything upside down for an exhausting five-day period that seemed much longer.

By any reckoning, it was not a typical week. Weekday and prime time pre-emptions collectively cost the networks between $15 million and $20 million in lost advertising revenue. CBS, which had at last been enjoying high ratings on its trouble-plagued baseball contract, suddenly saw its ratings plummet as viewers switched to the hearings. Fox Broadcasting Co. saw its fledgling Saturday morning kid's schedule get a big ratings boost as the other networks pre-empted their regular line-ups. The Public Broadcasting Service scored unusually high ratings for its unblinking coverage of the hearings. And local stations pre-empted their own news and syndicated programming to stick with the heated testimony.

Among the broadcast networks, NBC News pre-empted the most programming. The network aired about 30.5 hours of hearings over the five-day period, while ABC chalked up 23 hours and CBS tallied just under 13. NBC News Executive Vice President Don Browne said the network's decision to devote so much time to the story was based on what the news division saw as an unusual convergence of topics, including race, sex and government.

"Very rarely have we seen anything like this where all of these issues converged in one place at one time," said Browne. "It was just an extraordinary ongoing event that was more revealing than a thousand stories that we could have done individually. We hadn't seen a moment like that since Watergate."

Pre-emptions were costly not only for the networks but also for local stations, many of which stayed with the hearings in place of local news and syndicated programming.

"A lot of stations took a short-term hit on the lost inventory, but most stations decided it was in their best interest, from an image viewpoint, to carry the network live," said consultant Steve Ridge, vice president at Frank N. Magid Associates. "Local stations that were concerned about being the dominant source in their market needed to make that statement, regardless of the lost revenue."

At least one ABC affiliate, WCVB-TV's Boston, demanded that the network provide even more coverage than it had planned. On Sunday, Oct.13, as character witnesses were testifying on behalf of Thomas, ABC attempted to cut off its West Coast feed at 10 p.m. ET to enable a return to the usual prime time schedule. WCVB-TV news director, Emily Rooney, said ABC changed its mind and allowed stations to pick up the West Coast feed following threats that the Boston station would switch to a CNN feed in place of the network schedule. She was one of many news directors who placed great importance on coverage of the hearings.

"In the minds of many local editorial decisionmakers, the issues before the Supreme Court, and the nature of the Supreme Court itself, made it a story of strong interest," said Tim Rudell, vice president of Conus Washington. Audiences have gut-level reactions to Supreme Court stories, he added, because of the impact that the court has had on abortion rights and other concerns.

"It is much more of a local story when there is something dramatic happening with the Supreme Court than with any other activity in Washington," said Conus's Rudell.

The network news division had been hesitant to announce coverage plans at the outset, but their commitment to the story became clear when each presented at least nine hours of testimony on the opening day of the hearings on Friday, Oct. 11. More than 30 million homes watched the Thomas hearings on the broadcast networks on opening night, according to A.C. Nielsen data.

PBS, which presented about 44 hours of coverage in a joint arrangement with National Public Radio, scored some unusually high numbers. Public TV did particularly well on Sunday, Oct. 13, when the broadcast networks abandoned the hearings to return to regularly scheduled prime time programming. PBS scored an 11.4/17* on Sunday in 12 overnight markets, four times the usual 2-3 prime time rating for the service. Noncommercial station KCET-TV Los Angeles scored its highest-ever prime time rating with an average 11.4/18; WNET-TV New York also topped its own record with a 13.7/20, while KAET-TV Phoenix recorded a 17.7/27 Sunday night rating.

Fox Broadcasting also benefited from the altered network schedules, managing to chalk up high ratings for its Saturday morning children's lineup. The company last week boasted that its ratings were up 29% among kids 2-11 in the daypart, averaging a 3.6 season-to-date rating.

Hearings vs. baseball on CBS

Thomas coverage at times proved to be particularly problematic for CBS, which found itself contractually obligated to air post-season Major League Baseball. The post-season games on CBS so far have been a roller coaster of highs and lows for the network. Prior to the Thomas hearings, CBS post-season prime time baseball ratings were up about 6% over last year. But once the Thomas hearings began, naysayers were quick to label low playoff ratings as the latest problem in CBS's closely scrutinized, trouble-plagued $1.06-billion baseball contract.

On the opening night of the hearings, CBS found its Friday night American League playoff game up against coverage of Thomas's most dramatic testimony on ABC and NBC. CBS News anchor Dan Rather cut into the game via split-screen with four special reports, but many viewers stay tuned to competing sources for uninterrupted coverage. The Oct. 11 game wound up scoring record low 10.11 rating/9 share playoff number.

The following night's American League game scored even lower with a 9.0/17, while the National League playoff game earlier that afternoon had a 7.6 rating. Sunday afternoon's title-clinching American League game, which ran so long that it pre-empted the network's high-rated *60 Minutes*, had an 8.8 rating. Game four of the National League playoffs averaged an 11.3 on Sunday night, when a sizable chunk of the viewing audience tuned into PBS coverage of the Thomas hearings.

Once the Thomas hearings were out of the way, however, things once again began to look up for the CBS post-season baseball schedule. In its favor was the hotly contested National League playoffs, which went to a full seven-game series. On Wednesday night, the cliffhanging game six of the best-of-seven National League championship series scored an 18.3/31, the highest-rated playoff since 1988. The high rating helped CBS win the night, safely ahead of NBC's 13.1/22 and ABC's 11.6/19. In Atlanta, the game did a 51.0/71.

CBS wrapped up its playoff coverage on Thursday night, winning the night with a 19.8/32 national rating. In Atlanta the game did a 62.0/80. Preliminary 1991 playoff ratings were 12/22, up 2% from last year.

*Editor's Note: *The first number refers to the program's rating; the second number refers to its share.*

Cameras in the Court–Sort of
Rich Brown, BROADCASTING

As the William Kennedy Smith trial got underway last week, NBC News had some unexpected company in revealing the identity of the alleged rape victim in the case. While NBC News stood by its controversial decision of intentionally identifying the woman, CNN accidentally revealed her identity through some technical slip-ups.

The biggest problem in protecting the alleged victim's identity came from a gray dot that was intended to cover the face of the woman as she testified last Wednesday. The dot had been arranged by the court as a way of shielding her image on the press pool feed. But National Teleproduction, the company that was brought in to operate the dot, failed to keep up with her movements and revealed her face to a national live audience via CNN. To avoid further slip-ups, the cable network on Thursday covered the gray dot with a larger blue dot.

CNN slipped earlier in the week by accidentally telecasting the alleged victim's name during trial coverage.

Most media organizations, including CNN, have taken strong positions in not identifying the alleged victim. But that is not to say that NBC News has no allies on the issue.

"If the name is relevant in the story then we should have no hesitancy about using it," said David Bartlett, president, Radio-Television News Directors Association. "I agree entirely with [NBC News President] Michael Gartner that we are in the news dissemination business and not the news repression business. I am very impatient about the journalist as sociologist."

Press controversies aside, the trial proved to be a boon for cable networks CNN and the fledgling Court TV. Both managed to draw away some of the weekday audiences with their live coverage.

CNN saw its audiences build as the testimony continued throughout the week. The cable network on Monday averaged a 1.1 rating and 3.1 share on a 24-hour basis among cable households, representing 625,000 households. Its highest opening-day rating was from 4 p.m. to 5 p.m., when the network attracted a 2.5/6.2, or 1.46 million viewers.

By Wednesday, CNN's ratings had grown to a 1.7/5.3 on a 24-hour basis, representing more than 1 million homes. From 5 p.m. to 6 p.m., the network had a 5.1/11.4, representing more than 3 million homes. The Wednesday ratings more than doubled the 0.7 rating that the network has averaged on a 24-hour basis during the current quarter.

Court TV did not have ratings on its gavel-to-gavel coverage because Nielsen does not rate networks with under 10 million subscribers, according to a spokesman for the cable network. But a Warner Cable system in Cincinnati, which is able to monitor audience viewing, reportedly showed Court TV ratings more than tripling the numbers it had shown during the previous week. Court TV, which is the pool camera for the trial, has avoided problems in revealing the alleged victim's identity by blocking her image with an electronic mosaic.

The Media: Old Circus, New Context
Jonathan Alter, NEWSWEEK

The spectators were so rambunctious that they had to be restrained from carving their initials into the judge's chair. Photographers scrambled atop desks to snap hundreds of pictures of witnesses, and one newsreel cameraman secretly filmed part of the proceedings by using a hood to muffle the noise from his camera. With 141 reporters and 125 telegraph operators, the press horde exceeded the 150 accredited hacks in Palm Beach last week.

As the 1935 Lindbergh kidnapping trial suggests, courtroom media circuses are old hat. What has changed with the presence of live TV coverage is the collective mental lens applied to legal proceedings, real and fictional—all coming through on the same screen. How does Moira Lasch compare to Susan Dey on *L.A. Law*? It's a serious question for viewers.

'Front Page': The broadcasting of trials isn't completely new, though it was largely abandoned for 40 years. The famous 1925 Scopes "Monkey" trial, where Clarence Darrow battled William Jennings Bryan over the theory of evolution, was broadcast from Tennessee by Chicago-based WGN radio. And buying the story of witnesses—as *A Current Affair* bought Anne Mercer's—is out of *The Front Page*. It's true that there are now far more cameras at big trials. But in the old days, there were far more big daily newspapers. So it evens out.

What has changed most is simply context. If the press is better educated, better behaved and no sleazier than in the past, it is also creating a different version of reality. Live coverage is supposed to strip away the filter of print, and it does show more. But it distorts, too—juxtaposing confusing images, often unintentionally.

Consider the images conveyed by CNN, which tries to have it every which way. It interrupts its regular programming to cover the Smith trial gavel-to-gavel—ostensibly because of its news value. But then it interrupts the trial every few minutes—often at critical junctures—to air endless commercials, including, weirdly enough, one for Oliver Stone's upcoming movie *JFK* and another for St. John's University, where students were recently acquitted on rape charges. (The transition before the commercial break often includes a shot of William Smith pointing with outstretched arm in exactly the manner his uncle Jack made famous at presidential press conferences.) The big networks are airing the most graphic sexual testimony imaginable—as they did during the Anita Hill hearings. But they still refuse to allow condom ads, citing taste. Perhaps the most peculiar contextual moment came during the testimony of Sen. Edward Kennedy. Having crowded out most other news to cover the trial, CNN included a "News Update" crawl line under Kennedy's live appearance on the stand. It said: "Magic Johnson, C. Everett Koop to co-author safe sex guide."

Big Play: It all blends together. Is *Hard Copy* news? Plenty of viewers think so. Most distorting of all is the effect of live TV coverage on the relative play of stories. Imagine, for instance, if CNN and Court TV could have televised the trial of Manuel Noriega instead of the Smith case. Would the Noriega trial—which is, after all, the outgrowth of an American war—be covered by papers around the country with small wire-service accounts buried in back pages, as it is now? (The Smith case, by contrast, is given big play, including in NEWSWEEK.) The Noriega trial is not without news, including allegations of knowledge of drug trafficking by high-ranking U.S. officials. But it hasn't been certified as an important story by TV. By some Gresham's law of coverage, the bad too often drives out the good, first on TV, then in print. It's these choices, not the time-honored *Front Page* antics of tabloid reporters, that comprise the true journalistic legacy of the William Kennedy Smith case.

Cameras in the Court
Worksheet

1. Which of the following views of the judicial system have you experienced (check all that apply): (a) served on jury or testified in court, (b) watched TV shows or movies that presented fictional courtroom accounts (e.g., *Perry Mason, Absence of Malice*), (c) viewed pseudo-proceedings on *People's Court,* (d) witnessed real trials on network television. As a result, do you believe that you are well informed of our judicial system?

2. What are the potential negative aspects of Court-TV—live coverage of real trials—on (a) the viewer, (b) the accused, and (c) the victim?

3. The essay "Thomas Takes TV's Center Stage" revealed that Court–TV's coverage of the Senate confirmation hearings on Supreme Court Justice Clarence Thomas (which cost the network nothing but minimal production fees) stole a sizable audience from CBS's coverage of Major League Baseball playoffs (which was part of the network's $1.06-billion baseball contract). Was this a one-time-only phenomenon, or do you believe that court proceedings and trials—human drama and real face-to-face confrontation—are every bit the entertaining spectator sport that is baseball? Explain.

4. The CBS television network is currently having severe financial difficulties (see "Save CBS" in this text). One option for survival would be to abandon all the costly entertainment programming it offers (comedies, dramas, sports) and provide nothing but news/information programs (trials, debates, talk shows). Reality, after all, is less costly to program than fiction and fantasy. CNN, a 24-hour news network, is doing well and viewers flocked to the televised Kennedy trial and Thomas hearing. Would CBS as an all-news/information network work? Why or why not?

XIII

Media in Wartime

Suppose that the Nazis had invited American journalists into Germany during the second world war and, at the same time as ensuring that they were denied access to the concentration camps and other sites of Nazi atrocities, the German authorities had given them free rein to report the effects of allied bombing raids in heavily populated cities such as Dresden and Berlin. What would that have done to public support for the allied war effort and the fight against fascism? And should journalists, prevented from reporting first-hand on what the Nazis were doing to their victims, therefore have refrained from reporting the consequences of the allied bombing campaign on German civilians?

These are serious questions and point to a serious issue: What is the role of the American press during wartime? Are journalists propaganda machines working for the causes of their country, justifiably restricted in what and how they cover the war for the sake of public morale and military security? Are they potential tools for the enemy, cleverly offered selective insights into the destruction of property and prevalence of civilian casualties? Or are they third-party voyeurs, simply reporting the facts as they see it regardless of the outcome on public opinion, military success, or patriotic fervor? Is objective reporting even possible during wartime? The four essays in this chapter address these questions by reflecting on the Persian Gulf Crisis of 1991. The first essay, "The Storm and the Eye," was written immediately before the outbreak of "Desert Storm." It reports on the logistics of military rules for *governing* press activities. The second essay, "Just the Good News, Please," was written at the start of the conflict. It suggests that military *coordination* of the press is prohibiting but, nonetheless, a significant improvement over what transpired in Grenada in 1983, where reporters were barred from the island during the invasion, and in Panama in 1989, when the press was totally isolated from the action. "Who Won the Media War," examines the success of the various media that covered the war despite military *restrictions* and enemy influence. And finally, "Antihero: A Year After Desert Storm," offers a critical retrospective of press activity and suggests that the military bought and sold the American people on the war through its *manipulation* of the press.

The Storm and the Eye

Randall M. Sukow, BROADCASTING

The United States could be at war any time after tomorrow, Jan. 15. If fighting breaks out between Iraq and the international coalition in Saudi Arabia immediately after the United Nations deadline—or if it starts weeks later—TV and radio will be there in force.

"Certainly this is the most important story of a generation," said Ed Turner, executive vice president, CNN. "It's almost impossible to do too much on it, particularly since all we do is news and because of the global audience we have. People are hungry worldwide for information, opinion, analysis and commentary."

What sights and sounds will Americans receive? News executives coordinating the coverage and correspondents contacted by BROADCASTING provide a good picture.

On the day the U.S. mounts an offensive, land or air, CNN will go 24 hours on the story. The broadcast TV networks may follow suit.

Viewers switching channels will find almost the same report on every network. All media coverage will be pooled. A military escort will accompany each pool. A military censor will review all scripts and video.

At first it could be an almost pictureless war or video could be delayed for several hours. The networks have been told the Saudi government may tear down uplinks because they could be easy targets for Iraqi bombs and missiles. Video reports could be delayed by several hours while the networks seek alternate sites for uplinks. But it is expected to be a temporary inconvenience. The Pentagon is "convinced that after the first few days, the Iraqi air force and ground-to-aid [Scud] missiles will have been eliminated," said Timothy J. Russert, Washington bureau chief, NBC News.

No live radio or TV reports will be sent from combat. Microwave equipment for TV links will be too bulky and dangerous to install. Live radio depends on using military communications equipment, which is not expected to be made available.

Radio and TV reports may be vague. Pentagon rules for press coverage allow U.S. troop movements to be described only in general terms such as "company-size" or "multi-batallion." Damage and casualties to U.S. forces are to be described only as "light," "moderate" or "heavy."

By the time video starts airing, it will show blood and pain. Network executives and correspondents say they intend to cover "the horror of war."

The anchors will not be there. Only CNN's Bernard Shaw, in Amman, Jordan, last week, is planning to stay in the region this week. CBS's Dan Rather and NBC's Tom Brokaw had returned from the Middle East by last week; no decision has been made about possible return trips. There are no plans for ABC's Peter Jennings to leave New York.

Reports may continue to come from Baghdad, even if fighting begins. "We're going there purposely to be there for the Jan. 15 deadline," said Bart Tessler, vice president, news, Mutual/NBC Radio. Networks will allow correspondents to decide when conditions are too unsafe to remain.

To observant viewers, many pictures will seem to have less resolution and color clarity compared to normal news video. Lightweight, inexpensive "Hi8" (8 millimeter video format) camcorders will be used at the most dangerous pool locations.

Approximately 300-350 reporters, producers, cameramen and other technical personnel have been sent to the Middle East by the major U.S. TV and radio network news organizations. (For competitive reasons, most networks did not give specific numbers.) The largest group of broadcast reporters is in Saudi Arabia at Dhahran, a city on the coast of the Persian Gulf 200 miles south of the Kuwaiti border, and at the Saudi capital, Riyadh. Heavy media contingents are also in Baghdad, Amman and Cairo.

CNN has the largest contingent in the region—150 people. But by yesterday the number of CNN people in Saudi Arabia was expected to be 27-30, according to Jim Miller, a CNN producer in Dhahran. ABC, CBS and NBC are expected to have about the same number in Saudi Arabia. "The problem is with getting visas for some of the engineers. Until I get the visas, I can't tell for sure" how many people the network will have in Saudi Arabia, Miller said.

The radio networks in Saudi Arabia—AP Broadcast Services, ABC Radio, Mutual Broadcasting/NBC Radio and National Public Radio (NPR)—are "all one-man bands," said Doug Poling, CBS News radio correspondent there.

Earlier, NBC said its spending on Gulf coverage had returned to $1.2 million (its level of spending last August immediately after the invasion of Kuwait) from the $500,000-a-week rate of the past several months ("Closed Circuit," Jan. 7). Other TV networks refused to give exact numbers, but indicated their spending pattern has been similar to NBC's. "I question how you could spend initially $1 million a week, but it's not too far off," CNN's Turner said.

NPR has spent $200,000 on the story since last August. If fighting begins and lasts two months, "additional coverage, we believe, will cost us $500,000. That scale, for us, is a lot. Our news budget [for 1991] is about $13 million," said Bill Buzenbert, vice president, news and information.

C-SPAN sent crews to Saudi Arabia and Tel Aviv to complement its coverage of the congressional debate on the crisis. Expenses will be paid out of the existing international budget—$200,000 for the fiscal year ending April 1.

The expensive Middle East coverage comes at the same time network news divisions are suffering from an advertising slump, a combination that has led to across-the-board staff cutbacks in recent months. Expenses forced CBS Radio, which is usually unique among radio networks in sending a producer and reporter to cover virtually all stories, into sending Doug Poling solo to Saudi Arabia. "This is the first time I've been on a major assignment without a field producer," said Poling. "Maybe 10 years ago they would have put more people in here right away."

After the August invasion of Kuwait "the word 'money' never came up," said Bob McFarland, NBC deputy news director, New York (who was planning to be in Saudi Arabia before Jan. 15). "Budgetary concerns had crept in after a few weeks and it appeared that this would be a long-term story."

In spite of resources sent to the Gulf, broadcasters fear the quality of coverage could be marred by Pentagon censorship and the logistical nightmares caused by heat, sand, bombs and poison gas. The networks last week tried to solve the first problem through negotiations and second through technology.

A Jan. 4 meeting of the military and media executives at the Pentagon over the first 10-page list of rules for reporters in combat pools led to the issuance of a much shorter list last Tuesday (Jan. 8). The networks won several concessions but were unable to remove the Pentagon's demands for all combat coverage to be pooled and escorted by the military officers and for all news copy, audio and video to be submitted for review by the military before release.

Rules outlined last week by the Pentagon are "too restrictive and too paranoid," said CBS News's Don DeCesare, vice president, director of broadcast news. "I would relax a little if I were they and let us get about our business. Revealing plans to the enemy is not our mission in life and they know it."

DeCesare said the Pentagon restrictions have prompted CBS News to vigorously pursue, within the "bounds of safety and prudence," options to pool coverage. He declined to elaborate on those options. "We're taking on our own measures to cover the war, whether they want us to or not," he said.

"We're strongly opposed to what they're proposing to do, but I don't think we have a great deal of leverage at this point," said George Watson, Washington bureau chief, ABC News. "Ultimately, it's their battlefield."

Watson said ABC News's concerns about how the rules will affect coverage were heightened by several incidents during dry runs of the pools last week. In one case, he said, a military escort cut off an NBC correspondent's interview with a chaplain, a decision later overruled by the Joint Information Bureau in Dhahran.

Mike Mosher, NBC's Saudi Arabia bureau chief, based in Dhahran, downplayed the incident. "The military took one look at it and said they regretted the incident took place. There was nothing in there that violated any rule. They were very, very quick," he said. Mosher said the general working relationship between NBC News and the military has been good. There have been "no major disputes. There's been no tape taken away yet," he said.

Most broadcasters disputed the Pentagon's claim that military review of reports is needed to protect the security of U.S. troops. Mutual/NBC Radio's Tessler said inadvertent reporting of sensitive information is unlikely in the Gulf. Reporting from military-escorted pools "isn't the kind of situation where you let a reporter loose and you have total freedom and total access," he said.

CNN correspondent Carl Rochelle in Dhahran said reporters are "being allowed to get into areas where we could inadvertently make a picture of something that would give away a position or lose someone their life. In that case, it's all right to review it. What I would prefer is not to have restrictions at all, always."

Reporters differed when speculating on how close the Pentagon will let them get to combat. "I frankly think the military is going to take us closer than ever before," said NRP's Deborah Amos. "I think that after Grenada and Panama they decided they were even going to put us in harm's way. I'm not talking about intentionally trying to hurt us, but they think we want to cover it that closely and they're going to let us."

The greatest logistical nightmare for broadcasters involves the weight of the gear each member of a combat pool must carry. Everyone is issued a gas mask and chemical suit and must learn how to put them on before getting in a pool. Along with 40 pounds of gas mask and suit, everyone must carry their own equipment and a few toiletries. TV cameramen are expected to bear the heaviest load, 75 pounds.

All the TV networks have relieved some burden on the cameramen by equipping them with lightweight, inexpensive ($3,000) Sony Hi8 camcorders. "The Hi8 cameras that we've got are the professional models. It's not really a great deal smaller than the usual cameras that we use, but the supplemental equipment is much smaller," said Mosher.

Correspondents and producers said most of the equipment is holding up well to the desert's heat and sand. The hottest season has passed, they say. "At the height of the heat some of our cabling literally melted" during a taping of the *Today* show in Dhahran, NBC's McFarland said. "One of our producers was physically holding two pieces of cable to make it work." The next big worry is sand storms. "One suggestion that has been made is to put pantyhose over the tape recorders," said Steve Futtenberg, correspondent for Mutual/NBC Radio. "That will keep some of the dust away, but not all of it."

The (Logistical) Horrors of War

Determined to keep the video flowing back home, network producers and technicians were making contingency plans in case their satellite uplinks on the Persian Gulf coast are shut down, knocked out or jammed.

In addition to the possibility that Iraqi air or missile attacks might wipe out the ad hoc teleport, some were concerned the Saudis or the U.S. military might in the early days of fighting order the uplinks to stop transmitting for security reasons.

ABC-TV's Mitch Davis, pool producer for the networks, and others said informal warnings about the ordered shutdowns have come from military and other sources. Although few sources were taking the warnings seriously, all reported planning alternate ways to get their pictures out.

The broadcasting pool (which is using a unit operated by Washington-based Professional Video Services) and the networks have pointed their clustered uplinks at Intelsat 338 over the Atlantic Ocean, upon which ABC, CBS, CNN, NBC and the pool have each retained a three-month, full-time lease. (Last fall, Comsat and Intelsat opened a 338 spot beam to accommodate the traffic.)

Another alternate path for some broadcasters might be the British Broadcasting Corp. It has tentative permission to uplink from any forward division headquarters established in fighting, said Ken Oxley of BBC foreign operations. (U.S. broadcasters are barred from moving uplinks any closer to the front until Kuwait falls.)

If all else fails, said John Frazee, CBS vice president of news services, the broadcasters will have to carry videotape out of Saudi Arabia.

A subject of more immediate concern to the network operations people was the Saudi's ban, starting last Wednesday, on additional uplinks anywhere in the country. At press time, Davis was preparing to appeal the Saudi cutoff to allow the pool to complete already initiated deployment of a flyaway uplink at the capital city of Riyadh, expected to be a major briefing point.

Washington Lays Down the Rules of War

Broadcasters in the Middle East will abide by the "ground rules" and guidelines governing how and what they can videotape and what they may air—they have little choice—but that doesn't mean they like them.

Indeed, the heads of the four major U.S. television news organizations and the Radio-Television News Directors Association formally registered their objections and called for changes in letters to Defense Secretary Richard Cheney.

[T]he existing proposals go far beyond what is required to protect troop safety and mission security," said the network news presidents—ABC's Roone Arledge, CBS's Eric Ober, CNN's Tom Johnson and NBC's Michael Gartner—in a joint hand-delivered Jan. 9 letter. "Legitimate requirements of security do not require these rules," they said. "The workings of a free press argue strongly for their being abandoned."

The executives specifically cited the "security review" provision, which, they said, "set up cumbersome barriers to timely and responsible reporting and raise the specter of government censorship of a free press." The review process "may not be censorship in its purest form, but it compromises the free flow of information with official intrusion and government oversight," they said.

They also objected to the requirement that reporters have military escorts at their sides when at the front. "Of course, we shall rely on the assistance and advice of experts," he said. "But we must also retain our independence."

In a Jan. 10 letter, RTNDA President David Bartlett urged Cheney "to consider carefully whether prior review of pool material by military public affairs officers is really necessary for security, and whether more open coverage than is possible with escorted tight pools can be instituted once the military operation is underway."

"[W]e cannot condone any attempt by the military to use the guidelines to limit coverage, distort the news or hide embarrassing information that the American people are entitled to know." he said.

The current rules are far less restrictive and simpler than the original rules unilaterally imposed on reporters when the buildup began last summer. They reflect compromises made in intense negotiations between media representatives and Pentagon officials in Washington two weeks ago. They were released Jan. 8, although there were some reports late last week that the military was slow in implementing them.

The key points:

- "[Reporters] must remain with a military escort at all times, until released, and follow their instructions. . . . These instructions are not intended to hinder your reporting. They are intended to facilitate movement, insure safety and protect operational security.

- "Security at the source will be the policy. . . . [P]ool products will be subject to security review prior to release to determine whether they contain information that would jeopardize the operation or the security of U.S. or coalition forces. Material will not be withheld just because it is embarrassing or contains criticism. The public affairs officer on the scene will conduct the security review [but there are two levels of appeal].

- "Casualty photographs showing a recognizable face, name tag or other identifying feature or item should not be used before the next of kin have been notified. The anguish that sudden recognition at home can cause far outweighs the news value of the photograph, film or videotape."

Lost in the negotiations to amend the rules were, among other things, bans on reporters' buttonholing officers for impromptu interviews; coverage of religious services (out of deference to the Saudis), and pictures of all casualties. Also dropped was the requirement that all interviews with military personnel be "on the record."

The news personnel are not happy with the rules, but the rhetoric was less strident among the broadcast journalists in the field. "So far it's been OK," said Bob McFarland, NBC deputy news director. "We don't like to have tight controls put on us; we don't like that at all," he said. "On the other hand, even tight controls are better than nothing at all, which is what we ran into in Grenada. . . . There is an awareness on the part of the Pentagon that the media are here to stay."

Steve Futtenberg, correspondent for Mutual Broadcasting/NBC Radio, said he does not like the idea of the military reviewing everything he does. "But I think it's a fact of war," he said. "We all know there was very little censorship in Vietnam, but I can't see a major problem with the U.S. government not wanting certain facts coming out that would directly help its enemy," he said. "Censorship happens in many wars because the press can find out a great deal, and I think the military has a right to have censorship. The question is, will they do it fairly? I think there will be some battles, but the whole concept of censorship, overall, I think we're going to have to accept."

"In the end, we're going to cooperate," said CNN Executive Vice President Ed Turner, "but we're going to try to get them to be somewhat more lenient as to information we can release, because the fact of the matter is, one way or another, information secured by news agencies is going to get out."

Despite the continued griping about the rules, reporters have little alternative to participating in the military pools, said Tony Winton, a correspondent for the Associated Press Broadcast Services. "No one that I know is planning to get into a car and drive out to the front."

Just the Good News, Please
Debbie Nathan, THE PROGRESSIVE

When American troops began departing for Saudi Arabia last August, the Pentagon announced it would cooperate fully with the news media. Then it helped ship a national news pool to the desert and assigned the members dozens of public-information officers. The policy seemed to be an improvement over the one followed in Grenada in 1983, when reporters were bared from the island during the invasion, and in Panama in 1989, when the Southern Command at first isolated the press pool from combat areas.

Now, though, a growing number of reporters complain that the military is censoring sources, discouraging national press access to the field, and squelching critical coverage in favor of "Hi-Mom" reporting aimed at boosting pro-war sentiment at home.

Information officers, for instance, invariably accompany reporters into the field, where they monitor and even interrupt interviews. A recent ABC *Nightline* showed a reporter asking an officer whether civilians working with units will have to stay in the field if fighting breaks out. When the officer tried to answer, a public-affairs escort cut him off and forbade questions calling for speculation about "things that we don't know about necessarily."

In another sequence, an enlisted man started telling a correspondent his thoughts about praying in Saudi Arabia, where only Moslem rites are legal. "I will have my beliefs," the man was saying, when an information officer broke in and nixed any discussion of religion.

The military usually chalks up the censorship to concern for security. Correspondents covering Desert Shield generally comply willingly with ground rules ordering them not to report troop numbers and exact locations. But Deborah Amos, National Public Radio's Saudi Arabia correspondent, thinks the military's on-site editing about other matters is sometimes "arbitrary." She finds it frustrating that the Central Command's Joint Information Bureau in Dhahran doesn't honor journalists' requests to visit troops and units. Reporters wait weeks or months for approval and sometimes never get responses. ABC's John Laurence has had that experience; he believes the Bureau has black-listed him because he helped produce a Peter Jennings show last fall that described heat and sand problems with equipment and shortages of ammunition.

Soft, morale-boosting coverage is what the military likes to see. The television networks do their share—the quick segments featuring soldiers saying hi to their families sprinkled throughout the early-morning news programs are a case in point. But Amos and Laurence note that, in the field, the national press often gets squeezed out by reporters from local media. "Hometowners," as the military calls them, get much freer access to the field. A novel Pentagon program has so far invited about 450 reporters to travel to Saudi Arabia at military expense. Once there, the hometowners spend as long as four days billeting with units from their cities—Tucson, Buffalo, Monterrey, and the like. Even *The New York Times*, which maintains correspondent James LeMoune in Dhahran to cover the buildup, sent a metro reporter on a Pentagon junket to do hometowner coverage of a National Guard battalion's trip from Harlem to Desert Shield.

Hometowner coverage undoubtedly makes troops and their communities feel good. But skeptics wonder whether the military's enthusiastic promotion of this kind of news might be a repeat of former President Ronald Reagan's attempts to garner favorable coverage by inviting local rather than national reporters to news briefings.

Is the Pentagon hoping to capitalize on small-town sentimentality about "our boys" to further the Bush Administration's foreign-policy objectives? If so, are the U.S. media soft on the scheme?

Bob Locke, city editor of the *El Paso Times*, recently traveled to Saudi Arabia with a press pool sponsored by the 11th Air Defense Artillery Brigade and 3rd Armored Cavalry Regiment, out of nearby Fort Bliss. The *Times* is a Gannett newspaper in a city where a sixth of the population owes its livelihood to the military.

The paper, which normally forbids its staff to take free trips or meals from sources, nonetheless quickly accepted the Army's invitation. "We couldn't afford to send anyone otherwise," says Locke. The Saudi government does not issue tourist or visitors' visas, he adds, and *Times* editors heard that it's virtually impossible for journalists to get visas without U.S. military sponsorship.

Phil Pruitt, national editor for Gannett News Service, confirms that it took days of calls and visits to the Saudi Embassy to get his national correspondent a visa. But Pentagon-endorsed approvals for such hometowners as El Paso's Locke produce transit papers almost immediately. The Army provided Locke, along with a local radio-TV reporter and a cameraman, with training in nuclear/biological/chemical warfare and the etiquette of saluting. They were issued dogtags and G-12 status, equal to the rank of major, so they could commandeer jeeps and sleep in officers' tents.

This pool shared its copy and footage with all of El Paso's major media outlets. And the *Times* went further. It shared Locke's photographs with the Fort Bliss newspaper and gave the Army 8,000 reprints of his coverage for distribution to Fort Bliss units in Saudi Arabia and their families back home.

At least six Gannett newspapers have participated in the hometowner program. "I'm suspicious of it," says Pruitt. "I think [it's] a Defense Department PR attempt." To his knowledge, though, there have been no company-wide discussions at Gannett questioning the propriety of participating in the program.

Media interest groups haven't complained noisily about the access problems of national correspondents. This is partly because the press gauges its freedom to cover the military by how much fighting it gets to see—and so far Desert Shield isn't a combat zone but merely one of unprecedented buildup. Such organizations as the American Society of Newspaper Editors (ASNE) have confined complaints about troop access problems and censorship to meetings with Defense Department aides—chief Pentagon spokesman Pete Williams, for example.

Dick Schmidt, legal counsel to ASNE, feels that Williams, himself a former journalists, is pro-media and "wants to do everything possible to avoid Grenada." But others, even those who accept the Joint Information Bureau's current way of operating, worry that war in the Middle East could mean a repeat of the military's behavior toward the press during the invasions of Grenada and Panama.

"That's the worst possible case that we could have," Richard Pyle of the Associated Press said on *Nightline* last fall, "where the press would be taken to the desert equivalent of a golf course in Panama and stuck there while the fighting is going on someplace else."

Memories of the invasions of the 1980's haunt the media, but Desert Shield's real ghost is Vietnam. Reporters who covered the war there remember it as a journalistic paradise; almost anyone could take a commercial flight to Saigon. "If you were a free-lancer or small-towner," recalls ABC's Laurence, who covered Vietnam for CBS, "all you needed was a letter saying that your local paper would *consider* printing your stories. So anybody who knew an editor could get in."

Once in-country, a reporter could travel virtually anywhere by simply hitching a ride with a military jeep, helicopter, or C-130. And, though public-information officers were supposed to keep tabs, according to another veteran Vietnam reporter, "If a unit liked you, you could hang out with them and get lost in the woodwork."

Thus freed of escorts, journalists slept in the same barracks with troops, ate in mess halls with lieutenants and majors, flew low over Vietcong territory, and talked with local officials and peasants. They also accompanied troops in firefights and other dangerous situations—indeed, between 1961 and 1975, at least fifty-three correspondents died in Southeast Asia. The military made reporters sign a waiver releasing the Government from responsibility for injury and death. But, in exchange for the risk, they got an intimate view of the war.

That view, with its graphic pictures of mutilated bodies and demoralized soldiers, entered almost every American living room via the six-o'clock news. As public support for U.S. involvement in Vietnam eroded, many in the military became convinced that media bias and nightly pictures from the front were responsible. Ad-hoc attempts at censorship ensued. Laurence, for instance, was expelled from one company in 1970, after *CBS Reports* aired his film showing soldiers refusing orders. After a month, though, he was back with the troops.

Years later, officers and civilians in the Pentagon were still blaming journalists for the U.S. defeat in Vietnam, so it was not surprising that reporters were barred from Grenada during the invasion or that Admiral Joseph Metcalf III, head of the invasion task force, threatened to fire on any press boat trying to reach the island. In the midst of the national debate that followed the press embargo, President Reagan said at a press conference that, in Vietnam, the media had not been on "our side, militarily."

Press groups were irate at this treatment and threatened to sue Defense Secretary Caspar Weinberger for denying access to Grenada. The Joint Chiefs of Staff responded by creating a commission to recommend policy toward the media during future operations. It was chaired by retired General Winant Sidle, once head of the military's Saigon information office during the Vietnam war. Assuming authority on the post-Grenada commission, Sidle chastised Vietnam correspondents who had the temerity to act as mere reporters rather than Pentagon cheerleaders. "We had people," he remarked, "who thought they were on the side, watching the United States fight the North Vietnamese."

Media groups, meanwhile, abandoned plans to sue Weinberger after their attorneys suggested that such action might result in even worse restrictions. The Pentagon commission ultimately recommended that future fighting be covered by press pools with public-information escorts. The concept met with little protest from the press. When it was activated in Panama five years later, the Southern Command's isolation and manipulation of the press pool provoked only a flurry of media anger.

Now Operation Desert Shield appears to be dishing up more of the same. So far, the press is merely grumbling. Some wonder whether this is enough. "Journalists haven't challenged the restrictions by doing things like trying to get a way from the escorts, says Gannett's Pruitt. "If someone would do that, the issue would come up."

How easy would it be to flee the information officers? U.S. Navy Captain Michael Sherman, director of the Joint Information Bureau in Dhahran, has denied suggestions that the media's lack of access to Desert Shield reflects any Pentagon policy to slant coverage. Sherman and other military spokespeople blame the situation on Saudi Arabia's bleak, vast desert, which is difficult to maneuver in for well-equipped soldiers, not to mention reporters.

Besides the hometowners, there are about 330 members of the media in Dhahran every day, and only about thirty are taken on field trips. The others wait days or weeks for a turn. The long delays discourage free-lancers and correspondents from low-budget publications, who might manage to get visas but can't afford to hang around forever. National Public Radio has tried to fill Deborah Amos's down time: "We've tried to do a wedding, or a piece inside a Saudi family," says Middle Eastern editor Joyce Davis. "But so far we've had no luck—it's a closed society. So it makes no sense to go unless you have the money and time to wait for the military to cooperate."

Hometowner reporters, though, waste little or no time. Those participating in the program go directly from the United States to the field with their sponsoring units. The few others who come to Saudi Arabia independently usually hail from cities with big military bases, and their red tape is quickly cut by friendly public-affairs officers who are attached to those same bases when not with Desert Shield.

Joint Information Bureau director Sherman admits that he favors human-interest coverage, especially during holidays. Amos says the escort officers out of Dhahran were inundated with local reporters during Thanksgiving, giving rise to "lots of speculation" among her colleagues about whether the military was deliberately encouraging "war-fever" coverage.

"But I'm not convinced," she says. "If an officer has done his job correctly, he's got a bunch of troops who want war. It's twenty-year-olds who are psyched up. But I think that at the top, that's not their position.

Even if the Pentagon *is* trying to use local reporters to bang the war drums, some of the hometown television and newspaper coverage has been critical. David Garcia, a senior correspondent with El Paso's KTSM-AM-FM-TV, was a member of the Fort Bliss press tour to Desert Shield. He ate, slept, and worked in the foxholes with the troops, and came back trying to bring to the television screen a sense of the "insanity" of conditions he found in the field.

"It's horrible," he reported. "The boredom, the desolation. There are scorpions . . . you never get the sand out of you . . . it's freezing out there [sic] . . . your whole damned city moves, your tents collapse. I'm truly worried about how long the troops can hold out . . . they're going crazy."

Garcia says the local press pool took the trip "determined not to be victims of the military." The pool was so concerned not to be manipulated that its members avoided doing positive stories about equipment that impressed them. *El Paso Times* reporter Locke insisted that officers and NCOs leave whenever he interviewed a soldier. While much of his subsequent writing featured soldiers greeting their families or boasting about their weaponry and fighting prowess, Locke also quoted others blasting the Pentagon decision to cancel rotation and voicing eloquent reluctance to go to war.

What will happen if there's war? Sherman has said the Pentagon is considering setting up press pools to live with troops in combat. But NPR's Amos doubts reporters will be able to get out in the field as much as they need to. Other journalists are skeptical about an escorted pool system, but they haven't figured out what else could work in the Saudi desert.

"A lot of us talk about whether we could rent a car and just drive out to the war," says Amos. "It might be possible. Certainly, people are going to try."

Debbie Nathan, a free-lance writer in El Paso, writes often for Pacific News Service, The Village Voice, The Texas Observer, *and other publications.*

Who Won the Media War
Edwin Diamond, NEW YORK

An old Kuwaiti with an American flag made out of a pair of pajamas was celebrating the liberation of Kuwait City. "We give special thanks to Mr. Bush and all the allies," he said to the cameras. "The British, the French, the Egyptians, CNN. . . . "

The grateful Kuwaiti was on to something. There was the war and there was the coverage of the war. So much happened so fast that events began to blur together in a succession of video images: action and account, message and medium. For Americans at home, no less than for the crowds in Kuwait City, the Gulf War ended as it had begun: on television.

The buildup of forces in Saudi Arabia in the last months of 1990; the all-day debate on the war resolutions in the U.S. Congress; the first night of the war in the skies over Baghdad, described by Peter Arnett and CNN; the Soviet efforts to broker a cease-fire; the lightning assaults of the 100-hour ground campaign; the roundup of Iraqi troops; Saddam Hussein's generals arriving to accept Schwarzkopf's surrender terms—you saw it first on the home screen.

The biggest winners in the Gulf, of course, were George Bush, the Pentagon's AirLand doctrine, Schwarzkopf, "our" Arabs, and the troops in the field. There were some notable winners in the media as well. The journalists eventually conquered the obstacles of logistics, "censorship"— the dreaded pool system that evaporated when the latest satellite technology was deployed—and the press's own inflated sense of its importance.

Even the blitzkrieg of punditry unloosed on viewers and readers turned out, on balance, to do more good than harm. Henry Kissinger, William Safire, and others in a coalition of experts as unlikely as the allied force itself correctly called the turn of events. Newspaper op-ed pages frequently had fresher morning reading than the front pages, which served up news from the night before. In the ranks of television's guest experts, CBS News had the best inside scoop. Its man, Major General George Crist, wrote an internal memo on December 2 laying out why one of the best times for a land offensive would be February 22 or 23.

When the Dr. Strangeloves and think-tankers were wrong, however, they were spectacularly wrong. "No ground war," shouted John McLaughlin on the weekly poll-the-panel feature of the NBC's *The McLaughlin Group* just before the tanks rolled. The curse of the thinking classes was best personified by the omnipresent strategist Edward N. Luttwak (*Nightline, MacNeil/Lehrer*, and other sound-bite credits). Luttwak predicted in the *New York Times* on January 13 that U.S. Marines would die "inexcusably" in the event of a front attack on the formidable Iraqi positions. Five weeks later, also in the *Times*, Luttwak contradicted Luttwak, writing that predictions of tens of thousands of U.S. casualties in a ground attack were wrong because "the Marines will stage amphibious landings" in which "casualties should be low."

After the cease-fire, Schwarzkopf disclosed that he had used his amphibious forces as part of a plan to fool the Iraqis. Luttwak then told the *Washington Post* he had made his predictions because he wanted the allies to rely on air power.

Luttwak was honest enough to give part of the pundit game away. Too often, the ideologists' wish was father to the forecast. Writing in *The Nation* on the eve of what Saddam Hussein promised would be the "mother of all battles," columnist Alexander Cockburn saw little reason to doubt Saddam's genius. The attack on Kuwait, Cockburn explained, "will most likely be vigorously contested, house by house . . ." Further: ". . . just as the battle there could bog down, so too could the U.S. rush toward the rivers northwest of Basra come to grief . . . Iraqis will be fighting on their native soil, which itself will be unforgiving as the troops enter the marshy . . ." blah, blah, blah.

The journalists and news organizations who did best in their coverage and commentary of the Gulf War succeeded when they avoided any advocacy. The winners triumphed by returning to their truest purposes: gathering, sorting, and putting out the news wherever it could be found, in Baghdad as well as Washington.

Just as the allied military victory is redrawing the map of power in the Middle East, there is now a new postwar media landscape. CNN has become the preeminent world-news service and Peter Arnett its justly celebrated star. Among the old-line networks, the ascendancy of ABC News and Peter Jennings was certified by both critics and the audience. Jennings also won a personal battle, burying the canard with nine lives—that he has been less than evenhanded in his reporting on Israel.

Less noticeable is the realignment of functions and changing status among the newspapers and the news magazines. During the air war, "print became a bystander," say Jay Rosen of the Gannett Foundation Media Center. By the time the ground war began, traditional "pencil technology," and in particular *Time* and *Newsweek*, had found the right approach in an age of live battlefield TV.

There are also good reasons to feel renewed appreciation for the intelligence of the news audience. Readers and viewers, the opinion polls showed, were not overly upset by the military restrictions on "the public's right to know." The press, as Peter R. Kann, publisher of the *Wall Street Journal*, wrote, behaved rather patronizingly, as if it knew what was best.

It was, in fact, arrogant to assume that "they" out there couldn't grasp what "we" in the elite knew: that official news management, like rust, never sleeps; that the military command's twice-daily briefings were the Bush administration's way of trying to create "the messages of the day" and keep its spin on the story; that Peter Arnett's CNN cameras were taken to only the bombed-out sites the Iraqis wanted them to see; that the troops in the field weren't going to speak to reporters as openly as they might—about the food, their noncoms, or whether they were willing "to die for oil"—when a military escort officer was standing by.

The public's forbearance would have changed had the war gone badly. But in the absence of military cover-up and political deception—the real Vietnam syndrome—most Americans seemed satisfied.

Neither did they complain about the multiple streams of news. The round-the-clock coverage of briefings, reports from the field, and news conferences was alternately derided by the unreconstructed left for "promoting the government line" and scorned by the know-nothing right for "revealing military plans." Television and print did both—and the vast middle of the audience took it in stride. And they expressed their satisfaction across the board: CNN's ratings doubled on the weekend the ground campaign began. For the first two months of 1991, newsstand sales of the *Newsweek* war issues were almost double the usual number of copies sold in 1990.

CNN's "overnight" success story has been ten years in the making (*New York*, February 11). When the war started in January, the network had a staff of 90 in the Gulf region. While the three established networks were cutting back overseas bureaus, CNN was expanding its presence around the world. Arnett owned the Baghdad dateline, though not solely by pluck and luck. CNN had most-favored-network standing in Iraq well before the war.

Bill Blakemore of ABC News, Tom Aspell of NBC, and Betsy Aaron of CBS also worked their way into Baghdad. Only Arnett, however, had to put up with attacks while his back was turned. The chief sniper was Senator Alan Simpson, the "folksy" Wyoming Republican, who during the Gulf crisis made a second career of press-bating. Simpson had described Arnett as an Iraqi sympathizer and offhandedly threw in the "fact" that the former Mrs. Arnett, a Vietnamese woman, had a brother who, someone had alleged, may have been in the Vietcong. None of this slowed Arnett. Today, CNN is as familiar as old-line networks. News consumers know it's there, morning, noon, and past midnight.

At CBS and NBC, Dan Rather and Tom Brokaw also went out into the field, spending part of February anchoring their news programs and reporting live by satellite from Saudi Arabia. Later, when the ground campaign began, the two anchors moved north behind the allied troops advancing into Kuwait. These forays produced some memorable television. Viewers saw Rather—intense, crouching, illuminated only by a CBS camera—poking through Iraqi pillboxes and bunkers along the Kuwait City waterfront. He spoke in a low monotone, giving an inventory of the arms cache scattered throughout the abandoned positions. As he stepped over boxes of live ammunition (from Jordan) and an upright tea cup (nice David Lynch touch), the viewer tensed as well: Watch it, Dan! They might be booby-trapped!

Brokaw, too, pushed forward. He went past Kuwait City, north into Iraq, to the captured Iraqi air base where in front of the TV cameras, Schwarzkopf and his generals assembled to lay down the surrender terms to their opposites: the nightly news from Appomattox. A trooper thought he recognized the anchor: "Peter Jennings, right?" Brokaw took it in stride "We all look alike," he replied.

This time, the competing anchors and their shows did not look alike. Peter Jennings remained in New York, in suit and tie, in the studio. Rather and Brokaw did fine work, but Jennings did what a network anchor should do: In the middle of fast-changing events occurring on a global scale, he stayed in place. Night after night, Jennings called in his field correspondents, eliciting the latest news from them; he interrogated the resident ABC experts, guiding them away from Pentagonspeak. He provided stability: the heavy-duty anchor in the Gulf news storm. He remembered to thank people for their work.

Two days before the ground campaign began, on a Thursday night in the middle of all three of the network early-evening newscasts, the story of the Soviet "peace initiative" broke. Conflicting information was coming out of a half-dozen datelines. From Dhahran, Rather and Brokaw performed with their usual competence. But they were out of position. Jennings smoothly connected the live reports: from Moscow and the Soviet spokesman to Washington for White House reaction; next to the United Nations; then to Saudi Arabia.

To their credit, the three old-line networks expanded their early-evening broadcasts to one hour during the most intense phases of the Gulf story. By last week, they were back to 30 minutes again; the increased costs of covering the war, and the added loss of advertising revenues due to cancellations and preemptions, had left them financially spent and searching for ways to save money. NBC News, for example, reported that it was spending $1.5 million extra a week at the height of the crisis. All the networks may get relief from an unexpected source next year: The expenditures normally required to cover the 1992 presidential campaign may be *under* budget if there is no real challenge to George Bush.

TV sets were tuned to CNN and the other networks in the offices of newspapers and news magazines, as well. Print editors were among the first to acknowledge that they had to rethink some of their traditional formats in covering a story. Print organizations, unsurprisingly, tried to put extra energy into analysis and background stories. They also sought to capture some of the television imagery within their news columns, through the use of oversize photographs, battlefield maps, and full-page graphics depicting the troops and armaments.

As usual when print tries to look like television, *USA Today* made the boldest use of graphics. But these strategies worked more to the advantage of the news magazines, with their color photography, coated paper stock, and quality reproduction. The weeklies captured the most arresting images on their covers and, on inside pages, regularly displayed the pick of the photography over two full pages. But while *Time, Newsweek,* and *U.S. News & World Report* each pushed to cover the same big events with many of the same techniques, the results were not all the same. The Gulf coverage had the effect of sorting out the news magazines, the quickest and the smartest from merely the quick and the smart.

U.S. News, with its earlier weekend deadlines, was left behind in the coverage of the ground invasion. Its March 4 cover showed random rocket contrails and promised vaguely, "The Last Act." Inside, the photography had a similar shelf-like feeling: "U.S. troops in the desert prepared to deliver a stunning coup de grace to Saddam Hussein. . . ." By contrast, *Newsweek*'s March 4 issue went to the printer almost a day later than *U.S. News*'s. On *Newsweek*'s cover, a U.S. military policeman, 101st Screaming Eagles patch on his shoulder, knelt over an Iraqi POW. Inside,

Newsweek reported that the final offensive started at 4 a.m. desert time Sunday and that all the first day's objectives had been achieved.

Newsweek also out hustled *Time* with two pullout graphics useful enough to tack onto bulletin boards. *Time* did one war map, which appeared three weeks after *Newsweek*'s first effort. Handsome as the *Time* map was, it arrived in subscribers' hands almost simultaneously with the news that the fighting was over.

Newsweek's real edge came from its guest columnists, in particular David Hackworth (invariably identified as "America's most decorated living military man"). Hackworth described with chilling familiarity what it was like for Iraqi soldiers to be in a "target rich environment." "If the historical ratio of casualties to bomb tonnage holds true," Hackworth wrote *before* the ground campaign started, "I would not be surprised to learn that 50,000 Iraqis have been killed and more than 200,000 wounded after 37 days of the Gulf war." A week later, the newspapers were carrying stories with similar estimates.

Television did not make the traditional news-gathering job of newspapers any easier, either. The *New York Times* had long been a repository of "the record"—presidential news conferences, official reports, the documentary narrative. But after CNN has brought the Pentagon's briefings into homes live and in full, and after the evening-news shows have replayed key exchanges, who is still interested enough to read through texts fifteen hours later, especially if fresh news is coming in onscreen?

At times, the onrush of television coverage found newspapers stepping on their own lines. In the early edition of the *New York Times*, Washington bureau chief Howell Raines was quoted in a news story. Raines complained that political concerns were preventing the press from providing a more complete picture of the ground war. "We are over a month into this conflict," Raines said, "and we've never seen a photograph of a wounded American soldier." The story quoting Raines appeared on page A17 of the *Times*. On the facing page, A16, was a three-column photo with the caption "First Casualties. An American Soldier Wounded in the Early Fighting . . . Being Rushed to a Treatment Center." The photo-credit line read NBC NEWS.

The *Times* and other papers were able to compensate for print's disadvantages by enterprising reporting, working the phones, and trolling the sources. As early as December 28, Jack Nelson, the Washington bureau chief of the *Los Angeles Times*, offered a look into the mind of George Bush and the White House's realpolitik view of the war. Nelson quoted his sources: "The officials said that Bush assumes that the American public will be mainly concerned about the number of U.S. casualties, not the tens of thousands of Iraqis who stand to die or be maimed in a massive air assault." Nelson didn't judge the policy; he didn't argue with it. That was for others to do, or for him to do when he stepped out of his role as reporter.

Similarly, two months later, with the air war under way, Bob Woodward of the *Washington Post* called in some of his contacts inside the intelligence agencies. Woodward's interviews helped him develop a story on the conflicting American assessments of bombing damage; while U.S. Central Command in Saudi Arabia consistently used optimistic figures of success rates, the CIA, among others, took a more conservative view. Woodward reported the story in detail, leaving it to readers to tease out the obvious bureaucratic reasons for the infighting.

Both these minor scoops came from veteran reporters operating in familiar terrain in Washington. The press in Saudi Arabia was on more hostile ground. Last fall, the princes of the House of Saud informed the princes of the big media, including the *Times*, the *Washington Post*, *Time* and such, that they would get one visa per news organization: the *Times* getting the same treatment as the *Toledo Blade!* The press's "friends" in the Pentagon—the generals who had been company-grade officers in Vietnam—said they would intercede.

And so the military pool system was born. The hordes could enter. The *Times* had six people in Saudi Arabia. The TV networks, with their need for camera- and sound-people as well as satellite technicians, received all the visas they needed. More than 1,800 people were eventually accredited by the military's Joint Information Bureau (JIB). In exchange, the journalists would have to team up in pools—squads of seven to eighteen people who could go into the field after agreeing to major restrictions.

The pools quickly became a script for a bad musical comedy. At first escorts wouldn't let reporters talk to military chaplains (the Muslim host country might be offended). Pool TV and radio reporters interviewed Stealth pilots after a bombing run and immediately got their tapes cleared, distributed, and satellited. Two "pencils" in the same pool—Malcolm W. Browne of the *Times* and Frank Bruni of the Detroit *Free Press*—wrote up the same story only to have their materials held up 24 hours.

Still, non-poolers chafed at the pools' access. The unchosen started driving off on their own— "going unilateral," in JIB-ese. During the Khafji skirmish along the Saudi-Kuwait border, Brad Willis, the TV pool man from NBC, spotted some unilaterals and demanded that the military get them away from the scene. Poolman Rick David, also from NBC, phones his office in New York with a front-line report—before sharing his pool materials. NBC said there had been a "misunderstanding" and apologized.

Going unilateral could be dangerous, as Bob Simon and his CBS crew found out. They set off toward the Kuwait border on January 21 and had the bad luck to encounter an Iraqi patrol with its wits still about it. When the CBS men were released last week, after 40 days in Iraqi hands, Simon described how they had been accused of being "American spies" and had been beaten and cursed at by Iraqi intelligence officers ("Yehudi!"—"Jew!"—one officer yelled in Simon's face and then spit on him).

Going unilateral also meant risking arrest and detention . . . at the hands of the American authorities. Chris Hedtes of the *New York Times* was detained, but he also produced an excellent feature on the Harlem Hell Fighters, the National Guard transportation unit that arrived in Saudi Arabia last November. The Hell Fighters are composed in part of New York City police officers, firefighters and Transit Authority workers—many of them Vietnam veterans, all of them black. Hedges described a demoralized outfit, ill equipped and mistreated by their Regular Army officers. "Had it better in Vietnam," a Hell Fighters sergeant told Hedges.

Once the ground offensive began, however, the unilaterals swept north behind the troops. Their tank columns of choice were the Egyptians, the Saudis, and the Kuwaitis, forces less bothered about JIB rules. As the Iraqis gave up, the pool system made less and less sense. Field commanders were willing to let their stories be told by the Americans, especially those with TV cameras.

In this case, the security restrictions were no match for the satellite technology. Sandy Gall of ITN, Forrest Sawyer of ABC, and Richard Threlkeld of CBS moved north, pulled over to the side of the road, deployed their flyaway satellites, and broadcast live. Bob McKeown, a 40-year-old Canadian, had joined CBS last August and figured he'd have a walk-on role in the desert. But McKeown reached Kuwait City ahead of the opposition and relayed the first news of its liberation.

McKeown was hardly an Ernie Pyle or a Peter Arnett—the lone combat correspondent dropping into foxholes to interview the troops, then slogging back to a cablehead to transmit his copy. McKeown was accompanied by CBS cameraman David Green, soundman Andy Thompson, and satellite technician Ed Jackson. They drove north in three rental vehicles, transporting their satellite dish and the generator and fuel to power it.

The CBS crew represented the new face of war coverage. The Pentagon and the Dhahran briefers were able to manage a part of the allies' war news and control a flow of militarily correct images. As long as the war took place in the skies, the news managers were successful. Once the story became accessible via Land Rovers, the controllers lost their leverage.

And so the war that started with unilateral CNN in Baghdad ended with unilaterals in Kuwait. And at the Pentagon and in American homes, people watched television to see the news as it happened.

Antihero: A Year After Desert Storm
Danny Schechter, SPIN

Saddam Hussein still rules a devastated land. The Kuwaiti royal family is back on its throne with its own human-rights abuses a daily unwritten-about routine. Perhaps now, as public ardor cools and the yellow ribbons yellow, journalists can confront their own complicity in selling this war in the guise of reporting it. It is time to admit that major media institutions became willing collaborators of an orchestrated government policy.

R.W. Apple of the *New York Times* is livid at the way the Pentagon pool system deliberately interfered with the free flow of information. At a recent forum, he called the military minders incompetent and accused the government of curtailing freedom of the press. Jonathan Alter of *Newsweek* went so far as to call on his colleagues to risk jail and violate military restrictions the next time that journalists are corralled into pools. CNN's Bernard Shaw acknowledged to a university conference that the American people "never got the whole story."

This skepticism found more adherents because of how the war turned out—with what the UN has called "apocalyptic" damage in Iraq, a country that suffered as many as 200,000 military fatalities, many inflicted as their troops fled Kuwait at the U.S.'s request, only to be wiped out in what an Air Force pilot called a "turkey shoot"; with Hussein's massacre of the Kurds and the Shia Muslims; and nearly five million people displaced across the region.

The television news coverage of the war never showed us the scale of the suffering or prepared us for the cycle of upheavals, reprisals, and arms sales to follow.

Instead, it substituted images for information. Some journalists later said that the power of the mighty Iraqi army had been deliberately misrepresented and exaggerated; that only a minority of the munitions used were so-called smart weapons; that we may have been as responsible for the oil spills in the Gulf as Iraq; that the Patriots caused more damage than the Scuds; that there may have been no basis for the chemical weapons scare; that the real cost of the war could end up being ten times the official estimate, once you factor in veterans' benefits and war debt.

The packaging of this coverage—with its cost of military experts, nose cone footage, and absence of critical analysis—is the product of a television system that itself is rarely covered.

To get at how TV news gets at us, you have to put television itself into the kind of context that it rarely puts the issues it is covering. And unfortunately, the people who can do that best—the professionals who sit in at the network morning meetings that decide the story lineups, who decide which images to send our way, and who know what parts of their scripts get approved and what they have to cut out for reasons of time and content—are part of the news system themselves. It's hard to be reflective when you are caught up in the day-to-day, especially during those periods of crisis such as round-the-clock gulf coverage when the adrenaline rush has a contagious quality.

As an insider, you soon discover that corporate cultures exist within news organizations the way they do in other organizations—with unwritten rules steering you toward being part of the team. TV news organizations are structured into hierarchies and governed by codes of conduct that tend toward a sameness of approach, even a homogenization of what programmers call "product."

It hasn't always been this way. For years, the "big three" networks had worked hard to project distinctive identities. I once heard an executive describe the different network new organizations this way: CBS was referred to as "the Church"; NBC, "the Morgue"; and ABC, "the Asylum." Here's why: William Paley's CBS built itself on image and moral purpose—from the understated simplicity of its eye-like logo to its mystique as the network of Edward R. Murrow and Walter Cronkite. NBC was its staid alter ego with newsrooms known for the lowest decibel levels and the Waspiest decorum. ABC was considered the most aggressive and experimental, the new kid on the block, younger and more personality driver, the network of the famous and infamous (Barbara Walters, Howard Cosell, and even Geraldo Rivera).

Today, all of these differences are blurred,with Dan Rather's former producer at CBS producing ABC's Ted Koppel, with former NBC executives on ABC's payroll, and on and on. The networks' graphics may feature different colors and designs but their stories, their approach, and their "feel" are all pretty much the same. Even CNN, which came to life in the '80s, has essentially copied existing format. Its ability to "go live" has been its signature, but the content of CNN is the content of mainstream TV news—only there's more of it and it's global.

Why this sameness? A new book, David Altheide and Robert Snow's *Media Worlds in the Postjournalism Era*, offers a provocative explanation. The TV media, they say, has its own imperatives, what they call "media logic," turning the news world ultimately into a world of its own—with its own language, grammar, ideology, and interests. What is and isn't covered often has had much to do with how a program is seeking to position itself before the perceived or real demographics of a program's audience as the inherent importance of any one story.

"The journalism enterprise," Altheide and Snow contend, "especially TV news, essentially is reporting on itself; it addresses events that are cast in its own formats and frames of relevance, rather than attempting to understand the events on their own terms, and then trying to communicate the complexities and ambiguities of real-world condition."

During the Gulf War, a billion eyeballs around the world were glued to CNN, watching what the *Village Voice* writer Gary Indiana called "the Home Shopping Channel by other means"—made-for-TV Pentagon home videos which may have been designed as much for selling weapons systems to envious allies than bringing information to news-hungry Americans.

The war was the kind of story TV news organizations live for. It was a chance for them to show their stuff, prove their mettle, and make their reputations. (And today, sell their video cassettes!) Almost all of the super reporters of the Murrow era established their bona fides during World War II. Another generation of journalists catapulted to the top of the profession thanks to Vietnam. The Gulf War seemed to offer another such opportunity. For TV news organizations struggling to justify their outsize budgets to owners with bottom-line orientations, the war promised more resources and higher ratings. What more is there? Well, for starters, there is understanding. At the height of Desert Storm, a University of Massachusetts survey research team probed ordinary Americans for the basis of their jingoism and concluded that (1) most people actually know very little about the issues on which they had strong opinions, (2) they tended to echo government policy justifications, and (3) the more TV news they watched, the less they actually knew.

That's because news and truth were frequently worlds apart. The behind-the-scenes story of the politics and economics that created Hussein's power—including the role of the United States—was rarely told. In fact, a poll showed that 73 percent of the American people said they didn't know the U.S. was arming Hussein during the ten-year Iran-Iraq war. No wonder then that the events that led to the war and their context were barely explained.

It was barely treated in popular culture, either—the place where people tend to learn as much about reality these days as they do through news. When 41 prominent musicians remade John Lennon's antiwar anthem "Give Peace a Chance," a documentary expressing their ideas was never broadcast on MTV or other outlets. (*MTV News*, to its credit, did report on antiwar protests and the silence of the music industry overall.) In contrast, the "Voices That Care" song turned up in a send-off the the yellow-ribbon sentiment. Organizers tried to picture it as "nonpolitical" but the songwriter David Foster made no secret of his Republican sympathies. The song was given the full Top 40 treatment and a "making of" program ran nationally on Fox.

News organizations ran promo after promo, pimping off the war's popularity. *Time* and *Newsweek* pumped our souvenir editions; the line between news, entertainment, and merchandising began to disappear. In New York City, a daily newspaper helped pay for the "victory parade." (A local TV reporter was actually arrested when he tried to interview antiwar activists chanting on the sidelines.)

ABC tried to cash in one last time with a prime-time movie of the week salute to "the heroes of Desert Storm," complete with President Bush as the MC. Footage of the real events and dramatized material were intermixed. In a sense, this lack of distinction between fantasy and reality was consistent with the way network news treated the war. Only Karl Marx's dictum proved prophetic this time; history repeated itself as farce. The show was, to use a military metaphor, a total bomb.

The Reagan and Bush administrations knew something that Franklin Roosevelt understood well: Americans get mad at bad guys, not bad ideologies. Find a Hitler, or invent one, and you have the battle half won. So Qaddafi begat Noriega and Noriega begat Hussein. Demonization was rediscovered as a key tool of psychological mobilization. And to complete the circle, in this sales scenario, George "Wimp" Bush played Rambo, while the Pentagon produced a celebrity, too: Normal Schwarzkopf. With his outsize IQ and even more outsize torso, since slimmed down for his *Vanity Fair* portrait, Schwarzkopf was their antihero.

You'll recall how CNN's Peter Arnett became a target of right-wing criticism for his Baghdad reporting despite the network's constant efforts to point out that Arnett's stories were often being censored. Friends at CNN tell me that the network was very concerned about the well-orchestrated anti-Arnett campaign and were careful to insure that his reporting was surrounded by disclaimers and quickly followed by interviews with experts who treated Arnett as an advocate, not a journalist.

How CNN Fought the War, a new book by CNN's general-in-residence, retired major general Perry M. Smith, recounts his battle to keep the Pentagon position the dominant one, while operating inside CNN's Atlanta newsroom, a place that insiders often consider a news bunker. Smith explains how he waged his own war within the war to "balance" Arnett's "misleading" coverage. "Throughout this entire period of time," he writes, "I kept trying to figure out Peter Arnett. . . . The more I watched the Arnett coverage the more I talked to people who knew him well, the more I came to believe that he was a 'feeler.' In other words, Arnett is someone who empathizes with the people around him." Feeling and empathy are apparently considered a high crime and misdemeanor in some circles. Clearly his feelings were out of line with the official word.

There is another factor that brought the networks into line with government policy. January 1991 was not the best time for the networks to confront a popular President and his popular war. And the reasons were economic. A lot of smart network money was engaged in a massive lobbying effort to change the FCC's financial syndication rules.

Those rules limited the networks' rights to own and market their own programming, ostensibly to limit their power to monopolize the marketplace. This meant that program suppliers, not the networks, would make the big money when *The Cosby Show* and other profitable shows went into syndication. Needless to say, this arrangement leased the producers, but not the programmers. As television became more competitive, thanks to cable and VCR's, network profits began to plunge.

The Federal Communications Commission had the power to revise the rules, and it was dominated by a group of Reagan-Bush FCC appointees. One of the commissioners, James Quello, a former station manager of Detroit's ABC affiliate, was the network point man on the issue. Just before the war started, he made a very public point of criticizing aggressive questioning at Pentagon press briefings, labeling it as unpatriotic in a speech to the Oklahoma Broadcasters Association. What kind of signal do you think that sent to network higher-ups? What network big would want to antagonize the very administration it was then asking for a major financial dispensation?

A friend at one of television's top shows—a veteran producer who insists that his anonymity be protected—told me he proposed that broader debates be built into his network's Gulf War coverage. His executive producer agreed and invited him to draft a proposal.

He never received a response. When he complained months later, he was told that the nonresponse was his response. "Don't you know what was going on?" he was asked. He said he felt totally naive to learn that throughout this period, one of the key network executives, a prominent "fixer," was in the White House regularly, lobbying on the FCC rule change.

It was in this same period that Michael Gartner, president of NBC's news division, personally intervened to kill a story about civilian damage in Iraq, shot and produced by the network's long-time stringer Jon Alpert, one of the few independent journalists to regularly report for a network news program. Alpert was fired after 12 years. The circumstances were these: Thanks to an invitation from former attorney general Ramsey Clark, Alpert wangled a visa into Iraq at a time when NBC News could not get one for its own principal correspondent. Tom Brokaw's *Nightly News* program agreed to run his report but Gartner intervened, later telling Clark that he was considered a "loose cannon" and didn't want one of his people associating with the "Ramsey Clarks of the world."

Gartner says he never saw Alpert's piece so he was not censoring that specific story—and that network belt-tightening meant that free-lancers were no longer needed. But among journalists who examined the case there is no question that it was the content of Alpert's report—with its striking images of civilians in hospitals and people weeping over their dead—that doomed the report.

Slowly, as hard information snuck out from under the blanket of state censorship and news management, media organizations began to admit they had been had. Fifteen of the biggest media organizations wrote to Dick Cheney months after the war ended to protest the pool systems that the networks had helped create. Today, the Pentagon is negotiating with a committee of Washington bureau chiefs to rewrite the rules, not abolish them.

So as we celebrate the anniversary of Desert Storm, and await Schwarzkopf's five-million-dollar memoirs, many of our most thoughtful journalists know in their heart of hearts that truth was a major casualty of the Gulf War, and that there is nothing to prevent a rerun.

Danny Schechter is executive producer at Globalvision Inc., an independent production company whose projects have included the award-winning PBS series South Africa Now.

Media in Wartime
Worksheet

1. From the readings and your own recollections, do you believe the military's handling of the American press corps was more of a "governing," "coordination," "restriction," or "manipulation?" Explain your answer.

2. It has been argued that the "Hi Mom" coverage given the Persian Gulf crisis, as defined in the essay "Just the Good News, Please," was instrumental in keeping Americans "pro-war" throughout the conflict. Similarly, it has been argued that the explicit coverage of the horrors of Vietnam instigated public outcry and was instrumental in the termination of the war effort. Do you believe that the media have the power to influence public opinion during wartime to that extent? In other words, can the media lose or win wars? Explain.

3.   Along the same lines, the essay "Anti-hero" suggested that "the more TV news they [ordinary Americans] watched, the less they actually knew" about the Gulf War. Do you believe this to be true? If so, explain how this is possible. If you do not believe this to be true, why not?

4.   Not quite a month after the Iraqis overran Kuwait and U.S. forces were sent to Saudi Arabia, Murray Garnert, president of NBC news, wrote a letter to the op-ed page of the *Wall Street Journal.* It read: "Here's something you should know about that war . . .much of the news that you read or hear is being censored . . . and there is no excuse for this." What do you think? Should the American press corp quietly serve in the military's best interest by passing along censored and controlled information to the public during wartime? Or, like Mr. Gartner, do you believe that freedom of the press should exist in times of crisis and government censorship has no place?

XIV

Crisis Coverage

From the time you first picked up this book to your current arrival at this section of the text, accidents, tragedies and disasters will have happened locally, nationally and abroad. With rare exception, the dramatic and catastrophic incidents that influence and change our lives will have been experienced through mass media. Since their inception, we have relied on the mass media to inform and warn in times of emergency and urgency.

Such absolute reliance on any information source raises several important questions: (1) What is the optimal role of that source in warning and mitigation; (2) How does that source convey information about crisis, and how might it be employed in both natural and technological disasters; and (3) How might the source more accurately reflect the series of choices that disasters and accidents pose both to individuals and to social and political systems? When that information source is as particularly powerful and omnipresent as mass media, two additional questions must be raised: (4) Does media simply reflect crisis or does its very presence help create it; and (5) Is crisis occasionally created for media by individuals or groups seeking a world-wide audience?

All of these questions are addressed in the essays presented in this section. The first two, extracted from a special issue on crisis by *TV Guide*, focuses on one particular crisis: The Shiite hijacking of TWA Flight 847 in 1985. The first essay, entitled "The Coverage Itself," examines how television coverage of crisis can become part of that crisis. This essay describes the three stages of the crisis—the hijacking, the hostage crisis, and the political resolution—and evaluates television's function and dysfunction in each. Is television at its best in times of emergency? The second essay, "The Impact on Negotiations," evaluates whether television did more harm than good in its coverage of the hostage situation. Did television offer a global stage for the drama to unfold? Would the crisis have occurred without television coverage?

The final essay, "The Crisis Crisis," is a composite of two separate pieces that provide a critical overview of media coverage of crisis. Collectively, they suggest that media news has become synonymous with crisis, that news reports overemphasize and overaccentuate the evil state of world affairs, and the result is an induced state of fear, paranoia and sense of victimization by the media consumer.

261

TV and The Hostage Crisis:
The Coverage Itself
Edwin Diamond, TV GUIDE

"The terrorists won, right?" ABC News' Sam Donaldson pressed a former Reagan Administration official the day the 39 hostages from TWA Flight 847 were freed.

In the competitive, hyped atmosphere of American television coverage of the hijacking—a form of news treatment that might be called terrorvision—Donaldson's statement phrased as a question seemed perfectly understandable. TV news gave such dramatic, blow-by-blow, "this-just-in" coverage to the hijacking, it was only natural that, in TV's hands, the story became a kind of deadly game, with obvious winners and—by Donaldson's implication—apparent losers, such as Ronald Reagan, the U.S., Israel and Western ideas about the rule of law. A careful reviewing of the TV coverage, however, shows that one clear-cut loser may have been television itself.

After sampling the coverage of four U.S. networks over the 17-day period between the start of the hijacking on June 14 and the hostages' release on June 30—an exhaustive record of some 60 hours of TV viewing that includes selective materials ranging from two-minute bulletins to hour-long specials—our News Study Group at New York University found a startling, and disturbing, pattern. TV news people did much that they could be proud of: we saw individual examples of hard-working, intelligent anchors; dedicated, physically courageous field reporters; incisive commentators, concerned producers and feats of technical wizardry. But when the parts are added up, the TV system collectively went wrong. It was as if the too-potent mixture of organizational zeal and Mideast politics transformed moderate television into extremist terrorvision, in the fashion of Dr. Jekyll and Mr. Hyde. Thus, while ABC's George Will was decrying the "pornography of grief" on the screen, ABC—and the other networks—were piling on the shots of anxious hostages and their anguished families.

This schizophrenic pattern of individual journalistic achievement and collective news mindlessness can best be traced by seeing the story—with the benefit, of course, of hindsight—as a melodrama in three acts: the hijacking event, the hostage crisis, and the political resolution.

The Big Event. The first impression a viewer gets when replaying the TV coverage is one of the sheer news *strength* of ABC, CBS and NBC—and, to a lesser extent, CNN. These organizations assembled the pieces of the story with speed and competence. On June 14, Day 1 of the hijacking, for example, CBS offered special coverage on *CBS Morning News, CBS Evening News* and *Newsbreak*—plus 10 special reports, ranging from one to six minutes, during the broadcast day and a 30-minute news special at 11:30 P.M. The other networks were equally impressive at covering the breaking news; NBC had nine special reports totaling 38 minutes and 42 seconds on Day 1, plus its regular coverage.

The networks' evening newscasts quickly touched on all aspects of the story—the initial hijacking after flight 847 left Athens, the first landing at Beirut airport, the next leg to Algiers and the return to Beirut, which astoundingly, took place as the early evening newscasts were on the air. ABC's *World News Tonight* that evening was typical of the "routine" special performances the networks can mount. There were reports from London, Washington (the State Department, a terrorists "expert" from a think tank), and a Peter Jennings interview with Israel's ambassador to the UN. Then, from around the country, came the longest segment—and what would be one of the signatures of TV news during the next two and a half weeks—emotion-laden interviews with family members and friends of the American aboard the plane.

The most dramatic segment was an audio clip that all three network evening news shows began with: the voice of TWA pilot John Testrake beseeching the Beirut control tower to let him land

and then refuel: "They are beating the passengers! . . . They are threatening to kill them now! . . . We want the fuel now!"

Analysts often speak of "the fog of war"—the near-chaos of extended military engagements that make reliable accounts difficult to achieve. A similar cloud envelops long-running hostage stories.

There was considerable confusion at the start about whether the passengers with "Jewish-sounding names" were singled out (by passport inspection) and removed by the Shiites to be kept apart from the other Americans. This "Jewish list" varied, in network accounts quoting TWA and other sources, from six names to 12. In fact, only after all the hostages were freed did the actual story emerge. American men without U.S. passports or having a "military look"—for example, Navy man Robert Stethem—were special targets of the terrorists. Stethem was murdered; but another military man, Claude Whitmoyer, went unharmed. Whitmoyer held a top-secret clearance and worked with a key U.S. national-security group—information that at least two networks knew and withheld. TV reporters also knew more than they told about the movements of the U.S. anti-terrorist Delta Force, although they did report sketchy information about the size, general destination—and practical uselessness—of the unit.

At the time, however, some critics complained that such reporting tipped the terrorists to U.S. moves and hindered Delta Force. But we could find no responsible U.S. official who believed that these TV reports narrowed military options. As one Reagan White House aide declared in a discussion of National Security Council strategy sessions: "The TV media were not our villains."

Crisis Atmosphere. If individual reporters and news desks behaved with restraint and sensitivity to strictly military matters in the early days of the coverage, then other systemic forces drove the coverage more and more toward that true media villian, terrorvision, and effectively limited Ronald Reagan's political options.

The first factor was the superheated air of crisis that filled the screen. On Day 2, CBS did 13 special reports in addition to its *Newsbreaks* and expanded coverage on the Saturday evening news. On Day 3, CBS had 17 special reports in addition to its scheduled newscasts. Dan Rather was never more than a few moments away from the viewer that weekend, nor was Peter Jennings at ABC, NBC's Tom Brokaw cut short a family vacation in Africa and flew to Beirut.

The presence of these important media figures morning, noon and night signaled the importance of the hostage story. The magazine programs and the morning shows also joined in. *CBS Morning News* scrapped its usual feature format to become a two-hour-a-day Hostage Central with Bob Schieffer and Terence Smith. ABC's *Nightline*, which began during the Iranian hostage-taking and has since become as much a fixture of crisis journalism as footage of concerned officials, looked at the story every night for two weeks. Ted Koppel rounded up what we've come to regard as the "usual suspects"—terrorism experts (the same faces that appeared earlier in the evening), Mideast diplomats, media critics and the ubiquitous Henry Kissinger.

On the network evening shows, we found, on the average, almost 60 percent of air time in the period from June 14 to June 30 was devoted to the hostages and related stories, as if nothing else remotely as important was happening in the U.S. or the world. Even when the crisis desks were off the air, station-break promotions and teases—"Are positions hardening? Details later tonight"—stoked the crisis feeling. On CNN, the nonstop news network, the normal rotation of the 15 anchor teams gave a more matter-of-fact demeanor to the story. Still, CNN added its own melodrama by scrolling down the screen the names of hostages.

In part, all this exciting buildup and portentous delivery reflected the news judgement—a sensible one—that this was indeed a big story. In part, though, they reflected less sensible competitive pressures to be first with the most. And they signified that news organizations have the technical resources to pull a big story together and give it momentum even when nothing may be happening.

These resources kept the moment-to-moment crisis feeling at the top of the news and took some of the initiative away from the Administration policy-makers. But just as the networks, rather than Washington, controlled the public level of interest in the story—the White House tried at first, for example, to hold down coverage and later acknowledged its inability to do so—so, too, did the networks eventually lose their control over the story to two other entities. One was the terrorists' stand-ins, the Amal militia; the other, the hostages and their surrogates, their families and supporters.

Both the hostage-takers and the hostage-sufferers had what the TV system needed: good pictures. Serious journalists like ABC's Peter Jennings and his boss Roone Arledge may wince in private about the often maudling pictures of husbands and fathers expressing their desires for freedom, and wives and children reciprocating the anguish. Yet the images were riveting: what viewer wouldn't feel "those folks could be the people next door! They could be me!" The scenes were "good TV"—and ABC and the others are in the business of doing good TV.

Once TV fleshed out the terse bulletins with human faces and endowed the crisis with everyday emotions, Delta Force and all military options were dead. As CBS White House correspondent Lesley Stahl explained on *CBS Morning News*: "We [the TV networks] are an instrument for the hostages . . . We force the Administration to put their lives above policy."

The hostage families soon realized this. Many made themselves available to every talk show and interview that came their way, "to keep public awareness as high as we can," as the brother of one hostage told *The Boston Globe*. Conventional wisdom holds that TV arrogantly besieges hostage families. That may have been so in the past; today, we found, the families can take hostage a compliant TV system.

The other takers of TV, of course, were the Shiite Moslem terrorists and their Amal militia allies. It's a cliché now that the Shiites got the networks to carry their political message back to America. When the TV coverage is replayed, it's clear just how well the Shiite line was delivered. The original terrorists—in addition to murdering Robert Stethem—beat others. (Their alleged "moderate" accomplices later robbed passengers of money and jewelry.) It's shocking, even now, to see how quickly the coverage moved on from this thuggery—though Dan Rather, to his credit, got angry enough on camera to extemporize about how they took "somebody's son . . . beat the hell out of him and shot him to death. . . ."

Mostly, though, the TV system kept its collective cool, its vaunted "objectivity." On *ABC's World News Tonight* on June 21, Don Kladstrup reported on the Shiite Moslems, "the losers in life, the people who've been pushed from their homes in the South." Kladstrup interviewed an older man who, we were told, has two sons in an Israeli prison. "I sympathize with American families," this father says. "My sons are hostages, too."

Holding to its objectivity, TV was unable to strike a kind of "moral equivalence" that somehow made the kidnaping of 39 Americans who happened to be on an Athens-to-Rome flight the same as the removal to Israel of a group of Shiite Moslems detained by Israeli troops during their occupation of Southern Lebanon. On June 27, ABC's Charles Glass had an exclusive interview—arranged by Amal—with three hostages, including Allyn Conwell, who is an oil-company salesman based in Oman. Conwell referred to the Israeli-held prisoners as "hostages" and spoke of a "profound sympathy" for the Amal cause.

Such objective reporting can create a fog of its own. Fortunately, ABC commentator George Will cut through the murk. He called the Kladstrup report "heartrending" (which it was), but added that it was of little practical relevance: "If you're confronted, on the streets of Manhattan, with an armed fanatic, the problem is not to cure him; it's to cope with him."

During this crisis phase, our monitoring reveals, ABC gave more time to the hostage story than the other networks (the 24-hour all-news CNN excepted). ABC also had more exclusive interviews with selected hostages themselves. ABC, it's clear, got its exclusives for good journalistic reasons: it had people on the ground in Beirut, notably Glass and Julie Flint, who through the earlier agonies of the Lebanese civil war had developed excellent contacts with the various factions. They had in-country experience—the kind that journalism's critics are always urging news organizations to develop in their reporters. Among other firsts, Glass was able to approach the hijacked TWA plane on Day 6 and get an interview with Captain Testrake (both *Time* and *Newsweek* put an image from that interview, showing Testrake with a gun at his head, on their covers). Glass also did the long "sympathy" interview with Conwell (and two other hostages) and, working with ABC producer Derwin Johnson, got the extraordinary "dinner by the sea" on June 28. There, at Beirut's Summerland resort hotel, 14 hostages were seen dining with their Amal militia guards, including one billed by Peter Jennings as "security chief, Akif Haidar, who himself hijacked a Libyan airliner six years ago."

The surreal nature of some of the footage—on one occasion hostage Simon Grossmayer took a phone call from *Good Morning America*'s David Hartman at Amal headquarters—led to some disparaging remarks about ABC standing for the Amal Broadcasting Company.

That's an unwarranted shot. Yet it's clear that ABC treated the Lebanese Moslems differently than did CBS and NBC. On June 24, Day 11, all three evening news shows played the tape of an interview Amal conducted with eight hostages:

ABC's Peter Jennings: "Good evening. We have another opportunity today to see some of the hostages in Beirut. The videotape was made by a Lebanese cameraman working for a British news agency and made available to all the American networks."

CBS's Dan Rather (voice-over): "Videotape made and released by their captors. Good evening. . . . The Shiite Moslem kidnapers released the latest videotape of their victims. . . ." *Bill Radesker:* "These scenes recorded three days ago by Amal . . . the tape has been edited by Amal."

NBC's Roger Mudd: "Good evening. . . . The most dramatic information out of Beirut came in a series of brief interviews with eight other TWA hostages. The hostages volunteered almost no information. They were questioned by a member of the Amal. In the room at the time, but not seen in the pictures, are the Amal militia. The recording was done Thursday by a Visnews crew and held by the Amal until it was released tonight to the American networks."

The Day 11 story is like a journalism-textbook case: the same single picture, yet three sharply different captions. In ABC's "soft" account, the name Amal never appears. In Dan Rather's hard-nosed lead, tough words explode from the screen: captors, kidnapers, victims. Mudd's narration is neutral, more "factual." Not so incidentally, all three versions are true—like the blind men touching and describing the elephant, each account emphasized a different reality. But whether the narration took a hard or a soft line, each network used the tape in full. Much like the hostages' families, the Shiite Moslems had grapsed the lure of the picture: America, here are your husbands, sons, fathers—safe, so far. Give in and you can have them back.

Resolution and Reaction. During the crisis phase, the boisterous behavior of some camera people and mike-toting reporters forced the temporary postponement of one Amal-sponsored news conference. A "media circus," Roger Mudd called it on NBC that evening, expressing the general feeling. Our group is less disdainful, and more realistic. The journalistic grunts on the ground were following implicit orders; if they missed the good picture or the right sound bite, the high-and-mighty desks back at headquarters would send what the trade calls a rocket: "Where's ours, PLS?"

The real animal acts, in our opinion, involve such practices as flying families overseas and arranging hotel rooms for reunions—and for the cameras of the *Today* show, which picked up the tab. *Today*'s practice of paying for its news sources/guests is closer to entertainment show policies than to news operations.

Another questionable practice has to do with live, unedited interviews. It's valuable to see a news conference, say, as it happens—the story in the making. CNN, without the time constraints of the others, can let its cameras roll. In some of these situations, CNN triumphed; for example, with TWA stewardess Uli Derickson's news conference. But other times, CNN fell on its face: reporter Jim Clancy in the Beirut schoolyard interviewing the hostages was out of his league, with a style better suited to the 11 P.M. local news.

The sappiest use of live TV, however, came from people who should know better. David Hartman on ABC's *Good Morning America*, concluding a live interview with Nabih Berri on Day 15, asked earnestly of the Amal militia leader: "Any final words to President Reagan this morning?" It was exactly the kind of political matchmaking that has led to longstanding complaints about "TV diplomacy." Significantly, ABC's *World News Tonight* never used any live, unedited interviews with news sources, and sought to distance itself from what the "entertainment part of the company" did. Viewers, though, don't make all that many distinctions between a morning host and an evening anchor.

By the end of the crisis, it seems, the TV system had become more self-conscious about its role as a facilitator of events rather than mere recorder. With the hostages' safety assured, TV became a hall of mirrors; from early on the morning news until late evening on *Nightline*, still more experts looked at the role of TV looking at the hostage story (as this article does, holding up yet another mirror).

With the hostages home—and the dead buried—everything seemed to return to "normal." But, as viewers resumed their summer ways, the issues remained, and Attorney General Edwin Meese suggested that the networks consider delaying some reports of terrorist activity.

Whenever officials send such messages, broadcasters feel obliged to denounce Government control. But the choice isn't really between Soviet-style non-news and the present headless system. As one of the numerous specialists on terrorism pointed out on *World News Tonight* during the crisis, around the world people know American television's "great reputation for putting on anything that moves." Or, if network executives need a voice from within the reservation, they might look again at John Chancellor's commentary on *NBC Nightly News* on Day 12. "The fanatics want America in agony." Chancellor said. "They want public displays of grief. America brought to its knees . . . Let's not play into their hands."

So true, and yet does anyone dare to imagine the terrorvision scenario for the next hostage crisis?

Media critic Edwin Diamond is director of the News Study Group at New York University.

TV and The Hostage Crisis:
The Impact on Negotiations
Neil Hickey, TV GUIDE

Henry Kissinger
—Secretary of State, 1973–77

Television is often accused of letting the bias of its commentators affect the presentation of the story. This was not the case in Beirut. The problem was the nature of the story, plus the competitiveness of the medium, which gives hijackers an incentive to create and prolong such a situation in order to use television to get before the American public. It's a tough problem, because television, being a visual medium, goes after whatever pictures it can get. So the networks show the hostages and the hostage families when they can. Obviously, those are the people who have the least judgment of the situation's overall necessities.

One could argue that, in the long run, the best way to save lives is not to negotiate with kidnapers at all. If they win their demands, the incentive will be to grab another bunch of Americans in the future. But you can't expect the hostages or their families to have that view. And so the abstract requirement of saving American lives in the future is not necessarily the main priority of the hostages themselves and their families. This is a very complex issue, because if in any one situation the hijackers prevail and achieve most of their objectives, you create a premise that another hijacking will also be successful. And while you may then save some or all of the people being held at the moment, you are endangering the lives of future, potential victims. This is an objective problem and I don't know what television can do about it. You can't tell the networks not to show the hostages and their families. What they might perhaps do is explain that there are other considerations involved.

When they put on terrorists themselves, this is where I become worried. I do not advocate Government regulation or prescription. But perhaps the networks could agree among themselves that there are several things they will not do. They will not photograph the kidnapers stating their demands while holding hostages. I don't object to the simple reporting of demands. I object to letting the terrorists stage performances for American television during which they state their demands. That may create an incentive to kidnap people in order to get on television. I believe the networks might consider some self-limited guidelines. I'm emphatically not talking about Government censorship.

And, if at all possible, the networks should not show pictures of Americans, on display, under the control of terrorists. There's something indecent about having one group of Americans walk freely into a press conference and be free to leave, while another group of Americans is there under guard. I found it offensive to see a pilot on television with a gun held to his head and a guy putting a hand over his mouth. The networks wouldn't show a picture of an actual rape on television. There are some decencies that you must observe.

Another point to consider: when the network anchormen go on TV every hour, it creates a crisis atmosphere. If there's nothing new to report, why not just have a printed message run through the regular program saying: "There is nothing new to report, and when there is we will interrupt the program and bring it to you"?

I thought the anchormen were pretty responsible. I don't remember any interview that particularly outraged me. One big danger is that men like [Amal leader] Nabih Berri will act according to what they're saying on television rather than what they are saying, privately, to the United States.

I believe that self-restraint by television can take care of most of what concerns me.

Zbigniew Brzezinski
—National Security Adviser, 1977–81

Did TV help or hurt the situation? Let me speak to that from the vantage point of a close observer of the Beirut affair, but also as the crisis manager of the 1980 hostage problem in Tehran. I would say that television has three negatives and one potentially beneficial effect.

First, television tends to transform what is essentially a political issue into a personal drama. It prevents the Government from dealing with the situation as a political problem and forces it to think of it as a personal problem.

Second, television becomes a medium for conveying the kidnapers' demands and for permitting them to appeal directly to the American people over the head of the Government for the acceptance of the demands. It thus enhances the bargaining capacity of the kidnapers.

And third, television humanizes the enemy, thereby also making it more difficult for the Government to respond firmly.

The only possible beneficial effect is that, in the absence of any contact between the U.S. Government and the terrorists, television can fill a void that otherwise would have existed.

The networks could have exercised more restraint. Their performance was probably the consequence of uninhibited competitiveness and lack of judgment. I think crass commercialism does dominate the medium. And crass commercialism produces such consequences.

I think there should be some mechanism for voluntary communication between Government and the media in these cases. It's done during wartime. A kidnaping or an act of terrorism is something akin to a wartime situation, and I would have thought that patriotism—an old-fashioned word—would have played some role in guiding their decisions.

Alexander Haig
—Secretary of State, 1981–82

As always, coverage of a terrorist act has pluses and minuses. The minus is always that electronic coverage is the main vehicle for the portrayal of terrorist goals and aims, and therefore serves their purpose. The medium needs to assess this recent crisis from a standpoint of whether it is serving the expansion of terrorism or genuinely serving the information needs of the public. And that's a fine line that can best be determined by the medium itself. I would not be one who would suggest that guidelines be promoted by the Government.

When TV reporters interview kidnapers it inevitably complicates the job of the President. Also, it risks making international outlaws seem like responsible personalities. Television should avoid being used that way. But there's so much competition involved that it's almost naive to expect such a thing.

The emotional climate created by television in a hostage situation leads to national pronouncements in which the lives of the hostages take precedence over the broader interests of the American people. The first principle in a terrorist situation in my view should be: what is in the best interests of the American people as a whole, not a particular group of victims. TV tends to reverse those priorities. It certainly did in the recent crisis.

Dean Rusk
—Secretary of State, 1961–69

In the Beirut situation, the effect of television came out about neutral—no runs, no hits, no errors. It didn't help much or hurt much.

I was bemused by the fact that the networks brought in big experts to be interviewed, and they all retreated into generalities. A lot of that was a waste of time.

I don't think the television commentators pointed out sufficiently that, during news conferences with the hostages, their lives might have been at stake, guns could have been pointed at them and they were speaking under real duress.

I don't believe the media should have reported on the subject of our anti-terrorist Delta Force—where it was and where it was moving to. Still, I favor a high degree of freedom for the media in these things. Government is free to make suggestions, but it shouldn't clamp down in any way.

It was in very poor taste for reporters to go up to relatives of the hostages, put a microphone in their faces and say: "How do you feel?" How in hell did they think they should feel?

Hodding Carter III
—State Department spokesman, 1977–80

Was television a negative influence in this situation? No. Does it encourage terrorism? No. Terrorism is a product of this age. Was television irresponsible in some of its actions over there? Yes. Does that go with the territory? I'm afraid the answer is yes—the territory being a frantically competitive environment.

But I simply cannot buy the idea that television prolongs an agony. The hostages got out about as fast as they were going to get out. And if you read the polls, there is no indication that the American people were deluded by the terrorists.

Did television's presence make the President's job tougher? Absolutely. A free press in a crisis situation always makes life more difficult for a democratic Government. When I was the State Department spokesman, I did what anybody in an official capacity does in moments of stress. I said to the media: will you kindly shut up and leave us alone. I damn well beat up on the media when I was spokesman. And in retrospect, I was wrong. The interviews with the Ayatollah had no more to do with the outcome of that thing than the man in the moon. But they sure made our lives difficult. Some of the best information we got came from those interviews.

God knows television is an adolescent when it comes to the mature use of its power. Like an adolescent, it's given to really wretched excess and sometimes won't admit the impact of what it does. But it's no worse than the print press was about 50 years ago, when newspapers used to secretly take pictures of executions. I don't think the American people are idiots. They looked at those pictures of hostages giving press conferences and it enraged them. But it also gave them some sense of the condition of those people being held.

Jody Powell
—White House Press Secretary, 1977–81

The cause of excesses by television in reporting hostage situations is not ideological bias. It's motivated by money, which—as St. Paul said—is the root of all evil. Excess tends to play into the hands of the yahoos and people who don't believe in the First Amendment and the free flow of information. It undermines public support for the Constitutional guarantees that journalists need to do the job. The dumbest part of television's performance was the tendency to jeopardize those fundamental things in the interest of some very short-term strivings for ratings.

I don't think television's actions were in any sense damaging to the national interest—even the reporting of the deployment of the Delta team. Some journalists and First Amendment absolutists will argue, in the course of a debate: "It's not our job to worry about the consequences of our reporting. It's our job to report the news." They say that, but most of them don't act that way. Most of them would not report something they knew was going to get somebody killed. If they did, then I might change my view about not favoring Government sanctions against the media.

The Crisis Crisis
Peter Moore, PLAYBOY

Picture a crowded bar. Three television sets hang from the ceiling, tuned in to the network feed. This is a high-tech joint, so there are competing amusements, as well: MTV on wall-sized monitors, dueling jukeboxes, video games with synthetic voices. On top of this racket, there's the festive roar of conversation.

That is, until the news comes on. Talk stammers to a halt and eyes are cast upward; they dart from screen to screen. The anchor men begin to talk loudly, and they're talking crisis—drugs, vanishing rain forests, terrorism, Armageddon. They're inflating stories to ten times their natural size, decrying the end of the world. Their graphics are flashier than video games, their footage better than MTV, their high-tension talk scarier than s-f.

In the face of this onslaught, the patrons can't concentrate; they can't even think. Aghast, afraid, they gulp their drinks as the hysteria level rises.

When they've got a crisis to hawk, news magazines love to start stories in italics. In that type face, they can get away with anything: apocalyptic fiction that would otherwise be out of place in straight journalism, even overextended metaphors for American society like the one in the paragraphs above. Italic type can also clear the way for a single anecdote to stand in for the latest trend that's ravaging society, and it lays the groundwork for paragraphs that begin, "The sad story of Bob J. is all too familiar in America today. He represents an insidious epidemic that is sweeping. . . ."

As it so happens, America today is suffering an epidemic of nation-sweeping events unseen since the Biblical plagues in Egypt. In the attack of the killer trends, we are terrified on Monday by a crisis we scarcely knew existed the previous Friday, and Monday's dark portent, in turn, gives way to the next week's hysteria.

In horrific succession, herpes anxiety is overtaken by the plague of AIDS, which is followed by the shocking specter of Third World debt. After a brief but chilly nuclear winter, we are threatened by our own national debt crisis and devastated by starvation in Ethiopia; then it's back to our leaky ozone layer. Terrorists are suddenly in our midst, then the homeless—until all is swept away by crack mania.

The problems appear, the alarms sound, the cover stories and the special reports proliferate. Then the media lose interest, and it's on to the next disaster. The phenomenon is so pernicious, it's worthy of a cover story all its own: Call it the Crisis Crisis.

Nobody would tell you that our bloated national debt is a healthy sign, that AIDS is a passing annoyance or that crack is good for you. These are serious problems deserving of serious reporting and concerted follow-through—if only that would happen.

No, the Crisis Crisis is not a matter of what's reported, it's a matter of who reports the bad news and how it's reported. This new menace springs from the number of news outlets competing to force tragic trends down our throats and the vehemence with which they deliver the goods.

In the September 15, 1986, issue of *Time*, associate editor Evan Thomas told us that given the proliferation of drug abuse, "we really are in the midst of a national crisis." The previous spring, *Time* had decried the state of liability insurance in numbingly similar terms: "a rising flood of problems growing out of what has become a new national crisis." *Newsweek* easily matched the hysteria level of its competitor, asserting in the August 18, 1986, issue that radon gas is "the most dangerous source of radiation in America" (a window fan in contaminated homes turned out to be the solution). The radon scare followed a classic in slam-dunk Crisis Crisis delivery by no less a source than *Newsweek* editor in chief Richard M. Smith. In the June 16, 1986 edition, he wrote that drug abuse is "as pervasive and as dangerous in its way as the plagues of medieval times."

If the editor wanted to talk drug plague, he needed to look no further than the early 1900s, when cocaine use was far more commonplace than it is today. The editor was right to identify a plague, but it doesn't have anything to do with drugs, the use of which has remained pretty constant in the Eighties. The swarming critters gnawing on the landscape these days are not locusts but news-hungry journalists, and they are truly omnivorous beasts. Fueling their appetites is the intense competition for attention, both from the public and from the all-important advertisers.

It's no secret that *Newsweek*—the magazine that brought you the Hitler diaries—has been suffering a decline in ad pages. There's no dishonor in that; the past few years have been a tough time for many magazines. But when *Newsweek*'s bottom line dipped, its hysteria level rose; suddenly, sunshine could kill the sexy babe it put on its cover and unmarried 40-year-old women were "more likely to be killed by a terrorist" than to find a husband. *Newsweek* told us that Richard Nixon was "back" (now, *there's* a crisis), and the magazine has driven the cocaine band wagon from the start, with three 1986 cover stories on the subject.

As *The New Republic* recently asserted, "*Newsweek* has vowed to pursue the lonely struggle against crack no matter how much money it makes." And the results have been good: Its "Kids and Cocaine" cover sold 15 percent better than average, and "Cocaine—The Evil Empire," the February 25, 1985, granddaddy of drug hysteria, weighed in with a whopping 37 percent bonus on the newsstand.

Time was in there slugging as well, nearly matching *Newsweek*'s torrid pace on drug coverage with "The Enemy Within" and "Drugs on the Job," finding toxic waste in our water (and repeating a scary 1980 cover image in the process) and shrieking about the insurance crisis.

The television networks, suffering from a defection of 18 percent of their prime-time audience over the past eight years, may be the loudest contributors to the noise level. As ad revenues fall and corporate shake-ups rock the executive suites, news departments have become pressure points. The same competition that has escalated on-camera news positions into multimillion-dollar jobs is pushing these media superstars to lend their voices to inflated crises worthy of their inflated salaries.

So we watched Geraldo Rivera unveil *American Vice: The Doping of a Nation* (December 2, 1986), propelling the independent Chicago superstation WGN to a Nielsen rating of 18.1, doubling its average for the Tuesday prime-time period and trouncing the offerings from NBC and CBS in the Chicago market. On September 2, 1986, Dan Rather relived *48 Hours on Crack Street;* a few days later, Tom Brokaw toured *Cocaine Country.* Rather's descent into drug-trend hell earned the highest ratings of any documentary in the past six years; 15,000,000 people tuned in.

Crack use was then, and still is, a local—not a nationwide—phenomenon and nowhere near as deadly as, say, drunk driving. But that mattered less than the public's hunger to know about the new form of cocaine, and CBS mainlined the sordid goods straight into their living rooms. Not surprisingly, a *Newsweek* poll in the August 11, 1986, "Saying No!" issue showed that public perception of the drug crisis—skewed by media over bad—rated crack and cocaine as close seconds to alcohol as threats to society. And from the press coverage, who would know any different? During the Crisis Crisis, the boring old news about the high societal costs of alcohol abuse just won't play. Clearly, the networks and the news magazines had given their customers what they wanted, which is the first rule of merchandising. But when the product being sold is the news, that age-old hustle takes on a whole new meaning.

Never mind that the public may actually believe the hyperbole that they see and read. The greater problem is that impressionable Government officials in Washington may believe it. Our legislators must have watched all 17 hours of drug programming on network TV during the first half of last year, because they rushed through some spectacular—and probably unconstitutional—drug legislation during the pre-election rush last fall.

Before crack mania, Federal anti-drug initiatives had apportioned 1.8 billion dollars to catch dope smugglers, dealers and users, compared with $230,000,000 for education and rehabilitation of substance abusers, even though everyone from the President on down had said that we should attack this problem from the demand side. With the media drums pounding for action on the latest crisis, Congress responded to this serious problem not with a well-thought-out plan but with a proposed $900,000,000 worth of frenzied half measures and hocus-pocus. As New York Representative Charles Schumer said, "What happens is that this occurs in one seismic jump instead of a rational build-up. The down side is that you come up with policies too quickly and that the policies are aimed at looking good rather than solving the problem."

Savvy politicians play the hysteria game another way as well. Aware that the press is always up for a good scream, President Reagan and Secretary of State George Schultz were able to score points against the Evil Empire in the hours after the downing of KAL flight 007, charging that the Soviets willfully shot down a planeload of innocents. In *The Target Is Destroyed,* Seymour Hersh pointed out that the Russians had simply made a tragic mistake and that our Government intelligence gatherers knew it had been a mistake, as did the President and Shultz. They wouldn't admit that in the glare of a crisis, mind you; why waste the spotlight?

During the Qaddafi hysteria, the press was fully lathered to accept State Department-manufactured assertions of Libya's intended terrorist activities, and it ate up the fiction that our bombing raid had weakened "Mad Dog" Qaddafi's grip on his government. The crisis machinery was already in place and functioning, waiting for the next bit of news to pump up. In a telling bit of timing, the strike itself took place at two o'clock in the morning Libya time, which was seven o'clock in the evening New York time. And there was Dan Rather, encouraging his Tripoli correspondent to hold his microphone out the window so the American public could hear the 12 minutes of mayhem. At 7:20, Larry Speakes was in the pressroom, waging media war.

Reflecting on the whole mess, House Majority Leader Jim Wright told *The New York Times,* "One of the unfortunate by-products of the television age is the short attention span of the American public. We walk along fat, dumb and happy until a crisis grabs us by the throat. Once it is off the front burner of nightly television coverage, we go back to sleep."

So it is that the wave beyond the Crisis Crisis takes shape: dismissal by cover story. Once *Time* covers the famine in Ethiopia, we can forget about it. After *Newsweek* looks at nuclear war, the bombs disappear. Under the new system, crises will spend their few minutes in the spotlight, grant interviews all around and then gracefully retire, like Joe DiMaggio.

We're back in the bar again, as you can tell from this italic type. With all of the TVs blaring, the din of crisis-mongering has increased to a heavy-metal sonic boom. But the patrons no longer look frightened. They've stopped watching the monitors; they're numb to the very latest causes for hysteria. But that's what happens in noisy bars: Turn up the sound loud enough and you'll deafen the customers.

Victims of Press Stress
Lewis Grossberger, PLAYBOY

Stan H. and his wife, Gloria, slump dejectedly in the squalor of their once merely unkempt suburban home, their vacant eyes fixed on the television screen, their shaky hands clawing at the rising tide of newspapers and magazines. They both know that they are helpless victims of something awful, but they're not sure exactly what, as they haven't yet seen a thing about it in *Time* or *Newsweek.*

"Once we were a special kind of family," says Stan bitterly. "You know, a family not trapped in an ever-deepening nightmare spiral of fear, anguish and horror."

"Shh!" says Gloria. "The six-o'clock news is on. My God! They say the nation is caught in the viselike grip of a deadly drug crisis!"

"Forget that," says Stan, whimpering. "I just heard a bulletin on my Walkman. North America may soon be engulfed by a lethal cloud of PCBs, dioxins, radon gas, fluorocarbons, acid snow and gamma rays—and terrorists are behind it!"

Lost in their frenzy, they both begin to rock rhythmically back and forth, emitting the hackle-raising, defeated moan that is the characteristic cry of America's most pathetic individuals—the crisis-crisis victims. Such unfortunates have been exposed to so many crises, near crises and pseudo crises that their bullshit-immunity systems have broken down, leaving them defenseless against news-media penetration of the vulnerable, gray blob that is the human brain.

Stan, only recently the handsome, 40ish manager of a prosperous used-pet boutique, is now a gaunt, unemployed zombie of 58. Gloria, a rancid, gargoylelike caricature of the beauty queen and supermarket cheese demonstrator she once was, has the smudged fingers and blood-shot eyes of the hard-core news abuser. Their three children, Jane, 15, Bryant, ten, and little Willard (a wizened toddler sad beyond his years), are locked in the air-purified, multidisaster-resistant fallout shelter in the basement to protect them from the plague of virulent crises ravaging society.

"This is one screwed-up family," says Dr. Mumford Kittle, head of the Crisis Dependency Network, who is chained in the attic. "I thought we were making progress, but when I arrived for our session yesterday, Stan knocked me out and dragged me up here. Gloria had read a story about a wave of child abuse surging across America, and she suspects everyone. We're back to square one, treatmentwise."

Back downstairs, Gloria's digital wrist watch starts beeping; she stands bolt upright. "Testing!" she screams. "It's testing time!"

Scrambling to the basement, the panicky couple bursts into the fallout shelter. "OK, kids, fill up these specimen bottles," says Stan.

"You haven't succumbed to the nightmare of crack addiction, the number-one menace in the U.S. today, have you?" Gloria demands.

"Aw, Ma," Bryant whines. "You don't sniff it, you smoke it."

"Aha!" his mother cries. "How did you know that?"

"Dan Rather."

"Good God!" shouts Stan, stricken with terror. "Where's Jane?"

Bryant says that he saw his sister sneak off to school. "She had to," he says. "She's scared she'll become unemployable and end up a starving bag person roaming the streets of some overpopulated megalopolis, easy prey for psychotic killers, AIDS and the partnerless-single-woman syndrome."

"But school," Gloria sobs. "It's full of crime, illiteracy, rap music, satanic cults and secular-humanist values, whatever *they* are."

"We've got to save her," says Stan.

"You're right," says Gloria.

But neither moves toward the door. Instead, they resume that terrible moan, a sound so irritating that bystanders frequently become agitated to the point of homicide—a fact that, expert crisis theorists now believe, may result in America's worst crisis yet: a crisis-crisis-victim-victimization crisis.

XV

Children and Television

In 1955, when the British psychologist Hilde Himmelweit began her pioneering study, "Television and the Child," she could unequivocally assert that "there were few facts available about children's behavior and reactions to viewing." Thirty-five years later, one bibliographer compiled nearly 3000 English-language citations about children and television.

Nonetheless, most Americans treat television as just another piece of furniture. It is, after all, comfortable and familiar and seemingly harmless. Evidence of this can be found in the sheer quantity of television that parents allow their children to watch. According to recent Nielsen rating statistics (1990), children between 2-to-5 years old watch an average of 27:49 hours per week; children between 6-to-11 years old watch an average of 23:39 hours per week. Should parents be concerned that how much and what their children are watching on television might be hazardous to their mental, emotional and physical health? A review of the approximately 3000 published research articles offer equal support for both "yes" and "no." What's a parent to do?

The first essay reflects on the genuinely poor state of children's television, with an emphasis on violent content. "What TV Does to Kids" suggests that television pitches violence as the key to success and tells kids that the world is a mean, ugly, and scary place to live. The author concludes that "the quality of children's television is poorer than ever, and our children still sit in front of the television set and learn lessons that society may have cause to regret." The second essay implies that sufficient improvements will never be made because the networks are more concerned with the needs of advertisers than the needs of children. "Toys Are Programs Too" argues that children's television has become an exploitive, multi-billion dollar enterprise with the airing of product-first programming—that is, where first a toy is developed and then a 30 minute TV program is created based on that toy (e.g., *Strawberry Shortcake, Care Bears).* Clearly, these 30 minute long commercials are not operating in the child's best interest, but are serving to generate significant advertising revenue. The third essay explodes many of the myths surrounding television and children . . . many of which are found in the first two essays. "TV as Boob Tube: Bad Rap" cites governmental and scholarly reports that suggest that TV viewing is neither mindless nor necessarily harmful, if used correctly. The final essay, "How's TV Doing," is a compilation of opinions by experts on children and television. They suggest that television is doing much better, thank you. Here, we see that the quality and quantity of good children's programming is on the rise, with the networks becoming more responsive to the needs of children. The experts recommend that television still be handled with kid gloves until more and greater improvements are made.

What TV Does to Kids
Neala S. Schwartzberg, PARENTS

"Why is *GI Joe* your favorite show?" I asked a spunky towheaded six-year-old.

"Because it has a lot of fighting," he replied.

"What is the character GI Joe himself like?"

"He fights."

("Hold it"—the conversation is interrupted by his friend—"I have to go make more weapons.")

"Who would you like to be like when you grow up?"

"I want to be like Rambo because he has a big gun." The child starts to give me the specific name and type, but when I look puzzled, he describes it simply as "a big gun." "And when I grow up," he continues, "I want to shoot bad guys."

"What happens to the bad guys you shoot?"

"They die."

"And what happens to you?"

"Nothing."

The two cherub-faced children then formed their Construx into guns and grenades, armed themselves, and disappeared into the basement to play at war and killing.

We know that what we see on TV is fictional. But all too often we and our children take television not as a fun-house mirror, distorting life for our entertainment, but as a magic window on reality.

Some shows do give children very useful information. *Sesame Street* shows a new character making friends, a child with a new baby sister or brother. Other shows give information also, but much of it is of questionable utility.

How TV shapes kids' thoughts.

Unfortunately, the images children see through the TV "window" are so vivid and convincing that they affect their thoughts and ideas, the kinds of topics they talk about, and the games they play. The greater the consistencies in those images, in the "reality" presented, the greater the effects.

Television can and does change the way children see themselves and their roles, as well as the roles of others. Several researchers have reported, for example, that youngsters who watch more television with a stereotypical presentation of women have a more traditional perception of men's and women's roles.

And it is not a phenomenon restricted to young children, Alexis S. Tan, Ph.D., of the University of Washington in Seattle found that the beliefs of adolescent girls about the importance of physical beauty and youth were changed as a result of seeing a series of television commercials. One group saw commercials that used sex appeal, beauty, and youth as selling points. Another group saw commercials that used other techniques to promote products. The teens and preteens who saw the advertisements stressing youth and beauty were more likely to say that those characteristics were important to men. And it made being young and beautiful more important to them, too. They came away believing that these physical attributes were more "personally desirable," ranking them higher than intelligence and competence.

But the most disturbing effects are found in the area of televised violence. George Gerbner, Ph.D., dean of The Annenberg School of Communications at the University of Pennsylvania, has been studying the effects of television violence on children's perceptions of reality for years. He has found the distortions in the magic window to be very consistent.

Teaching might is right.

According to Dr. Gerbner, despite superficial changes, the symbolic environment—the images of the world presented to the viewer—is one of violence. And it is violence as a demonstration of power. Television depicts violence as the key to power; it is the way power is obtained and how it is exercised.

Unlike the real world in which power comes from many sources—wealth, a glib tongue, personal magnetism—in the realm of television our children are learning that violence and power are synonymous. It is the way you get people to follow your wishes. There is no clearer example of this kind of learning than the little boy who told me that he wants to be like Hulk Hogan "because he hurts people, and then they do what he wants."

Joseph R. Dominick, Ph.D., and Bradley S. Greenberg, Ph.D., of Michigan State University found that "the greater the level of exposure to television violence, the more the children were willing to use violence, to suggest it as a solution to conflict and to perceive it as effective."

What other practical lessons about the world around them do children extract from TV viewing? Dr. Gerbner reports with Larry Gross, Ph.D., professor of communications at The Annenberg School, that "young viewers who watch a lot of television are more likely to agree that it is 'almost always all right to hit someone if you are mad at them for a good reason.' " These children are also more likely to believe that most people just look out for themselves, take advantage of others, and cannot be trusted. Violence-laden television generates an exaggerated sense of danger and mistrust.

Distortions in children's perceptions of the world, brought about through TV depictions of reality, have also been found in their ideas about danger and crime. Gerbner's studies show that heavy viewers reveal a higher sense of personal risk and suspicion than do light viewers in the same demographic groups who were exposed to the same real risks of life.

Money talks.

Why do producers create and broadcasters air programs whose effects are going to be less than laudable? Because the forces of the marketplace are often stronger than the producers' and broadcasters' sense of social responsibility. Children's programs are aired when there is little else that can profitably fit into that time slot or when the programs are obtained at an extremely low cost.

One source of low-cost television is companies that hope to make their profit not from the sale of the shows themselves but from the toys that are the focus of the program. Toy manufacturers have literally invaded the television market by creating cartoons that are essentially 30-minute showcases for their products. And because the quality of the program is secondary to its ability to display and entice children into wanting the products, the quality of the programming depends on the social conscience and community interest of the manufacturer—a chancy affair at best.

The latest lure: interactive toys.

The newest development in the relationship between product and program is the interactive toy, a toy that is actually affected by the TV show itself. Mattel has developed several that will interact with a new life-action program, *Captain Power and the Soldiers of the Future*, and Axion has introduced *Techforce and The Moto Monsters*.

While both are labeled interactive, the toys and the ways they operate are as different as night and day. In the case of *Captain Power*, various action-figure accessories will be able to fire at on-screen enemies for points and be hit by enemy fire for point losses. With *Techforce*, figures actually move across the floor in response to commands embedded in the onscreen dialogue and can be programmed from a special computerized command console.

Although children can play with all the toys without the TV show, and watch the show without the toys, this intimate relationship, the very interactive nature of the toy, can easily exert a subtle but real pressure to depict situations compatible with the toys' unique abilities.

However fascinating and entrancing the technology behind them, these toys augur a deeper level of commercialism in children's television, drawing it farther away from the writer's imagination and creativity and closer to the necessities of the marketplace.

Futile attempts to redeem violent contents.

But regardless of the source of their shows and the financial incentives involved in their presentation, broadcasters and producers have attempted to bolster public acceptance of their programs. They have added moralistic messages tacked on at the end of violent cartoon shows, for example, in an attempt to convince their audience that the programs do have some redeeming social value. However, researchers such as Jerome L. Singer, Ph.D., at Yale University claim that the kids watching the shows often don't get that message. What they pick up on is the violence, and their play tends to be more aggressive after watching such programs.

How kids watch TV.

The way youngsters watch and understand a television show and the way they interpret what they see is crucial. In order for a child to become aware of the pro-social message underlying a program, he would need to sit down and watch most, if not all, of the program. This would be particularly important if the message was supposed to counteract the effect of aggressive content.

But children do not simply sit and watch an entire television show. They walk in and out of the room, play with a toy, or change the channel in the middle of a program. Carrie Heeter, Ph.D., and Bradley Greenberg, Ph.D., of Michigan State University found that children do a lot of channel changing, especially if they have a remote control selector or cable box. The researchers asked a sample of 1500 adults and 400 fifth and sixth graders about the way they watched television. The younger the viewer, the more likely he or she was to change channels. These "zappers," as Heeter and Greenberg call them, do less planning. They do not sit down with the intention of watching a particular show, but rather to watch television, so they catch bits and pieces of different shows as they move through the channels. They stop at the first program that looks good and then change the channel between shows, during shows, and at commercial breaks. Heeter and Greenberg found that zappers are less likely to watch a program from start to finish and often watch more than one show at a time. (Although interactive toys may focus kids' attention more on one program—an unfortunate prospect, since many of the shows the toys interact with are violent and some of the toys themselves are guns.)

But even if children sat down and watched a program from the opening scene to the closing credits, would they be able to understand and interpret what they saw? No, it seems they would not. They tend to remember the action—particularly the violent action.

What children remember from television programs.

In an admittedly unscientific experiment, I asked my six-year-old son to watch one of his favorite cartoons and remember all he could about it. The show, which seemed fairly uncomplicated when I simply watched it, became quite involved when I noted every event and element. Subplots and actions irrelevant to the main plot seemed to be included to stretch out the show's length.

My son recalled very little, two or three scenes that he told me about out of order, suggesting that he had not integrated the information into any linear, coherent representation.

I tried again with another series. This time he did better, but he had seen this episode before. When I sprang the question, "So, what was the show about?" without warning, and without first asking him to watch the whole episode, he could remember only the names of the characters and one scene: one of the characters sent out his pet to eat up the other character.

More formal research turns up similar results. W. Andrew Collins, Ph.D., director of the Institute of Child Development at the University of Minnesota, found that children in the early grades fail to organize and understand the scenes in a show and the way in which two scenes are related. They make fewer inferences about the relationships among program elements and fail to understand the links among the motives, acts, and consequences.

Suzanne Pingree, Ph.D., at the University of Wisconsin at Madison edited and simplified a family situation comedy and showed it to a group of preschoolers. She found that the characters' actions were remembered far better than scenes offering explanations of their actions. When she divided the show into segments, she discovered that children recalled most poorly the scenes recounting inner feelings and emotions to explain previous events.

It seems then that due to their TV viewing habits, our youngsters are less likely to pick up on the dialogue that promotes a more positive, or even more complete, understanding of the plot and story line. What they are catching is the physical actions and confrontations.

And even if they do watch the whole show, kids have difficulty fully understanding the entire thrust of the program, the theme or plot that guides and integrates the action. So again they are left with the physical actions dominating their recall.

What is real and what's not?

What children see on television is fiction. And how much can it affect them if they know that it isn't "real"? It all depends on how they think about reality.

Children may understand that what they see is made-up, but that does not stop them from believing it anyway. It now appears that even programs that are obviously fantasy can be judged by children as at least partly real.

Children's conception of reality is not one-dimensional, nor is it simple. They are used to getting "real" information from "unreal" sources. In children's television, for instance, words walk across the screen to form sentences. Animated characters demonstrate science, safety, and even nutrition. Puppets act out scenarios that the youngsters recognize as parallels to their own experiences.

Aimee Dorr, Ph.D., at UCLA interviewed youngsters in kindergarten through sixth grade as well as thirteen-year-olds, sixteen-year-olds, and adults about what they mean when they say something is "real," and how they decide what is "real" on TV.

Up until third grade, the majority of children had great difficulty in explaining what "real" meant. They said either they did not know, gave a synonym, or gave an idiosyncratic response. Around sixth grade, the children could describe what they meant by "real." Dorr found that about half used "real" to mean something that could possibly happen. To them, "real" meant "made-up but possible in real life."

Although by six or seven years of age youngsters generally know that television programs are "made-up," the more plausible a show appears, whether fantasy or not, the more likely it is to be taken as a representation of something that could happen. Children do not even evaluate a whole show as plausible or not. They evaluate separately the genre (cartoon, drama, comedy), the characters, what they do, and what happens to them. In other words, Dorr concludes, "Television content and its reality are thought about primarily in terms of incidents, events, or actions carried out by characters."

Why attempts to balance violence with pro-social messages fail.

So for many youngsters, attempts to pretty-up the violence with the fine words of justification and morality are not likely to do any good. The words and implications will be overlooked in their quest for and focus on the action. They are not apt to discount what they see if it seems plausible, even if television presents a distortion. And if they see characters they enjoy watching using violence to solve problems, they will view violence as an acceptable problem-solving method.

Could we make better television for children? Yes, we could. Research has shown that children do pick up pro-social messages from programs when the pro-social context is not overshadowed by aggression and violence. We could use TV to open up kids' worlds, to introduce them to the wonders of science and nature. The lessons of history could come alive through animation. Television could bring an appreciation for the cultures of others into our homes.

But we have allowed the content of one of the most powerful tools ever created to be controlled by the quest for profit rather than for excellence. The quality of children's television is poorer than ever, and our children still sit in front of the television set and learn lessons that society may have cause to regret.

Neala S. Schwartzberg, Ph.D., is an adjunct professor at Long Island University, C.W. Post College, a research psychologist, and the mother of a six-year-old son.

Toys Are Programs Too
Jan Cherubin, CHANNELS

Picture this: you're settle down in front of the television set awaiting the start of *Kraft Theater*. First you are beamed a recipe for tuna salad made with Kraft mayonnaise, and then, finally, *Kraft Theater* presents "A History of Sharp Cheddar."

Or this scenario from Action for Children's Television president Peggy Charren: a new series starring Bette Davis called *Marriott Hotel*, opening with Davis hailing a cab under the Marriott marquee.

Clearly, these examples of the gross commercialization of television are fictitious. Advertisers may wish for them, but programmers know that no intelligent being is going to watch a program-length commercial for Kraft Cheese or any other product. Even though Lucy may have smoked cigarettes on *I Love Lucy* to promote the sponsor, she never said, "Ricky, hand me a Philip Morris."

For children's television, however, this kind of exploitation is already a fact of life. Saturday mornings, after school, and even during prime time in certain weeks, children are shown half-hour animated programs based on products. On Saturday morning, between those fond old standbys *Tom and Jerry* and *Captain Kangaroo*, you'll find ABC's *Monchhichis* (a Japanese plush monkey), NBC's *Shirt Tales* (a Hallmark greeting-card figure and doll), ABC's *Rubik the Amazing Cube*, and *Pac-Man*. After school there's *G.I. Joe: A Real American Hero* and *He-Man and the Masters of the Universe*, both syndicated programs about boys' action dolls. Girl's dolls get their programs as well: *Strawberry Shortcake* and *Herself the Elf*. There's even plastic jewelry: *The Charmkins*.

Each one of these programs is actually a half-hour commercial, Peggy Charren insists, and her organization, ACT, has filed a complaint about them with the Federal Communications Commission. "We're not saying there's anything wrong with commercials. The fact is, some McDonald's commercials are nicer than the programs they interrupt. But *we know they're commercials.*"

If adults wouldn't put up with a series called *Marriott Hotel* for five minutes, why do they let their children watch program-length commercials? One reason is that children's toys are brought to life through animation, and thereby somewhat disguised. Another reason is that since popular television shows have historically spawned merchandise, parents can't always be sure whether it was the toy or the show that came first. From Davy Crockett coonskin caps to Flintstones vitamins, merchandisers have been trading on the icons of popular culture. It is only recently that the trend has reversed itself, with the toy as the *source* of the program. As one toy executive suggested, "We've simply speeded up the process." In essence, the process of love and identification has been so speeded up by the toy manufacturers and licensers that now, in children's television, the cart comes before the horse and the toy is the reason for the show. First the public gets the coonskin cap and then a show about Davy Crockett. Or—more likely these days—a show about a coonskin cap.

Alvin Ferleger, senior vice president of Taft Entertainment Co., doesn't see anything deceptive about product-first programming for kids. Taft Entertainment owns Hanna-Barbera and Ruby-Spears, television's two major animation houses and the producers of 73 percent of all Saturday-morning children's shows. Ferleger challenges Charren's logic by quoting her this way: "She says, 'If you start with an original on the air and it becomes a toy, fine; but if you start with a toy and it becomes a program, not fine, because then you might be persuaded to buy a toy.' But if a program is successful and inspires a toy, you buy the toy anyway. A three-year-old child today who first experiences *Sesame Street* by having a Big Bird doll put into her bed—well, as far as that child is concerned, she can't tell if the toy came first or the program came first."

But Charren objects to lumping *Sesame Street* in with product-based shows. "They didn't start out to sell Big Bird dolls. That character was created to attract inner-city kids."

Ferleger: "What makes our shows different from a commercial is that the character has a life that is totally independent of what that toy is. The Monchhichis don't sell themselves—they're deeply involved in plot."

Charren: "Telling a story and giving some character to the toys is still advertising, only with greater effectiveness than a 30-second spot has."

But the question of which came first, the toy or the TV character, is not as simple as it seems: the Smurfs, for example, have an extremely scrambled paternity. Americans first discovered them as tiny blue leprechaun-like dolls. Now they have their own Saturday-morning show, and Christmas specials to boot. The Smurfs are on Peggy Charren's hit list. But here's the catch: The Smurfs began as characters in a storybook by Belgian cartoonist Peyo. He sold the characters to an American licensing firm, Wallace Berrie, which in turn licensed the Smurf image to manufacturers of just about everything, including NBC and its animation producers. Charren now concedes that it might not belong on the hit list.

In 1969, the FCC passed a ruling that specifically addressed the problem of toys as TV stars. The focus of the ruling was a TV program based on Mattel's Hot Wheels. The complaint was filed against Mattel and ABC by the Trooper Corporation, a competing toy company. Topper was miffled at ABC for running what amount to a 30-minute commercial and logging it as a program.

The FCC found that: *There can be no doubt that in this program, Mattel receives commercial promotion for its products beyond the time logged for commercial advertising. Nor is there any doubt that the program was developed with this promotional value, as well as its entertainment value, in mind. The producer designed a format that promotes the product of a major television advertiser of toys; used the trade name of the product as the title of the program, thus identifying the product with the program, and sold the program to a network that broadcasts a substantial amount of advertising for the advertiser. We find this pattern disturbing; more disturbing than the question of whether the commercial time logged is adequate. For this pattern subordinates programming in the interest of the public to programming in the interest of salability.* Eventually, *Hot Wheels* was forced off the air.

In the early '70s, ACT and other children's television watchdog groups gained a number of victories. The broadcast industry agreed that children might be exploited by sophisticated advertising techniques, and adopted a strict code for advertising on children's shows. In 1974 the FCC issued a set of guidelines emphasizing the obligations of television broadcasters to serve the special needs of children, especially with regard to education.

But the atmosphere has changed radically since that time. Last December the FCC adopted the industry view that broadcasters should be able to determine how best to serve the needs of children. The commission also rejected ACT's petition for a prohibition against program-length commercials. This year more than 10 programs emulate the old *Hot Wheels* show, and the only action the FCC has taken on ACT's request was to send station managers a letter informing them of the complaint. But Charren is convinced the commission will have to do more. "There is a precedent in law. The FCC will either have to act on this or say that they are doing away with what was policy in the commission."

They might be willing to do just that. "The commission is moving toward deregulation," says Al Baxter, FCC chief of complaints and compliance, wearily and perhaps for the thousandth time. "Of course, if programs and commercials become so intertwined that they can't be distinguished, stations will have to consider their promise of how many minutes they devote to commercial time. And that will be weighed against their performance when their license renewal is considered." However, the FCC is almost certain to abolish the present limit of 16 minutes of commercial time per hour.

Squire Rushnell, ABC's vice president for children's television, defends his network's toys-as-TV-stars approach: "We look out in the marketplace and we see what kids are interested in." ABC's *Rubik the Amazing Cube*, for instance, is about a product, but the show is not exactly a promotional tool because it came to television only after sales of Rubik's Cube crested. "My feeling is that the question of intent is important." says Rushnell. "Is the intent of the program to be entertainment based on the idea with built-in popularity among children, or is the whole purpose to sell?"

"We can't deny that our TV specials are promotional tools," says Carole MacGilvray, president of General Mills marketing and design services (which, in association with American Greetings, produces the *Strawberry Shortcake* and *Care Bears* syndicated specials). Neither can Kenner, Hasbro, and Martel, all toy companies now producing programming. Said Jack Chojnacki, vice president for American Greetings' licensing division, when a *Strawberry Shortcake* special aired in 1981, "We told the writer, if you need new characters for the plot, keep in mind characters that can be greeting cards, dolls, merchandise."

American Greetings is second only to Hallmark in the greeting-card business. Like Hallmark, the company maintains a staff of artists who create original designs for their cards. More than 10 years ago, its art director, Tom Wilson, created his own comic-strip character, Ziggy. When American Greetings decided to use Ziggy on a card, it had to license the character from Universal, the newspaper syndicate. Not long after that transaction, Wilson and Chojnacki hit on the idea of establishing a separate licensing branch solely to develop characters with whom the public would immediately identify—characters that would be drawn on greeting cards and licensed to various manufacturers.

Strawberry Shortcake, their first stab, was not a comic-strip character, or an illustration of a storybook character, or an individual artist's cartoon, or a character rooted in folklore, or even a figure on a greeting card. She was a corporate creation, developed expressly for the purpose of licensing, and so far the licensing has brought in more than a billion dollars. It may be no exaggeration to say that Jack Chojnacki and Tom Wilson are two of the great marketing geniuses of the 20th century.

Any lingering doubt about whether American Greetings is devising program-length commercials should be dispelled by the fact that the networks rejected *Strawberry Shortcake* and the *Care Bears*. The networks have a policy against airing product-first shows. "No one at the networks sees *Strawberry Shortcake* as an acceptable program for television," says ABC's Squire Rushnell. "I might agree that some of the syndicated shows are intended to be commercials."

But the cartoon producers insist again and again that, as Alvin Ferleger puts it, "the important issue is not what the source of the program is, but whether it is valid entertainment, and whether there is socially useful information flowing through the program."

What of the entertainment value of these programs? Does the selling of toys get in the way of a good story line? Might the dramatization of a beloved storybook character actually have more substance than a show about a factory-made, history-less toy?

No fewer than five of the programs on Charren's hit list have the same story line. It goes like this: Very innocent, sweet, high-voiced creatures full of love and happiness and sunshine. (Elves, Monchhichis, Care Bears, Strawberry Shortcake and friends, and little Charmkin girls) live in a land full of happiness. But they are threatened by bad people in a dark land (a swamp, an underworld, or a land of no feelings). One member of the happy land is captured by the dark forces and the other happy creatures risk their lives to recapture their friend. Good prevails over evil, and they all go back to the happy land to celebrate.

This is a basic fairy-tale plot. But for five of these programs to follow identical plot lines calls into question the care with which this programming is produced. No one can take offense at the wonderfully moral, though unrealistic, premise of good prevailing over evil—it's pro-social; it's non-violent. Yet it is as if the producers bend over backward with cloying sweetness to compensate for the show's meaner intent: to sell toys. The result is insipid entertainment, even by juvenile standards.

The allegorical plots of toy-based programming are fine in and of themselves, but allegory allows only for one-dimensional characters that can easily be played by toys. The more interesting characters are invariably those nasty beings in the swamps and underworlds—the ones that didn't start out as cute toys. It's quite likely that children will lean toward those more felt characters for identification. So much for moral platitudes.

In an attempt to give obviously characterless characters some personality, the producers have labeled each elf, Charmkin, etc., with a different personality, a la Snow White's seven dwarfs. In the case of the Care Bears, their personalities are emblems "stitched on their stomachs," according to the advertisements. And during the first *Care Bear* special, one bear says, "10 Care Bears are better than one." Yes, and they cost more too.

It's worth noting that in the long-running cartoons of yesteryear, all the foibles and oddities familiar in a child's world were given their due. One-dimensional programming may actually prove to be short-lived programming, a fact that broadcasters might want to consider if they were unmoved by the which-came-first argument or the intent argument. While toy companies don't want programs to last too long—they want kids to throw out their old toys and buy new ones—the networks and syndicators ought to value a show that endures. It would be ironic, though scarcely surprising, if the same programmers who refused to give up toys-as-TV in order to protect the interests of children, did so in order to look out for their own interests as broadcasters.

Jan Cherubin is a staff writer for the Los Angeles Herald-Examiner.

TV as Boob Tube: Bad Rap
Bennett Daviss, TELEVISION & FAMILIES

The image is etched so deeply in our imaginations that it's almost become archetypal: A child sits, mouth agape, transfixed by a television set, accepting and absorbing everything that flickers over the screen. He doesn't hear the telephone ring; he doesn't hear his mother call him for supper. He sits helpless, addicted to a medium that is destroying his ability to concentrate, shriveling his imagination, and leaving him incapable of reading, homework, or any other activity that demands complex and sustained mental involvement. The child's mind is being shaped to fit the tube.

It's a powerful and frightening image, one that frames our anxious relationship with the world's most potent communications tool. But that image is based on nothing more than anecdotes, a few well-publicized surmises, and a handful of inconclusive research studies, many of them flawed. That's the conclusion of an exhaustive report sponsored by the U.S. Department of Education—the most thorough review ever undertaken of almost 40 years' research into the effects of television on children's mental development. Its verdict: there's no real evidence to support the popular idea that television makes kids dull. But there's also none to prove that it doesn't.

"It's a mistake, based on the evidence so far, to condemn the medium," says Dr. Daniel Anderson, professor of psychology at the University of Massachusetts at Amherst and a 16-year student of the effects of television on children. At the request of then-Secretary of Education William Bennett, Anderson and graduate student Patricia Collins spent nearly two years sifting through 165 studies from around the world and summarizing their findings in *The Impact on Children's Education: Television's Influence on Cognitive Development*, published in April 1988. "If the claims of the critics are true," Anderson says, "the effects of television are akin to those of lead poisoning. At this point, though, we don't think an alarm should sound over the influence of the medium—the idea that, in itself, watching television is a harmful thing. People have pushed that idea, but any convincing evidence is simply lacking. In some cases, alarmists' claims are flatly contradicted. In some areas of concern, there is no body of evidence; in others, the research that has been done just isn't very good."

Anderson cites two key wellsprings of the myth that television necessarily harms children's mental development. "First and foremost," he says, "in the early and mid-1970s several popular books were written taking a negative view of television. They were based on very little hard evidence, but they were convincingly written and they had a great deal of influence. One called *The Plug-In Drug* did more than any other to establish the idea that television is, in and of itself, a harmful medium." The book, which has survived more than a dozen printings and is still influential, marshals anecdotal evidence and conjectures from experts to argue that viewing creates "a changed state of consciousness" and transforms children into "television zombies." Author Marie Winn implies that the small screen bears substantial blame for social ills ranging from falling SAT scores to the drug epidemic.

"The deeper reason," Anderson adds, "is that this society's intellectual elite has always been suspicious of popular media, even though that view hasn't been supported by research. Every mass medium popular with children has been blamed for the problems of childhood—dime novels, comic books, movies, radio, television, and video games. Our local newspaper ran an editorial in the early 1800s declaring that children should only read geography and the Bible; novels were thought to weaken their moral fiber."

Since his report was published nearly 18 months ago, Anderson has had some direct experience with myth-making. His study circulated quietly among scholars and administrators for several months until the *Washington Post* printed an article about it last fall. Based on the *Post's* piece, the Associated Press published a national wire story that focused on a single sentence from Anderson's summary: "There is no evidence that homework done during television viewing is of lower quality than homework done in silence." According to Anderson, the AP article gave readers the impression that his paper "was promoting the idea that kids should do their homework in front of the television set, which was a complete misunderstanding of what we were saying. Newspapers wrote editorials denouncing us, and I got all sorts of angry letters." Stunned by such erroneous reports, Anderson took to the media to detail the ways in which his study exposes the seven most common misconceptions about television.

First, the report says, "Despite popular stereotypes of children just sitting and staring at the television, it is common for children to engage in other activities while viewing." Researchers find that kids typically look away from the television screen more than 100 times an hour to play, talk, read, eat, do their schoolwork, primp, or nap. "Observations of children spending time with television do not conform to the popular descriptions of the 'zombie' viewer," Anderson states. He points to several studies in which "the child is always seen as a passive recipient who is 'controlled' by factors such as rapid cutting, changes in color, and movement." Typically, the studies describe children as "fixated" and portray them as "involuntary" viewers. Anderson dismisses the claims: "Systematic research has not verified these notions."

Second, he takes on the question of alertness, attacking the kind of generalizations made, for example, in Kate Moody's 1980 *Growing Up On Television*. The author wrote, "Television does not arouse active attention; rather, TV viewing suppresses it." Anderson discloses that her evidence supporting the judgment "is anecdotal and is based on interviews with . . . 'experts' including . . . other journalists, a hypnotists . . . and a botanist." Actually, most of the studies on alertness reveal that kids are quite involved in the shows they watch. A 1987 report, for example, found that five-year-olds watching *Sesame Street* recalled 92 percent of the material that adults considered key in understanding the stories. Other studies discovered that many of those 100 or more looks away from the television each hour are used to speculate with family members about characters' motives and what turns the story might take—hardly evidence of "suppressed" attention. Writes Anderson: "Television viewing is, in many ways, as cognitively active as reading."

Third, Anderson tackles the notion of "overstimulation." Both Winn's and Moody's books quote the renowned pediatrician T. Berry Brazleton's claim that "television creates an environment that overwhelms and assaults the child" with rapidly shifting images, flashes of light and color, and so on. Most children, Brazleton says, cope with such overexcitement by dulling their minds. However, the theory holds, some don't. In the April 1976 *Journal of American Psychiatry*, physician Mathew Dumont writes," . . . the constant shifting of visual frames in television is related to the hyperkinetic syndrome . . . . the hyperactive child is attempting to recapture the dynamic quality of the television screen by rapidly changing his perceptual orientation. . . ."

Anderson aims special scorn at one of the most often-cited studies of television's complicity in creating hyperactive kids. In the prestigious *Journal of Communications* in October 1975, psychologists Dr. Werner Halpern published a paper he called "Turned-On Toddlers," in which he claimed that hyperactivity among a group of two-year-olds was "directly traceable to *Sesame Street*." Unfortunately, Halpern didn't bother to explain how, or offer any quantifiable data or controls. "The paper is completely inadequate in a scientific sense," Anderson laments, "but it got a tremendous amount of publicity and is cited in virtually all popular books about the effects of television. It was a really dumb paper, but it gave the whole idea a scientific veneer."

Fourth, Anderson vanquishes the idea that the time kids spend in front of television is stolen from more valuable and constructive pursuits. After reviewing relevant research, Anderson was able to state that "there is no consistent or strong evidence that television viewing displaces valuable cognitive activities." Most frequently, television-watching claims time from radio, comic books, and the movies, none of which have "been demonstrated to be more intellectually valuable than TV viewing.

"Everyone seems to imagine that if kids weren't watching television, they'd be doing their math homework or solving brainteasers," he adds. "Actually, they're just as likely to be out behind the garage smoking cigarettes or sitting on the lawn poking holes in the ground. There's a tendency to think about the negative effects of television without putting television in context."

The one "valuable cognitive activity" television may lessen is reading. Research in Canada and El Salvador indicates that children learn reading faster and more efficiently when their homes or towns don't have television. Other research shows that children who are light viewers tend to have better vocabularies than those who watch more TV, and Anderson also found reports suggesting that up to 10 or 12 hours of television a week—less than average—may actually help kids strengthen their reading skills and that, in any event, differences in reading abilities between light and heavy viewers tend to disappear as children grow. Although some kids may think watching TV is easier than reading and thus watch more than they read, no research has shown that television itself is any more responsible for that attitude than, for example, parents' own reading habits. "We found that kids weren't reading much before television and they're not doing much now," notes co-author Collins. "It doesn't mean that more reading wouldn't be good. It's just that TV isn't the culprit." Overall, then, "the effect of television on reading achievement appears to be small if it is, in fact, real," Anderson concludes.

Sixth, he found a smattering of evidence that "weakly indicates" that television might shorten children's attention spans, "yet the importance, generality, and nature of the effect is unknown." He points out, for example, that no one has answered the question of whether television shapes a child's attention span, or if the child's attention range was shortened by other factors and then "transferred" as an existing pattern to television-watching. On the other hand, Anderson admits that one study "convinced us that, under some circumstances, television can help kids' attentional skills." As an example, he cites the kind of puzzle that appears regularly in the Sunday comics pages and challenges kids to "find the 16 animals hidden in this farmyard scene"; camera zooms and other video techniques can help children learn to focus their attention on particular points in a scene by using the lens as a simulated focus of the viewer's own attention. Although he admits that "potential negative influences" on attention span "should be considered at least possible," he's quick to add that "the evidence just isn't there to support broad-brush claims and no one has really looked for it yet."

Finally, Anderson probes the often-repeated charge that television dulls kids' imaginations. It's a formidable case. When they're watching TV, kids can't "stop the action"—as they can when they're reading or fantasizing—to analyze or reflect on what's taking place, critics argue. In addition, by presenting a parade of concrete visual images, the small screen eliminates a child's need to supply his or her own. Just as bad television supplies entire populations of children with the same images and frames of reference, shrinking the number of imaginative new ones among kids in general.

Here, as in other areas, the evidence waffles. Some researchers have found that children use television's images as a launching pad for parallel fantasies while they watch. Others observed that youngsters were more imaginative in supplying endings to audiotaped stories than to videotaped ones. One study claims that children played less creatively after heavy television exposure than before it, while another reports that the most imaginative boys in a particular group of boys were also the heaviest viewers. "Television does not appear to interrupt the development of fantasy play or imaginativeness," Anderson sums up. "In fact, its incorporation as a common cultural experience into group play in preschool settings may help in forming friendships, promoting role-playing, and adding variety to play."

Ultimately, Anderson and Collins discovered that the evidence of television's effect on children's mental powers is simply too sparse to be in any way conclusive. "On the whole," they wrote, "there is no evidence that television, as a medium, either enhances or detracts from development of the intellect. In saying that television does not apparently damage a child's intellect, though, we're not also saying that TV is good for children."

Everyone seems to agree with Anderson and Collins that the evidence, when taken together, points in different—even opposite—directions. But that doesn't mean all observers share the report's value-free verdict. Some believe the medium's effects are more insidious and more progressive than the single sum of all the studies reviewed indicates. Among them: Dr. Jerome Singer and his wife Dorothy, co-directors of Yale University's Family Television Research and Consultation Center and two of the leading researchers in the area of children and television.

"Professor Anderson has not measured what sense children make of all of the rapid-fire shifts, cutaways, and interruptions that characterize U.S. commercial television," Dr. Singer points out in an April *New York Times* essay. "Several studies done at Yale and elsewhere suggest that children who are heavy viewers of television do not become more sophisticated about the medium. Compared to light viewers, they seem to have accumulated less general knowledge, they seem less able to follow the plots of TV dramas, they seem more prone to accept as possible the train-stopping or building-high leaps of superheroes, and they're less capable of explaining the function of commercials. Heavy viewers are also less likely to show imaginativeness or creativity. The fragmentary nature of television interferes with reflective thought and the careful mental repetition of the information presented. Modern cognitive psychology suggest that such processes are a necessary condition for the development of consciously accessible, voluntarily organized learning."

Singer backs his assertions with two decades of personal research. In a 1979 *Psychology Today* article, the Singers wrote, "Can television enhance or inhibit imagination in young children? We think the latter is true, and are increasingly disturbed about the emphasis in American television on extremely short action sequences, frequent interruptions, and drastic changes in the visual field. . . . it seems possible that [producers] are actually creating a psychological orientation in children that leads to a shortened attention span, a lack of reflectiveness, and an expectation of rapid change in the broader environment." As evidence, they offer the results of one of their own studies. A group of preschoolers was dosed daily with the tot-paced, very interactive *Mr. Rogers' Neighborhood.* After two weeks the Singers say, those children showed more imagination and more positive relationships with other kids than did a group watching a similar amount of the hectic *Sesame Street.*

Others, though, think Anderson and Singer are simply wrong to search for measurable scientific data. "Anderson's criticisms of many of the studies confirmed my skepticism of this kind of experiment generally," says *The Plug-In Drug* author Marie Winn. "I'm doubtful that any of these questions are going to be resolved through 'scientific' research." Indeed, Anderson and Collins do admit that an array of variables have to be anticipated and controlled in performing objective research on something as subtle and personal as television viewing. Instead, says Winn, "I rather favor a common-sense kind of approach" to gauging the ways in which television sculpts kids' minds.

For example, Anderson writes that "there are numerous possible explanations of the fact" that children who don't watch TV read better than those who do; he adds that to blame television itself for certain of the children's deficits "is purely conjecture at this point," based on the scant available data. Winn's evidence is both more visceral and less ambiguous. "I've heard from hundreds of teachers that when they read children a story without showing them pictures, the children are at a loss," she says. "They ask, 'What does the princess look like?', or 'What does the woodcutter's cottage look like?' They lack the practice, and therefore the ability, to visualize for themselves. Teachers who've bridged the entry of television say that children were better at visualizing before there was television. This is the kind of evidence that is more indicative to me." It's also the kind that less and less often can be measured objectively. After all, where can scientists still go to find children who don't watch television?

Ultimately, though, those who scrutinize the medium professionally do agree on a key point: regardless of the hardware's effects, the messages that the hardware delivers play a key role in shaping young viewers' ideas about themselves and the world. "It's clear that kids don't watch television with blank minds," Anderson says. "The evidence has grown, even since our report, that children take information from books. If parents would be alarmed to see their children reading pornography or Nazi propaganda, they ought to be just as concerned about what kinds of television programs their children are watching." Adds Dr. William Dietz, a pediatrician at Boston's New England Medical Center and a member of the American Academy of Pediatrics' subcommittee on children and television: "The conclusion that television viewing isn't mindless means that what children see presented on television, they're likely to incorporate into their own attitudes and behavior. That should strengthen the hand, and the resolve, of those actively engaged in trying to shape children's programming."

Too often, though, children's viewing isn't being shaped. Cartoon shows such as *Mutant Ninja Turtles* or *Masters of the Universe* don't offer much in the way of portable wisdom, and parents often don't help their kids interpret or modulate messages implicit in the deviant or sexual behavior common in adult programs. "Even if the content itself isn't memorable, things you learn in childhood become deeply ingrained," Anderson emphasizes. "These messages form the ways in which you think about the world. Traditionally, societies use stories to teach their children about expectations, about ways to deal with life's problems, about the values supported by the culture. Stories become metaphors, lessons used throughout life. Too few people are paying attention to the fact that television has become today's storyteller, and there's very little burden on producers to offer stories that reflect the most appropriate moral and ethical values of our society."

What message, then, should producers themselves draw from Anderson's research? "The audience is actively trying to comprehend what they see, and what they comprehend will stay with them," he say. "In every minute of their shows—even if they're intended purely as entertainment— producers are teaching kids, perhaps through formal techniques and clearly through content. It's a tremendous responsibility—and I hope they feel it."

Bennett Daviss is a freelance writer living in New England.

How's TV Doing?

Lee Margulies, TELEVISION & FAMILIES

DR. JOAN BABBOTT *is executive director of Planned Parenthood of Los Angeles.*

"I am vastly encouraged about the number of TV shows that are now willing to deal with the issues of contraception, abortion, wanted or unwanted pregnancies, the importance of being born loved, wanted and cared for. There was a *Cagney & Lacey* last year that was very good. There have been other good ones too that talked about some of the consequences of sexual activity, that showed the normalcy of budding sexuality and dealt with it sensitively.

"It's not nearly enough, however. Television could do a lot more about giving young people basic knowledge about their bodies and human sexuality and consequences. I'd like to see more programs that sock home to young people the seriousness of children having children, like the fact that something like 80% of the teenage girls who have babies don't finish high school.

"I'm 62 and I've had a lot of experience in this area. And my experience is that most youngsters really want to be responsible; they don't want to hurt each other. But they need help with talking about behavior—behavior that is not exploitive but is constructive and caring. They have basic needs for information—about families, about boy-girl relationships, about people who are gay and lesbian. All the media need to be much more helpful.

"Instead TV too often promotes the idea that sex has to be spontaneous and instant and unplanned. I wish they'd show that it's OK to think about contraception first. That doesn't have to take the romance out of it.

"Television has a perfect opportunity now to start talking about contraception because of AIDS. There is a real need to get information out about safe sex. And I think that idea of safety could be enlarged to include not just protecting yourself physically but also socially, emotionally and psychologically from an unwanted pregnancy."

DR. WILLIAM DIETZ *is chairman of the subcommittee on television and children of the American Academy of Pediatrics and is an associate professor of pediatrics at the Tufts University School of Medicine.*

"President Reagan's veto of the children's television bill that Congress had passed this year was a tragedy, because that measure for the first time would have built into law the responsibility that broadcasters have to air programs of educational and instructional benefit to children. And that's exactly what's missing from television: a commitment to produce quality shows for children.

"Now, I don't want to make that statement totally negative, because the market has shifted from three years ago, when 99% of what was made for children were program-length commercials. And the major networks have been more responsive to the needs of children, at least as represented by Saturday-morning programs, which I think are improving. One show I saw recently that I liked was *Pee-wee's Playhouse.* No one was put down or hurt; it was just wacky and enjoyable.

"But I'm not talking about shows like *The Cosby Show* and *Family Ties.* Those are good shows, but they're for the family. What we still lack are shows outside of Saturday morning that are specifically for children. PBS has some. *Degrassi Junior High* is a wonderful show, as is *Ramona,* both of which approach an age group for which programming has not been developed in the past—the 11- to 13-year-olds.

"VCRs have helped increase the options and the ability of parents to control what their children are viewing—at least their young children. I have a friend who tapes programs that he thinks are appropriate for his 5-year-old daughter and then turns those on whenever she wants to watch TV. That's quite an appropriate use of technology. Where it's missing, unfortunately, is with adolescents, for whom the VCR has basically opened up the adult world by way of the movies they now have access to. We haven't seen the full shakedown from that yet: Violent, aggressive behavior and sexuality are major issues for young people.

"I'm not about to argue that specific shows should or shouldn't be on, however; parents have to exercise their own discretion. What I would hope is that the people who work on children's shows, and the executives who buy them, would keep in mind every minute the thought that they are creating shows for their own children. Some do, I know; I wish every one of them would."

DIANA HUSS GREEN *is editor of* Parents' Choice *magazine, a review of children's media.*

"Through television, children today have an unprecedented amount of information and entertainment available to them. Television provides instant gratification in time, distance, and experience. That's both good and bad.

"On the good side, television has become much more tolerant. Kids are seeing all kinds of groups: black, white, old, disabled, homosexual—and are much more aware and knowledgeable than previous generations have ever been. They learn very early from the television that other people feel and respond as they do.

"On the other hand, television presents a fantasy view of incredible wealth, especially in the advertising. The way people are shown, with fine clothes and sleek cars, appears to be real. This fostering of materialism doesn't make life easier. It's very difficult for many children not to feel a great deal of anger that their own lives aren't like that.

"Yet I feel a little less threatened by television than I used to, because we are in control now. The consumer is clearly in the driver's seat.

"Cable is growing and the number of cassettes available for children is soaring. There is so much wonderful stuff out there. And the changing marketplace has surely made the networks more aware; there's little doubt that their programs are better. Look at *The Wonder Years, The Cosby Show, Muppet Babies, The Golden Girls, Jim Henson's Storyteller.* And then there's *Degrassi Junior High, Mr. Rogers, Sesame Street* and *Reading Rainbow* on public television. The sifting is everything."

BARBARA REISMAN *is executive director of the Child Care Action Campaign.*

"There are some excellent programs on television: *Sesame Street, Reading Rainbow, Square One, The Cosby Show, Family Ties,* some of the specials—even a show about day care (*Day by Day*), which is good. There aren't enough decent afterschool programs, though; that's a serious problem.

"Television is not a substitute for child care, however. If parents are using it as a babysitter because they're not there, it's a problem. It would be so much better if they could watch with their children to answer questions and discuss issues that are brought up. I remember sitting down to watch a *Family Ties* episode with my children and finding that it dealt with teen-age suicide! Parents need to be involved.

"I think it's wonderful that more programs are being produced that reflect what real American families look like—families where both parents work, single-parent families, families of different colors. Television should reflect the diversity of families as much as it can; it helps children affirm that their own experiences are what other people are experiencing too.

"Writers and producers forget sometimes that the medium is inherently educational: They are conveying messages to children. It would be good if the messages dealt with what is happening in real life. I know that's not their purpose—the programs are there to entertain—but in fact they do more than that, and I wish people would recognize they are talking on that responsibility when they create a show."

RICHARD BENNETT *is a family counselor in Gary, Ind. and publisher of the newsletter "Stepfamilies and Beyond."*

"I have a television show myself—a little interview show on cable called *Life's Dimensions*. The whole idea is to present people in a good light. So we bring on homemakers or quiltmakers or pipe carvers and they become celebrities for 30 minutes. I think we've made a real positive contribution to a lot of people.

"Entertainment television, tough, is a different ballgame. There is so little of it that has lasting value. It portrays everything in such a glamorized way that it becomes unreal. Everything comes out perfect.

"Take *The Brady Bunch*. That family is so perfect; it's a fantasy. You start dealing with real stepfamilies and you find there is a whole new set of feelings connected with anger and child support and visitation—things that aren't prevalent in nuclear families. I often feel, though I have no proof, that the tremendous perfection on television exacerbates some of the potential problems in the stepfamily.

"Mary Tyler Moore could be very helpful in her new show (*Annie McGuire*) if she did even one little stepfamily lesson per episode. There could be some discussion and a very positive message sent about the importance of making child support payments, for example. Another show might say, "If you're the noncustodial parent, visit your kids: They still need you."

"I think there's a tremendous amount of untapped education potential in television. There are lots of plays and historical subjects that they could build stories on. That to me would be a lot better than *Dallas* and some of the other shows that just present glamour.

"Programs like that help develop an attitude. When I was a kid, my mother controlled me by making me feel guilty. If I didn't go to church she would harp on it so much that I would feel bad. In our society right now, I think we have more of what clinically are called impulse disorders, or personality disorders, where kids feel bad or guilty about very little. I've seen hundreds of kids stealing or having sex at a very young age and feeling absolutely nothing bad about it at all. That bothers me. Television is a direct contribution factor with its emphasis on violence and people getting what they want and everything being perfect."

SUZANNE STUTMAN *is executive director of the Institute for Mental Health Initiatives.*

"Overall, I think television is a wonderful medium for translating all kinds of positive messages to kids. And specifically through entertainment programs, it can promote mental health for kids by modeling positive ways of handling difficult or stressful situations.

"I remember an episode of *The Flintstone Kids* in which the smart kid flunked his chemistry test. He saw himself for the first time as a failure and lost faith in his ability to become a scientist. His friends recognized his distress and intervened, telling him it wasn't the end of the world and to go at it again. His mother was also shown as supportive and nurturing. It was very good. It really showed how having a social support system and keeping the lines of communication open can encourage kids to bounce back.

"We need more of that. It would be terrific if we could have a number of people in the industry who looked closely at the ways characters portray anger and who asked themselves, 'Is this a way that seems constructive, or that can be modeled?' Obviously the more destructive anger and disappointment do not provide good models for the kids who are watching TV.

"Another question I'd stress is, 'Can we help the kids become better problem solvers?" A lot of the time what you see on the Saturday morning cartoons, for example, is the designated adult, whoever that might be, providing the solutions, or some magical force providing them. The thing we encourage is helping the children themselves become problem solvers, thinking through the predicament they found themselves in and taking some course of action that would solve the problem.

"Incidentally, people don't need to understand the psychological motivations of why a character is choosing to act in a particular way; all they need is to see a behavior modeled. Then maybe next time they've got a problem they'll remember someone trying this other approach and they'll imitate it. Some of the family sitcoms like *Growing Pains, Cosby* and *Family Ties* do a good job of modeling like this.

"I sometimes wonder, tough, if most television writers, like most of the general population, don't have the many varied options of dealing with anger in their own personal repertoire and therefore have difficulty showing them. You know, trying one thing, then if that doesn't work trying a second way, then a third if necessary. I would like to see much more of that—the idea that there is not one right way to handle a situation, that we all need lots of ways to handle predicaments or problems."

MARY HATWOOD FUTRELL *is president of the National Education Association.*

"Television has a lot of positive programs for young people. I'm very impressed with the *National Geographic* specials, for example, and the afterschool specials deal with a whole array of issues important to children—who they are, school, drugs, being home alone, developing friendships. They are also good educational programs—including, obviously, *Sesame Street*—and programs about history, science, other countries.

"My concern is in two areas: how much television children are watching and what they are watching.

"The first is not the fault of the television industry but rather of parents: Many are simply letting their children watch more than they should. There are lots of other ways those children could be spending their time, and the result is apparent to teachers: You can see that the more TV the child watches, often the lower their grades will be.

"Parents also bear much of the responsibility in the second area, for not telling their children, 'You are not allowed to watch certain kinds of programs.' There is a lot of very adult subject matter on television—a lot of sex and violence and profanity. But the television industry has to accept some of the blame, because the reality today is that parents can't always be home when their children turn on the TV, and they can't control what's on at a neighbors house.

"Frankly, I'm appalled at the amount of violence there is on television and how promiscuous things are. And they so rarely show the possible after-affects of casual sex or violence—the possibility of disease or pregnancy, or of long-term injury.

"I think the television industry has to exhibit more responsibility for what they portray and how they portray it. They must keep in mind that their audience is not only adults but also adolescents and pre-adolescents. I think they forgot that kids have to be taught the difference between fantasy and reality. It isn't a given, and a lot of what kids see on television leaves a deep impression. We have to remind them that 'what you see on TV is not necessary the way life is.'

"The industry, parents and educators have to work together. One of the things *The Cosby Show* does, for example, is to have a child psychologist as a consultant. He not only helps make the parent-child relationship more realistic but also makes sure the show is being sensitive to the audience that's watching. That's a way of being responsible."

XVI

Public Television

Since its inception, public television has been engaged in an ongoing fight for its very existence . . . for several reasons. To begin with, public television got a late start. The first noncommercial educational television license was awarded by the FCC in 1952, well after the advent of commercial television. It was not until fifteen years later, with 187 noncommercial stations already on the air, that the Carnegie Commission defined the purpose of public broadcasting—to "appeal to excellence in service of diversity"—in its report *Public Television: A Program For Action.*

Unfortunately, the report did not distinguish between public, educational or instructional broadcasting, thereby generating a form of television with many diverse identities and often conflicting goals. The report *did* note that, in order for noncommercial television to attain a competitive status with commercial television, "a well-financed and well-directed system, substantially larger and far more pervasive and effective than that which now exists in the United States, must be brought into being." However, this has not come into being. Regarding financing, the federal government has continued to cut the budget allocated to public television since it began issuing funds. Furthermore, public support through contributions has been extremely inadequate. Regarding the establishment of a well-directed system, Douglass Cater (one of the architects of public broadcasting) recently noted that public television is "hardly a system at all, but rather a variety of broadcasting arrangements bearing a common name."

The first essay in this section, "Old Enough to Get its Act Together," speaks of reasons to celebrate and lament the creation and subsequent poor performance of the marriage between "public" and "television." This essay describes the interworkings of public television, and what has kept it from reaching its potential of "excellence in service of diversity." The second essay presents an interview with William Lee Hanley, Jr., the former Chair of the Corporation for Public Broadcasting (CPB). In "You Can't Yank the Rug Out," the relationship between stations and the CPB—which is responsible for allocating and distributing federal dollars to public television stations—is discussed, and the finances behind public broadcasting are brought to light. The third and final essay, "Beyond Big Bird," examines the role, function, and future of public television in an increasingly competitive and diverse media marketplace. Is there room for public television in the era of direct satellite relays, VCRs, and cable saturation?

Old Enough To Get Its Act Together
Stuart Sucherman, CHANNELS

This is a season for celebrating public television—the idea, the extraordinary programs it has brought us and the people who support and work in it. Twenty years ago, the two words "public" and "broadcasting" were joined together by the Carnegie Commission, and in November of that same year Congress authorized the first federal funding for operations.

This is *not* a time, however, for overlooking the sad and blatant flaws in the way public TV is run. American public television keeps the phosphors glowing and occasionally sets the screen on fire. I've been proud to work in the system as a producer and as a station executive from the beginning. But when I compare its output today with the high hopes of 1967, I can say bluntly and fairly: The system doesn't work.

"It is a system no one in the outside world understands or can penetrate," former PBS president Larry Grossman said in a notably forthright speech this year. "It is a system that keeps public broadcasting at war with itself. It is a system that ensures that public television will remain mired in second-class status, with a top-heavy, expensive and stifling bureaucracy, a handicap in attracting or retaining truly creative and talented people, and an incapacity to make timely program decisions."

Public TV's primary problem has been the failure to find a way to decide upon and finance a consistent stream of top-drawer national programming. For this you can blame Congress, the public broadcasters or Americans at large. Imagine if, every night of the week, public TV had at least one series of the caliber of *The Jewel in the Crown, Cosmos* or *Vietnam: A Television History*—blockbusters that would make a splash in the public consciousness, lift the viewers' expectations, win larger audiences without resorting to the easy attractions of commercial TV and make the local PBS channel a solid viewing alternative. But, alas, it doesn't. Too often, by playing *Leave It to Beaver* reruns or wildlife films, it looks like an independent commercial station down on its luck.

Public TV has not yet disciplined itself to focus its funds where they would have the greatest audience impact, or spend them with the decisiveness and speed required in broadcasting. Most funds, including nearly two thirds of the federal appropriation distributed by the Corporation for Public Broadcasting (CPB), go to the local stations, which tend to put them into local facilities and staffing instead of into national programming—though less than 6 percent of their schedules, on average, is locally produced.

The result is a program decision-making and funding process that makes public TV producers endure years of delay, frustration and sheer mental torment. (A friend of mine suggested that they should take their case to Amnesty International.) Consider the stories of two important series developed in part by the respected journalist Stanley Karnow. The first was *Vietnam: A Television History*, an immense project aired by PBS in 1983, which was worthy of public television's original ambitions.

Karnow and Larry Grossman, then president of PBS, first talked about making such a series in 1976. PBS gave Karnow a small start-up grant and put him in contact with a producer named Dick Ellison and WGBH, the Boston public TV station, which was also contemplating a Vietnam series. Fund-raising began. Two years after Karnow spoke to Grossman, the project had been turned down by a myriad of corporations and by CPB. Karnow was at the end of his rope when he happened to bump into Joe Duffy, then head of the National Endowment for the Humanities.

Duffy's agency eventually managed to provide Karnow with about $1.2 million—about a third of the cash needed. WGBH courageously put up almost $1 million of the station's own funds. French and British broadcasters chipped in co-production funds. "Like so much of public television," says Karnow, "the program was about an American experience, and you had to go to Britain to get the story told."

The project's seven-year odyssey resulted in one of PBS' most important and controversial documentary series, which emboldened Karnow to try again. He proposed a series about the legacy of American colonialism in the Philippines. PBS gave Karnow a start on his $1.2 million budget, and he began looking for the rest. During his search, Marcos fell and Aquino came to power in the Philippines, making the project not only more timely but nearly mandatory for a serious journalistic medium.

In the twilight zone of public TV decision-making, however, the explosion in Manila made no difference. NEH judged his idea too journalistic, Karnow says. Corporations wouldn't help either. With no guarantee of full funding, Karnow and executive producer Drew Pearson began shooting in early 1985. Two years later they still have $400,000 to raise.

Karnow had proposed a timely journalistic idea well ahead of time, but the resulting series will probably stagger onto the PBS schedule in the winter of 1988–89. It will have missed its ideal air date by two years. The logical successor to one of public TV's most important projects will have taken five years of excruciating fund-raising.

Other proposals for series, equal in promise and timeliness, are abandoned in frustration at an earlier stage. Dick Ellison, Karnow's colleague on the *Vietnam* series, had gone on to propose a series with the working title *Who Are the Russians,* which would have taken an intimate look at the people most Americans regard as their primary global adversaries. The subjects, however, wouldn't stand still for public TV indecision. "The Russians refused to cooperate unless we had a firm financial commitment to the series," says Peter McGhee, WGBH's program manager for national productions. "Since we always had to present our requests with so much equivocation, we could never get them aboard." McGhee compares the situation to the tribulations in Homer's *Odyssey:* "It was like Penelope's tapestry, where every night the concept undid itself and we had to start over the next day."

The series would have been a wonderful primer as Americans struggle to come to grips with the enormous complexities of *glasnost.* But though the project had taken years and gotten commitments of some $500,000, WGBH dropped the idea and moved on. It was the public TV project's typical good news/bad news situation. The good news was that it had partial funding. The bad news was that it had partial funding.

Very few if any PBS projects have gotten full funding from one of the federal endowments, public broadcasting agencies, corporations or foundations that make grants. Small projects have the best chance of assembling funds from a mere two or three sources, which explains the grab-bag PBS schedule peppered with hard-to-promote one-shot specials and the often disjointed anthology series that try to group them.

"We're at a point where we don't need *more* programs on public television," says Nat Katzman, station manager of KQED, San Francisco. "What we do need is better programs. We have replaced some of the imports with domestic production. The next stage is to fund programs sufficiently to jack up the quality, and to invest in coherent series rather than depend as we do on anthologies."

There would be no reason, or excuse, for spending as much to produce PBS programs as NBC or CBS spends, but the present discrepancies show how tightly the purse strings bind public TV producers. In 1985–86, when the commercial networks' producers were spending $600,000 an hour, often much more, public TV producers spent just $130,000 an hour, on average, to make PBS public-affairs programs, and $195,000 an hour on drama and other cultural shows. While the commercial networks each laid out around $1 billion for broadcast rights, PBS funders spent $198 million.

Corporations, despite the prominence of their logos in underwriting credits, are vastly overrated as a source of production funds. Altogether they put up just $73 million for national productions on PBS in fiscal 1986—approximately equal to the new revenue of a single big-market commercial TV station. Fewer than 40 put up as much as $100,000 in 1985–86, and most of that had been selected to be highly noncontroversial. In the view of one fundraiser, most corporate executives expect little gain from underwriting a show on PBS and don't want to risk the money by giving it a try.

"There is a mythology that implies there is a massive amount of corporate dollars just lying there to be plucked up by the system if only we were just a little bit smarter or more aggressive," says Jay Iselin, former president of the New York public TV station WNET. "The reality is that a corporation has no identifiable interest, or the funding levels required are so high that any corporate contribution is supplementary and usually inadequate."

Collectively, the public TV stations are the second largest category of funders for PBS programming—$53 million in fiscal '86—but most of that is absorbed by continuing series such as *American Playhouse*, *Nova* and *Sesame Street*, vital for their schedules but not ideal for attracting and holding new audiences. Those same continuing series take a large share of the money available from the largest single backer of PBS programming, CPB, which spent $29 million of its federal appropriation in '86 and plans to spend $36 million this fiscal year.

To use the remainder of that kitty, CPB puts producers through a Kafkaesque bureaucratic fantasy called the Peer Review Process. In theory, production grants can be given out more wisely by consulting a panel of "peers." In practice, the money is dribbled out to satisfy a long list of political agendas. The process is designed not to be creative but to be politically correct.

Though the final decision rests with a professional program fund director, responsibility is obscured. "The members of the panel, kings and queens for a day, make decisions about which programs should be made but they have no continuing responsibility," objects award-winning documentarian Fred Wiseman, who has been bruised by the panel process. "If they make bad decisions, their jobs are not at stake." And in their hands, says WGBH president Henry Becton, the programs suffer: "All the elements, funders and producers end up pushing projects toward the middle, safe ground." It could be worse, of course: Not long ago, CPB was leaving its production funding decisions to the White House appointees on its board of directors.

In short, public TV has its backers, but none of them is an angel. With the exception of the stations themselves, the program funders scatter their largesse according to their own needs. Fortunately, public broadcasters have taken some tentative but encouraging steps to pool resources and coordinate decisions. This year CPB has put up $4 million, and the stations another $4 million, in a joint challenge fund unencumbered by peer review or bureaucratic nonsense. But a larger reallocation, and bigger changes in its ways of doing business, are required. I would recommend the following:

- *CPB should be abolished or drastically reorganized.* It has never lived up to its original promise, and has been entangled too often in ideological intrigues by the political appointees on its board. The new unit, with many fewer employees, would have nothing to do with programming—and little to do with "leading" the field, which ambitious CPB officials occasionally volunteer to do. Though public TV has a leadership vacuum, the last kind of leader it needs are hirelings of a political board.

- *All of the federal money should pass through CPB, or its successor, to local public TV and radio stations.* The responsibility for pulling up public TV by its bootstraps lies with the stations themselves—the same nonprofit, educational and state bodies that hold the licenses and are accountable for what goes on the air. Public television must address itself to its own salvation.

- *Funders must reallocate money to strengthen national programming and entrust the decision-making for a major part of it to a group of programmers who can lead, rather than follow, the system.* If the stations want to retake the high ground, they must put adequate funds in the hands of people—probably elected by the system for a renewable term—who are free to make the coherent, creative and courageous program decisions required to make a strong schedule.

The need to redirect funds toward national programming is so great that Larry Grossman has recommended earmarking all the federal money CPB receives: "Every dollar must be spent on programs designed for national distribution. Stations can pool their dollars in a national cooperative, giving them to PBS or anyone else who will create or commission national programming."

Earmarking could free up an additional $100 million for national programs—a 50 percent increase over total spending in recent years. It would require painful cutbacks by some local public broadcasters that are now overdependent on federal funds. Some small-city stations might have to consolidate into cost-efficient regional or state networks. But stations generally would benefit from a stronger PBS schedule. At last they would have the goods to build and keep their audiences.

In 1962, a Federal Communications Commission chairman declared that commercial television was a "vast wasteland." That widely shared opinion gave impetus to the development of public television five years later. Today, the commercial networks are still based on high-gloss escapism. If public TV didn't exist in 1987, we would have to invent it. Now we're ahead of the game: Public television has been invented already, but we haven't yet figured out how to make it work.

Stuart Sucherman is president of Hilton-Sucherman Productions and former executive producer of the PBS series The Constitution: That Delicate Balance.

You Can't Yank the Rug Out
William Lee Hanley, Jr., CHANNELS

Funding for 1988

Forty-four million bucks is a pretty good chunk of change to lose. The fact is that these monies have already been appropriated. We got advance funding simply because of production lead time, and stations have already made commitments knowing what their grants were going to be. The money was appropriated and the President signed the bills. I think we can make a very strong case that, "Look, there was a good reason for doing advance funding. You, Congress, agreed there should be advance funding because of the lead time involved in production and because of planning. Now you just can't yank the rug out from under us." Obviously we'll be trying to maintain what we got.

Every economist is saying the federal deficit is a ticking bomb. Something's got to give. We can say, "Yeah, but it shouldn't be us," but everybody in Washington is saying the same thing. In the final analysis, I don't know how we would stack up in Congress against Medicare.

Maybe we can address funding as part of a strategic plan: How can we best guarantee relatively constant or increasing funding for the system? If we've got to wage war with the President and Congress every year, it's a heck of a way to be doing business.

Selling Points

We can argue for funding in several manners. I don't think anybody disagrees that a role of the government is education! There is nothing more important than having an informed public. And virtually everything we're putting on, in radio and in television, is informative and educational.

Another emphasis has always been on local programming and local identification. I've talked about Arts & Entertainment and Nickelodeon coming along with competing programming on cable, but they aren't local in any way. They have no identification with a community. That's a distinctive thing. People do identify with Channel 13 here in New York.

A Crippled Board

There's been a major transition in the board, in that it was reduced a few years ago from a 15-person board down to 10. Lately we haven't been able to fill the 10-person board, which is tragic. We operated from March of '86 until November with five members. Then we got two more, so we're up to seven. Now we're looking at a situation where I go off the board in March, Rich [Richard Brookhiser] goes off in March, Sharon [Rockefeller, a two-term board member] can't be reappointed by law.

I can't say the White House is holding it up because I don't know. I know that Rick's and my [reappointment] papers are in process. They've known about these vacancies. I have talked to them. I know Senator Goldwater made several calls over there, saying, "Look, this is a disservice that you're doing."

Impact of the New Tax Law

Everybody has taken the attitude that the decrease in tax rates was going to be a disaster for all charitable contributions because the value of the deduction is lessened. I'm not sure that's going to prove out. I think more depends on the economy. In fact, when the top marginal rate was reduced from 70 percent to 50, a very substantial cut, in fact the opposite happened: Individual giving went up. Which I think says that people are giving for the right reasons, not just the tax benefit. They had more money in their pocket by virtue of the tax reduction and consequently they gave more.

Boosting Corporate Aid

Take a look at what was done with the '84 Olympics. Peter Ueberroth took something that has been around since 1896 and yet was able to create the perception that no corporation could do without sponsoring the games. I mean, he had Kodak and Fuji fighting like hell to be an official sponsor. He had corporations tripping over each other to participate.

Obviously, our situation is different. But we've got an event to capitalize on. It happens to be our 20th anniversary next November. [In November 1967, Congress adopted the Public Broadcasting Act, chartering CPB and authorizing the first regular federal funding to the field.] I hope we can make appeals directly to the CEOs of a lot of corporations that aren't involved with us now.

As you well know, the major sources of outside funding have been the Exxons and Mobils of the world, and with the situation in the oil industry, those funds are just in less supply. By the same token, there are other segments of the economy that have done awfully well, and I'm not sure we've done our job in attracting a broader base of funding.

A Strategic Plan

I guess the thrust of my interest is in developing two things. One is the marketing. The second is to work on what we don't have—a strategic plan. Which cannot come from just CPB. It's got to come from the system, from station managers, from PBS, from viewers.

We're talking about something structural, which really has to do with "What are we all about?" We do have a five-year plan that is periodically updated. I guess I've been on the board for three years, and we have dealt with it once, in really quite a perfunctory way, without a great deal of discussion.

One of the former board members once said to me when I was just coming on the board, "I don't know what you're going to find, but I think you'll find you spend a lot of time discussing what color to paint the closet"—nit-picky operational details.

Needed on Public TV

I think our programming is deficient in two areas. One is certainly children' programming. If you go to the networks, my Lord, there's nothing but four hours of commercials for toys. This has been a major initiative of the board for a couple of years and it's been very, very slow coming. We're still sort of riding on the success of *Sesame Street*. There was a series that in fact made a difference. Statistically it's been shown that if you measured people before *Sesame Street* and after *Sesame Street*, the level of achievement for those preschoolers was definitely raised. There are new programs like the new mathematics series, *Square One TV*, but I personally don't think there are enough on the horizon.

The second area is history. We did get at it with *The Constitution*. But you can think of innumerable things that should be done. History is, I think, a very, very neglected subject in our schools. It's sort of taught as, "Here's the history of Europe. These kings and those kings." And I'm speaking as a parent. I have done all I could with my children.

There is no history on the commercial networks and it's very limited on any of the other channels. Because it's difficult to produce. Here's an idea that somebody mentioned to me: Look at the history of this country through the eyes of the 40 presidents, but with a little bit different twist. Don't dwell on their politics. It would be sort of history and sociology. How did they grow up? We are told that Lincoln grew up in a log cabin in Illinois. What was Illinois like at that time?

Losing Must-Carry

It strikes me that if we are producing programming that people want, they are going to get it. If the loss of the Must-Carry regulations means that we're knocked off [cable systems previously required to carry public TV] in areas, that is a problem. Hopefully, the viewers will ask for it back. If we're really doing our job, people are going to demand it.

Where you've got three overlapping stations, without saying anything about any one of those stations. I'm not sure it's really in the best interests of the system as a whole to have a situation like that. Now you'll never get any one of those stations to say, "Well, gee, I'll turn in my license for the good of all."

The Proposed Content Analysis of Public TV

There isn't anybody who will disagree that we are charged with producing and airing programming that, taken as a whole, is objective and balanced.

I guess the problem I have, and maybe a lot of other people have, is: Whose view? How do you measure it? You could fill a room with 500 people and not get two to agree on what is objective. How you study it is a mystery to me.

PBS has appointed a committee that is doing sort of an in-house study, which I think is due to report out in April. My feeling is that we should wait and see what they're doing, what they say.

Beyond Big Bird
Charles Oliver, REASON

"One of the strengths of KCET is that when I turn it on, it isn't always something that I want to see," said one volunteer during the Los Angeles PBS station's March pledge drive. He summed up the attitude of many of public television's most devout supporters: It isn't always enjoyable, but dammit, PBS is important. In fact, PBS has looked pretty important over the past 10 months. In September, the network's series on the Civil War drew an incredible (by PBS standards) 12 percent of the national television audience. In October, PBS kicked off a $2-million ad campaign to promote the new season, including its first-ever ads on commercial television stations. And in November, the PBS board of directors took control of programming away from member stations and placed it in the hands of PBS Vice President Jennifer Lawson. The move promised to streamline an unwieldly system in which several different committees decided which programs were funded.

But beneath the surface successes, PBS appears to be in trouble. It isn't mortally ill, not by a long shot. But it is declining in importance. Indeed, long-term trends are at work that could spell the end of public television.

Before PBS, there was educational television. In 1949, the Federal Communications Commission reserved 242 channels for noncommercial instructional television. The next year, KUHT-TV in Houston went on the air as the nation's first educational station. By the early 1960s, there were 75 educational television stations on the air.

Educational television was pretty low-rent stuff. With little money to spend on programming, most stations relied on talking-head discussion shows, chalkboard-and-pointer instructional programs, and the occasional nature documentary.

PBS was supposed to counter all of this. In the preface to the 1967 Carnegie Corp. report that first proposed a public television system, E. B. White wrote that this system should be "the visual counterpart of the literary essay, should arouse our dreams, satisfy our hunger for beauty, take us on journeys, enable us to participate in events, present great drama and music, explore the sea and the sky and the woods and the hills."

In 1968 Lyndon Johnson created the Corporation for Public Broadcasting, which would pump money into public television and radio to create White's "visual counterpart of the literary essay." One year later, CPB and public television stations formed PBS to jointly produce and program new shows.

PBS was in many ways a model Great Society program: originated by ivory tower intellectuals, intended to achieve lofty goals, and given generous federal funds. And like many Great Society programs, PBS never quite lived up to its promise. The talking heads of educational television were simply interrupted every now and then by Cookie Monster or Julia Child.

The audience for it all was small. By the late 1970s, PBS usually averaged about 4.5 percent of the prime-time viewing audience. At the time, the lowest-rated of the three commercial networks could easily draw 15 percent.

Over the years, PBS's audience didn't grow, but public television itself did. The number of stations jumped from about 100 when the system began to about 300 in 1990. Today, public television is a $1-billion-a-year business. WNET, the member station in New York City, alone has an annual budget of more than $100 million. Perhaps most emblematic of the changes at PBS is the Washington, D.C. station, WETA. WETA started out in the home of one of its supporters, but now it has a $40-million annual budget, a skylighted complex in Arlington, Virginia, and Sharon Rockefeller (wife of Sen. Jay Rockefeller) as its president.

And as public television grew, the bureaucracy became more complex. An amalgam of alphabet organizations—CPB, PBS, NAPTS, EETN, PMN, and SECA being the most prominent—came together to fund programs and coordinate the actions of public television stations. Programming was particularly complicated. PBS itself could put shows into development through the PBS–CPB Program Challenge Fund. But programs were typically developed at a handful of large member stations—WGBH in Boston, WETA in Washington, D.C., and WNET in New York City being the most important. These stations drew their money from a variety of sources: the Corporation for Public Broadcasting, other stations through the Programming Cooperative, viewers, foundations, and corporations.

This complicated arrangement shielded the system from accountability. "The public television bureaucracy is certainly confusing to outsiders," notes conservative journalist David Horowitz, who is writing a book on PBS. "It seems designed so that everybody involved can avoid the responsibility for the programs. If you have some criticism of one of their shows, and you want to find out who is responsible for it, the response is always 'Well, funding was approved by this committee. And this group placed it on the schedule.' Or, 'It was produced by WGBH or by the BBC.' Everyone can pass the buck to someone else."

At least in the early days, there was arguably a need for public television. When PBS was formed, most households—except in a few big cities—could receive only the three networks. There was little variety in TV programming. The commercial stations stuck to sitcoms, shoot'em ups, the game shows. High culture and public affairs were almost nonexistent.

But even as the PBS bureaucracy was growing fat, changes in technology and in the marketplace were occurring that would challenge PBS's need to exist. The growth of independent commercial stations and the success of the VCR and compact disks gave people a greater choice in home entertainment. But the biggest problem for PBS is cable.

Thanks to those little boxes on top of their TVs, most people now have a large variety of channels to watch. The average viewer can choose from 30 channels, and that number will probably double by the end of the decade. As a result, PBS's share of the prime-time audience has declined by about 12 percent over the last decade, from its high of 4.5 percent to 4 percent in 1990. As cable channels develop, PBS's decline seems likely to continue, perhaps even to accelerate.

Many of the new channels just imitate—or more likely rerun—the programs offered by ABC, CBS, and NBC. But others have appropriated the kind of programming that was once unique to PBS, the programming that it was once argued must be subsidized by government because the market would not provide it. And, in most cases, the specialized channels give viewers more of what they're looking for.

PBS has *Nova* and *Nature*. But the Discovery Channel devotes most of its daily schedule to science and nature programming. PBS offers *Austin City Limits* and *Lonesome Pine*. But the Nashville Network gives country music fans 12 hours of music videos, live performances, and interviews each day.

Some PBS stations carry adult learning programs, but the Learning Channel specializes in educational shows. *The MacNeil/Lehrer News Hour* lets PBS viewers catch up with the news at dinner time each weekday, but CNN gives viewers the latest news around the clock. PBS lets us see *Masterpiece Theater* and *Great Performances*, but the Arts & Entertainment network offers fine arts and drama 24 hours a day.

PBS gives viewers *Wall Street Week* and the *Nightly Business Report*. But CNBC and FNN offer nothing but business and financial information. PBS has *Tony Brown's Journal*, a public-affairs program aimed at blacks, but ET targets *all* its news and entertainment programs specifically at blacks. Some PBS stations occasionally show classic films. But American Movie Classics and Ted Turner's TNT carry several different classic American and foreign films every day.

And when I watched a day's worth of KCET programming, the PBS affiliate clocked an average of 10 minutes of pledge breaks per hour—the longest was 19 minutes. Home Shopping Network begs for money 24 hours a day.

If the market now offers cultural and public-affairs programming, why should taxpayers continue to shell out $200 million a year for public television? And why should the FCC reserve a valuable share of the broadcast spectrum exclusively for public television programming? PBSers offer two reasons: PBS is free (unlike cable), and PBS still offers some programs that cable will not touch.

In fact, PBS does more than 90 percent of American homes, while cable reaches only 60 percent. But the people who most watch PBS are those who are most able to afford other forms of entertainment and information. They are better educated and more affluent than the typical couch potato.

In its audience breakdowns, PBS claims that its viewers are only slightly more affluent than the average TV audience. For example, PBS says that 32 percent of its audience earns less than $20,000 a year, compared to 36 percent for America as a whole. And 15 percent of PBS viewers earn over $60,000 a year, but for America as a whole the number is 13 percent.

These figures may be true if the broad demographic spectrum of people who plop their children down in front of *Sesame Street* is included. But the hard-core prime-time audience is decidedly upscale. In Memphis, Tennessee, for example, 68 percent of the subscribers to WNKO's viewer magazine have a household income of $50,000 or more; 62 percent have an investment portfolio of $50,000 or more; and 68 percent have a household net worth of $100,000 or more.

The figures are similar across the nation. Writer Andrew Ferguson notes that WETA's viewer magazine lures advertisers with promises of an upscale audience. "For these purposes," he says, "the station admits that its contributors have an average household income of $95,583, an average investment portfolio of $249,693, and an average household net worth of $627,663."

If PBS viewers are actually no richer or more influential than the average *Cheers* fan, he asks, why do all those Fortune 500 companies underwrite PBS shows? "As a WETA fund-raiser told me, 'They know that during prime time public television can deliver the demographic they want: affluent, highly educated, the movers and shakers, the socially conscious and well-informed.'" These aren't the sort of people who can't afford cable.

Still, Henry Becton, president of Boston's WGBH, contends that there are still certain types of programs that are unique to PBS. "The cable channels don't do opera or classical music," he says. "You won't find Peter Sellars doing Mozart on A&E."

Well, that's not exactly true. PBS may have a higher volume of classical music than cable, but one can find the classics on commercial channels. A&E's schedule has never been loaded with classical music, but it has offered viewers *Eugene Ormandy Conducts the Philadelphia Orchestra* and *Mahler: Songs of the Earth.*

And there's a very good reason that commercial channels don't carry more classical music. Richard Ottinger, CEO of the Georgia Public Television Network, notes that his network's audience for opera and classical music has fallen over the last decade, thanks largely to improvements in home stereo. "The quality of sound on television isn't that good," he says. "The people who like this type of music would rather listen to it on compact disk. On television the sound comes through a tinny little box."

As cable channels continue to multiply, finding a niche for PBS will become increasingly difficult. Ottinger, for example, wants the network to offer "more local coverage, more political coverage, and more service or how-to shows." But cable is filling even these niches. Almost every system sets aside one channel for community programming and coverage of city or county council meetings. Some larger systems even have 24-hour local-news channels. CNN and C-Span provide all the politics even the most voracious news junkie can stand. Finally, many channels offer some sort of how-to programs, and the Learning Channel specializes in information-you-can-use shows.

Richard Hutton, senior vice president for programming and production at WETA, offers another common solution: "We should focus on quality. Cable can't match us there. They have nothing like *The Civil War* or *Eyes on the Prize.*"

True enough. But cable is still in its infancy. As channels such as TNT and A&E begin to produce more of their own programs and gain more experience at making original programs, the quality of their shows will probably improve. In March, for example, *TV Guide* asked 11 experts to pick the best new shows for children. Most of the shows were on cable; some were on the networks. None were on PBS.

Besides, *quality* may be just a code word for "more expensive." If PBS's audience continues to decline and upscale viewers turn more to other forms of entertainment, it may become more difficult to get government and corporations to shell out money for PBS's "quality" programs.

In short, PBS insiders want to preserve their autonomy and government subsidies, but they can't seem to agree on the best strategy for doing that—or to come up with a strategy that will work. Becton offers a common solution: "We must remain unique and different from commercial channels."

The world is a much different place that it was 20 years ago, when PBS was taking its first steps. But the management of PBS has changed very little, and that limits the system's ability to find creative alternatives to commercial programming. "People tend to stay at PBS for a long time," says Bob Chitester, founder and former president of WQLN, the PBS station in Erie, Pennsylvania. "And the people at the top tend to have long tenure. There are station managers there who were there when I first started 20 years ago."

Like most government agencies, public television continues to operate much as it did when it was started, refusing to adapt to changing circumstances. Chitester contends that the network's schedule reflects PBS's lack of new ideas and reluctance to change. "If you look at the really important shows, you'll find that almost all of them are 15 to 20 years old," dating back to PBS's early years, he says. "*Sesame Street* is great, but there's no way for a new *Sesame Street* to evolve within the PBS system."

Two years ago, the board of directors created the position of "programming czar" to streamline the bureaucracy, stem eroding viewership, and push PBS into the 1990s. The post was given to Jennifer Lawson, who moved quickly to consolidate her authority. She ended funding for two low-rated PBS staples, the children's show *Newton's Apple* and the documentary series *American Masters*. She is developing a new children's game show and has announced plans to showcase more popular music.

Despite a general agreement that some sort of change must be made in PBS, some public television staffers, especially those at the local stations, regard attempts to reform the system with wariness. No one will criticize Lawson on the record. But privately some fear that her appointment, along with the more permissive rules for identifying corporate underwriters enacted six years ago, is part of a process of commercializing—or mainstreaming—PBS programming. Lawson denies this charge.

PBS producers, says Chitester, almost never ask if anyone else wants to see the shows they make. "I helped create programs that my mother wouldn't watch," he says. "It was fun and games at the taxpayers' expense." PBS producers fear that Lawson's changes may cost them the freedom to do what they want without worrying about attracting an audience. "One of the strengths of PBS is that it provides an outlet for different voices," Boston's Becton told *TV Guide*. "We need to offer an alternative to commercial television, and to do that we need a producer-driven system, not a schedule-driven system."

This difference between the mind-set at PBS and that of the cable channels was demonstrated in March, when the Discovery Channel picked up the British documentary *The Greenhouse Conspiracy* for broadcast in the United States. Aired in Britain last August, the documentary, which questions whether global warming is indeed occurring, drew tremendous praise from both reviewers and scientists.

But PBS declined to purchase the American rights, deeming the documentary too one-sided. PBS critics note that the system regularly shows one-sided documentaries, including several programs that uncritically accepted the direst global warming predictions. In response, one PBS executive told Media Watch, a conservative press watchdog group, "I'm not sure it's useful to include every single point of view in order to cover every base because you can come up with a program that's virtually impossible for the audience to sort out."

When PBS turned down *The Greenhouse Conspiracy*, Discovery jumped at the chance. "Politically, I'm not sure the views of the executives at the Discovery Channel differ from those at PBS," notes Richard Miniter, an environmental policy analyst at the Competitive Enterprise Institute who urged PBS to air the documentary. "But market forces compel the Discovery Channel to show things that don't necessarily conform to their world view. This was a very marketable product—a highly documented, well-crafted documentary that already had stirred up a controversy and gained quite a bit of publicity. The Discovery Channel has an interest in showing it that PBS didn't." Discovery will air the documentary in late June.

So what does the future hold for PBS? If Jennifer Lawson fails to stem the exodus of viewers, could we see the system privatized or abolished?

In 1981 the Reagan administration considered turning PBS into a scrambled, over-the-air subscription service, but it ultimately rejected the idea because the cost of the needed new equipment would far outweigh the revenue that the network could raise. Moreover, privatizing the system could easily lead to the demise of the network. Its staff, accustomed to Becton's "producer-driven" system, just wouldn't know how to cope in a profit-driven company.

"Most of the people in PBS management have worked their way up in the system or have come to it from academia. There aren't many people with commercial broadcasting backgrounds there," observes Chitester, who produced *Free to Choose*. "They couldn't readily adapt to a market system—producing shows that viewers want to see, rather than the programs they themselves want to see, trying to earn a profit. They wouldn't fit in in that type of environment."

Full commercialization or privatization of PBS seems unlikely. PBS remains popular on Capitol Hill. And while PBS is actually run by its staff, it has been very successful at loading its local boards of directors with community VIPs who want to help out *Sesame Street*. They form a very strong lobbying voice for public television.

Despite all of the controversy surrounding the National Endowment for the Arts, that program was never in danger of being abolished, and its budget was barely touched. If Congress continues funding Karen Finley, it certainly isn't going to cut the money for Big Bird.

But the pressures on PBS will continue to mount. Each year cable channels grow, both in number and in strength, drawing viewers and corporate dollars away from public television. Videotape and compact disks also cut into PBS's audience. Meanwhile, budget pressures at both the federal and state level will mean smaller budgets for public television. After adjusting for inflation, the federal contribution to PBS will decline slightly this year. Any many states have made nominal cuts in their funds for public television.

We can't count PBS out just yet. The existence of the Rural Electrification Administration and numerous other government agencies that have long outlived the problems they were created to solve indicates that PBS could be around for a very long time. But it isn't too farfetched to imagine the system slowly withering away.

Charles Oliver is assistant editor of Reason.

Public Television
Worksheet

1. Based on the three readings in this section, identify three major factors that are contributing to public television's failure to complete with its commercial counterparts.

2. Also from the readings, identify three things that public television needs to do (or do differently) to survive? What changes need to be made?

3.   College students are, for the most part, the smallest audience for public television programming. What would public TV need to do to attract your attention and regular viewership? Note: Your answer must be consistent with the goal of public television and operate with the realization that most public television money comes from the federal government and the viewing audience.

4.   Should the public pay for public television through a state tax? Do we have an obligation to keep public television alive, whether we watch it or not? Explain your answer.

XVII

International Media

The late-1980s and early-1990s have seen more international drama and upheaval in more parts of the globe than any time since World War II. The social and economic revolution in the Soviet Union, the political transformation of Eastern Europe, the death of the Ayatollah Khomeini, dissent and bloody repression in China, and gradual conciliation in Southern Africa and Lebanon all herald a redrawing of old international boundaries. And the American press, all the while, is doing its job of reporting the news from abroad to the reading and viewing public at home. How and how well it does so in comparison with media from other countries is the focus of this section.

The first essay, "News From the Global Village," written by the executive producer of *CNN World Report*, examines how new technologies shape and influence editorial content of the mass media and contribute to freedom of the press. Specific reference is given to the growth of international news exchanges that has accompanied the miniaturization of news gathering devices and ease of satellite transmission. The second essay, "Telling the West Bank Story," reveals how international news is regulated during time of war. The author illustrates the transformation that has taken place in the attitude of the Israeli government and public toward Israeli media coverage of the uprising in the West Bank and Gaza Strip. Tolerance and openness have been replaced by hostility and increasing press restrictions. The third essay also examines American media in foreign lands. However, "Unwilling Informants" explores the possible consequences that befall native informants who contribute to American media news reports, in this case Chinese citizens at the time of the Beijing massacre. The fourth and fifth essays examine whether freedom of the press is an international phenomenon in the 1990s. "How Free is the Press" offers a global sampler of the world's news media. "The New Censors" provides an interesting case study by examining the plight of native black journalists in South Africa during different phases of apartheid. It suggests that freedom of the press does not automatically occur with new-found individual freedoms.

News From the Global Village
Stuart H. Loory, GANNETT CENTER JOURNAL

In the offices of the *New York Herald Tribune* in 1959 there was a wire room that looked like it might have been a set for the movie *Young Tom Edison.* It was an unused relic. Two banks of old Underwood typewriters—the really limber kind that held their own with the early generations of IBM electrics—dominated the room. Next to each was a gooseneck lamp and a ticker from which the wire operators (I imagined them in green eyeshades and gartered shirtsleeves) once took incoming news from around the world, translating it from the dots and dashes into the abbreviated cable-ese that the rewrite men turned into finished newspaper copy.

As a young *Herald Tribune* reporter I used to stand in that room and let my mind wander. I imagined myself one with the great newspapermen of the past, with Lincoln Steffens, Richard Harding Davis and Sir Henry Stanley or, in delusions of grandeur, with Rudyard Kipling.

The analog dots and dashes are now digital switches, and my mind still wanders through journalistic history.

First stop: the newly convened class of 1958 at the Columbia University Graduate School of Journalism. Professor John Hohenberg projects his rhetoric through the huge old "newsroom." I listen rapt in the rear of the room as he explains the technological and economical underpinnings of the objective, fact-based tradition of American journalism. In the 19th century, Hohenberg says, the new telegraph made it possible to spread information from one end of the United States to the other with the speed of light. Because the telegraph was slow (the speed of light was in reality controlled by the speed of the operator's finger on the telegraph key) and the cost of transmission high, the premium was on brevity—just the facts.

When Samuel F. B. Morse's telegraph went international with the laying of the undersea cable, the British developed the so-called empire press rate. For a penny a word reporters could send material from anywhere in the empire to anywhere else, making it very cheap to transmit information. Because the British-ruled world was cheaper to cover and more accessible than other parts of the world, it got more coverage.

Second stop: the Democratic National Convention in Chicago, August 1968. Anti-war activists battle Mayor Daley's Chicago police in the city's lake-side parks and darkened streets. Anti-establishment politicians struggle in vain to gain control of the Democratic Party in the Chicago convention hall.

Less noticed is the communications revolution underway at the convention. Below the speaker's platform is a green-eye-shaded Morse code operator sending short messages to the *New York Daily News.* The first computer terminals are glowing next to him. The 19th and 21st centuries meet at the 1968 Democratic National Convention.

Third stop: the Reagan-Gorbachev summit meeting, Geneva, November 1985. On the down escalator of the Inter-Continental Hotel, one reporter shouts to another, going up, "Where's the nearest Radio Shack?" He's seeking to correct a problem with his Model 100 laptop computer, which is connected electronically through the hotel telephone to his U.S. editor.

Throughout the development of modern journalism, new technologies have shaped and influenced editorial content in the mass media. This has been more the case in the United States than in Europe. While the telegraph strongly influenced the development of reportage in the United States, political parties were the more important influence in Europe. The best newspapers there were party-owned, and analytical, interpretive and opinionated reportage rather than factual objectivity became the norm.

Coverage now still flows along the most accessible channels and is shaped by them. But the scope of this general rule has widened. As John Hohenberg said, in the same way that technology affected domestic U.S. news in the past, it affects international news today. The United States has taken the lead in new technologies of newsgathering and distribution, but journalists in other countries are rapidly awakening to the possibilities of satellites, miniature videotape cameras, fiber optics and computers, and will have a growing influence in the future.

American journalism has long had an impact on policymaking at federal, state and local levels by presenting news that sets an agenda, exposing situations that need correction, and stimulating the public to demand action from the nation's leaders. Information was once transmitted from one power center in Washington to another by the major newspapers circulating in the capital. More recently television news, primarily CNN, has filled that role. The executive and legislative branches increasingly exchange news and views via live, ubiquitous video coverage.

Advanced communications technology now makes it easy for international journalists to do for the entire world what domestic television and, to a lesser extent, newspapers now do in Washington. The corollary here is that television will have increasing significance for foreign policy making. Programs like ABC's *Nightline* and *Capital-to-Capital* and events like the "spacebridge" have demonstrated some of the possibilities. The steadily growing worldwide penetration of CNN—it is now carried to one-third of the earth's surface by a Soviet-built and -controlled satellite—is part of the picture. Former President Jimmy Carter said recently that all the embassies he has visited a broad carry CNN.

The United States is the best-covered nation in the world today, not only by American journalists but by those from abroad as well. The reason is simple: It is easier and cheaper to cover events here than anywhere else. The old empire press rate of the 19th century has been replaced by satellite tariffs, and the accessibility to satellites in this country is unmatched anywhere else.

For this reason journalists from other countries join Americans in orgies of news coverage that are often out of proportion to an event's true significance. For example, the American political party conventions are no longer crucial to the presidential nominating process or as a forum for party debate. The results in 1988 were known long before the delegates convened. The conventions are designed for the mass media. Each convention was as carefully scripted as a pre-glasnost Communist Party meeting in the Soviet Union. At the extraordinary 1988 Communist Party conference in Moscow, on the other hand, Mikhail Gorbachev outlined his plans for revolutionizing the Soviet Union, and these were analyzed, debated and examined from every angle. Yet the American conventions received far more international coverage than the Moscow meeting.

In recent months the Soviet government has made it far easier for journalists to operate in that country than before. There are once again direct-dial telephone lines going out of the country. Western television organizations can now "feed" their reports directly to a satellite from their offices rather than relying on the feedpoint at Soviet television, often at mortal risk in last-minute auto rides, to meet a deadline.

Whenever a country opens up in this fashion, the technological imperative goes to work. The number of organizations covering the Soviet Union has begun to increase as rapidly as the amount of coverage that each individual organization is offering. The facility of news transmission and increased coverage could help speed negotiations between East and West, perhaps spurring policy changes that are already in motion. This may contribute to a new definition of international relationships.

Our 19th-century predecessors shaped news coverage to fit the capabilities of technology, but they still made certain that the substance of the news was properly treated. Modern video journalism often gets so caught up in the gadgetry that it forgets the substance of the news. In the 19th century the new technology and economics of the telegraph dictated where stories would be covered and how the information would be transmitted; by the 1970s the ability to gather news electronically was also dictating *what* should be covered. At WNBC-TV in New York, where I was working when the first portable TV cameras were introduced in the city, the rule was that we had to have a live report on the 6 o'clock local news every day whether one was justified or not.

Last year when President Reagan visited Moscow, an ABC News crew hand-carried a portable microwave transmitter and antenna into the Kremlin, enabling Pierre Salinger to broadcast the arrival of the American president of a meeting with Gorbachev live to the United States. The electronic feat was remarkable—live from the interior of the Kremlin to the living rooms of America, but the content was the mere depiction of a man emerging from a car.

Since the international communications revolution began, the channels of information have been mainly controlled from Washington, New York, London, Paris and Bonn. In other words, the news does flow, as the developing nations have charged, from North to South, from industrialized to developing countries, from rich to poor. The United States Information Agency's WorldNet was a massive attempt to project the United States' point of view throughout the world, and the British, French and West Germany governments all have projects of similar intent, though simpler in concept.

There is nothing in modern technologies of communications that mandates this situation. Indeed, most of the nations of the world, including developing countries, are members of Intelsat and integrated into the growing international telecommunications network. Instead, politics and economics are the major barriers. In most of the world's nations, particularly developing countries, the organizations controlling satellite earth stations (known generically as the PTTs for "post, television and telegraphic") are working at cross purposes with the television organizations that produce the news. The government-owned PTTs insist on charging exorbitant rates for incoming and outgoing broadcasts. That makes it difficult for television news organizations, also government-owned in many cases, to maintain proper contact with the outside world. The governments that tolerate this conflict between competing bureaucracies have not yet discovered the compelling need for the free flow of international information.

Inside developing countries there is another economic problem of great importance—a lack of television sets and the electricity to run them. Ethiopia, for example, is a country of 40 million but has only 80,000 television sets. The situation is similar in Vietnam, where most of the population still has no electricity.

The political problems that obstruct the flow of information from developing countries to the rest of the world are several. In too many countries it is far too difficult for journalists to operate impartially. From Afghanistan to Zimbabwe journalists labor under restrictions that, if they do not amount to out-and-out censorship, at least demand tremendous self-restraint and crippling self-censorship. The broadcast authorities of Africa, Latin America and the Middle East have also been slow to set up regional news exchanges similar to those operating in Europe and East Asia today.

To a great extent the blame for one-way information flow lies not with the imperious attitudes of Western broadcasters, as developing nations have charged in such forums as UNESCO, but with their own policies and priorities. The developing countries fear the impact of Western industrialized nations generally. And that fear extends to within the Western community itself. In Europe some broadcasters fear that the United States will dominate their own markets if some protective barriers are not erected or other actions taken. At a recent meeting of the European Broadcasting Union News Working Party, a decision was taken to begin a transnational Euronews program in 1991 in which all of its members would participate.

But modern societies—and those trying to modernize—cannot erect lasting barriers. Technology will continue to create its own imperatives. Modern communications technology easily overcomes concrete walls, barbwire fences and restrictive legislation. The European Community can try as hard as it wants to keep American culture from dominating its television screens, but if the American product continues to be better and less expensive it will find its way into the market—if not via satellite, cable and broadcast channels, then via videotape or compact disc or who knows what other medium in the future.

Many Eastern European countries have already discovered this. In Prague, for example, one sees more and more baroque rooftops decorated with satellite dishes tuned to Western signals. The installation can be ordered in Prague which the locally manufactured dishes paid for in Czech crowns and imported low-noise amplifiers purchased in West German Deutschmarks. Many Czechs now have as much programming as an earth station owner in Paris. The Eastern European governments have lately recognized this reality, and most of them have abandoned their efforts to stem the tide of Western culture.

Cable News Network is now available in one hotel in Moscow and will soon be available throughout the city. Almost two years ago, well before Solidarity took control of the government, Polish television began broadcasting a nightly news program excerpted from CNN coverage in tandem with a program of excerpts from Soviet TV.

Ironically there has been a barrier to such international news coverage in the United States. Unlike newspapers, most American television news organizations have refused to accept news reports prepared by local journalists in foreign countries. That has prevented Americans from becoming as well informed as they might be.

But two years ago Ted Turner conceived the idea for the *CNN World Report*, a program that has since grown into the world's only global newscast and largest news exchange. The idea behind it is simple. CNN invites all the world's television news broadcasters to submit the news as they see it to a weekly program that is open-ended in length. CNN pledges to run that news unedited and uncensored. All contributors to the program in turn get the rights to use all of the material in each program. No money changes hands. Contributors pay the expense of getting their materials to the United States either by satellite or air freight. CNN pays the expense of getting the program back to them, either by satellite or air freight.

The result is a program of endless fascination, if not technological perfection. At this writing, *World Report* is celebrating its second anniversary and is still growing. On October 16, 1989, it added a half-hour weekday version. So far, 4,000 reports have appeared on the weekend edition, and the worst fears of traditional journalists—that the program would be a sounding board for the world's propagandists—have not been realized. Instead, the program has carried distinctly nontraditional interpretations of many news stories and has covered news that was otherwise not available.

During the program of October 15, for example, just before a special United Nation conference in Lausanne voted to ban ivory trade around the world, Zimbabwe Broadcasting Corporation submitted a report showing that elephants were overrunning farmers' fields in its country and causing famine; TV3 of Barcelona, Spain, submitted a poignant report on the problems of the aged in its country; Swedish Television presented a report on the release of the accused killer of Prime Minister Olof Palme saying that many Swedish citizens were relieved at the verdict because it showed that the criminal justice system still worked; and United Nations television reported on an effective new non-chemical way of wiping out the tsetse fly in Africa, using cow's urine and an ingenious trap.

Cultural chauvinism prohibits this kind of reportage from airing on the other U.S. networks unless it is presented by an American—or at least British—journalist. But we do the American people a grave disservice if we decide preemptively that only those brought up in the Judeo-Christian ethic, schooled in Western democracy and possessed of accents learned in Kansas City can report the news. The truth is that much information is editorially neutral, that many interpretations are in themselves news, and that our viewers can understand accented English and watch video that is something less than perfect.

International television news has grown in power in the past generation. In 1970 television reportage from Vietnam had already affected attitudes at home toward the war. By 1980 satellites were being used to create two-way, live conversations between the United States and the Soviet Union.

As 1990 approaches such "spacebridges" are commonplace and now the emphasis has shifted to global distribution. CNN, which did not exist as the 1980s began, has grown into a global network, its signal sold in 85 countries and available in all the world's nations.

So as changing technology makes our job easier and our output more compelling, journalists must also consider the attitudinal changes necessary to improve international news flow.

A couple of years ago Ted Koppel interviewed a climber atop Mount Everest live on *Nightline*. A program like that still requires a tremendous amount of planning and preparation, but by the year 2000 equipment will be so miniaturized and satellite transponders so readily available that reports from such remote locations could be set up in a matter of hours. We will be able to go live to anywhere in the world with the ease that a local television station now covers a rush-hour freeway accident. The equipment will be far smaller (perhaps using 8 mm tape rather than the half-inch that is currently standard) while offering much higher resolution than the two-inch tape that provides the best quality at present.

The continuing integration of computers and television will offer all sorts of possibilities for processing both images and facts. (In this season of dispute over the re-enactment of news events, just imagine what can be done in the future with computer "paint boxes" to gussy up the news quickly.)

As the technology improves, you can be sure that imaginative journalists will take advantage of the new opportunities. Julius Barnathan, vice president of ABC News, sees the development of multi-language broadcasts as one of the most important features of international communications as the century nears its end. One set of pictures will be accompanied by as many as eight narrations.

However, it may be easier to report live from the South Pole than to solve the political, economic, ethical and professional questions that will still be with us.

The political question will revolve around the matter of access to transnational audiences. Too many countries are concerned that their populations will be unduly influenced by television productions from outside their borders. The European Community's recent action in trying to set quotas for American television productions—though in the realm of cultural rather than informational programming—is a case in point.

Economically the PTTs will continue to try to control the transmission points, making access to satellites far more expensive and difficult than it need be. Once again the Europeans take the lead in this, but PTTs in the developing countries follow suit. The important issue here is that improving technology permits easier and easier satellite access from the location of an event, by-passing the PTTs. The PTTs are resisting the introduction of these so-called fly-away earth stations.

But even hese problems pale in comparison with the ethical and professional considerations. The questions of what we are going to cover—and how—receive the least amount of attention in our concentration on technique and technology.

Certainly we need to cover exciting events. (One of the knottiest questions of what to cover—too complicated for consideration here—is how to cover acts of terrorism.) And certainly we cannot become so dry and remote that we ignore the human element of the news. But international journalism has always been at its best when it served as a distant early warning system. In the electronic information age, we must not forget how to cover the worlds of ideas and politics that will shape the future of the planet.

In the year 2000 cameras and transmission equipment will be so small and sophisticated that within minutes of the order, live reports from anywhere in the world will be available. Imagine a search-and-destroy mission, Vietnam War-style, live in your living room. That will be possible. Imagine an impromptu exchange between the Soviet and American leaders during a time of crisis. That could be covered live with ease. Concealed cameras shooting in the worst lighting conditions will permit investigative reporting of a kind not possible now.

Technology will give future journalists ever greater power than they have now. Those journalists must not allow technology to overtake substance if they are to continue to be honest brokers of political ideas and ideals.

Stuart H. Loory is executive producer of the CNN World Report. *A former newspaper reporter and editor, he was the last Moscow bureau chief for the* New York Herald Tribune *and the first for* CNN.

Telling the West Bank Story
Joel Greenberg, COLUMBIA JOURNALISM REVIEW

On a cloudy day in mid-January a group of Israeli soldiers prepared to take on a crowd of Palestinian boys who were pelting them with stones at the al-Amari refugee camp in the West Bank. The soldiers stocked up on tear gas grenades and rubber bullets, and strapped on their helmets, in full view of a battery of television cameras lined up behind them.

Before charging the boys, a soldier turned to the camera crews and asked casually, "You guys have enough light? Can we get started?" The cameramen nodded, and the confrontation began.

It was a classic television chase scene. The troops hurled the tear gas grenades and ran toward the boys behind the billows of smoke, firing their rubber bullets as the stone-throwers disappeared into side alleys.

Four months later, one evening in mid-May, I filed a story on the latest leaflet published by the clandestine leadership of the Palestinian uprising in the occupied territories. A few minutes after the story reached the news desk, my editor told me it had been censored; not even the existence of the leaflet could be mentioned in the newspaper. It was the first time the military censor had banned publication in the Israeli press of such leaflets, containing instructions for protests and violent demonstrations. "We're doing everything we can to suppress these leaflets," the duty censor told me over the phone, "so we're supposed to allow them to be reproduced in the mass media?"

The two incidents illustrate the transformation that has taken place in the attitude of the Israeli government and public toward media coverage of the uprising in the West Bank and Gaza Strip. Tolerance and openness have been replaced by hostility and increasing press restrictions, as local and foreign journalists have dug up unsavory details of the ugly war betwen Israeli troops and Palestinians. The Palestinian uprising is seen by the government as a serious threat to state security, and it has decided that tough measures are needed to combat it, including limits on press freedom.

For reporters who, like myself, cover the West Bank, the changes have been incremental, seeming small when they happen, but significant when viewed in retrospect. We received an early hint of what was to come in the first week of the uprising (the second week in December), when a colleague and I reported on the vandalizing by border police of homes in the Balata refugee camp near the city of Nablus. In a subsequent briefing on the incident, a senior officer told us that the border police commander at the camp had been relieved of his duties. This piece of news was banned by the censor, apparently because it implied official admission of guilt. Similarly, the censor deleted from my copy a quote from the same senior officer, who had admitted that every killing of a Palestinian by the army "is a failure on our part." This censorship appeared to go well beyond strict security concerns.

On April 4, I filed a story about a Hebrew-language leaflet distributed by Arbas to Israeli soldiers in the West Bank, calling on them to desert. My paper ran the story without submitting it to the censor, but it was deleted by the censor from other papers, which had followed the rules, on the ground that publishing the contents of the leaflet could undermine the morale of the troops. *The Jerusalem Post* was reprimanded.

Later that month, a story reporting the de facto resignation of the Israeli-appointed Arab mayor of Nablus was censored. The reason was a conviction on the part of the authorities that any news about the departure of Palestinian civil servants could encourage others to step down, theatening the rupture of an important link in the Israeli military government in the territories. The definition of "security reasons"—the only ones for which the military censor may delete news copy—seemed to be expanding as the uprising wore on.

Access to areas in the West Bank and Gaza Strip was also being restricted. Declaration of "closed military zones"—i.e., closed to journalists—began in the Gaza Strip in early January and peaked on March 30, "Land Day," when Arabs in Israel and the occupied territories observed a day of protest against government expropriation of Arab lands. The entire West Bank and Gaza Strip were closed to journalists for the last four days of March, on the ground that the presence of television cameras and reporters encouraged rioting. Despite the absence of the media, Land Day proved to be the bloodiest day of the uprising: fourteen Palestinians were killed and more than one hundred wounded.

The closing off of certain areas has been taken as a challenge by local and foreign reporters, who have made it their business to get into precisely the zones from which they have been barred by the army. A basic tactic is to remove the "press" signs that Israeli reporters have been displaying on their windshields to deter Palestinian youths prepared to hurl rocks at any car with Israeli license plates. While removing the "press" sign makes you vulnerable to the rock-throwing, it gets you by the army checkpoints set up to keep reporters out.

A more difficult, but more interesting, task is to get into isolated villages that have been physically sealed off by the army as punishment for rioting. Those villages are surrounded by military roadblocks and ramparts of earth have been heaped by army bulldozers on all access roads. No one may enter or leave.

In mid-March, a colleague from the daily *Ha'aretz* and I paid separate visits to the town of Kabatiya in the northern West Bank, which had been under such an army siege for over a month, after its residents had lynched a local man thought to be collaborating with the Israelis. My colleague got in by riding a tractor that was smuggling in food supplies from a neighboring village. I entered by walking for half an hour along mountain paths leading from that same village.

Our stories ran on March 27 and 30. They showed that the people of Kabatiya were not only phyically cut off from the outside world; the army had also cut off their electricity, water, and cooking-fuel supplies. The stories described a town that had gone back a century in time, its residents collecting wood for cooking fires, drawing water from wells, and hunting animals in neighboring hills. The news brought a parliamentary question to the defense minister in the Knesset, and several days later the siege was lifted.

The need to get out into the field and see things for yourself has been made more urgent by the drying up of traditional sources of information for Israeli and foreign journalists. The official army spokesman, once a steady and largely reliable source of information on incidents in the occupied territories, has lost much of his credibility in the eyes of Israeli reporters. Since the start of the uprising, army reports have become increasingly incomplete and laconic; sometimes they are downright wrong. Often we have heard of incidents frist from Palestinian sources, not from the army. This has happened even when Palestinians have been killed or wounded in clashes with troops. Many incidents reported by Palestinians or witnessed by reporters are simply not mentioned by the army spokesman.

A classic case of this was the incident on February 5 in which Israeli soldiers using a bulldozer buried alive four Palestinian youths after a violent demonstation. The youths were rescued and they told their tale, which first appeared three days later in the daily *Hadashot*. At first the army discounted the report as untrue. Only after persistent questioning and publication of a follow-up investigation in the Jerusalem local weekly *Kot Ha'ir* was the incident officially confirmed; the soldiers were later court-martialed. Incidents such as this appear to be a result both of a deliberate attempt by the army to play down the extent of the unrest and of an inability of the army's information network to cope with the volume of reports streaming in from the field.

At the same time, Palestinian news sources are being restricted. Palestinians living at the scenes of major incidents are a vital source of information, whose reports can be compared with the army's. However, the barring of journalists from trouble spots has made it increasingly difficult to get their version of events.

On occasions when reporters *have* managed to slip into such areas, important details have emerged. On February 23 a Palestinian girl was shot and killed in the West Bank village of Baka Sharkiya. The army reported the death but said its circumstances were being investigated. I managed to slip through a military cordon into the village and heard an eyewitness report that the girl was killed by a Jewish settler. Earlier that month, reporters evaded army roadblocks to get into the village of Kaddum, where they heard accounts of another settler shooting, whose details had not been revealed by the army.

There have also been attempts to block off secondary Palestinian news sources. On March 30 the Palestine Press Service in East Jerusalem, which furnished foreign and local reporters with news tips provided by its many stringers in the occupied territories, was ordered closed for six months. The Israeli government press office, where most reporters have mailboxes, has banned distribution in these boxes of material from Palestinian institutions and organizations, arguing that a government office need not serve as a conduit for hostile Palestinian propaganda.

What has emerged from all this is a plain reality, often hidden here under the guise of "liaison" and "cooperation" between military and government officials and the press: when the chips are down, the interests of the government and the media are in conflict. Faced with what they see as a state of emergency, the authorities will have few qualms about limiting freedom of the press, notwithstanding Israel's reputation as an open society.

The developing conflict between the authorities and the press has emerged on all levels, from the offices of the Defense Ministry and army spokesmen in Tel Aviv to the military roadblocks in the West Bank. In the political realm, it has emerged in calls by right-wing politicians by banning the media from the territories altogether. It has also been reflected in growing expressions of antipress sentiment by broad sectors of the Israeli public.

Several recent incidents illustrate this increasing estrangement between Israelis and their media, and the danger faced by journalists here of being sucked into a conflict they are trying to cover dispassionately.

On the official level, journalists were recently warned by unnamed "defense sources" quoted in the local press that "measures" would be taken against them if they were responsible for "false" reports of events in the territories. One foreign radio reporter was called in by the army spokesman and ordered to apologize and to retract a report the spokesman had publicly denied.

There were more sinister developments in the political sphere. On Sunday, March 20, an Israeli army reservist was gunned down while on duty in Bethlehem. As he lay bleeding, he was photographed by an ABC television crew and by news photographers who were present in force in expectation of protest marches following church services. The shooting, the first killing of an Israeli since the uprising began, caused widespread feelings of outrage, which a rightwing member of parliament, Geula Cohen of the Tehiya party, tried to turn against the media. She charged that the newsmen may have had prior knowledge of the attack and had done nothing to prevent it, or even to provide assistance to the wounded soldier.

As it happened, the television crew had used a mobile phone in its car to call for help, but later publication of this fact did little to dispel the dark suspicions aroused by Cohen. She had, in effect, made the media accomplices in a killing.

The growing public animosity toward the media has been evident in the behavior of soldiers in the territories in their dealings with reporters. There have been numerous complaints by journalists of physical attacks on them by soldiers anxious to get them away from scenes of unrest. I was once roughly pushed back into my car when I got out to get a closer look at the bloodied face of a Palestinian youth who had been beaten. Verbal abuse from soldiers is also common. The reactions of the soldiers, who represent a cross section of Israeli society, seem to reflect a widespread belief that the press is concentrating on the negative, smearing the soldiers who are carrying out a tough job instead of giving them the backing they deserve. The media—particularly television—are, in addition, seen as provocateurs, troublemakers whose very presence can touch off a demonstration.

While Israeli journalists are increasingly perceived as enemies by other Israelis, they are often seen by Palestinians as being too closely identified with the Israeli authorities. After the lynching at Kabatiya, filmed by a Cable News Network crews, Israeli security authorities confiscated the film in order to use it to identify participants in the killing. CNN decided not to take legal action to recover the film after being told that, even if it were recovered, it could not be broadcast. Film taken from still photographers working for *Reuters, Time,* and *Newsweek* was also confiscated after the killing of the soldier in Bethlehem. These three news organizations regained their film after petitioning Israel's High Court of Justice. Concern was growing among journalists, who feared that use of their material for security purposes would endanger their lives, because they would be perceived by Palestinians as Israeli agents.

It is not uncommon for Palestinians to suspect that Israeli reporters asking them probing questions are in fact security agents. I have been asked several times by Palestinian youths to produce a press card. During a riot in Nablus, youths almost turned on a colleague of mine when they saw him taking notes in Hebrew.

A way out of this maze of partisanship has been to demonstrate publicly that one's journalistic work is not serving sinister aims, but can in fact be a constructive force. At least twice since the uprising began, it seems to me, this has been done successfully.

On April 6 a group of Israeli children from a West Bank settlement was attacked by a stone-throwing crowd in the Palestinian village of Beita. During the clash a Jewish girl was accidentally killed when the children's armed guard opened fire. Other children were hurt by stones and bullet fragments.

An NBC television crew, which arrived first on the scene, helped to rescue some of the children and called for help. But it did more than that. Its members appeared on Israel Television and told the Israeli public what they had done. This contributed significantly to improving the public's image of the media.

A second case occurred on February 25, when Israel Television broadcast footage shot by a CBS television crew showing Israeli soldiers beating two Palestinian prisoners in Nablus. The broadcast caused a wave of shock in Israel, though some right-wing groups said it proved why the media should be kept out of the territories.

CBS did more than make the film available to Israel TV. It gave it to the army, which used the footage to identify the soldiers involved, who were thereupon arrested. Israel's top West Bank commander ordered his entire staff of senior officers to view the film, and declared that "the army will not be a mob."

On these two occasions, journalists proved to Israelis that, beyond the daily public service of digging out the news, they were willing to become constructive actors in the scenes they were documenting. Such contributions, properly publicized, may help journalists avoid accusations of partisanship in the highly charged atmosphere of the Palestinian uprising.

Joel Greenberg covers the West Bank for The Jerusalem Post.

Unwilling Informants?
Jonathan Alter, NEWSWEEK

The appalling aftermath of the Beijing massacre is a reminder that the media can be used to imprison as well as liberate. The same Western TV transmissions that spread word of the democracy movement were later scanned by Chinese authorities to help round up suspects. But the dilemma for the press corps is not so much technological as moral. It reaches back to the very origins of what it means to cover the news. Like their predecessors in preliberalization China, today's journalists are trapped between reporting the story and avoiding complicity in the arrest of their sources. It's a tight spot.

The dangers are clearest in television. ABC News broadcast an eight-second sound bite from Xiao Bin, an eyewitness to the massacre. Five days later China's state television CCTV aired about 90 seconds of the same interview—suggesting that Chinese brass perhaps lifted the shot off a satellite feed of raw footage. CCTV followed with its own pictures of the same eyewitness under arrest, recanting his antigovernment comments. Shocked, ABC News moved immediately to scramble its satellite signal. The other networks began silhouetting or otherwise disguising the faces of Chinese departing from the party line. Newspapers, too, ran more anonymous quotes. NEWSWEEK changed the name of one of those who might be jeopardized.

Was there any way news organizations could have anticipated being used so cruelly? "We were totally taken by surprise," says Bob Murphy, vice president for news coverage for ABC News. "There had been no evidence of any repercussions." Before the crackdown, Chinese were emboldened as never before to speak openly. Still, there is plenty of precedent for repercussions after a crackdown is underway. Richard Bernstein, a *Time* correspondent in Beijing from 1979 to 1982, wrote a harrowing *New York Times Magazine* story last April about discovering that he had unwittingly helped send a dissident to jail for six years. "A lot of us have found out the hard way that we can get people in trouble with what seems to be innocent reporting activity," says Fox Butterfield, a *New York Times* reporter who inadvertently caused harm to Chinese sources in the early 1980s.

The dilemma goes to the heart of how journalists view themselves. Are they reporters first, or compassionate human beings? In a situation with complexities like those in China, the question cannot be addressed so squarely. At first glance, the argument for shutting down all contact with Chinese seems compelling. Why risk helping doom them to jail or even execution? In recent days even those Chinese who support the government entirely in interviews with Western reporters have found themselves interrogated afterward by security. Some media critics went so far as to criticize NBC News anchor Tom Brokaw for merely greeting passersby in the streets of Beijing.

Of course encouraging silence is exactly the effect that the Chinese government intends. "We are intimidated, because we don't want to get more people in trouble," said Kyle Gibson, an ABC News *Nightline* producer in Beijing. The result is not only journalistic impoverishment. It also means sacrificing the larger aim of many of the people who agree to talk, which is to get details of the massacre to the world. If they go uninterviewed, they are "protected," perhaps, but not fully represented, a position that may lack compassion in its own right.

Harsh price: There's no pat way to resolve this journalistic tension, which exists in many other repressive nations as well. Good reporters work on a case-by-case basis. When the subject in jeopardy seems careless or naive, he is often asked if he really wants his name used—and even if he says yes, is sometimes spared identification. The problem is that ultimately this weakens the reporting of the story. Readers are less likely to believe anonymous accounts. Particularly with Chinese authorities employing a Big Lie technique, bearing witness to the world seemed, for some Chinese, worth the harsh personal price.

One of the cruel ironies of journalism is that those who need the least protection often get the most—and vice versa. The high-ranking Washington official, simply trying to exercise self-serving spin control, almost always has his request for anonymity respected. Otherwise, he won't cooperate with the reporter in the first place. By contrast, the man in the street, less wise to the implications of his actions and less valuable to the reporter in the future, is more likely to see his name in print. Perhaps the China experience can reinforce the idea that "protecting sources" should take on more resonance when one is shielding them from torture and prison, than from political accountability. The most skillful and discreet reporters know how to manage that feat and cover the story at the same time.

How Free Is the Press? A Global Sampler
Peter Galliner, WORLD PRESS FREEDOM REVIEW

While journalists continued to face horrific physical risks in many parts of the world last year for simply attempting to carry out their professional duties, 1991 can be characterized as the year in which *economic* censorship hit hard. This phenomenon is best illustrated in the fledgling democracies of Eastern and Central Europe. Without the comfortable support they formerly received from the state, newly independent newspapers are encountering enormous problems merely surviving in the marketplace.

But the problem goes deeper. In many countries of Eastern Europe, newsprint supplies and distribution of publications remain firmly controlled by the state, and some ostensibly democratic governments could use this control to make sure that the media toe the official line.

One of the most graphic examples of the way economic problems have almost overshadowed those arising from government harassment is provided by Turkey. The country already had an inflation rate of around 70 percent when the Persian Gulf war forced most Turkish companies to reduce their advertising—a severe blow for the print media. These had been hit by intense competition between the newspapers and the state-run television company, which in 1991 added four new channels to its existing two, as well as the first private Turkish TV channel, which began broadcasting from Germany and attracted many advertisers.

The war in the Gulf constituted the first time that a war was covered live by television from behind enemy lines, giving an entirely misleading impression that press freedom had broken out there. The truth is otherwise. Kuwait, liberated from its Iraqi invaders, dashed hopes for a new breath of democracy by restoring censorship and instituting court cases against newspaper employees accused of collaborating with Baghdad. Some have been sentenced to death. Hundreds of Lebanese, Palestinian, Egyptian, and ethnic Iraqi journalists have been forced to leave Kuwait.

In August, a group of Soviet hard-liners attempted to depose President Mikhail Gorbachev—but the junta had not allowed for the people's thirst for democracy. The courage of the press, which miraculously managed to bring out photocopied versions of newspapers and distribute them in the streets at considerable risk, kept the public informed. The Soviet media emerged heroic and victorious.

Journalists elsewhere in the world continued to fall victim to assassins' bullets, official harassment, and general mistrust on behalf of the authorities. Nevertheless, there was a general feeling that journalists in Africa, in Eastern Europe, and in other places emerging from decades of repression were waking up to the fact that, in the words of the South African magazine *Work in Progress,* "The time has come for plain-speaking. Criticism, for us, is an act of loyalty."

The question remains, however, whether economic conditions will improve significantly to allow this correct and noble concept of independent journalism to flourish.

ALGERIA
The imposition of martial law in Algeria meant an end to the relative press freedom enjoyed since the end of 1989. A number of foreign journalists were expelled, and foreign publications were subjected to strict censorship by the military authorities. The formal end to the state of emergency, announced in late September, did not seem to have helped. But the situation for the domestic media looks more hopeful. Algerians are now permitted to receive French television, and the cables across the rooftops and satellite dishes show that this is an offer few can refuse.

CAMEROON

Cameroon has earned the reputation of a "hotbed" of confrontation among the one-party regime, the opposition, and the independent press. [See "Counting the Hours in Cameroon," *World Press Review*, January, 1992.] The authorities banned several newspapers. The private press has taken a strong stand, however, against President Paul Biya. More than 20 new weeklies have appeared on the newsstands.

CHILE

Press freedom is practically total in newly democratic Chile. Some prominent journalists face court cases, however, and the economic structure of the media world is still cause for concern. Cristian Edwards del Rio, the youngest son of the owner and editor of the country's largest daily, *El Mercurio*, has been missing—feared kidnapped—since September 10. Also in September, the Chilean government accused Manuel Cabieses, editor of the leftwing magazine *Punto Final*, of insulting the chief of staff of the army—former dictator General Augusto Pinochet. The magazine had published a montage featuring Pinochet blowing his nose on the Chilean flag, with the heading: Cynical and Sadistic.

J. Senen Conejeros, president of the Chilean College of Journalists, says "The main danger to press freedom lies in the continuing financial structure of the newspaper industry in Chile. An amazing 87 percent of the country's press is owned by two newspaper groups, the *El Mercurio* group and the *La Tercera* group. On top of that, *El Mercurio* controls 76 percent of the total advertising revenue of the written press; it also owns eight cable-television channels. In addition, the country's entire distribution system is in the hands of *El Mercurio* and *La Tercera*."

CHINA

Press freedom in China is non-existent. The Propaganda Department of the Communist Party has, for the past year, been conducting a quiet but thorough investigation of the political reliability of editors and reporters on China's main newspapers. Understandably, acts of journalistic defiance have been few and far between. The most sensational was the publication of an anti-government poem in the official Communist Party newspaper, the *People's Daily*, in March. Read horizontally, the poem was uncontroversial, but read diagonally, it called for the overthrow of Chinese Prime Minister Li Peng.

The youth and entertainment press traditionally have more flexibility than the main dailies. The *Beijing Youth News*, for example, ran a piece in October that candidly described the ridicule to which students who had been on military training were subjected by their peers at Beijing University when they returned to campus.

The foreign press in China has had another difficult year. In September, a British correspondent, Andrew Higgins of the *Independent*, was expelled after publishing a secret document that described measures to suppress nationalist unrest among ethnic Mongolians in China. Many foreign journalists continue to complain of surveillance, harassment, and obstruction.

COLOMBIA

Colombia remains a dangerous country for the free exercise of journalism. Six journalists were killed in 1991; several others were kidnapped, either by drug traffickers attempting to squeeze concessions from the government or by guerrillas trying to disseminate their ideology. Diana Turbay, editor of the magazine *Hoy Por Hoy*, was the first victim of 1991. She had been kidnapped with seven colleagues in September, 1990, by drug traffickers. In a confused police operation supposedly aimed at freeing the hostages, Turbay was killed.

On April 27, Julio Daniel Chaparro and Jaime Torres, a columnist and a photographer, respectively, of the daily *El Espectador*, were shot dead. They had been preparing a series on the most violent areas of Colombia, to examine how the people in these areas had overcome their problems.

ETHIOPIA

Ethiopia is a mixture of old Marxist thinking and creeping democratization. The flight of military strongman Mengistu Haile Mariam ushered in an era of civilian politicians led by Meles Zenawi, head of the country's transitional government. The new leader promised that in the new Ethiopia, journalists "will freely express different ideas."

In June, the new regime banned the Ethiopian Journalists' Association. On July 31, journalists working for the Ethiopian media were dismissed. Among those fired were Imeru Worku, editor in chief of *Addis Zemen*, the Amharic-language daily, and the heads of the government press department, TV, and radio. Twenty other media personnel were also fired after being accused of "spying" for the fallen regime.

The government must approve all advertising and news copy before it is published in the state-owned *Ethiopian Herald* and other publications. The Ministry of Information can still turn down advertisements, thus denying vital revenue to the country's newspapers, which already depend on heavy government subsidies. Foreign journalists are welcomed, but their movements are watched.

GREECE

The media year was dominated in Greece by the controversial new Anti-Terrorist Law, which bans the publication of statements by groups such as the November 17 Revolutionary Organization. Journalists and others consider the law unconstitutional for infringing on press freedom. The issue has sparked the biggest row over censorship in Greece since the military dictatorship of 1967–74 barred free reporting. Most journalists consider the law, and the arrests that followed it, to be "unacceptable acts of totalitarianism."

INDONESIA

While the media have been able to cover social conflicts more fully than hitherto, many problems are still strictly censored. One is the province of Atjeh, where killings and atrocities have been widespread following an upsurge of activity against Indonesian rule. In a report on Atjeh in June, the Asia Watch human-rights group quoted an editor in Medan as saying, "I'm not an editor anymore. I'm just a tailor. I have to take the information and sew it into something new." Two Atjeh newspapers, *Atjeh Post* and *Peristiwa*, were closed for "reasons of efficiency," but Asia Watch believes that the closures were related to the army's attempt to control the press in Atjeh.

Nothing of a critical nature on East Timor [occupied by Indonesia since July 1976] ever gets reported in Indonesia. Censorship was imposed at the last minute on the weekly *Tempo* of Jakarta to kill a report about young Timorese brought to Jakarta under false pretenses, thinking that they were to be offered well-paid jobs. The story was about dozens of Timorese who went to Parliament to present their complaints. Instructed to remove the item from its pages, the journal appeared on Saturday 7 with two blank columns, even though the contents page listed the item.

IRAN

The Islamic Republic of Iran, where some 40 journalists were reported to be in prison, distinguished itself for especially repressive policies and methods in 1991. The policy of massive purges, even within the official media, was pursued with increasing vigor and reached the country's leading daily newspaper, *Kayhan* (The Universe). Regarded as a critic of President Ali Akbar Hashemi Rafsanjani's policies, *Kayhan* was "brought under tighter Islamic control" with the appointment of Mehdi Nassiri, a former aide to the president, as the paper's executive editor. At least a quarter of the paper's editorial board was fired.

Elsewhere, reporters were kidnapped and beaten after "poking their noses" into sensitive issues. The government's anti-press campaign was part of a broader policy aimed at preventing intellectual dissent from becoming organized.

Nevertheless, the Islamic Republic continued to face many contradictions. The minister for Islamic guidance, Ayatollah Muhammad Khatami, pursued a relatively "liberal" policy by authorizing the publication of a number of new, strictly non-political weeklies and monthlies. He also tried to organize and lead the "liberal" faction within the official media by convening a conference in which the publishers and editors of the official and semi-official papers agreed to help one another against "attacks on constitutional liberties."

In September, the government imposed a total ban on all reports of disturbances in Teheran and the provinces, after reports in some newspapers that street battles had been fought between opponents of the regime and the Islamic Revolutionary Guard in many cities.

IRAQ

In Iraq, the regime of President Saddam Hussein promised a set of political reforms that included a loosening of control over the media. Saddam's son, Uday Hussein, was appointed editor in chief of the country's principal daily newspaper. The number of Iraqi journalists in prison in Baghdad was put at 13 by exile opposition groups in Europe.

ISRAEL

Pneumatic drills signaled the coming of the new age, as streets were being pried up for the insertion of television cables that are expected eventually to reach more than 60 percent of the country's 1.3 million households; 10 percent are already connected. Cable television will be available to all residents willing to pay about $200 for connection and $25 a month in fees.

The *Jerusalem Report*, an English-language weekly launched in 1990, reportedly suffered a $2-million loss in its first year of operation, but its executives hope to begin turning a profit by 1994. The weekly, which circulates abroad as well as in Israel, has won wide praise as a lively and credible journal.

KENYA

The country known for its buoyant, independent media continued to stifle the right to a free press. The authorities continued with their harassment of Gitobu Imanyara, editor in chief of the *Nairobi Law Monthly* [and *World Press Review*'s 1990 International Editor of the Year], who continued to attack the government's political record. His magazine was banned, and he was detained for three weeks without charge in the psychiatric wing of Kamiti Prison. Although in May the government released Imanyara, who was very ill, and withdrew all charges against him, his freedom of movement was curtailed. He was denied a passport.

In June, 1991, President Daniel arap Moi accused the top-selling *Daily Nation* and the country's number-three newspaper, the *Standard*, of being used by foreigners to destabilize Kenya. In September, Philip Ochieng, editor in chief of [ruling party's] *Kenya Times*, was fired after falling from grace among top politicians. The *Weekly Review*, published by Hilary Ng'weno, has a reputation as one of the continent's pioneers in the independent press, but its once-outspoken editorial coverage has become blunted—it is now pro-government. The *Weekly Review* does not want to lose its low-cost contract to use the state-owned Kenya Times Media Trust printing press. Additionally, it does not want to lose out on lucrative government advertising revenue.

Foreign publications critical of Kenya are regularly seized by the authorities.

KUWAIT

The return of the ruling Al-Sabah dynasty to Kuwait, after months of exile caused by the Iraqi invasion, did not produce the expected social and political reforms. The emirate was put under martial law, and all dissent was energetically repressed. By October, the Kuwaiti press, once the pride of the Arab world, was but a pale shadow of itself. A few newspapers had resumed publication inside the emirate, but others continued to be issued from Saudi Arabia, Egypt, or even London. A massive purge of "suspects" within the Kuwaiti media led to the expulsion of hundreds of Lebanese, Palestinian, Egyptian, and ethnic Iraqi journalists and technicians who were not only fired from their jobs but also forced to leave the country. The new witch hunt was even more ferocious than the anti-Shiite campaign launched by the emir in 1985–86.

LEBANON

In Lebanon, the restoration of relative calm and security, albeit under Syrian military occupation, allowed the press to regain part of the self-confidence it had lost during some 15 years of civil war. Lebanon is one of very few Arab countries with a large and lively pool of journalistic talent capable of doing a reasonable job, even under exceptionally difficult circumstances. Lebanese journalists continue to face the threat of being kidnapped or murdered by individuals or groups that do not share their political views. The Syrian military authorities, especially the notorious secret police, have made it plain by their actions that defiant journalists will not reach old age. Nevertheless, the Lebanese press in 1991 seemed to be slowly expanding the freedom that it had lost since the early 1970s.

NIGERIA

Angered by an "embarrassing article" on President Ibrahim Babangida and his wife, Mariam, in the evening daily *Lagos News*, the government ordered the arrest and detention of its editor, Ade Awoyemi, and news editor Kolade Alabi. The two men were released on $11,000 bail each on March 13, after three days in detention. They had to report daily to the police station. The police interrogators demanded the source of the story. The following day, 13 journalists on the newspaper were arrested, including Awoyemi. The federal government ordered the offices of the *Lagos News* to be sealed.

On May 29, security agents arrested four journalists working for the *African Guardian*, an independent Lagos newspaper. The reporters, accused of reporting the killing of two students in clashes with the armed forces, were released after 24 days. A photojournalist, Segun Olakitan of the *Nigerian Concord*, a daily paper, was assaulted by soldiers while covering bloody religious riots. He told his editor that the soldiers had damaged his camera, that he had been stopped by the army several times and frisked, and that his movement was restricted.

On June 29, the authorities deported William Keeling, Nigeria correspondent for the *Financial Times* of London; the government alleged that his reports could "sabotage the security" of Nigeria. One *FT* article was on the use of oil revenues by the government. Information Minister Alex Akinyele said that foreign journalists were picking up negative information from Nigerian newspapers. "I don't censor; there is no censorship at all," he said. "Let them write what they want to write. But if anybody does anything that is against the national interest, that person will have to answer questions. To criticize Nigeria is to criticize God."

THE PHILIPPINES

The Philippine media are growing more partisan. The seven-year-old *Philippine Daily Inquirer*, which has grabbed top circulation from the conservative, established *Manila Bulletin*, has gained a nationalist voice as definitive as the position it took in its infancy against former President Ferdinand Marcos. With a frankness refreshing in the Philippine press, the *Inquirer* published editorial after editorial against the continued presence of United States bases, the most controversial issue in 1991.

Journalists have not won a single court case against assailants. And in 1991, at least three media people were killed, bringing to 31 the total since Corazon Aquino assumed the presidency six years ago. That equals the record of the 14-year Marcos dictatorship.

POLAND

Poland in 1991 was a country with free and pluralistic media. The French publisher Hersant won bids to buy five dailies, and a Polish bank, BHK, bought 30-40-percent shares in eight dailies and weeklies. The trade union Solidarity was allowed to buy shares in seven dailies, and new political forces also increased their importance. A political party, the Center Alliance, bought *Express Wieczorny*, Poland's most popular afternoon paper, but other attempts by political parties to control publications were rejected.

Almost all editors in chief from the communist period were removed, and journalists from the underground press obtained positions of prominence. Competition, however, has caused many publications to fold.

The Roman Catholic church bitterly attacked the media in 1991, accusing them of "corruption and disinformation" and demanding a "return to universally accepted values." But the church seems to lack the political clout necessary to limit the press. On the other hand, the dissemination of rabidly anti-Semitic views by some fringe parties in the recent parliamentary elections reopened the debate on the limits of press freedom.

President Lech Walesa's threats to "take over the media," made during his electoral campaign, were not carried through, but a number of TV journalists unsympathetic to him were fired, and two critical TV news and commentary programs were closed down.

ROMANIA

The 1,000 new publications that have sprung up since the toppling of dictator Nicolae Ceausescu in December, 1989, face potentially crippling distribution costs and tenfold increases in the price of paper. To add to their woes, advertising revenue is still very low, as Western countries and corporations remain reluctant to invest in joint ventures.

As the Romanian hunger for information continues, a growing circulation war is under way. *Romania Libera*, the largest independent daily, continues to lead the group, followed closely by *Tineretul Liber* and *Adevarul*. Some newspapers have sent reporters and editors on learning stints to American, British, and French publications and academic institutions, but the level of journalism in Romania is still embryonic.

One positive move has been the formation of the AZR Higher School of Journalism, supported by the independent Romanian press, the United-States-based George Soros Foundation for an Open Society, and the International Media Fund in Washington. The school, located in Bucharest, has 140 students and offers programs in radio, television, and print media.

Under pressure from Western nations, particularly the United States, and after ignoring pleas for an independent station, the Romanian government gave permission for several hours of daily broadcasting on the second television channel at the end of official broadcasting time. The second channel is watched by only about 30 percent of the population and by far fewer after midnight, when the independent programs are shown.

SOUTH AFRICA

South Africa's "alternative" media have been undergoing a reassessment of their role in the runup to "the new South Africa." Once uncritically supportive of the banned and restricted liberation movements and of other organizations involved in "the struggle" against an authoritarian, racist government, these publications—mostly weekly—have, since restrictions were lifted on the groups and their members were allowed back into South Africa, begun to exercise a more independent attitude. The outside funding of these publications mainly from foreign governments, churches, and political foundations, has been drying up with the government's dismantling of apartheid and the growing perception that the need for the media to attack apartheid foundations is passing. Diminishing funds have brought pressure for these publications to broaden their appeal in the search for readers and self-sufficiency.

The differing ideologies among the liberation movements, once submerged as all fought together on a broad anti-apartheid front, have begun to surface, and the differences are now being stressed as the organizations vie with each other for support. This has resulted in newspapers' choosing between policies and criticizing some of the movements [see "Mau-Mauing South Africa's Media," *World Press Review*, October, 1991]. This, in turn, has resulted in greater pressure from the political organizations, especially those under attack, on the papers.

Punitive actions against the press by the government have been reduced substantially, although police continue to arrest journalists and photographers and raid newspaper offices for certain types of information. Legal harassment also continues. Journalists are frequently served with warrants demanding that they disclose their sources of information for published stories.

The use of formal court procedures to harass newspapers has been stepped up in the past year. When *Vrye Weekblad*, the "alternative" Afrikaans/English paper, published claims by former security police captain Dirk Coetzee that he had been supplied with special poisons by the head of the police forensic laboratories, Lieutenant-General Lothar Neethling, to assassinate anti-apartheid government opponents. Neethling promptly sued the paper for $357,000 (and the *Weekly Mail*, which also published the claims, for half that sum). *Vrye Weekblad* raised the money to defend the action, partly through the French government and the Media Defense Trust—and won. The paper would have gone out of business if it had lost the case.

On several occasions in 1991, people obtained Supreme Court injunctions preventing newspapers from publishing stories about their activities. Most of the decisions were later reversed; in one instance, one of the litigants was deported from the country after the story appeared. There is concern in media and legal circles that this form of "judicial censorship" is on the increase.

A major event during the year was publication of the government-appointed task-force report on television and radio broadcasting, which proposed a restructuring of TV and radio services. The stated purpose was to open up broadcasting, to "depoliticize" it and free it of government control, but critics say that the proposals provide the opportunity for the government to exercise even greater control over the electronic media than exists now.

THE SOVIET UNION

Turmoil beset the Soviet media in 1991. The year saw both newspapers and television embroiled in firings and resignations, accusations and denials, and the purging and alleged witch-hunting that has threatened to muzzle or even kill off entire papers and TV channels. Ideological stance, complicity, and downright political vengeance have been at the root of the changes. Developments in the Soviet Union in 1991 will inevitably be seen in terms of before and after the coup attempt. The Soviet press had not only to observe the political shifts but also to respond to them.

Traditionally conservative newspapers such as *Sovetskaya Rossiya* and *Krasnaya Zvezda*, the armed forces publication, criticized Lithuanian "nationalists" and heaved sighs of relief that "order was being restored" when troops moved into the republic. The popular TV talk show *Vzglyad* was taken off the air at the beginning of January, 1991, by the chief of Gosteleradio (the state radio and television committee), Leonid Kravchenko, *Vzglyad*, with its lively young hosts and often-controversial revelations, was at the forefront of *glasnost*, tackling issues that were taboo a few years before.

At the same time, footage of events in Vilnius, Lithuania, was allegedly not shown, despite a request to do so from the Supreme Soviet. Fewer dissenting voices were given air time, and *Vremya*, the main evening news program, became more like its old pre-*perestroika* self: dull and wooden. *Vremya* chose not to criticize the shootings in Vilnius, preferring to highlight the plight of ethnic Russians living in Lithuania.

The coup attempt had Soviet media chiefs facing a difficult choice: conform or defy. True, no one knew during those three crucial days what the consequences of defiance might be. Nevertheless, editors of newspapers closed by order of the coup leaders took their lives into their own hands. Although they could not physically print normal editions of their papers—the presses were sealed and surrounded by tanks—makeshift editions sprang up all over Moscow. Hastily prepared photocopies of typed articles and faxes of Russian President Boris Yeltsin's condemnatory resolutions appeared in shop windows and in the subway, where they were devoured by crowds of Muscovites hungry for news.

Other papers remained open and printed the junta's decrees word for word, even expressing support for them. These newspapers, including *Pravda*, were later closed for several days by Russian President Boris Yeltsin. He made it clear that papers that had been Communist Party mouthpieces would have to clean up their acts. Deprived of Communist Party funding, *Pravda* was forced to take the humiliating step of appealing to its readers for cash to save the paper. Like others, it was at pains to persuade the public that it was not implicated in supporting the coup. Lenin's sculpted face and the exhortation, "Proletarians of the World, Unite!" disappeared from the top of *Pravda's* front page almost overnight.

Change and symbols of change are, however, two different things, Newspapers and TV programs can still be closed down by a command from on high.

TURKEY

The Turkish press encountered severe financial problems in 1991. The virtual bankruptcy of Asil Nadir, who owned about a third of the Turkish print media, had a crushing effect on the Turkish press. About 1,000 journalists lost their jobs, and as many were left without pay for many months. The professional organizations of journalists proved unable to protect the rights of their members during this crisis. Newspaper owners did not fully abide by the collective agreements signed with the journalists' unions.

The most positive development of the year was the lifting of certain articles of the Turkish penal code that had hitherto seriously curbed the freedom of expression and the press in Turkey. The Anti-Terror Law, adopted by Parliament in April, 1991, legalized communist and religious propaganda and stipulated the "conditional release" of prisoners, including nearly 30 journalists who had been sentenced to many years in jail. Cases of harassment and outright beating of journalists by security forces continued. The police failed to track down the assassins of distinguished journalist Cetin Emec and of well-known author Turan Dursun, who were shot to death by gunmen in 1990.

UGANDA

Ugandan newspaper publishers appealed to President Yoweri Museveni for a freer press and for an end to the government monopoly on television and radio broadcasting. The Uganda Newspaper Editors and Proprietors Association presented a memorandum to the chairman of Uganda's constitutional commission, Justice Ben Odoki. Its 15-point memorandum included demands for freedom of expression and information, the ending of the government monopoly on broadcasting, and the right to protect the source of information; defense of "public-interest" cases in which the state prosecutes for the disclosure of information; the banning of newspapers and searching of their offices only through a court order; the outlawing of press censorship; and the right of newspapers to hold in their archives documents that would be considered seditious.

YUGOSLAVIA

Without doubt, the blackest of black spots for the press in 1991 was Yugoslavia. Both sides in the Serbo-Croatian war appear to have deliberately singled out journalists for attack. As many as 20 journalists were killed or wounded. On July 26, Egon Scotland, a reporter for the Munich daily *Sudeutsche Zeitung*, was shot dead near Glina in Croatia—allegedly by Servian insurgents. Stejpan Penic, a radio producer and correspondent for the Croatian newspaper *Glas Slavonije*, was reportedly murdered by Serbian nationalists. Pierre Blanchet, 47, a correspondent for the French newsmagazine *Le Nouvel Observateur*, and Damien Rudin, a Swiss radio reporter, were killed by a land mine. Peter Brysky, a freelance Canadian photographer, was killed by a mortar shell south of Zagreb.

Serbian rebels in the field, whose only information comes from Belgrade's state-run press, believe that non-Serbian journalists are either Croatian or German agents.

ZIMBABWE

The state-controlled media came under fire from some 200 journalists who accused it of pandering to the ruling elite, of excessive self-censorship, and of frustrating independent-minded journalists. At a seminar in Harare in March, the journalists said that radio and television services were openly controlled by the government, while the major group, Zimbabwe Newspapers, which publishes the main daily, the *Herald*, and several other papers that were theoretically independent, was actually controlled by the state. The journalists alleged that the state-controlled media had been "hijacked by bogus journalists" from the civil service who ended up frustrating professional journalists.

The New Censors
Juliette Kayyem, THE NEW REPUBLIC

Early Wednesday morning, October 23, gunmen entered a train station in Nancefield, Sowerto, and began shooting on the platform and into a commuter train. By 6:15 that morning, as the train traveled on to four other stations en route to Johannesburg, nine passengers lay dead. The massacre was a hot story for *The Soewetan,* the newspaper that covers the township. The paper routinely reported the incident, and cited the far from unwarranted conclusion of the police investigation that members of the Inkatha Freedom Party had something to do with it. But this was South Africa, and the IFP—a real power in the township—publicly attacked *The Sowetan* for the story.

The incident serves as an emblem of the difficulties black journalists face in the new South Africa. Banned, harassed, and arrested in the days of apartheid, black journalists seem at first, in color and profession, double beneficiaries of political reform. Yet the path toward constitutional representation and political power has been a vexing process. For reporters and photographers on *The Sowetan,* the country's largest daily, the new South Africa has its own occupational hazards— and the pressures against free speech and reporting now come from within the black community, rather than from outside it.

Back in the 1980s the greatest danger to black journalists came from the white minority. As described in William Finnegan's *Dateline Soweto,* black reporters were by definition political activists. Daring to report or photograph apartheid violence or township life defied censorship laws and brought down government harassment. Even in the old days, however, black journalists faced threats from the community they covered—a kind of censorship Finnegan barely mentioned in his book. Now as black political parties compete, and as violence spreads throughout the townships, black reporters work with ever more common threats of verbal and physical intimidation by township residents, hostel dwellers, and activists.

Reporters are threatened with being necklaced as they try to cover a story; a photographer is manhandled when he tells a crowd which newspaper he works for; an editor, accused of fostering division, must move his wife and children to a neighbor's house when he receives a bomb threat. The result of these pressures on journalists is simple: in a recent forum on the new censorship sponsored by the South African Institute of Race Relations, some black reporters suggested that only 60 percent of the information black newspapers report is factual. Journalists are, for example, often compelled by party activists to inflate numbers of those present at political rallies. Or, in many cases, reporters will simply not cover sensitive issues—for example, whether boycotting school has harmed the black community. And no black newspaper discusses the culture of political intolerance that makes it difficult to cover any issue objectively.

Several years ago *The Sowetan* was embroiled in a political fight that ended in a mass boycott of the paper. *The Sowetan* had chosen to cover the meetings of smaller political organizations, such as the Azanian People's Organization (AZAPO) and the Pan Africanist Congress (PAC). "Several prominent activists," as senior assistant editor Thami Mazwai calls them, claimed that the paper was wasting space on parties that were insignificant. More interesting than the boycott itself is Mazwai's description. The villains of censorship always are "prominent activists," or "certain organizations." To name them might incite more trouble.

To make matters worse, there's no culture among readers and potential readers that might demand or support an independent paper. A recent survey conducted by the Department of Political Science at the University of Stellenbosch asked 270 black South Africans about their acceptance of differing political ideas. When asked whether to allow "newspapers to write about the policies of . . . [the respondent's least-liked group, e.g., the National Party, the African National Congress, etc.]," 40 percent answered "definitely not."

The Sowetan is non-aligned. It has to be. Its editorial page hasn't endorsed the ANC, Inkatha, AZAPO, or the PAC. To do so would be suicide. Sello Rabothatha, *The Sowetan*'s news editor, knows that many of his senior journalists and editors have different political ideologies. If the paper were to endorse any political party, says Rabothatha, "there would be a number of resignations here." But such prissiness inevitably undercuts the edge of the newspaper's contribution to public debate.

The news content is also often bland. In an attempt to calm a volatile community, and, according to Rabothatha, "to make Soweto seem more normal than not," *The Sowetan* often behaves like a small-town paper. Front-page coverage of township violence is shared with a *Sowetan* wedding photo essay titled "Looking at the Brighter Side of Life" and an entry clue for the paper's "Stick a Pic" competition for a leather lounge.

This small-town feel, despite 1.6 million readers, is very much a consequence of the fact that the black journalists and editors live in Soweto. When there is violence, the second concern is the story. The first concern, says Robert Magwaza, photography editor, is "that your mother and wife were not on that train." He is toying with the idea of moving out of Soweto altogether. The law at last permits it; and he can now afford it. He fears for his wife and children's safety. But he also worries that he will betray the paper, and his friends, if he leaves. And yet the personal proximity of the newspaper's reporters to the unrest in the township means that, when readers are displeased, a reporter is an easy target. Themba Molege, a political reporter, has to be escorted to Zulu-dominated hostels by IFP members for fear of his safety. Rabothatha acknowledges that "they not only threaten you, but they know what car we drive, where we live, our wives' names, how many children we have."

Black photographers are particularly at risk. Mbuzeni Zulu, who, when the paper needs a lead story, is sent out into me township just to "look for action" (he's rarely disappointed), has often been turned away when he has tried to cover political rallies. His face, and camera, are now known to work for *The Sowetan*.

Admittedly, reporters from *The Sowetan* can easily mesh into the crowd, being less conspicuous in the township than their white counterparts. But one of the enduring ironies of apartheid is that blacks are often in a weaker position as reporters than whites. Blacks, according to Len Maseko, deputy news editor, still find it hard to say no to white reporters, although they'll ignore fellow blacks. When *Sowetan* staffers tried to question a Zulu man who'd been shot by police during an Inkatha rally, the man refused to answer any questions. Black reporters went outside the hospital room and grabbed a white colleague. The white reporter wasn't interested in the injured man's story, but he was able to solicit the answers for *The Sowetan*.

Integrating *The Sowetan*'s reporting staff might be one way to steel the newspaper's nerve, but it can bring more troubles in its wake. Already, *The Sowetan*'s black journalists are wary of their white management, Argus, South Africa's newspaper conglomerate. Lately Argus has started to pay more attention to the paper, which it used to leave more or less alone. Its recent hire—an Afrikaner managing editor, Deon du Plessis—has stirred resentment. Each morning, it's du Plessis's job to send a critique of the morning paper to all editors and writers. He comments on everything from bad layout to bad English. He talks of the "emergence of market factor on black journalism": it is his hope to turn the paper into something more than a township rag. Predictably perhaps, many black journalists, who spoke on condition of anonymity, have taken umbrage. Says one reporter, "It gives a bad impression, this large white guy, looking like he runs the place." Since du Plessis took over, the editorial page of *The Sowetan* has become, as one reporter says, "more white, less liberation struggle." Du Plessis and his nominal superior, editor Aggrey Klaaste, who's black, co-author the editorial page, but, as another reporter comments, "Feon definitely has the final say on it." The implication is that Agrus acknowledges the political significance of *The Sowetan* and now wants to have greater domination over the paper.

Between its white owners and its black audience, *The Sowetan* is now fighting for its integrity. Freedom of expression has a paltry history in South Africa. In the old days the National Party never shied from censoring the press. In the new South Africa, black journalists face conflicts with their readers, their paymaster, the political groups they cover—and work in a climate of violence few American journalists could even contemplate. That press freedom has survived at all it perhaps a wonder. That it will flourish in the new South Africa is looking more doubtful by the day.

Juliette Kayyem is a free-lance writer in Johannesburg.

International Media
Worksheet

1. Do you believe that modern media have made the world smaller and more accessible because we can see into our international neighbors' backyard? Or, do you believe that modern media have created fences and barriers between us and our international neighbors because we can see into their backyards and don't often like what we see? Explain your answer.

2. Much of what we know about the people in other countries is from what our media tells us or by examining the nature of their media. Do you believe that our *National Enquirer* is a reflection of the American people? Explain.

3. "How Free is the Press" discusses the varying degrees of freedom in the world's newspapers and broadcast outlets. Do you believe that *all* the world's press should be free, regardless of individual governments' ideologies? Explain.

4. The First Amendment gives American journalists the freedom to criticize and question our government and government officials. Do you believe that this same freedom applies to our journalists when dealing with foreign governments and government officials? Explain. Are there any unique circumstances where your belief does not apply?